# THIS IS ANFIELD

THE ILLUSTRATED HISTORY OF LIVERPOOL FOOTBALL CLUB'S
OFFICIAL MATCHDAY PROGRAMME

# THIS IS ANFIELD

THE ILLUSTRATED HISTORY OF LIVERPOOL FOOTBALL CLUB'S
OFFICIAL MATCHDAY PROGRAMME

**Reach** Sport

Hardback edition first published in Great Britain in 2023

**www.reachsport.com**
**@reach_sport**

Reach Sport is a part of Reach PLC Ltd, 5 St Paul's Square, Liverpool, L3 9SJ
One Canada Square, Canary Wharf, London, E15 5AP

**Hardback ISBN:** 9781914197673

**Writers and researchers:** Andy Marsden and David Cottrell
**Designer:** Colin Sumpter
**Production editor:** Roy Gilfoyle
**Cover design:** Glen Hind

**Photographic acknowledgements:**
Liverpool Football Club, Getty Images, Mirrorpix

Printed and bound by Bell & Bain.

Every effort has been made to trace the copyright.
Any oversight will be rectified in future editions.

CONTENTS

# GET WITH THE PROGRAMME

**T**oday's official Liverpool FC matchday programme is a thorough undertaking. Published up to 30 times a season, it endeavours at all times to be eye-catching and engaging, informative and entertaining; hitting the strictest print deadlines while staying fresh and original in an age of instant digital consumption; reflecting the club's values and traditions while reaching out to its legions of fans around the world with clear, intelligent and meaningful content.

Its editorial team liaises closely with the press office assisting the playing and coaching staff at the AXA Training Centre, building strong relationships and rapport, as well as working alongside the club's official website and TV channel, PR and communications, licensing, retail and ticketing departments.

Passion shines through the publication – just as it does on the pitch, in the dugout and in the Anfield stands.

The matchday programme has its own special heritage. It's as old as the football club itself, and this book tells its story from the publications for the earliest Liverpool FC fixtures to the latest editions in a modern era which, on and off the pitch, has been truly exceptional – even by Anfield's amazing standards.

The bulk of this book's images and information come from Andy Marsden's personal collection. Andy is a fan who previously published his own, limited-edition guide to Reds programmes since the Second World War, with profits from its sale going towards LFC Foundation's life-changing projects in communities at home and abroad.

"For as long as I can remember," he says, "a huge part of my life has revolved around Liverpool FC and programme-collecting.

"It was thanks to my dad that I became a Red. I was born in Liverpool on the morning of an FA Cup final and a few years later he also gave me my first football programme, from the 1971 final against Arsenal.

"Then in 1973 I was lucky enough to attend my first home match. It was against Leeds United and that was also when I got my first copy of 'The Anfield Review' [the old title of the matchday programme]. In those days it cost five pence, there were 16 pages plus a 24-page 'League Football' insert. I was hooked. It was the start of my programme collecting.

"I look back at that programme from time to time and the memories come flooding back: I was in the old Main Stand and can remember the sights and sounds, the Kop flooding forward when Kevin Keegan scored, how big everything seemed.

"That's the thing with programmes – they are a portal to the past, a piece of affordable history that anyone can own."

And this, dear reader, is the ultimate time-capsule for anyone with a love for LFC. Read on, reminisce, and enjoy!

# CHAPTER 1

# THE EARLY
# YEARS

The matchday programme was there from the start, when Liverpool Football Club was born after a dispute with Anfield's original tenants

**O**nce upon a time there was a chap called John Houlding who dabbled in politics and owned a brewery in the big port-city of Liverpool. When a football club called Everton refused to pay more rent for the land he owned at Anfield, they left and Houlding formed a new club instead: Liverpool.

Houlding sent 'committee member' John McKenna – in charge of team affairs with WE Barclay – north of the border for players. He returned with a team of Scotsmen who donned a blue-and-white kit left behind by the former tenants and, on Thursday 1 September 1892, they played a friendly against Rotherham Town. The score: 7-1.

Two days later, this 'Team of Macs' would play its first competitive match, at home to Higher Walton in the Lancashire League. They won 8-0.

Around the same time a flag was hoisted above Houlding's ground. It bore, as one local newspaper put it, "the liver [bird], which proudly waves over the field of battle and seems to beam on its patrons with a hopeful smile." The story of Liverpool Football Club had begun.

Copies of the programmes from that first season, 1892-93, have survived to this day. Four pages each, they are surprisingly informative with reports from previous fixtures and the laws of the game to educate those new to football.

The following season, the club was elected to the Football League and went on to win the Second Division. They then beat Newton Heath (now Manchester United) 2-0 at Blackburn's Ewood Park in a 'Test match' to determine who would play in England's top-flight.

Over successive seasons Liverpool were relegated and promoted again, this time consolidating their First Division status under new boss Tom Watson, changing to red shirts, and signing defender Alex Raisbeck from Hibs – the Virgil van Dijk of his era who would become captain of the team and one of LFC's first stars.

At the turn of the century the headlines were all about the Boer War in South Africa and a fierce battle at Spion Kop (from the Dutch for 'Lookout Hill') where the British suffered a harrowing defeat, and within a handful of years a vast new terrace would be constructed at Anfield, adopting the name of the battle site.

In 1901, three months after the death of Queen Victoria, Liverpool were crowned champions for the very first time, pipping three-time winners Sunderland by two points after a 12-match unbeaten run. Three seasons later, though, the Reds were relegated, having been without injured striker Sam Raybould for 9 fixtures. Once again they bounced back at the first attempt – with goalkeeper Ned Doig, signed at the age of 37, an ever-present – and in 1905-06 they were champions for a second time, four points clear of Preston North End.

Liverpool and Everton now published a joint-programme – a venture which would last until the end of the 1934-35 season after 1,200 issues. When one first team was at home, the neighbour's reserves would be playing across Stanley Park. Each 16-page programme included the line-ups for both games along with 'Anfield Happenings', 'Everton Jottings', 'Personalia' – news about players, fixture lists and a brief look at the visitors – and 'Round the Theatres' and 'Round the Halls', reviewing local shows and concerts.

There was a scare for the Reds at the end of 1908-09 when they had to win at new champions Newcastle to stay up, but the following season they were second behind Aston Villa with

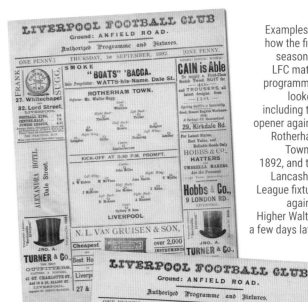

Examples of how the first season of LFC match programmes looked, including the opener against Rotherham Town in 1892, and the Lancashire League fixture against Higher Walton a few days later

Bootle-born striker Jack Parkinson firing 30 goals and future skipper Donald Mackinlay joining from Scots club Newton Villa.

By then, the Port of Liverpool Building – the first of the so-called 'Three Graces' on the city's waterfront – had been completed and the Royal Liver Building and Cunard Building would soon follow, while Britain's first Woolworths store had opened its doors on Liverpool's Church Street.

In 1911-12, for the second time in three seasons, Watson's men left it late to maintain their top-flight status, unbeaten in the last four fixtures to end the campaign in 17th. But the only story around the world was the sinking of the Liverpool-registered passenger ship, RMS Titanic.

Later in the year the Reds signed Irishman Elisha Scott, set to become an Anfield legend between the posts, and in April 1914 they reached their first FA Cup final but lost 1-0 to Burnley at the old Crystal Palace stadium in London, now long-gone.

In the last season of 'normal' football before the First World War began, Everton were champions as the Reds languished in

13th despite a 24-goal contribution from Fred Pagnam.

With regular competitions suspended, Liverpool played in a regional league for Lancashire – the programme shrinking in size due to paper-rationing – while around the country women's matches, contested by factory and munitions workers, were staged to raise funds for the war effort.

By the cessation of hostilities, on 11 November 1918, thirteen players registered with Liverpool Football Club were known to have been killed in action.

The First Division resumed in 1919-20 and for Liverpool it was a season of two halves, slumping to bottom by December but recovering to finish fourth under new manager David Ashworth. They were fourth again in 1920-21 with Harry Chambers scoring 22 goals – he'd be top scorer for LFC from 1919 to 1923. By which time the Reds were crowned champions twice!

They hit top spot on Saturday 17 December 1921 with a home win over Manchester United and (but for one weekend) stayed there; the following season they went top in mid-September 1922 and remained there under Matt McQueen, a club director and former player who replaced Ashworth as boss midway through the campaign.

The remainder of the decade saw Herbert Chapman's Huddersfield Town achieve a treble of titles, the Reds beat Manchester United 5-0 and Everton 5-1 at Anfield in the space of one September week in 1925, and a young South African called Gordon Hodgson score his first hat-trick for the side a year later, at home to Sheffield United.

The *Football Echo* described him as "a cute, strong, combining forward who can give and take a bump with impunity." For seven out of eight seasons between 1927 and 1935 he'd be the team's leading marksman.

In August 1928 the 'Spion Kop New Stand' was opened – the first roofed terrace of its kind in the country – before Liverpool's match with Bury, and a special souvenir programme was produced to mark the occasion.

At the start of the Thirties the city of Liverpool's population peaked at 850,000. On Saturday 11 February 1933 a young Reds team beat Everton 7-4 at Anfield – the highest-ever score in this fixture – and in September a new star was born when another South African, outside-right Berry Nieuwenhuys, provided two assists on his debut in a 3-0 triumph at Tottenham then scored in Liverpool's 3-2 win over Everton the next week.

Goalkeeper Scott bowed out with a farewell speech at Anfield in May 1934 after 468 appearances over 22 years. He was succeeded by Arthur Riley, a South African who'd joined alongside Gordon Hodgson and would clock up almost 350 appearances of his own in a relatively fallow era for the Reds.

Liverpool ceased collaborating with Everton and launched their own matchday programme at the beginning of the 1935-36 season with club honours proudly blazoned on the cover.

Meanwhile, George Patterson stepped down as boss after eight years, to be replaced by Southampton's George Kay in the summer of 1936 – the same year as the Jarrow March to London against unemployment.

There was a record attendance of 300,000 for the Grand National at Aintree in 1937 (including eleven-year-old Princess Elizabeth) while across the ocean Joe Louis became world heavyweight boxing champion.

For season 1938-39 the programme took on a new identity when former *Liverpool Echo and Daily Post* sports editor Ernest 'Bee' Edwards was appointed editor. He introduced new features,

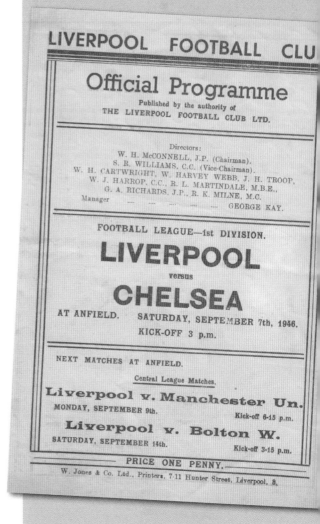

In the first true post-WW2 season the Reds beat Chelsea 7-4 and this was the programme cover

competitions, and humour coupled with his brilliant writing. He even persuaded former goalie Elisha Scott to be 'An Editor for A Day' in the issue for the game against Arsenal.

On New Year's Eve 1938 the Reds hosted Preston North End at Anfield, with Matt Busby skippering the Reds and Bill Shankly in the visiting XI. Final score: Liverpool 4 Preston 1.

Nine months later, the outbreak of war caused the abandonment of the League after three fixtures, and a depleted Liverpool played in the quickly-arranged 'Western Division' and 'War League Cup'. Subsequently there were two regional leagues, North and South, with no trophies or medals and winners decided by goal-average rather than points.

Owing to paper shortages, a single-sheet programme was printed – initially on card then on low-grade paper – relaying team line-ups, match officials, the next home fixture, and on the reverse the occasional 'Manager's Bulletin' or thoughts from the 'Board'.

The club was keen to point out it was 'the only programme published by the authority of the Liverpool Football Club Co., Ltd'

The covers of the Liverpool Senior Cup final programme from June 1947 and the Charlton league game in November 1948 (below)

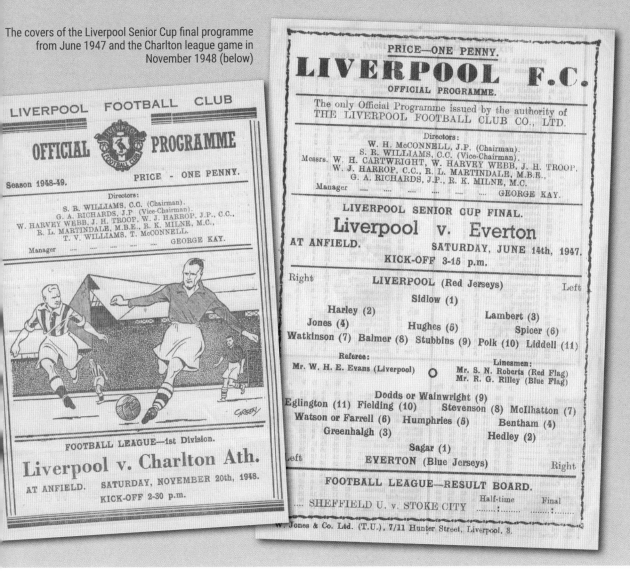

**LIVERPOOL FOOTBALL CLUB**

**OFFICIAL PROGRAMME**

Season 1948-49.    PRICE - ONE PENNY.

Directors:
S. R. WILLIAMS, C.C. (Chairman).
G. A. RICHARDS, J.P (Vice-Chairman).
W. HARVEY WEBB, J. H. TROOP, W. J. HARROP, J.P., C.C.,
R. L. MARTINDALE, M.B.E., R. K. MILNE, M.C.,
T. V. WILLIAMS, T. McCONNELL.

Manager ............    GEORGE KAY.

FOOTBALL LEAGUE—1st Division.

**Liverpool v. Charlton Ath.**

AT ANFIELD.    SATURDAY, NOVEMBER 20th, 1948.
KICK-OFF 2-30 p.m.

---

PRICE—ONE PENNY.

**LIVERPOOL F.C.**

OFFICIAL PROGRAMME.

The only Official Programme issued by the authority of
THE LIVERPOOL FOOTBALL CLUB CO., LTD.

Directors:
W. H. McCONNELL, J.P. (Chairman).
S. R. WILLIAMS, C.C. (Vice-Chairman).
Messrs. W. H. CARTWRIGHT, W. HARVEY WEBB, J. H. TROOP,
W. J. HARROP, C.C., R. L. MARTINDALE, M.B.E.,
G. A. RICHARDS, J.P., R. K. MILNE, M.C.

Manager ............    GEORGE KAY.

**LIVERPOOL SENIOR CUP FINAL.**

**Liverpool v. Everton**

AT ANFIELD.    SATURDAY, JUNE 14th, 1947.
KICK-OFF 3-15 p.m.

Right    LIVERPOOL (Red Jerseys)    Left
Sidlow (1)
Harley (2)    Lambert (3)
Jones (4)    Hughes (5)    Spicer (6)
Watkinson (7)  Balmer (8)  Stubbins (9)  Polk (10)  Liddell (11)

Referee:    Linesmen:
Mr. W. H. E. Evans (Liverpool)  O  Mr. S. N. Roberts (Red Flag)
Mr. R. G. Rilley (Blue Flag)

Dodds or Wainwright (9)
Eglington (11) Fielding (10)    Stevenson (8) McIlhatton (7)
Watson or Farrell (6)  Humphries (5)    Bentham (4)
Greenhalgh (3)    Hedley (2)
Sagar (1)
Left    EVERTON (Blue Jerseys)    Right

**FOOTBALL LEAGUE—RESULT BOARD.**

.... SHEFFIELD U. v. STOKE CITY    Half-time    Final
.......:........    .......:........

W. Jones & Co. Ltd. (T.U.), 7/11 Hunter Street, Liverpool. 3.

---

n part to thwart pirate programme-sellers who operated close to he ground.

Due to the war effort, teams were able to use guest players from other clubs to help fulfil their fixtures, namely professionals serving in the armed forces and stationed nearby. Look carefully at the single-sheet programme for the match with Everton in May 1942 and wearing the number 4 shirt you'll find Bill Shankly (although his surname is misspelt). This was his one and only appearance in a Liverpool shirt.

The fifth season of wartime football, 1943-44, saw local lad Laurie Hughes feature for the Reds at centre-half; in time he'd become the first LFC player to appear in a World Cup finals.

By the end of the war, eleven of Liverpool's players had lost their lives, while the so-called May Blitz of 1941 had devastated the city of Liverpool and its docklands. Peacetime brought the return of large crowds, and on Saturday 29 December 1945 the Reds drew 2-2 with Everton at Goodison Park in front of 60,926.

In 1946, ahead of the first 'proper' season since the war, at the suggestion of chairman William H McConnell the Reds toured

North America to play exhibition matches while beefing up on steaks away from food-rationed Britain. They returned to win their fifth title and first since 1923, although they had to wait until mid-June to be confirmed as champions.

The average Anfield gate topped 40,000 for the first time and among the new crowd favourites was Albert Stubbins, signed from Newcastle, who was the club's equal top-scorer in the league with Jack Balmer on 24 goals apiece.

The latter half of the decade saw a relaxation on paper-rationing and a matchday programme increasing to eight then 16 pages, printed in red ink on white paper. Among the new features were guest columnists from newspapers, a few adverts, and 'Our Weekly Pen Picture' – soon to be renamed 'Our Portrait Gallery' – dedicated to a current player.

On Saturday 25 March 1950, the Reds met Everton in the FA Cup semi-final at Maine Road (the second of five last-four meetings to date with the neighbours). It finished 2-0 with Bob Paisley and Billy Liddell on target. But the road to Wembley ended in heartache with a 2-0 defeat by Arsenal in the FA Cup final.

When Liverpool and Burnley met for a friendly in 1914, four days after the FA Cup final between the teams, proceeds from the match were donated to the Theatrical Gala Fund – hence the title on the front cover

In the early 1900s, adverts were often for men's clothing, and Beaty Brothers dominated the cover until the outbreak of the First World War for a programme shared by Liverpool and Everton

There was a splash of colour on this 1934 cover for the match against Tranmere Rovers

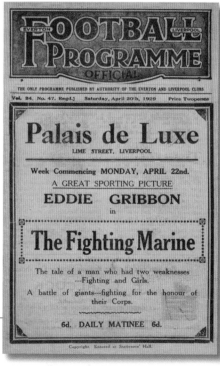

By 1929 the programme cost twopence and the Sunderland edition advertised a show at the Palais de Luxe cinema

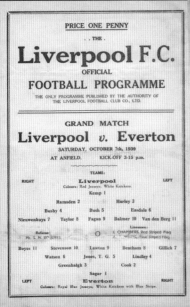

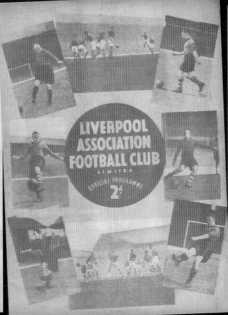

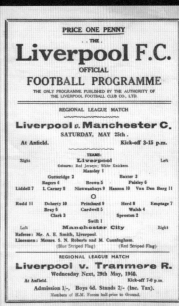

Just over a month after Britain entered World War II, Liverpool had Matt Busby and Jack Balmer in their line-up for a match against Everton

There were lots of pictures on the cover of the Leicester programme in March 1939, a selection chosen by editor Ernest Edwards to last the whole season

There was a regional league match against Manchester City in May 1940 where Liverpool wore 'red jerseys, white knickers'

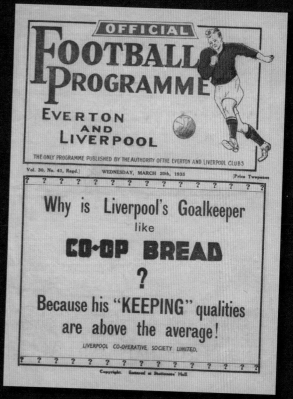

Having previously shared a programme with Everton, the club went solo, starting with this Manchester City issue in September 1935

A slice of fun in an advert on the cover of the Everton programme in March 1935

## NOTES.

IT is hoped that a programme issued in this form will be appreciated by our supporters.

Everything possible will be done to ensure that the information given on the front page, as to the names and positions of the various teams, visiting Anfield Road, is correct.

Occasionally, however, alterations take place after going to press, when too late to make corrections.

These programmes should not be thrown away, but should be preserved, as they will form an interesting record of the doings of both teams, and also contain a list of fixtures, etc., up to date.

The ground is in good order, and the committee earnestly beg spectators to refrain from crossing the field, either before or after the matches. Nothing is gained by crowding on the field, but on wet days the damage is great, and the ground rendered almost unfit for play.

Every one should carefully study the

## "OFF-SIDE" RULE,

For it is of the utmost importance that the proper interpretation should be clearly understood. The vital point, and perhaps the one most frequently overlooked, is, that it is the position of a player at the moment the ball has been played by one of his own side, that determines whether or not he is "off-side," and not his position when he secures the ball. To be in play, one must either be behind the player, on his own side, or have three opponents between him and the opposite goal *at the moment the ball was played.* Any one "off-side" at the moment when the ball was played, must not under any circumstances either play the ball or interfere with an opponent doing so till he is put in play. Now, a player once "off-side" can be put in play in *two ways only*, these are,—the playing of the ball by an opponent, or by one of his own side nearer the opposite goal; of course no one is "off-side" when the ball has been played by an opponent, whatever his position may be. According to the old Scotch interpretation of the rule, a player "off-side" was put in play whenever he got three opponents in front of him, whether the ball had been played or not, but now the playing of the ball is the one thing needful.

THE above is a portrait of our esteemed president, MR. JOHN HOULDING. To know him is to like him, though there are some who are hostile to him, because they never tried to know him.

He is a man of energy, determination, and honesty of purpose, and under his presidency the LIVERPOOL CLUB is sure to prosper, in the same way as the EVERTON CLUB did.

May he long be spared to take part in the many good works in which he is engaged in his native city.

Some excerpts from the Reds' first programme (v Rotherham Town in September 1892), including an appeal for fans not to go on the pitch, an explanation of the offside rule and a portrait of club president John Houlding, which declared that 'to know him is to like him, though there are some who are hostile to him'

A message from George Patterson, secretary-manager, at the start of the 1935-36 season asked fans for "a little patience and forbearance" as well as "a continuance of vocal encouragement"

## CLUB GOSSIP
### By THE SECRETARY-MANAGER

With the opening of a new season past successes and failures are again overshadowed by the vision of brighter things in the future. We commence our first column in the new programme by thanking all our loyal and enthusiastic followers for their magnificent and unswerving support in the past and trust that their renewed confidence will be duly merited when the final curtain is run down on 1935-36.

We are pleased to say we have a happy, contented and enthusiastic staff of players, fit and eager to bring honours to the Club if at all possible and no effort will be spared by the Board to foster that spirit of goodwill among them, and also to acquire any additional playing strength which may be found necessary as the season progresses. Our well-equipped ground is the envy of many visiting Club Officials and players, and it is our intention to have a team which will arouse equally envious glances from our colleagues in the First Division.

"Rome was not built in a day" and only one team can win the championship each year, therefore, we would appeal to all spectators for a little patience and forbearance and for a continuance of that vocal encouragement which means so much to the Club and players alike. We can assure you

the players give of their best but, being human, they are bound to have an "off" day occasionally. Many a good player has been ruined by well intentioned but misguided enthusiasts who barracked when a little encouragement would have been so beneficial. Now "Kopites" keep up your vocal reputation!

We hope from week to week to give some interesting information in these columns, together with a brief resume of the away matches played the previous week.

Against Manchester City on Wednesday, our forecast of a hard and fast game duly materialised. While congratulating the City on their victory, we feel that Dame Fortune did not smile on us when the shot by "Nivvy" which appeared to all the players, and most of the spectators, to be over the line, was not allowed by the Referee. Had a goal been allowed at this junction it might have conceivably changed the course of the game. We can, however, console ourselves that we were defeated by a really good side who, if they maintain that standard, must be strong challengers for the League Championship.

## NEILLS FOR HATS AND CAPS

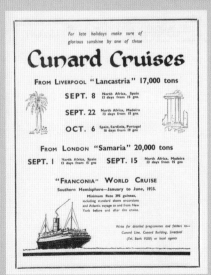

In 1934 Cunard Cruises were advertising holidays to North Africa and the Mediterranean from the port of Liverpool

Dashing pictures of the players in 1909, including the legendary Alex Raisbeck

The Birmingham programme in March 1934 reminded fans of the chance to see the marvellous new Mersey Tunnel

View from Walton Breck Road—Kemlyn Road Corner.

## FIRST DIVISION MATCH.

### LIVERPOOL

*v.*

### BURY.

LIVERPOOL.

R.         SCOTT         L.

JACKSON      MacKINLAY

MORRISON   DAVIDSON   BROMILOW

EDMED MILLER WHITEHURST McDOUGALL HOPKIN

O

AMOS  BALL  SMITH (J.R.)  BULLOCK  ROBBIE

PRATT   BRADSHAW (T.)   ROBINSON

THOMPSON   BRADSHAW (G.)

L.       RICHARDSON       R.

BURY.

Kick-off 3-15.          Referee: H. E. HALL.

Linesmen: H. CARTLIDGE and T. BROWN.

### THE GREAT SPION KOP

In August 1928 the club had a special programme for the Bury match to mark the opening of the first 'roofed-in' Kop, including pictures and facts

# Liverpool Association Football Club.

FIRST DIVISION CHAMPIONS 1901, 1906, 1922, 1923.
SECOND DIVISION CHAMPIONS 1894, 1896, 1905.
Highest Total First Division Points since the War, viz. : 433.

## Souvenir of the Opening

## . . of the completed . .

## Spion Kop New Stand.

## Epic Features of the New Spion Kop Stand.

The first roofed-in Kop in the country.

\* \* \*

It is 425 feet long by 131 feet wide, and is 80 feet high. A new stand in entirety, only the cinder hill beneath the centre portion and three post-war concrete staircases now remain of the old Kop of two years ago.

\* \* \*

Two-thirds of its possible 28,000 spectators can see the game without a single intervening stanchion.

\* \* \*

The cost is greatly increased thereby, but so is the efficiency and the pleasure of the One Shilling Spectator and Supporter of the Club.

\* \* \*

No other ground offers 45,000 of its accommodation, all under cover, at One Shilling Fare.

\* \* \*

The outside walls and six internal stanchions of the Kop carry 45,500 square feet of roof, over one acre; under which 91 subsidy houses of standard type could be packed together in one layer.

\* \* \*

The length of one truss and cantilever is 131 feet. Second comes those of West Ham United at 100, and at Everton, 55 feet.

\* \* \*

The Cantilever alone is a 51 feet overhang, compared to 38 at West Ham, 25 at Leicester, 15 at Everton.

## FIND Mr. KOPITE

### THERE IS A SEASON TICKET FOR THE FIRST MAN TO PICK HIM OUT.

Our competition for the season ticket continues.

You've got to find "Mr. Kopite" to-day, and if you have a Programme in your keeping and are first to approach him, thus: "You are Mr. Kopite, I claim the season ticket prize"—you win.

I am asked to give some notion of his whereabouts, etc.

Let us take down his particulars, as the comics say:

He is rather pale-faced; of good number of years-of-life; wears a trilby hat; slightly bent-stance; deep set eyes. He will walk around the ground, taking up his position in good time for the game—whether on the Kop, in the Paddock, on Kemlyn Road Stand, or the Grandstand, no one can say at the moment.

Challenge your neighbour; he may be the Mystic Missing Link.

The winner will visit the club's offices after the game and stake his claim with the officials for the gift of a season ticket.

#### YOU MAY KOP IT.

And now, lads of Spion Kop, let me beg you to leave the oranges at home for the kiddies. This throwing business has gone too far; the accumulation of complaint against you from referees and visiting teams will lead to trouble for the club if you do not cease-fire.

You are entitled to your view of a defender, or a referee, but you are not entitled to throw anything. Besides it makes such a litter about the place!

You have been warned; you have been requested; now, come on sports, let us have no more of this greengrocery business on the Kop.

On with the game; have your fill of enjoyment, but don't let us suck it and see when you think things are not going well with the Reds!

In 1938 if you found the mystery 'Mr Kopite' you could win a season-ticket!

# Our Honours.

**The English Cup** — Won by Everton at the Crystal Palace, April 21st, 1906.

**The League Champion Cup** — Won by Liverpool by consistent good play during the Season 1905-6.

**The Sheriff of London Shield.** (Presented by Sir Thomas Dewar) Won by Liverpool at Fulham, where they beat the Corinthians by 5-1 April 28th, 1906.

## DEWAR'S "White Label" WHISKY.

### RESULT TABLES UP TO SATURDAY.

Liverpool and Everton's combined honours list from the 1905-06 season looked pretty impressive

## THE COMPLETION OF THE ANFIELD GROUND.

The ground is in splendid condition and the new stand makes the ground look complete. The players come from the centre of it instead of the South East corner, and their new quarters are much more comfortable. The Board room, secretary's office, and general office, are fitted up very tastefully, and to Mr. Watson the change from his old quarters must be most agreeable. There are baths for players, a gymnasium, and a billiard room, so that every comfort is provided.

By the way I must congratulate Will Dunlop upon his successful essay as referee.

Changes to the Main Stand were lauded in the Villa programme in September 1908

# LIVERPOOL'S NEW GROUND.

The changes that have taken place at Anfield Road will delight those who have visited that enclosure in years gone by. For a long time the triangular piece of waste ground at the Walton Breck Road entrance was a source of discomfort to many. In wet weather it formed a muddy embankment, which had to be crossed, and if the day was fine it was used as a playground for a lot of youths who did not profess any consideration for passers-by. Oftentimes, too, it was occupied by travelling shows, and the blaring tones of the organs which are the proud possession of such things were not a source of delight to the man with a musical ear. Another relic of the past which has disappeared is the old bottle neck exit at Kemlyn Road, which is something to be devoutly thankful for. Now a handsome and substantial wall has been erected, and the exits and entrances will be as near perfection as possible.

The first thing that strikes one on entering the ground is the huge terracing which is rising at the west end. Already there are forty steps completed, but eventually there will be one hundred, and it will accommodate about 20,000 people. The terracing is continued along the two sides, but, of course, it does not rise to anything like the height it does at the west end. For the moment the Anfield Road stand has not been interfered with, but terracing has been carried round to join it, and what was wasted space has been utilised fully. To make those standing comfortable barriers have been erected, and they are Leitch's patent barriers, which are absolutely unbreakable.

The grand stand has been removed to the opposite side, where the old original small stand used to be. That has gone for ever, but the substitute has been altered and improved so that everybody who has a seat thereon will be comfortable, and able to have a perfect view of the game.

In days to come a new stand will be built, and then the ground will be complete, but that is not yet. The playing pitch looks very fine, and if the sods have knitted together it will vie with Goodison Park for perfection. It has been moved considerably over, and a portion of the new playing pitch is where the big stand was in former years. To enable it to be carried over, the ground had to be raised nearly three feet, and an immense quantity of earth had to be obtained in order to bring it up to the necessary level. The corners have been rounded, so that there is a chance of seeing the game from every standpoint.

I suppose everybody to-day will be going to see for themselves, but I doubt whether many of the assembled thousands will really understand the magnitude of the work undertaken. The accomplishment is seen and will be appreciated, but how it was done can only be known to those who have watched its progress from time to time. The amount that has been tipped there reaches thousands of tons, and to obtain this alone, and to get it properly distributed is a great thing in itself. But when one remembers that everything had to be pulled down before the work of re-construction could be commenced, and that time was limited, then one realises that almost a miracle has been accomplished.

The Liverpool directors were fortunate in obtaining the services of Mr. Arch. Leitch, of London and Glasgow, the experienced ground architect, who has been responsible for many of the finest grounds in the kingdom, including Fulham, Chelsea, and Bramall Lane. He has designed the ground, and I think everybody will agree that he has made the very best use of the site. He has given great attention to it, and must himself feel pleased at the result of his labours. He has been ably assisted by the clerk of the works, Mr. George Nelson, and the directors, from the chairman downwards, have displayed a great interest in every step. Indeed, certain of the gentlemen connected with the club, such as Messrs. E. Berry, J. Fare, Briggs, Ramsay, and T. Watson, seemed to live on the ground, for they were always there. Another year must elapse before the scheme is fully carried out, but when complete the ground will be a picture.

## ANNOUNCEMENT.

Owing to the re-construction of the ground, the score board is not yet ready. As far as possible half and full-time results will be sent round on slate.

There were changes aplenty to the ground in 1906, as explained in September's Stoke programme

## PERSONALIA.

### William Dunlop, Liverpool F.C.

We are delighted to-day to once again present to our readers William Dunlop, Liverpool's left full back, who has served the club so faithfully and well for over a dozen years. The occasion is the benefit granted to this player, and we only re-iterate our previous declarations—in so doing doubtless expressing the hope of thousands—that he deserves a bumper. There are some men who perform brilliantly in their various positions in the field, but there never was one who year in year out has given such whole-hearted service as Dunlop has to Liverpool. He always plays to win, and no matter what the odds are he is prepared to do his level best with that object in view. All who have followed the varied fortunes of the Liverpool club can testify to this, and we hope those who profess to admire the character of the man and the ability of the player will not be content with lip service only, but will show their appreciation in the right way. Every one can do something, and each according to his pocket ought to do what he can. We have no wish to labour the question, but hope to chronicle the fact next week that Dunlop has been fully and worthily recompensed.

A few brief remarks about Dunlop's career will not be out of place here. He comes from Hurlford, in Ayrshire, that nursery of footballers, which for its size and the number of its inhabitants has probably produced more players than any other similar place. He played for the team of his native village in his early teens, and even then his position was at left full back. From Hurlford he progressed through Kilmarnock to Paisley Abercorn. While with the latter he was chosen to play for Ayrshire against Glasgow, and also for the Rest of the Second League against the Champions—the Hibernians. In 1894 he crossed the border, and Liverpool made no mistake when they secured his services.

He assisted them through their initial year in the Second Division, through the transitory time in the First League, and then again to become champions of the Second Division. But after this he was for a time kept on one side, first through a poisoned ankle, then through the form shown by Wilkie. The deterioration of the latter meant once again the advancement of Dunlop, and ever since—for ten years—he has held his place. He is the one member of the old school left, and he is a fitting representative. When after the disastrous season of 1903-04 Liverpool for the third time had to fight their way through the troublous waters of the Second Division, Dunlop was foremost in the fray, and he had the satisfaction of helping to establish the unique record held by Liverpool of being Champions of the two Divisions of the League in successive seasons. When Liverpool's re-entry into the First League was assured, there never was a prouder man than Dunlop, except on the day when the First League Championship was annexed.

Dunlop is a vigorous back, and he kicks wonderfully in any position. He is also a rare cover goal, and many a time his head has proved useful on the goal line. International honours in his case were belated, but "everything comes to him who waits." So it certainly proved to the left back, for last April he had the satisfaction of being chosen for Scotland against England, and figuring on the side of the winning team. Thus he after being passed over many times reaped the reward long since due to him.

Dunlop comes of a family of seven brothers, but he is the only one who has taken up football as a profession. In private life Dunlop is modest and unassuming. He has a passion for music—in common with others of his family—and is a clever performer on the violin.

He is well equipped physically, being 5ft. 9nin. in height, and weighing 12 stone. Such is a brief *resumé* of to-day's popular *beneficiare.*

The following biographical details of to-day's beneficiare. William Dunlop, have, we believe, never before been published. We have, therefore, pleasure in affording our readers a chance of perusing them, and merely remark that they are copyright throughout the civilised world.

| | | |
|---|---|---|
| Also in Liverpool and Bootle :- | | |
| Born | 1876 | ? |
| Short-coated | 1876 | ? |
| Mumps | 1878 | |
| Knickerbockered | 1879 | |
| Allowed to play football | 1882 | |
| Measles | 1886 | |
| Trousered | 1890 | |
| First smoke | 1890 | |
| First sick headache | 1890 | |
| First joined Hurlford | 1891 | |
| Ditto, Kilmarnock | 1892 | |
| Ditto, Paisley Abercorn | 1894 | |
| Ditto, Liverpool | 1894 | |
| First wore red jersey | 1894 | |
| First time League player | 1895 | |
| First Test Match | 1895 | |
| First time ought to have been International | 1899 | |
| No. of kicks made in League football | 396.875 | |
| First time actually was International | 1905 | |
| Height in socks | 5ft. 9½in. | |
| Ditto, on stilts | 27ft. | |
| Weight before meals | 12st. | |
| Ditto, after meals | | variable |
| Second benefit | 1906 | |
| Estimated receipts from same | £15,000 | |
| Amount not received | £14,700 | |

| | |
|---|---|
| Grand total | 426.875 ?? variable |

Audited and found fairly correct,
Smith and Jones,
Shattered Accountants.

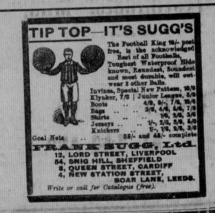
In October 1906 the page of 'Personalia' gave us lots of information on left-back William Dunlop, including the years he first had mumps, had his first smoke – and how tall he'd be on stilts!

A 1938 competition in many issues to find nicknames came up with 'Boomerang' for Jack Balmer

'Club Gossip' in August 1936 brought news of a new manager, George Kay, joining from Southampton

The Preston programme in March 1937 used an image of a memorial tablet in honour of John McKenna

The 1909 Lincoln programme informs fans of the latest melodramatic theatre production in town

# LIVERPOOL FOOTBALL CLUB. SEASON 1935-36
## DIRECTORS, OFFICIALS AND PLAYERS

[Photograph by courtesy of Carbonora Co., 59a Lime Street, Liverpool.

**BACK ROW**—F. Rogers, B. Nieuwenhuys, B. E. Dabbs, J. Browning, L. L. Carr, J. W. Tennant, R. G. Neal, J. Harley, T. W. Bush.
**THIRD ROW**—C. Wilson (Trainer), T. Bradshaw, N. Low, R. J. Glassey, R. E. Savage, J. McDougall, A. J. Riley, E. Blenkinsop (Captain), S. Kane, T. C. F. Johnson, T. Cooper (Vice-Captain), B. Ramsden, E. V. Wright, G. Hodgson, E. Longworth (Asst. Trainer).
**SECOND ROW**—G. S. Patterson (Secretary-Manager), Mr. G. A. Richards (Director), Mr. W. H. McConnell (Director) Mr. W. Harvey Webb (Director), Mr. J. H. Troop (Vice Chairman), Mr. W. J. Harrop (Chairman), Mr. W. H. Cartwright (Director), Mr. J. Asbury (Director), Mr. R. L. Martindale (Director), Mr. S. R. Williams (Director), J. C. Rouse (Asst. Secretary), J. Hewitt (Asst. Trainer).
**FRONT ROW**—F. Howe, A. Hanson, H. Taylor, S. Roberts.

Team photos from 1935-36 (above) and 1905-06 (right)

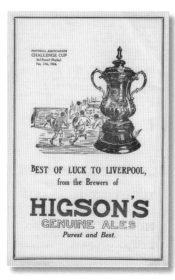

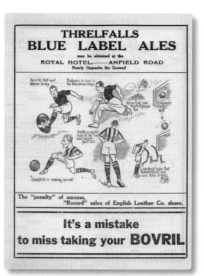

Adverts for Higson's ales (1924), Threlfalls ales (1932) and Jack Sharp sports outfitter (1909)

# CLUB GOSSIP

It is felt that a short description of the tour to the Canary Islands might be of interest to readers.

Three Directors, the Manager, fourteen players and the Trainer comprised the party which set sail on S.S. "Adda" on May 8th, arriving at Las Palmas on the 14th. Thanks to the Captain and his Officers the passage was thoroughly enjoyable, amid ideal weather, though on the first day the dining room had many notable absentees, in fact the party was at one meal only five strong. Some of the players, though not actually sick, took the precaution of staying down below to avoid possible comments as to how far they could "shoot"!

They eventually recovered their sea-legs and proceeded to entertain the other passengers with their gymnastics and punch-ball displays and participation in the various deck games.

Itinerary cards, giving the personnel of the party with dates of arrivals and departures and fixtures to be played, were in great demand by passengers and crew and we were kept very busy autographing them.

On arrival at Las Palmas we were driven to the Hotel Metropole which became our Headquarters for the next 12 days. The open-air bathing pool and miniature golf course attached to the Hotel were well patronised, and in the evenings the card rooms and billiards in the adjoining British Club were thoroughly appreciated, particularly as our lack of acquaintance with the Spanish language made the cinemas and theatre no attraction whatever. One or two evenings were spent at the open-air boxing matches.

We had several interesting motor tours around the Island, but a chara journey to what is known as "The Crater" at a height of 6000 ft. above sea level was anything but enjoyable, due to the fact that the driver of the vehicle was a super "speed-hog." Although ascending narrow winding roads with a huge drop on one side he never slowed down or changed gear, and the more the boys bawled (!) at him, the worse he became. He took their shouts and threats (not understanding English or Scotch) as an indication to "carry on," and consequently we all spent a most uncomfortable time. Bradshaw's face was a study, while several others took a position denoting they were ready to "jump for it" if anything untoward occurred. Happily we returned without a scar but there were no future drives outside the confines of Las Palmas.

The actual games have been fully reported, and require no comment except to say that the only game we did not win was drawn 2-2, thanks to ludicrous refereeing. One of our forwards beat four opponents and his final shot was luckily diverted by the goalkeeper to another forward who placed it in the net. The referee's verdict was offside! nuff sed! In the same game he refused to grant the home team's absurd claim for a penalty and he was thereupon hailed with a veritable shower of cushions from the seats in the paddock and stands. It was highly amusing to see the players and linesmen removing the "debris" for fully five minutes before the game could be restarted.

The return journey was in many respects similar to the outward passage except that the training was dispensed with. The S.S. "Accra" is a well appointed boat, but was uncomfortably crowded and therefore the trip was not as enjoyable as on the S.S. "Adda," although the Captain and Officers of the "Accra" were equally as obliging as their confreres on the "Adda."

'Club Gossip' in the Aston Villa programme of November 1935 gave a fascinating insight into a club trip to the Canary Islands in May of that year

A line-up from the Cardiff issue in April 1922 shows legendary names including Elisha Scott and Harry Chambers. The Reds won 5-1 with Chambers netting a hat-trick and two days later they beat Burnley to be crowned champions

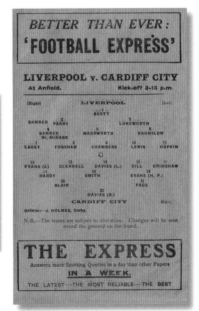

The Stockport County programme of January 1915 included this appeal for more men to join the war effort

Pages from the final programme before World War II intervened, v Chelsea in September 1939

Liverpool's line-up for the 1942 Liverpool Senior Cup final included Bill Shankly (mis-spelled as 'Shankley'). It was a double-header so also counted as a league game

February 1942's game against Sheffield United had a 'Board Room Comment' about recent events, including an illness to captain Matt Busby

## MANAGER'S BULLETIN.

Anfield supporters will be very pleased to hear that the Directors of the Club have offered to send a team entirely composed of our Service players to play games in Germany, Belgium and France for the benefit of any of the Forces Charities.

The Liverpool Club will cover the expenses incurred on this tour.

As we were the first professional club whose players joined up practically "en bloc" in the Territorial Army in August, 1939, we regard it as a signal honour to be the first League Club to play in the European War Zone.

"Red" supporters in the B.L.A., who have followed the progress of the Liverpool Club with great interest, will, I am sure, give a warm welcome to our team when we reach the other side of the Channel.

The exact date has not yet been arranged, but we are awaiting further news about the matter from the Football Association.

The Season has been extended to May 26th, and during this period we are expecting Blackpool and Derby County to pay a visit to Anfield.

On VE + 1 Day we have arranged to play Preston North End at Anfield Road.

Our visit to Derby on Whit Monday will be full of interest, as we are still in the running for the League Championship.

GEORGE KAY.

In May 1945 manager George Kay expressed his pride in sending a team to play in a "war zone"

### LINKS WITH THE LIVERPOOL FOOTBALL CLUB.

#### MR. MATT. McQUEEN.

Mr. Matt. McQueen was laid to rest at Anfield Cemetery on Tuesday. The Rev. James Jackson, our former Captain, performed the last rites with rare taste and solemnity—he paid tribute to the sturdy man of Anfield, and he called for our remembrance of the widow and children left behind. A number of old-time players were present at the service and in the officials one noticed the Club's Chairman, Mr. W. H. McConnell, with Directors W. Harvey Webb and S. R. Williams, together with Messrs. Geo. Kay (Manager), J. C. Rouse, Geo. Patterson, Dr. Curwin, Bert Riley, Andy McGuigan, groundsmen and gate-checkers, etc. It was a simple ceremony, sincere in every note, and typifying the life of Matt. McQueen, who was a relentless, stern, straight and forthright man.

Matt. McQueen came to Liverpool from his bonny Scottish Leven and grew up with the Liverpool Football Club, for whom he played in every position. In the old days it was argued that a good player could play in any position. That was a fallacy, but Matt. McQueen was the man to whom the phrase applied, because he ran the whole gamut of football; think of his links with the Anfield Club—there was not a point at which he had not had effort and success. He was a player in every position, including goal, when the Liverpool team was termed "the team of Macs"; he was a competent Referee; he was a valued Director of the Club, and at one time became its Manager. The name of Matt. McQueen and Liverpool Football Club will be associated for all time. By his works we knew him.

#### LIVERPOOL F.C. FIXTURES, 1944.

| 1944. | | | Goals. | | |
|---|---|---|---|---|---|
| | | | F | A | P |
| Aug. 26—Stockport County | ... | A | 3 | 2 | 2 |
| Sept. 2—Stockport County | ... | H | 2 | 0 | 2 |
| „ 9—Manchester City | ... | H | 2 | 2 | 1 |
| „ 16—Manchester City | ... | A | 2 | 2 | 1 |
| „ 23—Crewe Alexandra | ... | A | 1 | 4 | 0 |
| „ 30—Crewe Alexandra | ... | H | 1 | 4 | 0 |
| Oct. 7—Wrexham | ... | H | | | |
| „ 14—Wrexham | ... | A | | | |
| „ 21—Everton | ... | A | | | |
| „ 28—Everton | ... | H | | | |

| 1944. | | | Goals. | | |
|---|---|---|---|---|---|
| | | | F | A | P |
| Nov. 4—Manchester United | ... | H | | | |
| „ 11—Manchester United | ... | A | | | |
| „ 18—Bury | ... | A | | | |
| „ 25—Bury | ... | H | | | |
| Dec. 2—Chester | ... | H | | | |
| „ 9—Chester | ... | A | | | |
| „ 16—Tranmere Rovers | ... | A | | | |
| „ 23—Tranmere Rovers | ... | H | | | |

SCORERS.
Done, 4; Welsh, 2; Dix, 2; Fagan, 1; Nieuwenhuys, 1; Eastham, 1.

There was a tribute to legendary club figure Matt McQueen in the Wrexham single-sheet issue in 1944

## THE ROYAL AIR FORCE.

### EXCHANGE YOUR OVERALLS FOR FLYING KIT.

### AIR CREW APPEAL.

An opportunity for fit men between the ages of 17½ and 39 to exchange their overalls for flying kit is being provided at the moment on Merseyside by an extensive Recruiting Campaign. No matter what your occupation, reserved or unreserved, if you come within the age limits and are fit, you may be considered for flying duties. Here then, is a chance to strike a direct blow back at the enemy.

The R.A.F. are running daily and nightly express services to German cities and Enemy Occupied Territory, and you are asked to book your seats for these trips and see you "get a front seat too"!

Air power will no doubt be a deciding factor in the victorious ending for us of this war and the intensive bombing of German war industries which is now going on is crippling the enemy before munitions and implements of war can reach their Armed Forces.

At the moment we hold predominancy in the air and with the help of our Allies and our Dominions overseas, the R.A.F. are not only going to maintain that predominancy but to steadily increase it. As Fighter and Bomber Aircraft come from the factories, we need the trained flying crews to take them over.

The permanent Recruiting Office for the Liverpool district is at Renshaw Hall, Renshaw Street, open daily from 9 a.m. to 6 p.m., and two temporary Recruiting Kiosks are now open at Messrs. T. J. Hughes, London Road, Liverpool, and Messrs. Allansons Stores, Grange Road, Birkenhead, where enquiries can be made and application forms filled in. So come along you men who want a chance to strike a direct blow for the cause of FREEDOM and VICTORY. Many trades are also open on the Ground Staff, age limits 18 to 55.

The Everton programme in November 1943 was used to try and help recruit more men for the RAF

**LIVERPOOL FOOTBALL CLUB.**

**FOOTBALL LEAGUE (Division I)—CHAMPIONS 1946-47.**

By courtesy of the Liverpool Evening Express.

The Preston programme of August 1947 was a chance to show a group photo of the previous season's league champions

**FROM THE BOARD ROOM** (continued).

At this juncture it is appropriate to point out to the schoolboys that it is essential that on entering the ground they pass immediately to the "Boys Pen," where they will be free from all danger and injury. The accommodation set aside for them is undoubtedly one of the best positions on the ground, and unless they carry out these instructions it may be necessary to remove their enclosure to a more remote part of the ground.

To assist them it has been decided that in future their turnstiles will be opened at least 30 minutes prior to the other stiles, to enable them to gain admission to the pen before the adult spectators are admitted.

On Saturday next, the 28th September, we have another home League fixture with Leeds United, kick-off 3 p.m. We advise spectators to arrive early to avoid last minute crushes and would earnestly appeal to spectators on the popular portions to close towards the centre and leave the entrances clear for those who come later.

It would also assist greatly in expediting admission if **spectators will please tender the correct money at the turnstiles.**

September 1946's match against Everton had a 'Board Room' column that advised schoolboys to head straight to the 'Boys Pen' when they get in the ground – and asked all fans to tender the correct change at turnstiles

## FROM THE BOARD ROOM.

To old and new supporters we extend a hearty welcome. It is difficult to realise that seven years have elapsed since that Wednesday evening, 30th August, 1939, when Middlesbrough opened our home programme for 1939/40. Less than four hours before the match most of our playing staff had received telegrams to report for Military service, and eight of the team had returned from Army headquarters with their uniform—some with non-commissioned rank. Although the clouds of war were hanging over players and spectators alike, the game was an interesting one, full of thrills, etc., with Liverpool winning by four goals to one. Taylor 2, Balmer and Van Den Berg being our scorers.

To-day we welcome Middlesbrough, who play football of the best type, and with Manager David Jack at their helm, one can visualise new tactics that have been practised to perfection. Their team contains players who took part in pre-war football, and those who have made good during the war years. On Saturday next, Chelsea are visitors, and a great welcome will await Tommy Lawton, who, although a member of our Goodison rivals for many years, was always a popular figure at Anfield. The kick-off is 3 o'clock.

Now that football is restored to its pre-war basis, the games will prove to be much harder and keener than those played during the war years—with promotion and relegation once more in operation. All clubs will be anxious to place on the field teams good enough to provide attractive football for their loyal supporters. For our part, you can rest assured that every effort will be made to strengthen the team to make it one of the foremost in the land. Many overtures have been made for prominent players, but our efforts to date have not been successful.

Despite war-time restrictions rapid strides have been made during the close season to bring the ground and stands to their pre-war condition. Many repairs have been effected, but the Directors are anxious at all times to provide for the comfort of the spectators, and everything will be done, provided the necessary permits can be obtained to still further improve the accommodation.

The first league match at Anfield following World War II took place on Wednesday 4 September 1946 against Middlesbrough, with the board promising that the ground was back to 'pre-war condition'

LIVERPOOL FOOTBALL CLUB

Official Programme

Published by the authority of
THE LIVERPOOL FOOTBALL CLUB. LTD.

Directors:
W. H. McCONNELL, J.P. (Chairman).
S. R. WILLIAMS, C.C. (Vice-Chairman).
Messrs. W. H. CARTWRIGHT, W. HARVEY WEBB, J. H. TROOP,
W. J. HARROP, C.C., R. L. MARTINDALE, M.D.B.,
G. A. RICHARDS, J.P., R. K. MILNE, M.C.
Manager ——GEORGE KAY.

FOOTBALL LEAGUE—1st DIVISION.

**Liverpool**
*versus*
**Middlesbrough**

AT ANFIELD. WEDNESDAY, SEPTEMBER 4th
KICK-OFF 6-30. p.m.

NEXT MATCH.
FOOTBALL LEAGUE—1st DIVISION.
**Liverpool v. Chelsea**
AT ANFIELD. SATURDAY, SEPTEMBER 7th.
KICK-OFF 3 p.m.

PRICE ONE PENNY.

W. Jones & Co. Ltd., Printers, 7-11 Hunter Street, Liverpool, 3.

## DO YOU KNOW.

Elisha Scott and his brother Billy, kept goal for Ireland in 54 International matches. 'Lisha was "capped" on 31 occasions.

\* \* \* \*

No fewer than fifteen clubs have regained 1st Division status after being relegated the previous season, Bolton Wanderers performing the feat on three occasions.

\* \* \* \*

The record attendance for any match played in England outside of London. F.A. Cup—6th Round—Manchester City v. Stoke City, at Manchester, on March 3rd, 1934, when 84,569 spectators paid for admission.

\* \* \* \*

The Football League fined Newcastle United £750 for playing weak teams in seven matches in 1924. Newcastle United defeated Aston Villa in the F.A. Cup Final that year.

\* \* \* \*

Aston Villa and Blackburn Rovers have each won the F.A. Cup on six occasions.

**'Kick-off' with a HIGSONS**
*The BEER for YOU!*

BREWED IN LIVERPOOL SINCE 1780

The Middlesbrough programme in 1946 included some top trivia to entertain its readers

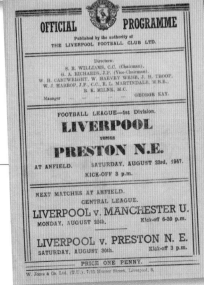

OFFICIAL PROGRAMME
Published by the authority of
THE LIVERPOOL FOOTBALL CLUB LTD.

Directors:
S. R. WILLIAMS, C.C. (Chairman).
G. A. RICHARDS, J.P. (Vice-Chairman).
W. H. CARTWRIGHT, W. HARVEY WEBB, J. B. TROOP.
W. J. HARROP, J.P., C.C., R. L. MARTINDALE, M.B.E.,
R. K. MILNE, M.C.
Manager ...... GEORGE KAY.

FOOTBALL LEAGUE—1st Division.
**LIVERPOOL**
versus
**PRESTON N.E.**
AT ANFIELD.    SATURDAY, AUGUST 23rd, 1947.
KICK-OFF 3 p.m.

NEXT MATCHES AT ANFIELD.
CENTRAL LEAGUE.
LIVERPOOL v. MANCHESTER U.
MONDAY, AUGUST 25th.    Kick-off 6-30 p.m.

LIVERPOOL v. PRESTON N. E.
SATURDAY, AUGUST 30th.    Kick-off 3 p.m.

PRICE ONE PENNY.

W. Jones & Co. Ltd. (T.U.), 7/11 Hunter Street, Liverpool, 8.

The Preston cover from August 1947 had black type as a mark of respect for the death of LFC chairman WH McConnell

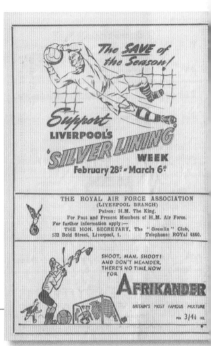

*The SAVE of the Season!*
Support LIVERPOOL'S 'SILVER LINING' WEEK
February 28th – March 6th

THE ROYAL AIR FORCE ASSOCIATION
(LIVERPOOL BRANCH)
Patron: H.M. The King.
For Past and Present Members of H.M. Air Force.
For further information apply:—
THE HON. SECRETARY, The "Gremlin" Club,
132 Bold Street, Liverpool, 1.    Telephone: ROYal 4840.

SHOOT, MAN, SHOOT!
AND DON'T MEANDER,
THERE'S NO TIME NOW
FOR
**AFRIKANDER**
BRITAIN'S MOST FAMOUS MIXTURE
per 3/4 oz.

Adverts in 1948 included one for 'silver lining week' to encourage post-war saving

IMPORTANT NOTICE.

Season Tickets, 1948-49

Season ticket holders must indicate to the Club Offices, Anfield Road, ON OR BEFORE SATURDAY, 15th May, 1948, if it is their intention to renew their tickets for 1948/9.

Applications to state Stand, Row and Seat No. for which the ticket is available and be accompanied by remittance, viz.:—

RESERVED, BUT NOT NUMBERED - £3 10 0.
RESERVED AND NUMBERED - - £4 0 0.

NO NEW APPLICATIONS CAN BE ACCEPTED AT THE PRESENT TIME.

THE ROYAL AIR FORCE ASSOCIATION
(LIVERPOOL BRANCH)
Patron: H.M. The King.
For Past and Present Members of H.M. Air Force.
For further information apply:—
THE HON. SECRETARY, The "Gremlin" Club,
132 Bold Street, Liverpool, 1.    Telephone: ROYal 4840.

SHOOT, MAN, SHOOT!
AND DON'T MEANDER,
THERE'S NO TIME NOW
FOR
**AFRIKANDER**
BRITAIN'S MOST FAMOUS MIXTURE
per 3/7

A reminder from the end of the 1947-48 campaign for fans to renew their season tickets in good time

## PLAYING STAFF—Season 1949/50.

| Name. | Date Signed. | Birthplace. | Previous Club. | Height. | Weight. st. lbs. |
|---|---|---|---|---|---|
| Sidlow, C. | 21/ 2/46 | Colwyn Bay | Wolverhampton W. | 6ft. 1in. | 13 10 |
| Minshull, R. | 28/ 9/46 | Bolton | S'port High Park | 5ft. 10½in. | 11 10 |
| Crossley, R. | 16/ 6/47 | Hebden Bridge | Army | 5ft. 10½in. | 11 3 |
| Ashcroft, C. T. | 29/12/45 | Chorley | Eccleston Jrs. | 6ft. 2in. | 12 1 |
| | | | | | |
| Lambert, R. | 18/ 7/39 | Bagilt | Flint Schoolboys | 5ft. 9½in. | 12 3 |
| Shepherd, J. W. | 8/12/45 | Liverpool | Elm Bank, L'pool | 5ft. 8½in. | 11 4 |
| Cadden, J. Y. | 12/ 6/48 | Glasgow | Brooklyn, U.S.A. | 6ft. 0in. | 13 5 |
| Parr, S. V. | 5/ 5/48 | Bamber Bridge | Farrington Villa | 5ft. 8½in. | 11 10 |
| White, G. | 4/11/48 | Philadelphia | Vale of Leven | 6ft. 0in. | 12 9 |
| Seddon, K. J. | 8/12/45 | Bolton | | 6ft. 0in. | 11 7 |
| Liddell, T. | 21/ 6/49 | Dunfermline | Lochore Welfare | 5ft. 10in. | 12 2 |
| | | | | | |
| Taylor, P. H. | 11/ 3/36 | Bristol | Bristol Rovers | 5ft. 9½in. | 11 2 |
| Jones, W. H. | 22/ 9/38 | Whaley Bridge | Harfield St. Matt. | 5ft. 11in. | 13 2 |
| Paisley, R. | 8/ 5/39 | Hetton le Hole | Bishop Auckland | 5ft. 6½in. | 11 3 |
| Hughes, L. | 19/ 2/43 | Liverpool | Tranmere Rovers | 6ft. 0in. | 12 4 |
| Spicer, E. W. | 4/10/39 | Liverpool | Liverpool Schools | 5ft. 10in. | 13 2 |
| Williams, R. | 7/ 8/45 | Liverpool | Local | 5ft. 6in. | 11 10 |
| Coppack, J. | 5/ 5/48 | Liverpool | Connahs Quay Jrs. | 5ft. 9in. | 11 7 |
| Heydon, J. | 30/12/48 | Birkenhead | Everton | 5ft. 10in. | 13 1 |
| Saunders, R. | 19/ 5/48 | Salford | Hull City | 5ft. 6in. | 10 2 |
| | | | | | |
| Payne, J. B. | 3/11/44 | Liverpool | Bootle A.T.C. | 5ft. 7½in. | 9 13 |
| Balmer, J. | 28/ 9/35 | Liverpool | Everton | 5ft. 10in. | 10 12 |
| Stubbins, A. | 12/ 9/46 | Wallsend | Newcastle United | 5ft. 11in. | 12 10 |
| Done, C. | 10/ 1/38 | Liverpool | Bootle B.B. | 6ft. 0in. | 12 12 |
| Liddell, W. B. | 17/ 4/39 | Dunfermline | Lochgelly Violet | 5ft. 10½in. | 12 9 |
| Fagan, W. | 22/10/37 | Musselburgh | Preston N.E. | 5ft. 9½in. | 12 13 |
| Brierley, K. | 26/ 2/48 | Oldham | Oldham Athletic | 5ft. 7½in. | 10 6 |
| Baron, K. | 25/ 8/45 | Preston | Preston N.E. | 5ft. 6in. | 10 7 |
| McLeod, T. | 18/10/45 | Musselburgh | B.A.O.R. | 5ft. 9in. | 10 5 |
| Shannon, L. | 7/11/44 | Liverpool | Local | 5ft. 8in. | 10 5 |
| Watkinson, W. | 20/ 2/46 | Prescot | Prescot Cables | 5ft. 9½in. | 11 13 |
| Williams, R. R. | 14/10/45 | Liverpool | Local | 5ft. 10½in. | 11 11 |
| Swift, K. | 14/ 8/45 | Liverpool | Local | 5ft. 9½in. | 11 12 |
| Christie, F. | 20/ 3/49 | Scone, Perth | Scone Jrs. | 6ft. 0in. | 12 4 |
| Wright, R. K. | 14/ 6/47 | Liverpool | Local | 5ft. 6½in. | 10 1 |
| Glazzard, M. | 28/ 5/49 | Ellesmere Port | Ellesmere Pt. Jrs. | 5ft. 11in. | 11 8 |
| Shield, S. M. | 30/ 4/49 | Denny | Cowdenbeath | 5ft. 8in. | 11 3 |

The squad list from the 1949-50 season included details of players' height, weight and former club

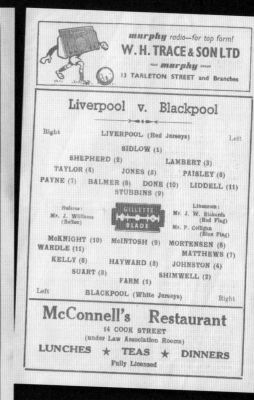

**W. H. TRACE & SON LTD**
*murphy* radio—for top form!
— *murphy* —
13 TARLETON STREET and Branches

### Liverpool v. Blackpool

Right — LIVERPOOL (Red Jerseys) — Left

SIDLOW (1)
SHEPHERD (2)    LAMBERT (3)
TAYLOR (4)   JONES (5)   PAISLEY (6)
PAYNE (7)   BALMER (8)   DONE (10)   LIDDELL (11)
STUBBINS (9)

Referee: Mr. J. Williams (Bolton)

Linesmen: Mr. J. W. Richards (Red Flag)   Mr. P. Colligan (Blue Flag)

McKNIGHT (10)   McINTOSH (9)   MORTENSEN (8)
WARDLE (11)     MATTHEWS (7)
KELLY (6)   HAYWARD (5)   JOHNSTON (4)
SUART (3)    SHIMWELL (2)
FARM (1)

Left — BLACKPOOL (White Jerseys) — Right

### McConnell's Restaurant
14 COOK STREET
(under Law Association Rooms)
LUNCHES ★ TEAS ★ DINNERS
Fully Licensed

This team line-up from the fixture against Blackpool in February 1949 saw legends on both sides as the likes of Billy Liddell, Albert Stubbins and goalscorer Jack Balmer faced Tangerines stars Stanley Matthews, Jimmy McIntosh and Stan Mortensen. The game finished 1-1

**ow to get the Autographs of your favourite players**

ou can be certain of getting the autographs of ur favourite Liverpool players. All you have do is to collect 12 Pal Hollow Ground razor ade wrappers. Send them with your name and dress, the name of your favourite player and nny stamp (to cover postage) to:—PAL LADES (Football), 79 Davies Street, London, .1. In return you will receive a handsome, rsonally signed card. Start collecting Pal wrappers today. Soon you will have a full set of your favourite players' autographs. The wrappers are easy to get because every man who shaves with a Pal Hollow Ground Blade recognizes its famous *"feather touch"* and goes on using these extra sharp blue blades.

**PAL** HOLLOW GROUND BLADES **3** for **6ᵈ**

PAL razor blades would send you player autographs in return for used wrappers in 1949

## FROM THE BOARD ROOM.

Hello everybody ! Here we are again at the commencement of a new Season, although it appears only a few days since we were cheering the announcement over the "mike" that the Championship Cup had returned to Anfield after an absence of twenty-four years.

The hearty congratulations of the Directors have already been extended to the players personally, but we feel it should be placed on record how much the Board, and our legion of supporters, appreciate their splendid achievement in winning five and drawing one of the last six League matches, particularly as four of the games were on opponents' grounds. Such a performance, coming as it did after their unfortunate dismissal from the F.A. Cup in the replayed semi-final, speaks volumes for the determination and team spirit of all those who took part in the concluding games when injuries and International matches deprived us of the services of Billy Liddell, Phil Taylor and Bob Paisley for the majority of these games. Eddie Spicer, Bob Priday and Bill Watkinson filled the vacancies with great credit.

League honours were supplemented by the winning of both the Lancs. F.A. Cup and the Liverpool Senior Cup—a fitting climax to a most successful season.

---

All our players have reported fit and well, eager for the fray, and fully determined to do their utmost to retain possession of the League trophy for another Season, and thus equal the record of six Division I. championships held by Aston Villa and Sunderland.

To-day, we welcome our old friends from Preston, who always provide good football and a hard encounter. They were one of the original twelve teams when the League was founded in 1888. They won the Championship during the first two Seasons (1888/89 and 1889/90), but their only League honours since that date have been the championships of the Second Division in 1904 and 1913.

The board of directors used their column for the first match of the 1947-48 season (a 3-1 win against Preston in August) to publicly congratulate the team on being champions

It is our sad duty to officially record the death of our Chairman, Mr. W. H. McConnell, which occurred suddenly at Dyserth on August 7th, and to express our deep sense of loss of one who rendered very valuable service to the Club as Director and then Chairman during a period of 18 years.

Mr. McConnell joined the Board in 1929, realising then the beginning of a life long ambition, and from the onset he took the keenest interest in all the activities of the Club of which he had always been a fanatical supporter. Mr. McConnell's ability and enthusiasm led him further into Football Administration for he was elected to the Management Committee of the Central League, played an active part in the Liverpool County Association, and was greatly interested in Youth Football, particularly in the Bootle area.

That Mr. McConnell should be taken just on the eve of the Official Celebration of the Club's past Season's honours, and what to him would have been one of the greatest moments of his life, was doubly tragic.

Much more might be written about him, about his kindness, his wit, his happy knack of making friends, his services to the Liverpool Club, but it cannot be summed up better than in the words of the Rev. James Jackson, our old Captain, who in a beautiful reference at the funeral service said "Mr. McConnell was a sportsman beloved by players, officials and spectators."

No man could wish a finer epitaph.

The Late
W. H. McCONNELL.

An obituary to chairman William McConnell appeared in the Preston programme, 16 days after his death in 1947

In what might be termed "the good old days" pigeons were used by pressmen for the purpose of sending their reports of matches to their offices, and, as a consequence, some little time had to elapse before the papers were on sale in the streets. Even to-day, the sporting writers at most grounds are handicapped for, after reserving telephones in private premises in the vicinity, have to employ messengers to go to and fro to transmit their "copy." The Directors have, at all times, appreciated the value of the press and have now decided to install several additional telephones in our Press Box, which will enable National and Visiting Press to send their reports of matches to their respective papers in the minimum of time and with every convenience. The new telephones will be available for the International League game.

In September 1948 the board reported on the extra phones that had been installed to help the press

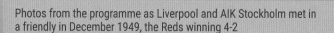

Photos from the programme as Liverpool and AIK Stockholm met in a friendly in December 1949, the Reds winning 4-2

## BILLY LIDDELL.

Billy Liddell, the epitome of dynamic action in football, who is now in his eleventh year as an Anfield player, is regarded today as the greatest striking force in the game, and there is no doubt that he is having his greatest season to date — a series of thrilling, match-winning displays which have not only helped to take Liverpool back to the No. 1 position they occupied at the end of season 1946/7, but simply forced the Scottish International Selectors to recall him at a time when their main objective was to place their destiny in the hands of the Home Scots rather than Anglos. Liddell's tremendous driving urge which enabled us to conquer a stubborn Birmingham, Middlesbrough, Fulham, Charlton Athletic and Aston Villa, and enabled the "Reds" to stage that thrill-a second rally against Newcastle United which kept the unbeaten record intact, has carried him back into the International sphere, and while his greatest games have been for his club, there is no doubt that Scotland will need him if they make the trip to Rio de Janiero next summer. In this modern age of high transfer fees, Billy's price in the market could not be valued, and yet he did not cost Liverpool a penny piece when they signed him on amateur forms at the age of 15. He was then playing for Lochgelly Violet, a Fifeshire junior club, and the condition of his signing was that he would be allowed to continue with his studies in an accountant's office.

It was in the Northern Mid-Week League side that Billy first helped the club when he joined them in July, 1938, and such was the progress he made that in April, 1939, he was signed as a professional.

As crisis in the glorious, colourful career of Liddell came in 1939 when he severely injured a knee in playing Blackburn "A" that is was feared his career might be finished. Expert attention was given to this "Wonder Boy" and he made a marvellous recovery and proved such an incisive forward for Liverpool during the early days of war football that the Scottish F.A. selected him to play in his first International in April, 1942. Matt Busby was there too to encourage him, and Scotland beat England at Hampden Park by five goals to four. Billy scored the first goal of the game and helped to give Jock Dodds a hat-trick.

Continued on next page.

## BILLY LIDDELL (continued)

Liddell did so well that in the October of that year he played for his country in a goalless draw with England at Wembley, and played again at Hampden Park in April, 1943. There would have been another honour too, but he had the misfortune to crack a small ankle bone when playing in a Royal Air Force game and had to withdraw, but on 3rd February, 1945, he played against England at Villa Park — his last war-time international. He played in the Victory Internationals against England, Wales and Ireland in 1946, and in 1946/7 received his first full international caps against Wales and Ireland. He went on to play against all the three home countries in 1947/8, and that season was crowned by the greatest honour of his time — his place in the Great Britain team which conquered the Rest of Europe. That very selection made Liddell as admittedly the greatest outside left in football, and . . . . since then he has more than cofirmed that opinion and fact.

One of Billy's secrets of success is that he is as deadly with his right foot as he is with his left, and so can change direction at top speed in the twinkling of an eye, beat an opposing back on the inside or outside, and centre or shoot from any position without having first to manoeuvre the ball to a favourite foot.

Liddell has no peer as a genuine club man, and has willingly played at centre-forward and inside forward when the occasion has demanded and Liverpool's needs were pressing. His desire is to serve his club at his best where ever he is needed, and there is no doubt that this great young footballer is carving for himself a special niche in football's Hall of Fame.

Not including today's match, Billy has played in 127 League games and scored 35 goals.

"All the BEST!" BENT'S Famous ALES and STONE STOUT

famous for quality
for over 100 Years

BENTS - BREWE...
LIVERPOOL & STO...

Portraits of the star players appeared in programmes during the 1949-50 season

---

### THIS WEEK'S SPECIAL FEATURE.

By RANGER, "Liverpool Echo."

Good morning, everybody. First let me wish you the season's greetings. In these days of austerity I'm afraid it won't be as merry a Christmas as some we've had, but let's make the most of it, and be thankful that things aren't any worse. As for the New Year, here's my hope that for all of you it will be a happy and healthy one, and more prosperous than that just ending.

In matters football we are at the half-way stage. So far as the Reds are concerned, it would be idle to pretend that their programme has been entirely satisfactory. After last year's League Championship and brilliant F.A. Cup run we entertained rosy dreams of another season of outstanding success. While events have not gone according to plan, we can take comfort from the evidence of an improvement in the offing, and hope that the second half of the season will see them again in the ascendancy.

The points difference separating clubs in the middle portion of the table is so small that a comparatively limited run of success would lift them well up the chart, and they can yet finish in a very respectable position.

What about the Cup? Last season's failure at the penultimate hurdle was a real blow. After all these years it looked as if success was at last to crown Anfield's striving. Instead, we had to postpone the pleasure of celebrating a Wembley victory. I wonder what this season holds? Much depends on the luck of the draw, and certainly the Reds would seem to have been favoured in this respect for their third round tie on January 10th, when Notts Forest come to Anfield. I haven't forgotten how Forest upset Manchester United's apple-cart in the fourth round at Maine Road last January, at a time when United were challenging for the League leadership.

All the same, I can't see them repeating the dose at Liverpool's expense in three weeks' time, and look to the Reds to go further ahead.

Liverpool have an abundance of that fighting spirit which is a real asset in the "death or glory" atmosphere of a cup-tie. If they can reproduce it unimpaired at cup successive hurdle they should again do well. The one thing they must guard against is underestimating the calibre of their opponents. Cup games are great levellers. All start from scratch, no matter what their League record or position. Each game is just eleven players against eleven others, and as a rule the minor clubs, with less at stake, are prepared to take greater chances.

In the past, Liverpool have sometimes shown a tendency to play down to the level of their opponents, and to rise to the heights when their prospects have looked less promising. The former tendency is a dangerous one in a cup-tie. Often a single goal is all that is needed to sway the issue.

The visit of Arsenal to-day gives us a sight of the side which is recapturing some of the old glamour of the halcyon days of Herbert Chapman. At one time is looked as though the Highbury lads were going to make the championship a one-horse race. Since then they had proved themselves subject to human frailties the same as others, and the fight is far from being won yet.

No matter who wins to-day, I hope we shall be able to go home to our Christmas dinners satisfied by a good exhibition of first-class football, fought in the clean sporting spirit which has characterised all Liverpool's games this season.

Good luck, good health, and the best of everything to you all during this festive season and throughout 1948.

---

FOOTBALL MATCH.

## Liverpool v. A.I.K. of Stockholm

AT ANFIELD.   MONDAY, 5th DECEMBER, 1949.

KICK-OFF 2-15 p.m.

**Prices of Admission:**

Ground 1/3d., Paddock 2/3d., Stands 5/-. Reserved and Numbered 3/6d. and 3/- (inc. Tax). ALL PAY.

Applications for reserved seats (5/-) to be sent to the Club Offices, Anfield Road, Liverpool, 4.

The upcoming friendly with AIK Stockholm was advertised in the Leicester programme in November 1949

Liverpool Echo columnist 'Ranger' had an article in the Christmas Day programme in 1947 which talked about austerity – and the Reds' chances in the upcoming FA Cup tie with Nottingham Forest

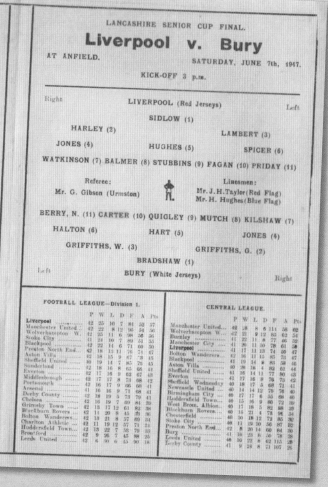

## From The Board Room.

The hearty congratulations of all our supporters must be tendered to the team for its magnificent display at Wolverhampton last Saturday. The whole team played delightful football and thoroughly deserved their victory.

Those who were unable to be present certainly missed an epic match and the two goals scored were the acme of perfection.

The club's performances in away games since the semi-final at Manchester have well merited our position as League leaders with 57 points, including twelve away victories.

To-day's game versus Bury recalls memories of our early days when Bury were our chief opponents. In our first season—1892-93—we won the Lancashire League, beating Bury by a narrow margin and securing election to the 2nd Division of the Football League. The following season we gained promotion to the 1st Division and Bury were elected to the 2nd Division, and both clubs have retained their Football League membership, although Bury have had a chequered career—whereas we have retained membership of Division I for the past 42 years.

It is interesting to recall that Bury were our visitors in the League match in 1928, when the covered Spion Kop at Anfield was officially opened by the League President, the late Mr. John McKenna.

Next week we meet our local rivals, Everton, in the Final of the Liverpool Senior Cup, which should prove a grand finale to a most successful season in which we reached the semi-final of the F.A. Cup and can only lose League honours on a small fraction of goal average. The score at Sheffield in the vital match with Stoke City will be announced every 15 minutes. Our kick-off will be at 3-15 p.m.

### LANCASHIRE SENIOR CUP FINAL.
# Liverpool v. Bury

AT ANFIELD. SATURDAY, JUNE 7th, 1947.
KICK-OFF 3 p.m.

The programme for the Lancashire Senior Cup final v Bury in June 1947 (which was won 2-1) gave the board a chance to hail the players who had won their last league game of the season at Wolves to put them in pole position for the championship

Last season an appeal was made to spectators to refrain from giving gratuitous advice to our players which, we are pleased to record, had the desired effect. Unfortunately a small section of the spectators are again expressing their discontent rather volubly, particularly behind the goals, with the result that the team is giving better displays away from home than before their own spectators. This is evidenced by the fact that we have gained five points in the last three away games, whereas in a similar number of games at home we have dropped five points. We therefore appeal to spectators to give the players a fair chance and not discourage them by disparaging remarks.

By January 1948 some fans were not quite so happy, prompting this request in the programme for the 4-1 win against Nottingham Forest

# CHAPTER 2

# 1950s

A decade that began with a cup final and finished with the
appointment of one of the most important figures in the club's history

LIVERPOOL FOOTBALL CLUB

SEASON 1950/51

No. 1 **Official** Programme

Directors:
G. A. RICHARDS, J.P. (Chairman).
E. K. MILNE, M.C. (Vice-Chairman)
W. HARVEY WEBB, J.P., T. POOL, W. P. HARROP, J.P., C.C.
B. L. MARTINDALE, M.B.E., J.P., Aldermen R. R. WILLIAMS.
T. V. WILLIAMS, T. McCONNELL.

Manager: GEORGE KAY   Secretary: J. C. ROUSE

FOOTBALL LEAGUE — FIRST DIVISION.

Liverpool v. Manchester Un.

AT ANFIELD.   WEDNESDAY, 23rd AUGUST, 1950.
KICK - OFF 6-30 p.m.

PRICE - TWO PENCE.

No. 26

LIVERPOOL
SEASON 1955-56
FOOTBALL CLUB

Directors:
W. J. HARROP, J.P. (Chairman).
T. V. WILLIAMS (Vice-Chairman)
B. L. MARTINDALE, M.B.E., J.P.
G. A. RICHARDS, J.P.      T. McCONNELL.
H. ROBSON ROBERTS      H. CARTWRIGHT.
S. E. REAKES, J.P.        E. J. HILL.
D. WELSH (Manager)       J. S. McINNES (Secretary).

F.A. CHALLENGE CUP—3rd ROUND
Liverpool v. Accrington S.
AT ANFIELD
SATURDAY, 7th JANUARY, 1956
Kick-off 2-15 p.m.

OFFICIAL PROGRAMME
PRICE   THREEPENCE

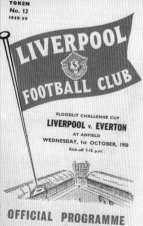

TOKEN
No. 12
1958/59

LIVERPOOL
FOOTBALL CLUB

FLOODLIT CHALLENGE CUP

LIVERPOOL v. EVERTON

AT ANFIELD
WEDNESDAY, 1st OCTOBER, 1958
Kick-off 7-15 p.m.

OFFICIAL PROGRAMME

PRICE THREEPENCE

Twopence to cross the Mersey. Twopence, then threepence, to buy your copy of the pocket-sized Liverpool FC 'official programme' in the Fifties, which carried an action illustration, rendered in red ink, on its front for most of the decade. Today, if you possess an issue in particularly good condition, it could well be a 'directors copy' – these were printed on glossier paper and have stood the test of time far better than the typical stock used for those on general sale around Anfield.

The decade had begun with the premiere of the musical *Carousel*, featuring the song *You'll Never Walk Alone*, in London's West End, and an FA Cup final, ending in defeat for Liverpool against Arsenal, at Wembley Stadium. On the pitch it got steadily worse. In 1950-51 the Reds finished ninth in the top flight and dropped to eleventh the following season, despite 19 goals from Billy Liddell. This was the third of seven seasons, between 1949-50 and 1957-58, in which the great Scot would finish as Liverpool's leading scorer.

The 1951-52 campaign was also notable for Anfield's record attendance: 61,905 for a fourth-round FA Cup tie with Wolverhampton Wanderers on Saturday 2 February 1952, won 2-1 thanks to early goals from Bob Paisley and Cyril Done. Four days later, the country and the commonwealth had a new queen, Elizabeth II.

Liverpool would finish 17th in 1952-53, two points off the drop – they'd been third at the start of November 1952 – and they were dumped out of the FA Cup at Gateshead in the third round. New faces included full-back Ronnie Moran, winger Alan A'Court and striker Louis Bimpson.

The unthinkable happened over Easter weekend in April 1954 when Liverpool were relegated (while Everton were promoted), rock-bottom with 28 points from 42 fixtures. It would take eight long years to bounce back up. The day before the season's last home game, an academic 4-1 win over Middlesbrough, former Reds manager George Kay died aged 66.

The front cover of the programme had always included the words 'First Division' but this was dropped from the cover during 1952-53 and 'Second Division' never appeared during the wilderness years.

On Saturday 21 August 1954 almost 50,000 at Anfield saw Liverpool beat Doncaster Rovers 3-2 in their opening game in the Second Division and all the goals came from a 6ft Welsh-Italian striker called Antonio Camilio Rowley, or Tony Rowley for short. He'd net another five in 12 more appearances that season, but the standout scorer in 1954-55 was John Evans with 33 in all competitions, including five versus Bristol Rovers in September 1954 – a feat only four other LFC players have managed before or after (John Miller in 1892, Andy McGuigan in 1902, Ian Rush in 1983 and Robbie Fowler in 1993).

In that first season in the second tier the Reds came eleventh (while Chelsea were top-flight champions – their first and only time until 2004-05).

While Elvis Presley scored his first no1 with *Heartbreak Hotel*, and Real Madrid won the first of five consecutive European Cups, it was third spot and an agonising whiff of promotion for Liverpool in 1955-56 plus elimination from the FA Cup at the hands of Manchester City in a fifth-round replay – with the referee blowing the final whistle at a snowy Anfield just before Billy Liddell hammered in an equaliser.

The day before, club chairman WJ Harrop died and vice-

Liverpool played German side FC Saarbrucken at Anfield in May 1951 as part of the Festival of Britain when scores of continental teams were invited over

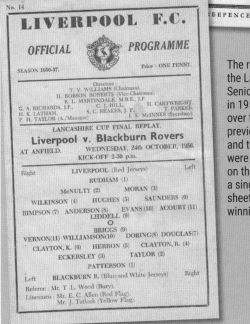

The replay for the Lancashire Senior Cup final in 1956 was held over from the previous season and the line-ups were printed on the front of a single-sided sheet, the Reds winning 2-0

chairman TV Williams succeeded him, while at the end of the season manager Don Welsh stood down to be replaced by former Reds right-half Phil Taylor.

Liverpool were third again in 1956-57, a point behind runners-up Nottingham Forest and eight off champions Leicester City. Ronnie Moran was a league ever-present.

The Reds finished fourth the following season, having been to for most of mid-November to mid-January. Billy Liddell was aga the goal-machine with 21 in the league – no wonder the team was dubbed 'Liddellpool'.

The 1957-58 campaign also saw floodlights installed at Anfield. This enabled the club to move Saturday kick-off times

# LIVERPOOL F.C.—SEASON 1952-53

Anfield hosted a South Africa touring party in October 1953. Between the two line-ups (left) is a football advertising the famous Jack Sharp sports shop in the city – for many years it supplied kits for the Reds and other sides

the later time of 3.15pm, giving spectators who worked in the morning a greater chance to make it to Anfield for the start of the match.

Prior to this, kick-off times had ranged from 2.15pm to 3pm depending on the time of year. But it was a period overshadowed by the awful news of the Munich air disaster of Thursday 6 February 1958.

There was a new arrival for 1958-59 in the shape of 20-year-old forward Roger Hunt who signed from Stockton Heath as Liverpool finished fourth in the Second Division and went out of the FA Cup at non-league Worcester City in the third round.

Tuesday 1 December 1959, though, was the day when everything changed for LFC. Manager Phil Taylor had resigned and the club appointed Bill Shankly, previously boss of Huddersfield Town, as his successor.

"When I come to Liverpool I shall be taking my jacket off and I shall expect everybody to take their jackets off," warned the Scot. "The First Division is where Liverpool should be, and that is where I aim to put them."

In turn Taylor told the press: "Please tell Mr Shankly that I wish him all the luck in the world – I hope his highest ambitions are realised."

The Reds reached third at the end of that 1959-60 season with Hunt scoring 21 league goals.

## OUR TRIBUTE TO BERT RILEY.

It is with a measure of regret that we have to record the closing of forty-two years of glorious service to the club by Mr. Bert Riley, our Chief Groundsman and one of the greatest and most loyal servants ever to work for the Liverpool Club. Bert is going into a well-earned retirement and while we shall feel the loss more than anyone others throughout the country will miss the kindly help and advice he always has been so willing to give.

We regard Bert Riley as " the king of groundsmen," and the vacancy he leaves will be difficult to fill. He has absolutely been " wedded " to Anfield and throughout the years has given us a playing area of which we have been proud.

The club appreciated that when Bert was first appointed in May, 1908, in succession to A. Clements that here was a man of knowledge and ideas, and the Directors decided to give him a free hand to implement his ideas. Never was a wiser decision made. Working closely with the Grounds Committee during his service Bert Riley has given Anfield a playing arena second to none in the whole country.

Possibly it was Bert's keen knowledge of cricket pitches which laid the foundations for his success. He was, you know, a cricket professional bowler with the West Derby club as a young man. A good cricketer he was too. His love of cricket remains as strong as ever and he is a staunch supporter of Lancashire to this day. Bert Riley has prepared Anfield for football matches as carefully and thoroughly as groundsmen at Old Trafford, Lords and the Oval have prepared wickets for Test matches.

Conscientious to a degree Bert Riley has " nursed " Anfield, and many is the time he has been seen working on the pitch at midnight during the summer weeding and tending the grass. He used to like working quietly at night carrying on his campaign to master the bogy of every groundsman—the dreaded " knot grass." This weed which so quickly strangles the grass itself has not yet been conquered by any groundman, but an unrelenting campaign carried out in the Riley way has checked it. All other weeds have fallen to the Riley campaign of devastation in fact just before the season opened Bert challenged anyone to find any weed at Anfield apart from an odd root of " knot grass."

Inoffensive, likeable and thorough the Club Directors paid tribute to Bert Riley on his 70th birthday by making him a presentation, and we know that every follower of the club will join in wishing him a long and happy retirement. He has earned it by faithful service and industry.

There was a glowing tribute to Liverpool's 'king of groundsmen' in September 1950 as Bert Riley retired after 42 years of service

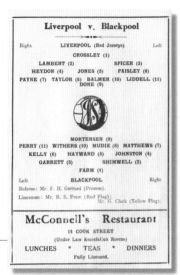

A team line-up in 1950 included
Bob Paisley and Billy Liddell

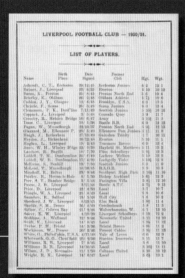

The squad list in 1950-51 included
the height and weight of every player

## IMPORTANT REMINDERS TO ALL SECTIONS OF OUR SUPPORTERS.

1. Season Ticket holders are requested to occupy their seats at least 15 minutes before the advertised time of kick-off.

2. Please tender the correct admission money at the turnstiles. This will facilitate immediate admission to the ground, and thus prevent congestions.

3. Early comers are asked to move quickly to the centres of the various enclosures, leaving the passages clear.

4. Do not purchase any "Pirate" programmes outside the ground. The Official Programme can be obtained inside the turnstiles only.

5. Please patronise the advertisers who have helped us to publish a 16-page programme at the low cost of 2d.—one of the best and cheapest in the country.

6. The "Kop Roar" should be copied in all parts of the ground. The players appreciate this encouragement.

A list of reminders in 1950 requested that fans all around the ground replicate the 'Kop Roar'

A Gent's new left hand glove, made by Messrs. Dents, was found in 'Block E' of the stand at Norwich, and, as the seats in this section were allocated to our club, it is thought it may belong to one of our supporters. The glove is now in the 'custody' of the Norwich City Police, and can be recovered by applying to them.

In January 1951 the loss of a fan's glove away to Norwich was handily reported by the programme

## FROM THE BOARD ROOM.

The team was very unfortunate to lose at Charlton Athletic last Saturday, for the high standard of its play fully merited at least one point. Uytenbogarrdt, the South African goalkeeper, deputising for Bartram, was fortunate on several occasions, due principally to his height of 6 feet 4½ ins. Bobby Paisley had all the ill-luck of the match, for he might have scored on three occasions with worthy efforts. It was certainly not the "Reds" (playing in white by the way) day, but providing they serve up similar displays, attractive on the floor passes with interchanging of positions, points should soon come our way.

Bill Jones, the most versatile of footballers, played in his original position of inside right and was a great success, while Laurie Hughes at centre-half proved he is quite fit again, and gave the opposing centre-forward — Jepson, of Sweden, very little scope, although the latter scored the only goal of the match from a scramble.

\*      \*      \*      \*

It is with regret that the Board annouce that Mr. George Kay has resigned his position as Manager of the Club owing to continued ill health. In accepting the resignation the Directors desire to express their sincere appreciation of the excellent and whole hearted services he has rendered since his appointment in 1936.

During his 15 years association with the Club, Mr. Kay has always enjoyed the utmost confidence of the Board, Players and Staff.

Mr. Kay has been ill for some months, and it was on medical advice that the Board reluctantly accepted the resignation. He lived for football, and his club in particular, and he was a sincere friend to every player.

His first successes came in 1946/7 season when the "Reds" won the First Division Championship of The Football League and were narrowly beaten by Burnley in the replayed Semi-Final of F.A. Cup at Manchester. In April last he was a very proud man when he led his players on to the Wembley turf for presentation to His Majesty The King. It must have brought back many happy memories of the occasion when he captained West Ham United in the first Cup Final to be played at Wembley — in 1923. Unfortunately his ambition to bring back the Cup to Anfield for the first time was not realised, but he had the satisfaction to know that his team played the most sportsmanlike football ever played in a final tie. It may now be known that Mr. Kay had to remain in bed for the two days immediate to that match, and he was a sick man when the players took the field.

Mr. Kay was one of the finest readers of a game, and his tactical talks to the players were of immense value.

All associated with the Club look forward to the day when Mr. Kay will have sufficiently recovered to be able to come to Anfield and enjoy our matches without the responsibility and worry which is the portion of a Managerial position.

'From The Board Room' was the club's way of speaking to fans in the 1950s and in February 1951 it was announced that manager George Kay was stepping down

### From The Boardroom

Football players will be happy to hear the final whistle this afternoon, for the majority will have taken part in three hard games within the short space of four days. In addition they have had many hours of travelling, which does not ease their task. We hope their endeavours on the field have brought good entertainment to all sports lovers.

With the completion of the Easter holiday programme, some light may shine on the promotion and relegation problems, although it is quite likely these questions will not be settled until the last day of the season—May 3rd. The next two weeks will certainly be a trying time for several Club Managements.

As we have had to go to press rather early for to-day's League encounter with Manchester City, we are unable to give any reports of the two games in Manchester on Good Friday and Saturday, but we hope our total points are now in excess of 40. We obtained our second double of the season when we defeated Stoke City at Anfield on Grand National evening—the other being against Huddersfield Town, and the goals scored by Bob Paisley and Kevin Baron helped the club to reach the sixth position in the League Table.

The arrangements for our forthcoming tour to the Continent are now completed. The party will travel by air to Dusseldorf on Tuesday, May 6th, and play the following matches :—

    May  7—F.C. Rot Weiss at Essen.
      „  14—K.F. Austria at Vienna.
      „  18—B.C. Augsburg at Augsburg.
      „  22—Club Athletico at Madrid.

In addition to the above programme the Gibraltar Football Association extended an invitation to us to play two matches on "the Rock."

Our Captain, Phil Taylor, was operated on in a local nursing home on Tuesday for the removal of a cartilage, and we are pleased to report he is progressing favourably. We send Phil our best wishes for a speedy recovery.

Our replayed Liverpool Senior Cup Semi-final with Southport will be played at Anfield on Wednesday next, 16th inst., kick-off 3 p.m. This game should prove very interesting for the winners will meet Everton in the Final on the 30th April. We are hopeful that we may be the victors for it will give us the one opportunity this season of playing our friendly rivals from Goodison Park. Such a match would attract a large attendance, for there is no doubt the supporters of the " Reds " and " Blues " have missed their " Derby " games this year.

We complete our "home" programme with the visit of Tottenham Hotspur to Anfield on Saturday next, 19th inst.—kick-off 3 p.m. The " Spurs," in addition to having eyes on the leading position in the First Division, are anxious for the revenge of their defeat at White Hart Lane earlier in the season. On that occasion Billy Liddell was in most exhilarating form scoring the three goals which brought us such a fine victory.

Applications are now invited for the renewals of season tickets for 1952/3, and a form for this purpose is set out on another page of this programme. Owing to the increase in the entertainment duty, the Directors regret they have been compelled to increase the charges, viz.:
    Reserved Seats—£5. 5. 0.    Unreserved Seats—£4. 10. 0.

The Easter fixtures, a European tour and Phil Taylor's knee operation were among the topics covered in 'From The Boardroom' in April 1952

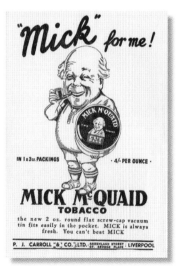

Restaurants vied for space with tobacco in the programme ads of the Fifties

# FROM THE BOARDROOM

The decision of the Chancellor of the Exchequer to abolish Entertainment Tax on Football and so bring our National Winter Sport into line with its Summer counterpart, Cricket, has been heartily welcomed by all Club Managements. The relief afforded will be a life-saver to many Clubs who had found it increasingly difficult year by year to carry on under this crippling burden.

News of the removal of 'Entertainment Tax' was warmly greeted in April 1957

## Tonight's The Night!

### By Mr. H. CARTWRIGHT
### (Chairman of the Floodlighting Sub-Committee)

Although it is only tonight that our supporters see the culmination of the decision of the Liverpool F.C. Board to erect floodlighting at Anfield, a decision taken about twelve months or so ago, the matter has never been far from the minds of the Directors for several years.

Long before I had the privilege of joining the Board it had been considered from time to time, and those then charged with responsibility for the club's well-being weighed up all the arguments, both for and against, with scrupulous care and thoroughness. For reasons which were sound and prudent, however, it was decided, on each of these occasions, to hold the project in abeyance. But last year it was felt that the time was ripe for this innovation, and that a start should be made as soon as possible.

Once having come to this decision no time was lost. My colleagues appointed me as Chairman of a small sub-committtee which was charged with the task of getting estimates, comparing various schemes, and generally seeing to it that everything was ready for the autumn of this year. My colleagues and I, after closely examining the installations of other clubs and consulting the leading technical experts, put forward what we considered the most suitable scheme for our needs at Anfield. This in due course received the approval of the full Board, which in its turn gave every encouragement to ensure that the work should proceed with all possible speed.

A start was made last May, as soon as the football season had ended, and gradually we had the satisfaction of seeing the job proceed steadily from stage to stage, until this evening floodlit football at Anfield becomes not a dream, but a reality.

My colleagues on the Board feel, as I do, that the time and money spent on this project will prove well worth while. While floodlighting at the moment is a novelty, and excellent gates are expected for the various special and very attractive matches which we are to stage in mid-week, this is not the only consideration we have in mind. Your Directors are of opinion that we shall also derive much benefit from the fact that we shall now be able to start our Saturday games during the winter months at the standardised time of 3-15, thus giving many of our followers who could not attend for the earlier kick-off a chance to get to the ground in time.

Floodlights were first used at Anfield in October 1957 for a special 'Floodlit Cup' tie against Everton

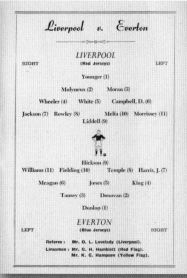

A team line-up page (above) and a handy guide to bus routes home (below)

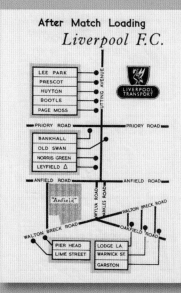

# LIVERPOOL FOOTBALL CLUB
## SEASON 1959-60

### Directors:
**T. V. WILLIAMS** (Chairman)

**H. ROBSON ROBERTS** (Vice-Chairman)

R. L. MARTINDALE, M.B.E., J.P.

G. A. RICHARDS, J.P.

H. CARTWRIGHT

S. C. REAKES, J.P.

C. J. HILL

H. K. LATHAM

T. PARKER

**W. SHANKLY** (Manager)        J. S. McINNES (Secretary)

## From the Boardroom

We extend a warm and hearty welcome to our new Manager, Mr. W. Shankly, who has assumed his duties at Anfield this week. Mr. Shankly was previously with Huddersfield Town where he took over from Andy Beattie with whom he was a stalwart player in pre-war days with Preston North End. Mr. Shankly witnessed the Central League team in their 5-0 victory over Manchester City last week, and today has his first view of the League side under his charge.

---

### F.A. CHALLENGE CUP—3rd ROUND
### LIVERPOOL v. LEYTON ORIENT
#### Saturday, 9th January, 1960

ADMISSION:

GROUND AND PADDOCK ... ... ... Pay at Stiles.

STANDS (Ticket only) ... ... ... ... Centre Stands 7/6
Wing Stands 6/-

Shareholders may apply for One Ticket at 7/6 for each Season Ticket held, and for 6/- Tickets in respect of their Shareholding allocation as per previous Home Cup-ties.

Season Ticket Holders except those of "F" and "B" Stands may apply for One Ticket at 7/6 for each Season Ticket held. "F" Stand Season Ticket Holders who will be accommodated in "A" Stand for this Tie, and "B" Stand Season Ticket Holders may apply for One Ticket at 6/- for each Season Ticket held.

All applications must be received at the Club Offices, Anfield Road, not later than Saturday, 2nd January, and must be accompanied by No. 1 Voucher duly completed, stamped addressed envelope and appropriate remittance.

The balance of 6/- Tickets will be available to the General Public who must also apply not later than Saturday, 2nd January, 1960.

**ALL APPLICATIONS BY POST. NO PERSONAL APPLICATIONS.**

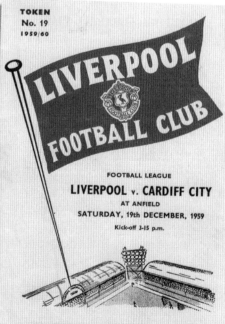

TOKEN
No. 19
1959/60

**LIVERPOOL FOOTBALL CLUB**

FOOTBALL LEAGUE

**LIVERPOOL v. CARDIFF CITY**

AT ANFIELD

SATURDAY, 19th DECEMBER, 1959

Kick-off 3-15 p.m.

**OFFICIAL PROGRAMME**

PRICE THREEPENCE

'Mr W Shankly' took charge of his first Liverpool match on 19 December 1959 and the 'Boardroom' extended him a 'hearty welcome' in the Cardiff programme

# CHAPTER 3

# 1960s

As Shankly helped his Sixties stars move back to the top table of English football, they had a programme worthy of champions

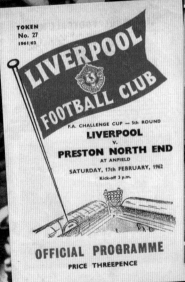

TOKEN
No. 27
1961/62

LIVERPOOL
FOOTBALL CLUB

F.A. CHALLENGE CUP — 5th ROUND
**LIVERPOOL**
v.
**PRESTON NORTH END**
AT ANFIELD
SATURDAY, 17th FEBRUARY, 1962
Kick-off 3 p.m.

**OFFICIAL PROGRAMME**
PRICE THREEPENCE

OFFICIAL PROGRAMME

**LIVERPOOL**

EUROPEAN CUP
SEMI-FINAL
(1st Leg)

**LIVERPOOL**
V
**F.C. Internazionale**

AT ANFIELD
TUESDAY, 4th MAY 1965
KICK OFF 7.30 P.M.

PRICE **4ᴅ**

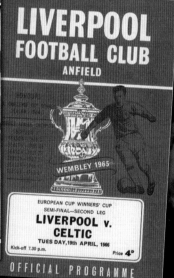

**LIVERPOOL**
FOOTBALL CLUB
ANFIELD

WEMBLEY 1965

EUROPEAN CUP WINNERS' CUP
SEMI-FINAL—SECOND LEG
**LIVERPOOL v.
CELTIC**
TUESDAY, 19th APRIL, 1966
Kick-off 7.30 p.m.          Price **4ᴅ**

OFFICIAL PROGRAMME

'Anfield Personalities', including this one with Gerry Byrne, was a regular which appeared in the 1961-62 season programmes

I f you fancied a swift one with your Sixties matchday programme, then it was 'UP THE REDS!' and 'DOWN WITH HIGSONS!' according to a regular advert inside for Liverpool's favourite local brewers of the time.

This was the decade which transformed Britain from post-war recovery to pop-culture revolution, and for the programme there was a progression from a 'pamphlet' to a larger, more substantial publication.

In time the front cover would evolve from the classic image of the LFC flag emerging from the gable-roofed Main Stand, with a floodlight pylon in the corner, to an all-red affair – surely at Bill Shankly's behest – with an illustration of a player in action.

Inside there were black-and-white team photos, player interviews and profiles, 'pen pictures' of the visiting team, and messages 'from the boardroom' or the chairman, with the manager's say yet to be an established regular. By the midway point of the 1960s each issue contained a nationwide Football League insert with its own colour cover.

Liverpool still wore white shorts when they were third in the Second Division at the end of 1960-61, with striker Dave Hickson, signed from Everton just before Shankly's arrival, scoring 16 goals. The following season, boosted by summer signings Ian St John and Ron Yeats, the Reds were top from start to finish. Eight points clear of runners-up Leyton Orient, they returned to the top flight after eight long years.

Shankly reflected: "When I was asked to become manager in November 1959, do you know why I accepted? It was because

**FIXTURES 1963**

| 1963 | FOOTBALL LEAGUE | | F | A | 1963 | CENTRAL LEAGUE | | F | A |
|---|---|---|---|---|---|---|---|---|---|
| Aug. | 24—Blackburn R. | A | 2 | 1 | Aug. | 24—Manchester C. | H | 2 | 0 |
| " | 28—Nottingham F. | H | 1 | 2 | " | 27—Bury | A | 0 | 0 |
| " | 31—Blackpool | H | 1 | 2 | " | 31—Blackpool | A | 2 | 3 |
| Sept. | 2—Nottingham F. | A | 0 | 0 | Sept. | 2—Bury | H | 2 | 3 |
| " | 7—Chelsea | A | 3 | 1 | " | 7—Blackburn R. | H | 4 | 1 |
| " | 9—Wolves | A | 3 | 1 | " | 11—Wolves | A | 1 | 4 |
| " | 14—West Ham Utd. | H | 1 | 2 | " | 14—Barnsley | A | 3 | 1 |
| " | 18—Wolves | H | 6 | 0 | " | 21—Sheffield Utd. | H | 2 | 1 |
| " | 21—Sheffield Utd. | A | 0 | 3 | " | 23—Wolves | H | 3 | 0 |
| " | 28—Everton | H | 2 | 1 | " | 28—Everton | A | 0 | 3 |
| Oct. | 5—Aston Villa | A | 2 | 1 | Oct. | 2—West Brom. A. | A | 2 | 1 |
| " | 9—Sheffield Wed. | H | 5 | 2 | " | 5—Aston Villa | A | 0 | 1 |
| " | 19—West Brom. A. | H | 3 | 1 | " | 12—Sheffield W. | H | 5 | 2 |
| " | 26—Ipswich Town | A | 2 | 1 | " | 19—Chesterfield | A | 3 | 0 |
| Nov. | 2—Leicester City | H | 0 | 1 | " | 26—Burnley | H | 0 | 0 |
| " | 9—Bolton W. | A | 2 | 1 | Nov. | 2—Manchester U. | A | 2 | 0 |
| " | 16—Fulham | H | 2 | 0 | " | 9—Preston N.E. | H | 3 | 0 |
| " | 23—Manchester U. | A | 1 | 0 | " | 23—Derby County | H | 2 | 2 |
| Dec. | 7—Arsenal | A | 1 | 1 | " | 30—Huddersfield T. | A | 1 | 0 |
| " | 14—Blackburn R. | H | 1 | 2 | Dec. | 7—Newcastle U. | H | 4 | 1 |
| " | 21—Blackpool | A | | | " | 14—Manchester C. | A | 2 | 4 |
| " | 26—Stoke City | H | | | " | 21—Blackpool | H | | |
| " | 28—Stoke City | A | | | " | 26—Stoke C. | A | | |
| | | | | | " | 28—Stoke C. | H | | |

These fixtures are the Copyright of the Football League Ltd., Regd., Office: Lytham, St. Annes, Lancs., and must not be reproduced, in whole or part, except by written consent of The Football League Ltd.

W. Jones & Co., 29 Seel Street, Liverpool 1

A big celebratory can of Threlfalls was looking more and more desirable as the fixtures counted down in the 1963-64 season

I had played at Anfield and knew what it was like to have that Kop to beat as well as the team. And I knew that the people who produced that roar were just like myself, who lived for the game and to whom football was their abiding passion. Football is my life – and that's how it is with them."

There was FA Cup semi-final heartache the following season – defeated by new bogey-team Leicester City – along with a creditable eighth-place, but it was merely a prelude to greater things.

In 1963-64, as The Beatles landed their first no1 with *Please Please Me*, the Reds were champions with a sixth First Division title, finishing four points ahead of runners-up Manchester United, having moved into top spot on 30 March 1964 and stayed there. They were crowned on Saturday 18 April 1964 with a 5-0 win over Arsenal in front of close on 50,000 fans – singing fans – at Anfield, with thousands locked out.

St John and strike-partner Roger Hunt scored over 50 league goals between them and there were three ever-presents: Ian Callaghan, Gordon Milne and Peter Thompson.

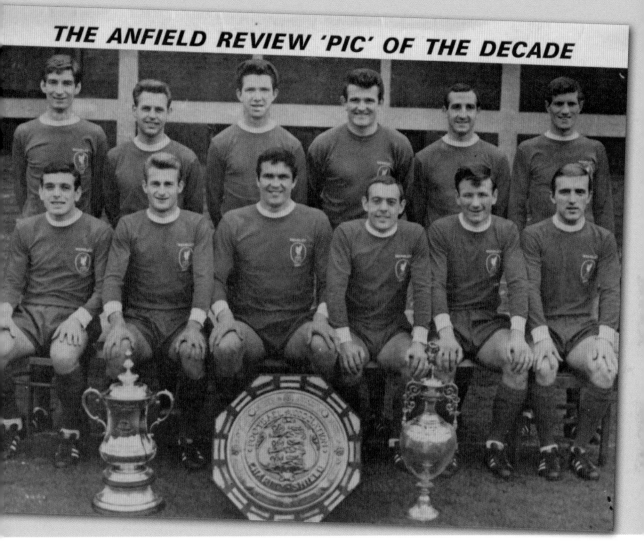

# THE ANFIELD REVIEW 'PIC' OF THE DECADE

In 1964-65 they were FA Cup winners – at last! The all-red Reds beat Leeds United 2-1 at Wembley and upon their return the scenes in the city were unprecedented. One senior police officer told the *Liverpool Daily Post*: "This makes the Beatles' homecoming look like a vicarage tea party."

Two days later, on a tide of Anfield emotion Liverpool beat Inter Milan 3-1 in the first leg of their European Cup semi-final, but the Italian champions would controversially progress 4-3 on aggregate.

What a time to be a Liverpool fan. Season 1965-66 – champions again! Shankly's boys finished six points clear of runners-up Leeds United, clinching title no7 with a 2-1 win over Chelsea at Anfield on 30 April 1966. Roger Hunt got the goals, bringing his total to 32 – the sixth of nine seasons in which he'd be top scorer.

In the European Cup Winners' Cup they beat Celtic in a 'Battle of Britain' last-four, two-legged tie but came unstuck to Borussia Dortmund in the soggy Glasgow final. Bill, of course, felt the best team lost.

After England's glory in the 1966 World Cup finals, the Reds beat neighbours and FA Cup holders Everton at Goodison Park in the Charity Shield, got knocked out of the European Cup by an Ajax side featuring a young Johan Cruyff, and were fifth in the league.

They were third in 1967-68, three points off champions Manchester City, and there were defeats to West Bromwich Albion and Ferencvaros in an FA Cup sixth-round second replay and Fairs Cup third-round tie respectively.

The decade drew to a close with men on the moon and Liverpool still shining back on Earth, but they were runners-up to Don Revie's Leeds United in the league in 1968-69, were eliminated from the Fairs Cup on a coin-toss to Athletic Bilbao, and lost an FA Cup fifth-round replay to those Leicester bogeymen.

Season 1969-70 saw them finish fifth and knocked out of the FA Cup at Second Division Watford in the tournament's quarter-finals.

But the trophy-winning fun had only just begun.

TOKEN
No. 10
1960/61

# LIVERPOOL FOOTBALL CLUB

FLOODLIGHT CHALLENGE CUP—FIRST LEG

## LIVERPOOL v. EVERTON

AT ANFIELD

WEDNESDAY, 5th OCTOBER 1960

Kick-off 7.15 p.m.

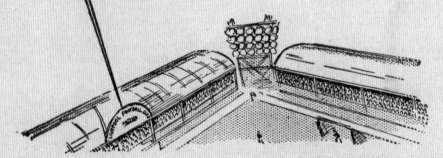

# OFFICIAL PROGRAMME

## PRICE THREEPENCE

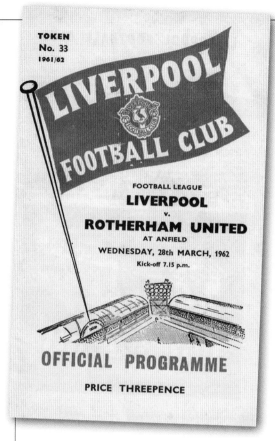

Covers for the 1961-62 campaign were the same style as the season before

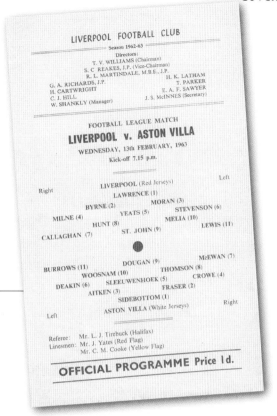

There was only time to produce a single-sheet programme for the hastily re-arranged fixture with Aston Villa in February 1963

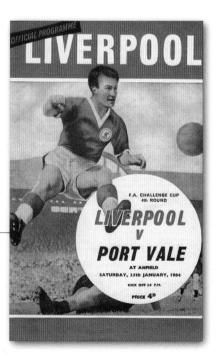

This Kop-backdrop action shot featured on the cover of the 1963-64 programmes

One bright moment – literally – to emerge from the Second Division wilderness years was a regular two-legged tie against the neighbours, played from seasons 1957-58 to 1961-62 under the Anfield floodlights.

The Reds forked out £12,000 to have the new technology installed at the ground, with the *Liverpool Echo* publishing a souvenir edition in October 1957 with a cartoon of a street vendor selling sunglasses in team colours! The first such Floodlit Challenge Cup tie also marked the 75th anniversary of the Liverpool County FA.

In October 1960 (far left), in front of 30,000 fans, the Reds won 3-1 thanks to goals from ex-Blue Dave Hickson, Roger Hunt and Johnny Morrissey. The *Echo* reported: "Liverpool may not be in Division One, but they were back where they belonged for ninety minutes last night.

"They left the impression that if they do regain their status they will be perfectly at home. They played some gorgeous stuff of the kind which gave the impression that there were fifteen of them and only eleven in blue!"

The second leg was actually held over to the following season and it ended 2-2 at Goodison Park in October 1961.

The cover for the Sheffield Wednesday game in April 1966 gave a reminder of the FA Cup success of the season before

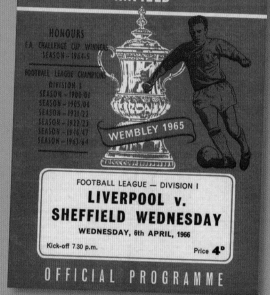

There were two covers for the Cologne European Cup second round home leg after the original game was postponed in 1965

For the first half of the 1965-66 season, including the European tie with Juventus, the same cover image was used as the season before

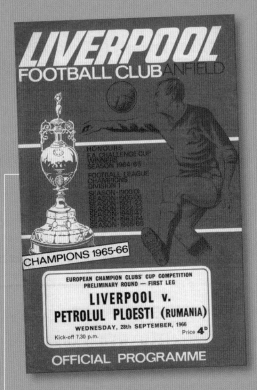

The club's pride at being Division One champions was on display on the cover of the 1966-67 programmes

Fans at the first home game of the 1969-70 season, against Chelsea, would have seen a cover with the words 'ANFIELD REVIEW' superimposed over a picture of expectant Reds supporters – before Bill Shankly's men went on to win the game 4-1

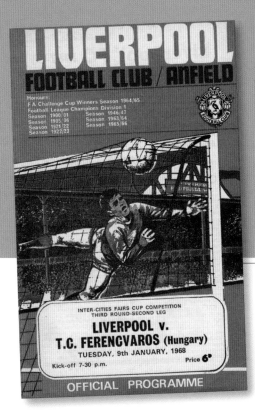

Pick that one out! An illustration of a goalkeeper watching the ball hit the back of the net adorned 1967-68 covers, including this one for the return match of a Fairs Cup tie with Hungarian side Ferencvaros

# Liverpool FC 1964/65

### Directors:

T. V. WILLIAMS (President)

S. C. REAKES, J.P. (Chairman)

H. CARTWRIGHT (Vice-Chairman)

R. L. MARTINDALE, M.B.E., J.P.       H. K. LATHAM

C. J. HILL      E. A. F. SAWYER      T. PARKER

W. SHANKLY (Manager)      J. S. McINNES (Secretary)

# From the Boardroom

### WELCOME TO F.C. INTERNAZIONALE

ON this the First Leg of the Semi-Final of the European Champion Clubs' Cup Competition, we extend a sincere and warm welcome to the Directors, Officials, Players and Supporters of the Inter-Milan Club, the present Holders of this Trophy. This is the first occasion in which an Italian Club has taken part in a match at Anfield.

It will no doubt be remembered that last season, F.C. Internazionale, after a goal-less draw at Goodison Park, obtained victory over Everton, our friendly rivals from across the Park, by the only goal of the match in the Second Leg in Milan.

---

On this occasion, the last game at Anfield for the season, the Players, Manager, Staff and Directors thank the Spectators for their loyal support during the season.

The Players, one and all, continuously praise the enthusiastic support which they receive from all sides. The musical honours from the 'Kop' are, of course, an added attraction, but it is the number of those cheering the team that arouses admiration.

Our first venture into the European Cup has brought a wealth of experience, including a match abandoned only minutes before the kick-off time. An evening such as this made history. What might have been a real crisis was minimised by the patience and good sense of our Spectators.

---

### F.A. CHALLENGE CUP

At long last this coveted Trophy, which has eluded us throughout our history from 1892, has been won. The magnificent achievement of the team at Wembley on Saturday last, in securing victory in extra-time after a goal-less ninety minutes, received a wonderful and fantastic acclaim on the return to Liverpool on Sunday evening, surely the greatest welcome to any team in the history of the game.

---

To all Supporters, from Season Ticket Holders in the 'posh' places, down to the Boys' Pen, we wish you a good holiday season and look forward to having you with us for the Season 1965/66, which opens in August.

The 'Boardroom' was given its first chance to welcome the Italian champions – and also hail an FA Cup triumph – in May 1965

# Liverpool FC 1965-66

**Directors:**

T. V. WILLIAMS (President)
S. C. REAKES, J.P. (Chairman)
H. CARTWRIGHT (Vice-Chairman)

| | | |
|---|---|---|
| R. L. MARTINDALE, M.B.E. J.P. | C. J. HILL | H. K. LATHAM |
| E. A. F. SAWYER | J. H. SMITH, F.C.A. | H. E. ROBERTS |
| W. SHANKLY (Manager) | | P. B. ROBINSON (Secretary) |

## A Message from the Chairman

THIS being our last home game, I would like to take the opportunity of expressing, on behalf of myself and my directorial colleagues, our deep appreciation of the splendid efforts of our players and officials—not only throughout this season, but also during previous campaigns.

The Liverpool Football club can look back with pride on the achievements of the past five years, which rank as the most successful period in our history. I hope it will not be regarded as out of place if I briefly mention the senior distinctions which have been gained during this period. In 1961-62 we topped the Second Division after heading the table throughout the season. In 1962-63 we reached the semi-final of the F.A. Cup, and twelve months later won the First Division championship as well as appearing in the last eight for the F.A. Cup.

Last season, of course, the club's ambition of bringing the F.A. Cup to Anfield for the first time was realised, and in addition to this our players reached the semi-final of the European Cup. This season we have got through to the Final of the European Cup Winners' Cup tournament and have been leading in the First Division for the last five months.

The Board is also most appreciative of the achievements of our reserve teams over the last few years. These contain the players upon whom we shall rely to maintain our reputation in the years ahead, and to fill any vacancies arising in the senior eleven through causes beyond our control.

The honours I have mentioned, while most gratifying, are not the only way in which the Liverpool club has enhanced its reputation, both at home and abroad. Equally gratifying has been the high technical ability and entertainment value of the football produced and the clean and sportsmanlike behaviour of our players.

Simultaneously with the Board's efforts to achieve playing success the comfort and convenience of our supporters has always been kept well in mind. Our two new stands and other improvements are concrete evidence of this, and we shall continue to do everything possible in this direction in future.

We have so often expressed our appreciation of the support given us by the public of Liverpool that I do not propose to stress that unduly on this occasion, though I should be lacking in my duty if I did not once more take the opportunity of thanking our followers for their wonderful loyalty and enthusiasm, which is so deeply appreciated by players, officials, and all connected with the club.

It would be invidious of me to single out individual players for special mention, for all have done remarkably well and each has contributed to the utmost of his ability. I would, however, like to express appreciation of the efforts of our "back-

*A Message from the Chairman—continued*

room" staff—to Mr. Bill Shankly and his able assistants, and to our secretary, Mr. Peter Robinson, who has done such a splendid job in his first season at Anfield.

Although we look back today on five years of splendid achievement, we have no intention of resting on our laurels! The Board is always looking ahead and taking stock of the current position, and our supporters can rest assured that every possible step will be taken to ensure that this new and successful era is maintained, so that in the years ahead our supporters can be prouder still of the club to which they give such heartening loyalty.

S. C. REAKES, *Chairman*

## CAN YOU ANSWER THESE?

1. How many players figured in our team (League matches only) when we won the First Division championship in 1946-47? Would you say it was over or under twenty-four?
2. In the 1946-47 season our team had an excellent away record. Can you recall whether it reached the double figure bracket in away victories?
3. When we won the senior championship two seasons ago we utilised the services of seventeen players in League games. How many of these played in all forty-two matches, and who were they?
4. When was the last occasion that four Liverpool forwards achieved double figures as scorers in League games in one season?
5. Thirteen years ago our last game of the season was against Chelsea at Anfield, and a very vital match it was. Why?
6. Chelsea's admission to the Football League sixty years ago was decidedly unusual. Why?

### ANSWERS

1. It was just over that figure: twenty-six to be exact.
2. Yes. Twelve away games were won and four drawn.
3. Three did so, namely, Gordon Milne, Ian Callaghan, and Peter Thompson.
4. At that time five clubs, including Liverpool, were dependent on the result of their concluding matches to avoid relegation. We defeated Chelsea 2-0, which lifted the team to the seventeenth position.
5. Three did so, namely, Gordon Milne, Ian Callaghan, and Peter Thompson.
6. Unlike the usual procedure, where clubs come into the League from a lower sphere, Chelsea were elected members of the Second Division without having played a single match in any sphere of football.

---

The mid-Sixties – imagine being a Kopite back then – and similar in many ways to the trophy-laden rollercoaster ride of the Jürgen Klopp era.

The apex was arguably the European Cup semi-final with world champions Inter Milan in May 1965, three days after the Reds had won the FA Cup for the first time ever.

Anfield's turnstiles were closed 90 minutes before kick-off with 54,000 inside to witness their heroes win 3-1. Even the Italian newspaper *Corriere Della Sera* noted 'the moving, colourful, picturesque and electrifying support' from the terraces.

# Liverpool FC 1964/65

**Directors:**

T. V. WILLIAMS (President)
S. C. REAKES, J.P. (Chairman)
H. CARTWRIGHT (Vice-Chairman)

| | |
|---|---|
| R. L. MARTINDALE, M.B.E., J.P. | H. K. LATHAM |
| C. J. HILL | T. PARKER |
| W. SHANKLY (Manager) | E. A. F. SAWYER |
| | J. S. McINNES (Secretary) |

## The passing of a well-known figure

It is with deep regret that all connected with Football in Liverpool, and indeed throughout the country, learned that our Director, G. A. Richards, Esq., J.P., had passed away at 9 p.m. on Wednesday last.

Mr. Richards had been a Director from 1934, but had been a life-long Liverpudlian, and Shareholder for many years before being elected to the Board. He held the Chairmanship for three years from 1950 to 1953. Due to an injury received in France during the 1914/1918 war, Mr. Richards had to restrict his sporting activities to bowls, but was a knowledgeable spectator of both football and top class cricket.

Possessing an excellent memory, our late colleague could recite the history of Clubs — Teams and Players — for many years back, and this not only made enjoyable company when travelling with the team, but was helpful at many a Board Meeting.

To Mrs. Richards and to the family of four daughters we offer our deep and sincere sympathy.

## From the Boardroom

EUROPEAN CHAMPIONS CUP

**LIVERPOOL v. 1. FC KOLN**

ALL connected with our Club regret the last minute postponement of the game last Wednesday. Had the Officials been able to visualise the game not being played, how much trouble and exasperation could have been avoided. Once it was learned that the Referee had thought of a postponement it was agreed that those who had paid, should see the re-arranged game without paying again.

The Club had tickets for such an emergency already in stock, but giving them out was a major difficulty, and the help given by the Police in marshalling the spectators is readily acknowledged. In the end, although there were frustrations and disappointments, we believe that 90 per cent. of those present were satisfied. Complaints which came in were varied, but those who said we should have kept the entrance money and had a second gate were in the minority.

Inconveniences and annoyance to many residents in stock, but after consultation with the Police in regard to such inconveniences will be minimised.

March 3rd was the first time in the history of the Club that we have faced such an emergency and all concerned, Management, Officials and Spectators hope it will be the last, but note has been taken of difficulties which had to be overcome at such short notice.

---

There was a special message from club chairman Sid Reakes in 1966 in which he thanked the Anfield crowd for "their wonderful loyalty and enthusiam"

'Inconveniences and annoyance' were recognised in 1965 after the European Cup home tie with Cologne fell victim to a late postponement – it was eventually played five weeks after the first leg

# Liverpool FC 1962/63

**Directors:**

T. V. WILLIAMS (Chairman)
S. C. REAKES, J.P. (Vice-Chairman)
R. L. MARTINDALE, M.B.E., J.P.

G. A. RICHARDS, J.P.
H. CARTWRIGHT
C. J. HILL
W. SHANKLY (Manager)

H. K. LATHAM
T. PARKER
E. A. F. SAWYER
J. S. McINNES (Secretary)

## Chairman's Welcome

NEVER since I became chairman of the club has it given me such pleasure to write a foreword to the beginning of the season as I derive from penning this message today. Like our splendid body of loyal supporters, I have lived for the day when Liverpool would regain membership of the First Division. It has been a long time coming, but, as so many famous clubs have found in the past, it is much harder getting out of the Second Division than some people think.

First and foremost to-day I would like to pay a public tribute to all who contributed to our promotion success last season, and particularly to the players, who fought so courageously right from the outset and whose team spirit and loyalty was outstanding.

Our belief in their ability to maintain a strong position in the First Division this winter is evident from the fact that we shall be relying on them again in the months ahead, and have every confidence in them. Should it turn out, however, either through injury or other causes, that strengthening appears necessary, our supporters can rest assured that every possible effort will be made to ensure that the team which represents Liverpool will bear favourable comparison with any in the country. No club can stand still, but must ever be on the lookout for possible contingencies, and seek to guard against them. This your directors will do, and indeed, much has gone on behind the scenes in the last few months with this end in view, though obviously this is not the place to go into details.

It may be noticed that I have not singled out any player for individual mention, simply because I feel that our success last season, as already stated, was founded on all-round team effort. Certain players received more limelight than others, which is natural enough, but every single member of the side played his part to the utmost of his ability and gave whole-hearted endeavour, and in that respect all deserve equal praise. Similar praise is also due to the Central League side and the "A" and "B" teams, all of whom did exceptionally well, and last, but not least, to the Manager, the training and coaching staff, and those behind the scenes in the office.

I cannot close without again expressing the grateful thanks of the Board to our loyal supporters, who have stood by us through thick and thin and thoroughly deserve the higher class of football which will be offered for their entertainment this coming winter. The support we receive is the envy of many other clubs. I trust it will long continue that way, and on my part I can assure you all that the Board will do everything in its power to deserve it.

T. V. WILLIAMS.

Chairman TV Williams couldn't hide his joy when addressing fans at the first game back in the First Division in August 1962

A tribute to Bill Shankly's team from the men in suits at the end of the 1961-62 season

# LIVERPOOL FOOTBALL CLUB

## SEASON 1961-62

**Directors:**

T. V. WILLIAMS (Chairman)
S. C. REAKES, J.P. (Vice-Chairman)
R. L. MARTINDALE, M.B.E., J.P.

G. A. RICHARDS, J.P.
H. CARTWRIGHT
C. J. HILL
W. SHANKLY (Manager)

H. K. LATHAM
T. PARKER
E. A. F. SAWYER
J. S. McINNES (Secretary)

## From the Boardroom

The Championship of the 2nd Division having been won and our aim of promotion to the premier sphere thus achieved, we would like to pay tribute to our Manager, Staff and Players for the great efforts they have made to realise this ambition.

We would also thank our followers for the wonderful support afforded to the team, not only at Anfield but also for away matches.

After the game this evening the League President, Mr. J. Richards, will present the Championship Trophy and Medals to our team.

The Central League team who have also had a very good season, and have been in the running for Championship honours most of the way, and a victory against Newcastle United on Saturday last will have clinched the Runners-up position to Burnley.

# Liverpool FC 1968-69

*DIRECTORS*

T. V. WILLIAMS (President)
H. CARTWRIGHT (Chairman)

S. C. REAKES, J.P.
J. H. SMITH, F.C.A.
W. SHANKLY (Manager)

C. J. HILL
H. E. ROBERTS

E. A. F. SAWYER
Ald. A. B. COLLINS, M.B.E.
P. B. ROBINSON (Secretary)

## From the Boardroom

IT must be a unique occasion in the history of Liverpool that we should be playing a fifth round FA Cup-tie on the day scheduled for the sixth round. Yet that was the outcome of our seven-times postponed game with Leicester City.

The frustration of such a long run of bad luck is felt by everybody connected with the club—directors, management, staff, players and supporters. All of them have suffered in one way or another. By earning tonight's replay the team have gone some way towards making the long wait worthwhile and giving us the chance of a quarter final place.

The doubts about the possibilities of playing the match at Leicester created a new routine at Anfield. Instead of the players reporting for a 10 a.m. training session they were at the ground at 9 a.m. with bags packed, not knowing whether they would be needed or not.

On the mornings we waited for the result of a referee's inspection there were two motor coaches ticking over in the club car park; one to take the party to Leicester, the other to go to the Melwood training ground.

And there were other inconveniences. Our manager, Mr. Shankly, made two trips to Leicester to be present at the pitch inspections, and the staff had to make a lot of hurried arrangements in the knowledge that they may be wasting their time.

One day was spent trying to arrange four hotel bookings. One was needed for a hoped-for date at Leicester and another for the following date in case the first one was not needed.

In addition, as we did not know our possible sixth round opponents, hotel accommodation had to be found for a game at either Mansfield or West Ham. Arrangements for a replay at Leicester had to be made and, of course, this changed as frequently as the day of the proposed first game.

All this was caused by the despair of the British public—the weather. In addition to the difficulties of the Cup-tie it also affected the work required in staging a normal League fixture. The recent home game with Nottingham Forest is an example. The day before the match our staff arrived at Anfield to discover that the pitch was covered in snow to a depth of three or four inches.

If we were to get the Forest match on just over 24 hours later a lot of work and organisation had to be done.

In less than an hour a labour force of 50 men, plus a snow-clearing machine, were at the ground. Their instructions were to remove most of the snow but to ensure they left a thin covering to act as a cushion and a protection against frost.

We knew that Forest were due to leave Nottingham at 2.30 and we were anxious to let them know what was happening before they left. A referee's opinion was needed but the nearest—Mr. A. W. Jones of Aughton—was out of town and would not be back in time.

Efforts were then made to contact Mr. S. J. Kayley of Preston and he was eventually traced to Southport where he

2

In 1969 heavy snow delayed Liverpool's FA Cup tie at Leicester from 8 February to 1 March, followed by an Anfield replay

# Liverpool FC 1964/65

## From the Boardroom

ON this, the first occasion on which a European Cup Match is being played at Anfield, we extend a warm welcome to the K.R. Football Club of Iceland, in the return match of the Preliminary Round of this years' Competition.

In the first game at Reykjavik, a month ago, we gained a 5-0 lead, after being one goal in front at the interval, in a match which was played in the most sporting spirit throughout, with hardly a foul during the full ninety minutes.

On that occasion, our party enjoyed themselves immensely, the hospitality and kindnesses afforded being second to none, and we trust that our visitors of this evening, after their stay in Liverpool, will take back to Reykjavik, many happy memories of their first visit to this City.

In our home League match against Blackpool, the Seasiders led by one goal at the interval, but this was equalised in the second half by a brilliant goal from Peter Thompson, from a pass by Gordon Wallace. Blackpool restored their lead with a goal from their centre-forward, but with just over ten minutes to play, Roger Hunt headed in a cross from Gordon Wallace to secure a share of the spoils.

At Leicester on Wednesday evening last, we suffered our third away defeat of the present campaign, the home team recording goals in each half, the first after ten minutes play and the second ten minutes before the end. In this game we displayed something like our form of last Season, with however nothing to show for our efforts, as regards goals, outplaying the home team for long spells.

The Central League team lost by the only goal of the game at Blackburn, and in the match with Chesterfield at Anfield a week ago, sustained their second home reverse with an odd goal in five defeat, after having the great bulk of the play. Both our counters were secured by Alan A'court.

1964 saw the 'Boardroom' able to talk about a home European Cup tie for the first time when Icelandic outfit KR Reykjavik were the visitors to Anfield

# MEMORY CORNER

Every time I have played at Anfield against Coventry City since they were promoted I have scored.

I know they have been here only twice, but you can't blame a winger who is not a tremendous goal grabber for savouring the memory.

Coventry came here on 30 December, 1967, after they came up, and were a goal down in only 17 minutes. Dietmar Bruck had the ball near the corner of the Anfield Road penalty area and lost it—to me. I moved along the edge of the 'box' and as goalkeeper Bill Glazier came out I squeezed the ball between him and the post to give us a one-goal win.

We beat them 2-0 when they were here last November, although with four minutes to go were hanging on to a goal by Geoff Strong. Then we got another with the type of move that rarely comes off in modern football. It started just outside our penalty area and finished in Coventry's.

Ian St. John pushed a ball out to Alun

* * * * * * * * * * * * * * * * * * * *
IAN CALLAGHAN explains why he is on a hat-trick against Coventry City today.
* * * * * * * * * * * * * * * * * * * *

Evans on the right wing near the entrance to the players' tunnel. Alun returned it to Ian and moved along the wing, drawing a defender to him to create a space in the middle. That's where I went and moved forward—fast.

Suddenly I was just outside the penalty area with the ball at my feet. Ian had hit a glorious pass along the ground that travelled about 25 yards and swerved round a Coventry player's foot. It left me with only Glazier to beat and I can still see the Kop erupting as the ball hit the net.

*Ian Callaghan*

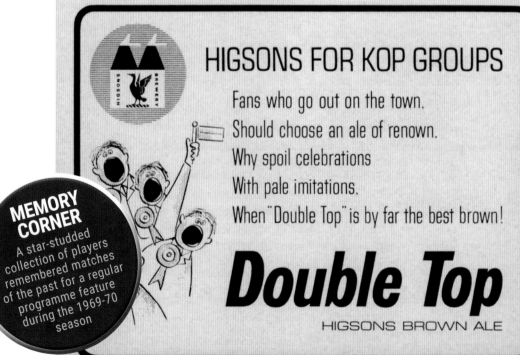
**MEMORY CORNER**
A star-studded collection of players remembered matches of the past for a regular programme feature during the 1969-70 season

# MEMORY CORNER

✱ BOBBY GRAHAM looks back to a great
✱ game with Manchester United on 6 April
✱ last year.
✱✱✱✱✱✱✱✱✱✱✱✱✱✱✱✱✱

Games between Liverpool and Manchester United are usually a bit different. Both clubs have done so well over the past few years that meetings between them are among the highlights of the season.

The match at Old Trafford in April last year certainly was. And I'm not boasting, for I didn't even play in it. But I was substitute, so I got a good look at the game.

United were the First Division champions and the league leaders at the time, so we knew it was not going to be exactly a pushover for us. It looked even less like one two minutes after the kick-off. We were a goal down.

George Best chased a ball into our defence, it broke for him as he went into a tackle with Emlyn Hughes and he ran on to push it past Tommy Lawrence. Four minutes later it would have been 2-0 but for a great save by Tommy from a typical thunderbolt shot by Bobby Charlton.

Yet from that start Liverpool hit back to win with the best performance I have seen from them against United.

Ten minutes after Tommy's save the score was 2-1 for us. With the United defence in something of a tangle Tony Hateley got the ball to Roger Hunt, and although he was angled Roger hit the ball well wide of Alex Stepney and into the net.

Ronnie Yeats scored the second, stabbing the ball into the goal after his header hit the post.

The second half was all Liverpool's. They were in such control I had no doubts they would come away with two points—and they did. It was a wonderful exhibition by our lads who, having fought their way back into the game, made sure United didn't do the same.

---

# MEM C

✱ It's
✱ Ch
✱
✱✱✱✱

My first European game was almost exactly five years ago—on 25 November 1964. It was against Anderlecht in the European Cup and some people still believe it is Liverpool's best performance against Continental opposition.

Although we had met Reykjavik earlier—I did not play against them—this class of competition was largely unknown to us.

Anderlecht had just provided the bulk of the Belgian team which had held England to a draw at Wembley, so we gathered we were up against something special. We were right.

Yet Mr. Shankly had something special up his sleeve too. He had seen Belgium against England and drafted

After had a sh scored. T Roger m after the great hea

That's you are games a Belgium.

It was a and a gre Liverpool

---

# ME

It was 21 April, 1962, and we had a home match with Southampton. Although there were still five games to play we knew that if we won we not only ensured promotion, we clinched the Second Division championship as well.

What a terrible day it was for weather. The rain was very heavy and the light so bad that although it was a Saturday afternoon game the floodlights had to be switched on in the second half.

When Alan A'Court hit the post in the first few minutes it might have been taken

---

*Anfield Review*

# MEMORY CORNER

✱ WILLIE STEVENSON of Stoke City,
✱ returns to the Anfield scene with a
✱ memory of 4 April 1966.
✱✱✱✱✱✱✱✱✱✱✱✱✱✱✱✱✱✱

Easter is always the crucial time for teams chasing titles or trying to avoid relegation. In 1966 Liverpool went into the holiday programme with eyes on the championship, and our first game was against Sheffield Wednesday at Anfield.

It was played on the Wednesday night before Good Friday and the Sheffield club had been good enough to agree to the match even though they were in the middle of a heavy fixture programme. They had reached the semi-final of the F.A. Cup.

We were seven points clear at the top of the table with seven games to go. The match against Sheffield Wednesday was the first of three in six days and we wanted to get off to a good start.

I think we showed that by the way we set off against Wednesday. Within minutes of the kick-off their goalkeeper was leaping all over the place saving shots and headers, and we thought we should have had a penalty when Gerry Young handled the ball.

After about 25 minutes we scored. Ian Callaghan crossed a ball that was just too

high for Roger Hunt. But Roger jumped anyway, just to confuse the defenders, and the ball came through to me. I put it in the net and it turned out to be the winner. I remember the move well because it was one we had practised, the forwards moving to Ian's cross leaving me room behind them.

How we didn't get more I don't know. It was a typical Anfield display by Liverpool in which Wednesday, according to the following day's papers, were roasted. Still, one goal was enough, and we were more than happy to have two more points towards that championship win.

*Willy Stevenson*

---

Four games from the end of the season we needed only two points to win the championship. But three of those games were away and the visit of Arsenal was our only chance to clinch the title as we wanted—in front of our home crowd.

I think that day showed the football world that Liverpool had arrived as a team. It certainly proved the Kop had arrived as a crowd.

Our fans were fantastic that afternoon and I doubt if they have ever put on a greater performance. The television cameras were here for the first Match of the Day and captured the amazing scenes for the rest of the country.

The match got off to a great start for us with a goal after only seven minutes by Ian St. John. Yet we looked as if we might lose it when Arsenal gained a penalty. But Tommy Lawrence made a great save from George Eastham's kick,

✱ GERRY BYRNE recalls one of the most
✱ memorable days in Anfield's history. It
✱ was on April 18, 1964 and Arsenal were
✱ the visitors.
✱✱✱✱✱✱✱✱✱✱✱✱✱✱✱✱✱

and we were two up at half time with a header by Alf Arrowsmith.

Two goals early in the second half by Peter Thompson made certain of the result and Roger Hunt added the fifth.

It was a great performance that led to a memorable lap of honour by the players and a sing-song in the dressing room.

That day must surely be one of the most remarkable at Anfield over the past few years. I'm glad I was part of it and always think of it when Arsenal are the visitors.

*Gerry Byrne*

---

# MEMOR COR

When we ran out at Roker Park that night we knew we were about to play a vital game. We had won our first three matches of the season and, like us, Sunderland were fancied for promotion.

Right from the start I felt we were the better side and after 26 minutes we scored. Alan A'Court fired in a shot at Wakeham, the Sunderland goalkeeper, he could only parry it and the ball dropped at my feet for an easy goal.

Thirteen minutes later we were two up, Ian St. John heading in a centre by Jimmy Melia. Incidentally, that was Ian's first League goal for Liverpool.

Brian Clough, the present Derby manager, pulled one back for Sunderland

✱ ROGER HUNT
✱ Second Divisio
✱
✱✱✱✱✱✱✱✱

We waited an third goal whe A'Court took th before leaving me In the last minu again to give us out of eight and

The Sunderlan great reception a we would get pro season. And they

Photograph by courtesy of Mercury Press Agency Ltd.

**Ian St. John on duty at the Radio Merseyside Studios. Ian has his own record request programme every Thursday.**

Ian St John was pictured in the studio for his Radio Merseyside show in 1968

The likes of Roger Hunt, Ian Callaghan and Gerry Byrne were on the squad lists in both 1960 and 1969

### LIVERPOOL FOOTBALL CLUB
### PROFESSIONAL PLAYING STAFF
#### SEASON 1960/61

| Name | Birthplace | Date Signed | Former Club | Ht. | Wt. |
|---|---|---|---|---|---|
| **Goalkeepers** | | | | | |
| Lawrence, T. | Culcheth | 30.10.57 | Local | 5.11 | 12.5 |
| Slater, R. | Musselburgh | 12.6.59 | Falkirk | 5.8½ | 10.12 |
| **Full-backs** | | | | | |
| Byrne, G. | Liverpool | 30.8.55 | L'pool Schools | 5.10 | 12.0 |
| Jones, A. P. | Flint | 29.4.57 | Flint Schools | 5.11 | 10.7 |
| Molyneux, J. A. | Warrington | 23.6.55 | Chester | 5.10 | 13.3 |
| Moran, R. | Liverpool | 7.1.52 | Crosby Schools | 5.9½ | 13.4 |
| Parry, J. E. | Flint | 27.5.57 | Flint Schools | 5.11 | 11.9 |
| **Half-backs** | | | | | |
| Campbell, R. | Liverpool | 11.5.55 | L'pool Schools | 5.9 | 12.0 |
| Ferns, P. (S) | Liverpool | 24.3.58 | Local | 5.10 | 11.11 |
| Leishman, T. | Stenhousemuir | 20.11.59 | St. Mirren | 6.0 | 11.5 |
| Nicholson, J. P. | Liverpool | 7.1.57 | Local | 5.11 | 11.11 |
| Wheeler, J. E. | Crosby | 8.9.56 | Bolton W. | 5.9 | 12.1 |
| White, D. | Scunthorpe | 10.11.55 | Scunthorpe U. | 5.10½ | 12.1 |
| Davies, R. | Capetown | 17.11.59 | Hibbs. Capetown | 6.1 | 11.3 |
| **Fowards** | | | | | |
| A'Court, A. | Rainhill | 24.9.52 | Prescot Cel. | 5.8 | 11.1 |
| Arnell, A. J. | Chichester | 22.3.55 | Sussex Youth | 6.1 | 13.5 |
| Banks, A. | Liverpool | 5.5.58 | Rankin Boys | 5.8 | 11.0 |
| Callaghan, I. | Liverpool | 28.3.60 | L'pool Schools | 5.6½ | 10.8 |
| Carlin, W. (P) | Liverpool | 5.5.58 | L'pool Schools | 5.6 | 9.4 |
| Green, P. A. | Birkenhead | 26.1.60 | New Brighton | 5.11 | 11.11 |
| Hickson, D. | Salford | 6.11.59 | Everton | 5.10 | 12.6 |
| Hunt, R. | Golbourne | 29.7.59 | Stockton Heath | 5.8½ | 11.10 |
| Lewis, K. | Ellesmere Port | 16.6.60 | Sheffield Utd. | 5.11 | 11.0 |
| Liddell, W. B. | Dunfermline | 17.4.39 | Lochgelly V. | 5.10½ | 12.3 |
| Melia, J. | Liverpool | 1.11.54 | L'pool Schools | 5.8½ | 10.12 |
| Morrissey, J. | Liverpool | 29.4.57 | L'pool Schools | 5.6 | 11.4 |
| Harrower, J. | Alva | 3.1.58 | Hibernian | 5.9 | 12.6 |
| Twist, F. (P) | Liverpool | 31.7.58 | L'pool Schools | 5.7 | 9.10 |

(P) Part Time     (S) Service Player

Ronnie Yeats, our tallest and heaviest first team player

Ian Callaghan (left) is the shortest and Bobby Graham the lightest

*Anfield Review* 11

## Who...when...where...what?

QUESTIONS stem from interest, and no supporters are more interested in their team than Liverpool's. We get bombarded with questions about all our players. Where was he born? When did he sign? How tall is he? What is his weight?

In a bid to provide the answers we have tabulated this information about all our professional staff and reproduce it here. Cut it out, put it in your pocket and it can help you win a lot of arguments.

| | Date Signed | Previous Club | Birthplace | Ht. | Wt. |
|---|---|---|---|---|---|
| **GOALKEEPERS** | | | | Ft. ins. | St. lb. |
| Ray Clemence | 12.6.67 | Scunthorpe U. | Skegness | 5 11½ | 12 0 |
| Tommy Lawrence | 30.10.57 | Amateur | Dailly | 5 11 | 13 12 |
| Graham Lloyd | 10.1.67 | Schoolboy | Liverpool | 5 9 | 11 0 |
| Philip Dando | 22.9.69 | Amateur | Liverpool | 5 9 | 10 0 |
| **FULL BACKS** | | | | | |
| Gerry Byrne | 30.8.55 | Schoolboy | Liverpool | 5 9 | 12 0 |
| Chris Lawler | 20.10.60 | Schoolboy | Liverpool | 6 0 | 12 10 |
| Kevin Marsh | 29.3.66 | Schoolboy | Liverpool | 6 0 | 11 2 |
| Geoff Strong | 7.11.64 | Arsenal | Kirkcaton | 5 10 | 11 2 |
| Peter Wall | 6.10.66 | Wrexham | Shrewsbury | 5 11 | 12 4 |
| John Webb | 17.2.69 | Schoolboy | Liverpool | 5 7½ | 10 4 |
| **HALF BACKS** | | | | | |
| Roy Evans | 5.10.65 | Schoolboy | Bootle | 5 7 | 11 0 |
| Emlyn Hughes | 28.2.67 | Blackpool | Barrow-in-Furness | 5 10½ | 11 13 |
| Larry Lloyd | 22.4.69 | Bristol Rovers | Bristol | 6 2 | 12 4 |
| Alec Lindsay | 13.3.69 | Bury | Bury | 5 8 | 10 10 |
| Ian Ross | 25.2.69 | Schoolboy | Liverpool | 5 8 | 10 3 |
| Tommy Smith | 18.8.65 | Amateur | Glasgow | 5 9½ | 11 9 |
| Ron Yeats | 5.4.62 | Dundee U. | Aberdeen | 6 2 | 14 5 |
| Denis Walsh | 24.9.69 | Schoolboy | Dublin | 5 10 | 10 11 |
| **FORWARDS** | | | | | |
| Phil Boersma | 11.9.68 | Amateur | Liverpool | 5 10½ | 11 7 |
| Ian Callaghan | 28.3.60 | Schoolboy | Liverpool | 5 7 | 11 1 |
| Brian Hall | 26.6.68 | Amateur | Glasgow | 5 7 | 10 6 |
| Roger Hunt | 29.7.59 | Stockton H. | Golborne | 5 9 | 12 1 |
| Doug Livermore | 9.1.65 | Schoolboy | Liverpool | 5 8½ | 10 5 |
| Bobby Graham | 24.1.61 | Amateur | Motherwell | 5 7½ | 10 7 |
| Stephen Marshall | 25.2.69 | Schoolboy | Bootle | 5 8 | 10 0 |
| Stephen Peplow | 20.3.64 | Schoolboy | Liverpool | 5 8½ | 10 4 |
| Ian St. John | 2.5.61 | Motherwell | Motherwell | 5 7½ | 11 9 |
| Peter Thompson | 14.8.63 | Preston N.E. | Carlisle | 5 9 | 11 10 |
| Alun Evans | 17.9.68 | Wolves | Kidderminster | 5 9 | 11 0 |

🚉 **British Rail**

### LIVERPOOL TO LONDON

| DAY RETURN | 76/- | — | PERIOD RETURN | 100/- |
|---|---|---|---|---|

# CHOICE of the WEEK

## ALUN EVANS (Liverpool F.C.)

*HOW DOES IT FEEL to be Britain's costliest soccer teenager? Ask the lad who carries the title, Liverpool F.C.'s blond-haired youngster, Alun Evans, and he will explain in a matter-of-fact way:* "I've got used to it now. I was a little worried at first, but I have settled down so well at Anfield, that I never think about that fee."

☐ The "experts" raised an eyebrow when shrewd Bill Shankly paid out a fee reported to be around £100,000 for the 18-year-old Wolves reserve who had only a handful of League games behind him.

☐ Now those very same "experts" praise the Anfield chief for pulling off one of the best buys of the season.

☐ The move itself came as a bit of a shock to Evans, who despite his Welsh name, was born in England. "I knew something was in the

**Above: Alun tucks into a hearty lunch at the Anfield club's canteen. His appetite receives the nod of approval from manager Bill Shankly.**

air," he says, "but suddenly I found myself a Liverpool player. There were a few regrets at first about leaving friends from the Midlands, but I soon settled in at Anfield."

■ Alun shares digs with team mates Emlyn Hughes and Peter Wall. Hughes, previous holder of that "costliest teenager" title, is another Englishman with a Welsh name.

☐ The tie up between the two goes deeper than that, for while Evans' father was a War-time Welsh soccer international, Hughes' father earned international recognition for Wales . . . at Rugby Union.

☐ Evans' spare time these days is taken up with exploring his new surrounds. "*I like to stroll round Liverpool finding out just where things are. I'm still a new boy in these parts, but gradually I'm beginning to know the place. It's a great place, too, when you start to get your bearings.*"

☐ Anfield's Kop-ites, among the most critical of fans in the game, quickly took to their new hero after the youngster had burst on the scene by scoring three goals in his first two matches.

☐ Evans shares an equally healthy respect for the Anfield patrons. "I enjoyed playing at Liverpool last season for Wolves and I realised then just what a sporting crowd they were. They gave me a tremendous welcome here and I am very grateful to them. **They've made a difference to my football.**"

☐ Evans' greatest moment in his short career with Liverpool was his return to Molineux when he scored twice in Liverpool's 6—0 win, to silence those Wolves fans who had jeered him only four weeks previously.

☐ "I was thrilled by the way things went," he recalls. "I saw some of the Wolves players afterwards and they pulled my leg, but I could stand it after that game."

☐ Alun Evans, the youngster who started the season as a First Division reserve, and six weeks later took Anfield by storm, looks like justifying the expensive tag he wears.

■ *IT'S NO WONDER HE IS CHOICE OF THE WEEK FAR BEYOND THE CITY LIMITS OF LIVERPOOL.*

### Vital Statistics

**A schoolboy international, signed professional forms for Wolves in September 1966 and won Youth honours while at Molineux. Moved to Liverpool in September 1968. Born at Bewdley, Worcestershire, the son of the former West Bromwich player and Welsh international.**

### WHAT CHOICE OF THE WEEK IS ALL ABOUT

☐ *"Choice of the Week" features the player our readers most want to hear about . . . be he established star or a young up-and-coming hopeful. You tell us whom you'd like us to feature, and we'll do our best to oblige. Write to: Choice of the Week, Football League Review, Lytham St. Annes, Lancs.*

☐ *Votes are now flooding in. Heading the lists are youngsters like Dave Thomas (Burnley), Malcolm Manley (Leicester), Chris Garland (Bristol City) and Colin Sullivan (Plymouth) together with stars like Bobbie Charlton and Bobby Moore. Who's your choice?*

An interview with dynamic young striker Alun Evans appeared in the Football League Review insert (more about this later in the chapter) in 1968

# LIDDELL HAS ADDED LUSTRE TO LIVERPOOL'S NAME

**by Mr. T. V. WILLIAMS**
*Chairman,* LIVERPOOL FOOTBALL CLUB

I have been asked to write something about Billy Liddell for this evening's programme, which is a task I undertake with the greatest pleasure. I cannot do better than repeat what I wrote for the foreword of Billy's book, which is to be published next month. This is what I said then, and what I have much pleasure in saying again on this auspicious occasion:

"I have known hundreds of footballers in my time, many of them wonderful players and loyal club men, but throughout my long experience I have never known a man whom I have admired and respected more than Billy Liddell, both on and off the field. Since the days when he joined Liverpool as a sixteen-year-old amateur I have followed his career with the greatest interest, and also watched the growth of his splendid character and personality. In my official capacity I have been in much closer contact with him than most people, and the more I have seen of him the greater has been my admiration. Billy Liddell's ability as a footballer needs no recommendation from me. His records and achievements speak for themselves. Never once throughout his long service with Liverpool has he given the club a moment's anxiety. Whatever he has been asked to do he has done willingly and with good grace, content with the know-ledge that even if it was occasionally not just what he would have preferred, it was for the good of the Liverpool club, which has always been his primary aim. He has added much lustre to Liverpool's name by his sporting behaviour on the field, the high standard of his play, and his scoring exploits. Never have I seen Liddell guilty of a deliberate foul, of arguing with the referee, or anything else which would tend to lower the reputation of himself, his club, or football in general.

"Off the field he is just as much an example. He is a clean-living man who, without parading his religious beliefs, seeks to lead a true Christian life.

"As he says himself in his book, football has been good to him, and in turn he tries to help others. He works hard for many Church and charitable causes, and gives pleasure to patients in hospital by regular visits. The welfare of young people is close to his heart, and his scope in this direction was considerably increased when he was made a Justice of the Peace, an honour which, as far as I am aware, has only once before been bestowed on a professional footballer while still earning his living at the game.

"Billy is a non-smoker and teetotaller, but not a bigoted one. It is simply that neither relaxation appeals to him. From his pictures and demeanour on the field you might think he was a very dour person, but I see him often when football duties are not on his mind, and he has a light-hearted side to his nature of which many folk are not aware.

"Billy Liddell has been a credit to the game throughout his long career. Football would be all the better for many more of his stamp."

That, as I have mentioned earlier, is what I wrote as a foreword to the story of Billy Liddell's Soccer life. All that remains now is for me to wish him a bumper Testimonial tonight and the best of good luck in the future. He deserves it.

**LIDDELL LOVE**
There were warm words for Liverpool icon Billy Liddell from club chairman TV Williams in the Scot's testimonial programme in 1960

Grateful acknowledgment is due to the 'Liverpool Echo' and The Provincial Press, Southport for their timely assistance in supplying photographs—W.B.L.

# ANFIELD PERSONALITIES
## No. 2. IAN ST. JOHN

*Photo by courtesy of "Liverpool Echo"*

Signed from Motherwell on May 2 this year, Ian St. John made his first appearance in our colours a week later, in the Liverpool Senior Cup final against Everton at Goodison Park, and scored all our three goals in that game, which Everton won 4-3. He went on the tour of Czecho-slovakia, scoring four goals in the four matches played there, and then made his Football League debut in the opening match of the current campaign, in which he speedily showed his great capabilities. Ian started his career with Douglas Water Thistle, a Lanarkshire junior club, joining Motherwell when he was 17. He made his League debut for Motherwell four years ago, and during his career with them played in all five forward positions. In his second season he was top scorer in Scottish football, and got his first cap when chosen to lead Scotland's attack against West Germany. He has played for his country now on seven occasions, all at centre-forward. Prior to becoming a full-time player he served his time as an engineer in a Motherwell factory.

Ian St. John has already delighted the club's supporters with his splendid ball control, his clever passes, and the general excellence of his all-round play. He has quickly settled down in English football, despite its faster tempo, and we look forward [to many] years of first-class service from this stylish and attractive player.

**ANFIELD PERSONALITIES**

As players' profiles grew, more individual features would appear in the programme, such as these from various 1961-62 editions

# ANFIELD PERSONALITIES
## No. 3. RONNIE YEATS

*Photo by courtesy of "Liverpool Echo"*

Let us clear one thing up about Ronnie first of all. He pronounces his name to rhyme with "Bates", not "beats". Born in Aberdeen, he learned the rudiments of the game with Aberdeen Lads Club, eventually signing for Dundee United in November 1957, at the age of 19. He was then a big strapping youngster, admirably fitted for the duties of centre-half, and within a month of joining the Dens Park staff he was drafted into the first team. He still has happy memories of his debut, for Dundee United that day defeated East Stirling 7-0. Once given this chance to show what he could do, Ronnie Yeats proved his ability in such convincing fashion that he remained automatic choice for the rest of his stay with Dundee United, until we had the good fortune to secure his signature in July this year.

Ronnie played for Scotland's Youth team on three occasions, and has been reserve for both the Under-23 and full Scottish international team. One of these days, and in the not very distant future, we hope he will join Ian St. John as a "full" internationalist. He is the tallest player we have had on our books for a long time, but uses his height and weight with scrupulous fairness. Like Ian St. John, he has quickly become a great favourite with our supporters, and has done splendid work, in conjunction with his fellow-defenders, in keeping the "goals against" column to a very low figure. We wish him a long and happy career with us.

# ANFIELD PERSONALITIES

## No. 1. DICK WHITE (Captain)

Dick White, secured from Scunthorpe in November 1955, spent most of his time for the first eighteen months in the Central League side, but came into the senior side for the first time on March 10, 1956, when he deputised for Laurie Hughes—off with a cracked rib—against Barnsley at Barnsley, and also in the next two games. Then Roy Saunders was indisposed and Dick carried on for another five games at right-half, always shaping most promisingly. The following winter he had another five senior outings, filling the breach again when the centre-half and right-half positions were vacant through injuries. When the 1957-58 season began, Laurie Hughes was taken ill a couple of days before the kick-off, and into the breach once more stepped Dick White—but this time with a different result. He was now a mature and consistent player, and so well did he fill the pivotal position that he became an automatic choice for four seasons, during which he missed only two League games. This season the acquisition of Ronnie Yeats as centre-half left the way open to further strengthen the rearguard by switching Dick to right-back, where he has performed with his customary skill, consistency, and whole-heartedness. He has also shouldered the responsibilities of captaincy with equal satisfaction.

# ANFIELD PERSONALITIES

## No. 11 IAN CALLAGHAN

Although he is the 'babe' of the team, both in age and experience, young Ian Callaghan has quite an old head—in a football sense—on his youthful shoulders. A most likeable lad, Ian is rapidly making a name for himself as a top-class winger, and as he is anxious and willing to learn all he can from those best qualified to help him he should make still further progress as he absorbs experience and knowledge. A native of Liverpool, and a member of the City Boys' team, Ian came to Anfield straight from school, signing his first amateur form for us exactly four years ago this week. Almost from the start it was obvious that he was a player likely to make good in the highest grade, and after displaying his prowess in the Colts and Junior teams he was introduced to Central League football on January 9, 1960, against Leeds United Reserves at Elland Road. After only four Central League games Ian got his big chance in the first team in the home game with Bristol Rovers on April 16 the same year, taking over at outside-right from no less a player than Bill Liddell. Including the Senior Cup game with Everton, Ian had five first-team outings before the season ended, shaping most promisingly in them all. Last winter he acted as deputy to Kevin Lewis, making seven appearances in League and Cup matches, all at outside-right except one appearance on the opposite wing in the League Cup replay with Luton at Luton. He also occupied both wing positions in the Central League side, scoring 11 goals in 35 games. At the start of the current campaign he was again second string to Kevin Lewis, but was called upon for senior duty in the game against Preston North End at Deepdale on November 4, since when he has been earning much praise for his consistent displays. Ian is a boy with a bright future, but still as modest and unassuming as the day he first joined us.

# ANFIELD PERSONALITIES

## No. 8 ROGER HUNT

*Photo by courtesy of "Liverpool Echo"*

Providing he steers clear of injury, which all at Anfield fervently hope, it seems certain that Roger Hunt is going to establish a new individual scoring record for the club this season. The total Roger has to beat is that set up by Gordon Hodgson in the First Division in 1930-31, when the South African scored 36 goals in 40 League matches. Roger is well on the way towards that figure, and has only to maintain his present "average" during the second half of the season to make sure of becoming our new record-holder.

A native of Culcheth, he joined the Anfield staff from Stockton Heath, signing his first professional form in July two years ago. After five Central League games at the start of 1959-60 season, in which he scored seven goals, he was given his initial first-team outing, against Scunthorpe United at Anfield. On that occasion he was at centre-forward. Then he had two games at inside-left, after which he was switched to inside-right and began to prove his ability in no uncertain fashion. That season he finished as joint leading scorer with Dave Hickson, getting 21 goals in 36 League outings. Last winter he scored 15 goals in 32 games, while this season, of course, he has been showing not only splendid opportunism, but also proving that he possesses other attributes, such as good ball control, a keen positional sense, and a very fine turn of speed. While he undoubtedly owes much to the chances created by the men alongside him, Roger is now a top-class player in his own right, and a great future is before him. We congratulate both Roger and Jimmy Melia on their invitation to join the England party in special training sessions at Lilleshall next week, which we sincerely hope is a pointer to honours in the near future.

# ANFIELD PERSONALITIES

## No. 18. CHRIS LAWLER

During our long history many brilliant centre-halves have worn our colours, and if Chris Lawler continues to make the same steady progress in the future that he has done over the past year or so it seems certain that one day he will add his name to the list of his illustrious and talented predecessors. A native of Liverpool, Chris rose to be captain of England's Schoolboy international team, and later added the distinction of also being captain of his country's Youth team. Though only just over 18, the promise he showed as a Schoolboy and Youth international is now being tested and confirmed in the much sterner ranks of Central League football, where he is earning regular commendation for his solid and consistent displays. Naturally he is now finding himself up against much more experienced and frequently very much older players, some of them with extensive First or Second Division experience, and the fact that he has been more than holding his own in company of this class is a happy augury for his future.

Chris joined our ground staff on leaving school, and quickly progressed through the club's junior teams to his present Central League position. Measuring 5 ft. 11 in. and weighing just over 11 stone, he is ideally built for the berth, and his stylish and intelligent play is not the only pleasing factor of his work. Considering he has been a professional for so short a time Chris has made splendid progress, which we hope will continue in the years ahead. We wish him the best of good fortune in the future.

# ANFIELD PERSONALITIES
## No. 6. BERT SLATER

*Photo by courtesy of "Liverpool Echo"*

As most of our followers are doubtless aware, our telegraphic address is "Goalkeeper, Liverpool", a constant reminder of the many brilliant custodians we have had on our books over the years. Bert Slater is a worthy addition to that long list, which includes such famous names as Ted Doig, Sam Hardy, Elisha Scott Kenny Campbell, Cyril Sidlow, Tommy Younger, Arthur Riley and Doug Rudham—all of whom, like Bert Slater, played for their country. Bert has yet to get his first full Scottish cap, though that is an honour we hope will come his way in the not-too-distant future. In the past he has played for Scotland's Under-23 team and also their "B" eleven, and on the form he has been displaying this season must surely be in the minds of Scotland's Selectors for further honours. Bert, a native of Musselburgh (Midlothian), started his career with the little known Broughton Star, but it was not long before he was attracting the attention of bigger clubs. He chose Falkirk, and made his debut in their first team at the age of 17, soon after joining them. He spent over five years with the Brockville Park club, being automatic choice, except when injured, throughout that period. We signed him in the summer of 1959, at the same time that Tommy Younger went to Falkirk as their player-manager, and since making his debut in English football he has, apart from one short period, been a regular first-team player. Compared with the average goalkeeper, Bert is not over-blessed with height, but neither were some of our previous custodians who made their names famous wherever football is played. Bert makes up for lack of inches by amazing agility, wonderful anticipation and safe handling.

# ANFIELD PERSONALITIES
## No. 9 GORDON MILNE

*Photo by courtesy of "Liverpool Echo"*

Though Gordon Milne is often referred to as a Scot, this is not correct. He was born at Preston, while his father Jimmy was on the playing staff of North End, of which club he is now, of course, the manager. Jimmy Milne joined Preston in 1932, and was a playing colleague of our own manager, Mr. Shankly, in pre-war days. They were also near neighbours, and Mr. Shankly has known Gordon Milne since he was a child. He has always had a high regard for his football ability, and had been trying to add Gordon to the playing strength at Anfield for some time before he actually pulled off the deal. That was in August last year, after Johnny Wheeler had been injured in the game against Middlesbrough at Ayresome Park. Gordon made his League debut for us, 24 hours after his signing, in the mid-week game against Southampton. After eight outings—two of them at left-half—he dropped out of the team for a short while when Johnny Wheeler had recovered, but it was not very long before he was back again for another nine League and Cup matches. Altogether he played in 20 first-team games last season, and this season, in which he has been showing splendid form throughout, he is an ever-present. Gordon first signed for Preston at the age of sixteen, spending some time on their ground staff before becoming a professional in 1956. He made his League debut in September, 1956, but it was not until two years later that he became a regular first-team selection. In addition to playing in both wing-half positions, he also had some outings at inside-right, where he did quite well. In addition to playing for Preston, Gordon also turned out regularly for the Army while doing his National Service and has made one F.A. appearance. He has fitted into the scheme of things at Anfield splendidly, and we look forward to many years of first-class service from him.

*Photograph by courtesy of Mercury Press Agency Ltd.*

**Bobby Graham heads the ball over the Manchester City goalkeeper Ken Mulhearn to score our first goal of the season.**

Bobby Graham scored the first of the Reds' goals in a 2-1 win over Manchester City in August 1968, while (below) an eventful few days for Emlyn Hughes in 1969 were illustrated by an Anfield goal against Manchester United

## The Anfield Review 'Pic' of the Week

*Photograph by Liverpool Daily Post*

**It has been a memorable month for Emlyn Hughes, with goals against Everton and Manchester United (above) and his first Wembley appearance for England—all in eight days.**

*Anfield Review* **13**

# Geoff Strong's last-minute winner against Coventry

'PIC' OF THE WEEK

*Anfield Review* 13

Picture by Charles Owens, *Daily Mirror*

Geoff Strong lifts the ball over the head of Coventry goalkeeper Bill Glazier to get the points that put us at the top of the First Division.

Everyone loves a late Anfield winner, so this Geoff Strong effort to claim the two points against Coventry City in September 1969 was picked out. Below, there's a great view of Roger Hunt's goal against Stoke City's England keeper Gordon Banks in a 3-1 win that same month

## The Anfield Review 'Pic' of the Week

Photo by Charles Owens, *Daily Mirror*

*Anfield Review* 13

It takes a good shot, well hit and well directed, to beat Gordon Banks. Here is Roger Hunt proving it with our first goal against Stoke City in our last home match.

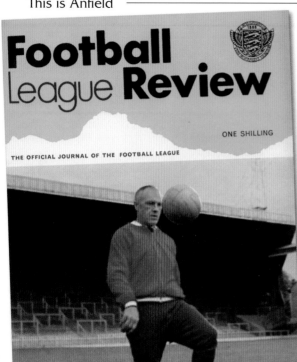

*Examples from season 1967-68 of the 'Football League Review' – later known as 'League Football' – which was stapled into the centre-pages. It was the mouthpiece for the Football League and 202 different copies appeared in the Liverpool FC matchday programme before the publication ceased. Sales of the programme reportedly doubled as a result.*

An attractive colour photo of the stars on display at Anfield in 1968 appeared in the Football League Review in the Everton programme of October that year

LIVERPOOL F.C.
*Division One 1968-69*

Back row :— GEOFFREY STRONG ☐ RAYMOND CLEMENCE ☐ THOMAS LAWRENCE ☐ GERALD BYRNE
Middle row :—ROBERT GRAHAM ☐ TONY HATELEY (now with Coventry City) ☐ THOMAS WALL ☐ IAN ROSS
ALFRED ARROWSMITH ☐ PETER THOMPSON
Front row :— IAN CALLAGHAN ☐ EMLYN HUGHES ☐ ROGER HUNT ☐ RONALD YEATS ☐ IAN ST. JOHN
THOMAS SMITH ☐ CHRISTOPHER LAWLER

# CLUB CALL

## Liverpool F.C.
## Anfield Road,
## Liverpool, 14.

AMONG THE top six clubs for success and support, Liverpool in 12 glorious seasons have averaged exactly 53 points, with 324 in six Second Division seasons and 312 since returning to where they belong.

☐ During this phenomenal phase the proud Anfielders have added to their many achievements a fourth Second Division championship in 11 seasons altogether, their sixth and seventh triumphs as League Champions and the club's first FA Cup win in three Finals.

☐ This was a 2—1 success in extra time against Leeds United three years ago. Twice previously Liverpool were finalists with the reigning monarch present—in 1914 when Burnley scored the only goal in the last Final at the Crystal Palace, and in 1950, when Arsenal won 2—0.

☐ Never blessed with much Cup luck, Liverpool nevertheless can claim eight semi-final appearances. Their last League title win (1965-66) was by the club's record First Division points total of 61, and remarkable also for the fact that only 34 goals were conceded.

☐ Liverpool's points total of 62 when promoted as champions after eight postwar seasons in Division Two was also their highest in that company, and they had their best goals total (99) for 66 years.

☐ Their goals record is 106 on gaining promotion at their first attempt in 1896. Liverpool's League championship years started in 1901, their eighth season, a success repeated in 1906, 1922, 1923, 1947, 1964 and 1966.

"HONEST" John McKenna, Football League president, 1910-1936, often spoke of his beloved Liverpool's stout hearts during his reign as chairman. Another of Anfield's famous men, secretary Tom Watson, went into print with "We always seem to be fighting for something."

☐ Their successors, not least manager Bill Shankly, would endorse those sentiments with ". . . and not often losing!" And so says all the Kop (identity tune: "We are the greatest!").

☐ Liverpool, in fact, were born fighting—to justify their arrival as an offshoot of "Papa" Everton in 1892.

☐ Welcomed to the Lancashire League, Liverpool's lusty "babes" promptly won the Championship and made it a "double" by annexing the Cup which, alas, was stolen from them and cost the club £127 to replace it.

☐ The following season Liverpool were warmly welcomed into The League's enlarged Second Division and straightaway rocketed out of it as undefeated champions with 50 of a maximum 56 points (goals 77-18). They also beat the then "Invincibles," Preston North End, by 3—2 in the F.A. Cup.

☐ Just as promotion was gained by winning a Test match, First Division status was forfeited by losing one 12 months later. Typically, Liverpool swallowed their disappointment and fought back to rout the "Dismal Jimmies" by scoring 106 goals to 32 in 30 matches.

☐ The "team of Macs," as they were called (through the many Scots on their staff), progressed to become League runners-up in 1899, and champions early in the new century.

☐ Surprisingly, Liverpool were relegated as next to bottom club in 1904, but once again proved themselves at their best when on their mettle.

☐ Up again at the first attempt, as Second Division champions for the third time in three seasons, they stormed on to win The League title the following April with 58 points.

☐ Liverpool's next First Division stay was for as many as 38 seasons.

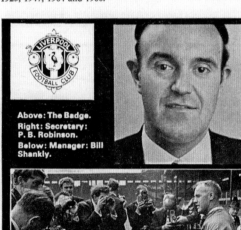

Above: The Badge.
Right: Secretary: P. B. Robinson.
Below: Manager: Bill Shankly.

## FOUGHT THEIR WAY TO FAME

By gum, that was good, says Liverpool FC manager Bill Shankly as he finishes a big meal in the club canteen at Anfield. But they won't be serving Christmas fare there this year. Say the club : this is a staff canteen and the boys have to be careful with their diet. So no Christmas pud or turkey, or cigars. "Just the plain, good food that footballers need to give them the protein essential to their requirements", says Bill. Mind you the club will give the players and their families presents and a staff party . . . as most clubs do. All clubs give their players a present, many give the families presents. Many hold special parties . . . on the lines of Arsenal FC who hold a special Christmas staff party in their Gunners Restaurant. Everyone goes, from the Chairman and Board of Directors down to the telephone girl in the office.

A shot of Bill Shankly accompanied a piece on the club's canteen arrangements at Christmas in 1968

EVERYTHING happened to Liverpool F.C. goalkeeper Tommy Lawrence the day he went to St James' Park, Newcastle. The home side have just scored and the hell-bent throwers have just showered him in paper . . . and now a dog runs across his sights. It's all in the day of a top-class goalkeeper.

Tommy Lawrence had to deal with toilet roll and a rogue dog on the pitch at Newcastle!

There was an interesting take on the club's history in the 'Club Call' feature in the Chelsea programme in 1968

Peter Robinson

# POLITICS IS MY ESCAPE HATCH

# MAN and MANager

## BILL SHANKLY (Liverpool F.C.)

HE GRINNED mischievously over his lunch in the spotless club canteen at Liverpool FC's Anfield Road Ground. "Don't believe those people who tell you I'm so football crazy I have no other interests," Bill Shankly insisted. "When Liverpool aren't winning I'm a political student."

☐ The fast-talking, tremendously likeable Scot wasn't kidding either. "Football today demands everything from everybody in it. You can't split up your interests into little parcels and think that the game is something which happens to you when you get to the ground.

☐ "A manager, players too, are of little use to their clubs if they aren't thoroughly dedicated. My enthusiasm for football is as uncomplicated now as it was when I went to Preston North End as a raw and slightly overawed youth of 17. Some people try to take the mickey out of me for it, but I am a happy man inside because my life is my work and my work is my life. It's a lucky man who can say that, and I'm thankful for it."

■ **So what about the political twist?**

☐ Bill Shankly let us into a secret. "If I had time for something outside my football then it would be politics, and why not . . . politics is the stuff of life.

■ "What politicians and political parties do everywhere matters very much to all of us. Power, government, administration . . . it's all so very intriguing and I often wish I had more time to keep up with it and current affairs.

☐ "So when my team is in a bad patch (anything less than top of the League is a bad patch to Bill), "I offset my frustrations. When my team wins I stick to reading the sports pages, but when we lose I turn to the front pages. I relax in thinking about politics. **It works wonders for me."**

☐ And he means it. That doesn't mean he involves himself with party lines. "I like to dissect what every political line of thought really means, I like to pick the bones out of policies, seeking the strong points and analysing the weak ones. It relaxes me for my real job."

■ What of the game itself? Nothing annoys Bill Shankly more than those who complicate it by talking in ciphers: "inventing words like wall-ball and sweeper-up and link-man and the rest of the clap-trap."

☐ "It's the same basic game I used to play," the Liverpool boss argues. "Arsenal played 4–2–4 in the thirties and our team at Preston in the late thirties operated most of the systems you find with the so-called modern labels of today.

☐ "The only thing which advances is training methods, diet, team work . . . they're the things which have improved football. But the clever-clever boys who think football wasn't discovered until the Hungarians hit Britain in the early fifties are still wet behind the ears."

## VITAL STATISTICS

Born in Glenbuck, Ayrshire. Signed for Preston North End on July 20, 1933 and was a one-club man. Member of the 1938 Cup-winning team and won many Scottish international caps. Became manager of Carlisle United in 1949, moved to Grimsby two years later and tried Workington in 1954. A year later took over as assistant manager at Huddersfield, taking full control a year later. Went to Anfield in 1960 starting a success story that began with the Second Division title in 1961-2 and went on to two League crowns and an F.A. Cup win.

*Football League Review* 9

## Star Supporter

### KEN DODD (Liverpool F.C.)

KEN DODD was four years old when his uncle took him to watch Liverpool play Everton—and he's been a supporter of the Reds ever since.

☐ "I would like to say," he reflects ruminatively, "how tickled H'I am when I'm watching Liverpool. What about you, madam? Have you ever been tickled when watching Liverpool?"

☐ Most Liverpudlians —which includes those Everton folk, of course—are keen footballers, as schoolboys. Ken was no exception. But he never pursued the sport after leaving school. He is the first to admit that this was chiefly because of his prominent teeth.

☐ He was scared stiff of breaking them—and a good thing, too, for those teeth, together with the spiky hair, have become one of his most valuable assets as a showbiz star. "I was the only member of our family who could eat a tomato through a tennis racquet," is one his favourite stage quips.

■ But on a more serious note—and no-one can be MORE serious than Doddy when he is away from the atmosphere of the theatre—he really does get a tremendous kick from the atmosphere of football in general . . . and Anfield in particular.

☐ He's no stranger to the Liverpool club, on training days, and he knows the lads well. Two or three years ago, when he played the Christmas season at a Liverpool theatre, he bowed in on opening night with Billy Liddell, Ian St. John and Ron Yeats—as a four-piece beat group!

☐ The cheers and counter-cheers at this spectacle were reminiscent of any Liverpool-Everton game. And don't think that—when away from the Anfield fanatics—Doddy has no admiration for rivals Everton.

■ "They help to make Merseyside the most exciting of all Soccer centres—and I bow to no-one in making this assertion," he says.

☐ Doddy supports the game wherever he goes. He is a shareholder of Walsall F.C. "I opened their new Clubhouse a couple of years ago," he grins, "and the fee I asked for was one share in the club. I got it."

Other 'Football League Review' pages from 1968 included quotes from celebrity fan Ken Dodd – and a focus on Bill Shankly's fascination with politics, which he described as "the stuff of life"

Anfield Review 3

*Introducing*

# YOUR NEW REVIEW . . .

A PROGRAMME that is bright, colourful, informative and interesting not only on club matters, but on the national scene as well. That is what the modern soccer supporter wants and the Liverpool fan in particular deserves. We believe the new-style **Anfield Review** more than answers the challenge.

It has been designed to keep you in the picture with what goes on at Anfield, in all levels, and incorporates the **Football League Review** with its wide coverage, in words and pictures, of what goes on at other clubs.

**From us to you** . . . is the official editorial of the club with news and views on current topics. Your information about the visitors is in a new-style "red carpet welcome" feature.

The **ABC of Anfield** will introduce the stars of our A, B and Central League teams and keep you informed on their progress and results so that when they make the first team they won't arrive as 'unknowns' to our fans.

For the benefit of our supporters who travel away there is a page on "**how to get there**" with a map, route and railway guide.

**Memory Corner** will recall great games, players, occasions and goals involving Liverpool and the visiting team while **The Captain's Table** is laid out for the youngsters. It will feature an article, with autographed action picture, of the visiting skipper. Paste it in your scrapbook and at the end of the season you will have a complete dossier on every First Division captain.

### Two programmes for the price of one

**Records Review** will solve your arguments —and probably start some.

In addition to these regular features there will be pictures and topical articles, all adding up to what we feel is the type of programme you want.

Pride of place in the *Review* must be the front cover and we have devoted it to the people who have played a full part in achieving the fame and success recently enjoyed by the club—the supporters.

We are grateful to Syndication International (*Daily Mirror*) for use of a picture which captures perfectly the mood of our fans, our ground, our club and the Anfield Review. We hope you enjoy it.

### In your next 'Review'. . .

BILL SHANKLY talks about his hopes and plans for the new season; your ticket arrangements for the European Fairs Cup-tie with Dundalk, and an advance booking chart for all First Division clubs. PLUS the regular features.

### RECORDS REVIEW

Liverpool's 10-1 victory over Rotherham Town in 1896 was their best-ever—and still is. Their biggest defeat was 9-1 at Birmingham City on December 11, 1954.

*Leads with television rental*

**Telephcne: ROYal 9105**

---

Anfield Review 3

# Your view of the Anfield Review . . .

A FTER only two issues the Anfield Review seems to have been accepted as part of the Liverpool club scene.

Congratulations have poured into the club offices by letter, phone call and word of mouth. Inevitably, different features appeal to different people, but the important thing is that most fans seem to have found something they like.

Here is a selection of views of what YOU think about YOUR REVIEW.

**BRAINWAVE**
"Everyone is talking about the new-style programme and all declare it first class. I consider it a brainwave to have the team sheet and half-time scoreboard together on the back page, a convenient spot. We will now be able to get the information we want without a search." A. E. Jones, 38 Snaefell Avenue.

**A CRITICISM**
"I like the new-style programme. Only criticism is that the colour is not full-blooded Anfield red." Stan Kelly, Priory House, Alcester, Warwickshire.

Don't worry, we hope to get the red you want soon.

**ABC IS OK**
"The A B C pages will prove very welcome. I'm

sure many supporters will be only too pleased to follow the fortunes of Liverpool's other teams." J. Williams, Queens Drive, Liverpool.

**THE BEST**
"I would like to say that, as a Liverpool supporter for the past 30 years, the new programme is the best I have seen." T. M. Murray, 119 Radway Road, Huyton.

**ENJOYABLE**
"I was delighted to see an article by Bill Shankly in the Anfield Review. I am sure I am speaking for all my mates on the Kop when I say I found the article most enjoyable and look forward to some more." One of the Kopites.

**THAT TABLE**
"I'm looking forward to having a full album of the First Division captains, and a lot of my

pals are starting to collect them too." Master Brian Henderson, Widnes.

**MEMORABLE**
"I'm sure Memory Corner will bring back many happy memories to all supporters, and it will be interesting to read the players' views on some of the great matches we have seen at Anfield." Fred Corcoran, New Chester Road, Cheshire.

**IN YOUR NEXT REVIEW . . .**
Are you compiling a Captains' Table . . . following Records Review . . . collecting the club crests . . . keeping the autographs . . . reading Memory Corner? If you're only doing one of these things you won't want to miss the next Anfield Review. There is something in it for you.

*Leads with television rental*

**Telephcne: ROYal 9105**

The club were keen to promote the new-look programme in 1969 – and revealed fan reaction

---

## EUROPEAN CUP COMPETITION

# LIVERPOOL v. REYKJAVIK

### AT ANFIELD, MONDAY, 14th SEPTEMBER, 1964

#### Kick-off 7.30 p.m.

For the above match, STANDS ONLY will be ticketed at the following charges:

| | |
|---|---|
| Kemlyn Road Stand and Main Stand Block "C" | 10/- |
| Main Stand Blocks "B" and "D" | 9/- |
| Main Stand Blocks "A" and "E" | 8/- |

POSTAL APPLICATIONS for Stand Tickets will be accepted from Shareholders and Season Ticket Holders only, who must apply **not later than Friday, 4th September 1964**, allocation as per previous Home Cup-ties.

Shareholders on Holding, may apply for 8/- Stand Tickets only, and should quote number of shares held. Season Ticket Holders must enclose **No. 1 Voucher duly completed**. Where possible Ticket Holders will be allocated Seat in Stand for which their Season Ticket is valid, but this cannot be guaranteed.

ALL ENVELOPES should be marked "EUROPEAN CUP" in top left corner and must be accompanied by **Stamped Addressed Envelope and Correct Remittance**.

NO POSTAL APPLICATIONS WILL BE ACCEPTED FROM THE GENERAL PUBLIC. The balance of Stand Tickets, if any, will be sold to personal applicants only at a time and date to be announced later.

ADMISSION TO THE PADDOCK AND GROUND will be by payment at the Turnstiles on the day of the Match, charges as follows:

| | |
|---|---|
| Paddock 5/- | Ground 3/6 (Minimum allowed by E.U.F.A.) |
| | Boys' Pen 2/- |

The ticket details for the club's first home European match in September 1964 were printed in the Leeds programme 12 days earlier

Anfield has changed gradually over the decades, with each side of the stadium undergoing redevelopment up to the present day. In 1963 it was the turn of Kemlyn Road to acquire a new cantilevered stand – as reported in the programme (right), while in 1965 the Anfield Road stand was rebuilt and given a roof, and in 1971 the Main Stand underwent extensive redesign.

When the Main Stand was spectacularly expanded in 2016 the club stressed how important it has always been to "retain the heart and spirit of Anfield and the city of Liverpool itself...

"We've learned that it's possible to take a hallowed sporting ground, upgrade it and end up with the best of all worlds; a stadium that retains the essence of what made it special while providing an improved experience for everyone."

The Anfield Road is the latest side of the ground to undergo a major upgrade ready for the 2023-24 season.

# KEMLYN ROAD STAND

In order that our New Stand at Kemlyn Road will be ready for the commencement of Season 1963/64, work has to be commenced on Sunday, 28th April, and in consequence, the Kemlyn Road Stand and the Terracing in front of same will not be in use for our Football League matches against Sheffield Wednesday on Monday, 29th April, and Birmingham City on Wednesday, 8th May.

For these matches, Season Ticket Holders and those who have purchased tickets for the Kemlyn Road Stand, will be accommodated in "A" Stand. We regret this inconvenience to Ticket Holders, but feel all will appreciate the circumstances, and crave your indulgence in this matter.

Tickets for "A" Stand will be forwarded by post to Holders of Season and Match Tickets, and in this connection, any change of address should be notified to this Office immediately.

We apologise to the regular patrons of "A" Stand for thus depriving them of their customary viewpoint, but feel sure that all will understand the position.

———————

We would also announce that for the Sheffield Wednesday game on 29th April, Turnstiles at the Kemlyn Road/Anfield Road corner will not be in operation and admittance to Anfield Road End will be obtained via Turnstiles at Garage Corner and Middle of Anfield Road End. An announcement regarding Turnstiles for the Birmingham City match will be made later.

A notice for fans in April 1963

The bootroom boys promoted the club's own rock, which was on sale at Anfield in 1969

*It's Liverpool through and through!*

British Rail

SATURDAY, 22 NOVEMBER
LEEDS UNITED v. LIVERPOOL
FOOTBALL LEAGUE—DIVISION 1
Lime Street depart 11.30, Leeds City arrive 13.30, return from Leeds at 17.38
LEEDS 23/- (No half fares)
Seats limited, book in advance. Tickets obtainable only at Lime Street Booking Office.

*Photograph by Courtesy of Mercury Press Agency Ltd.*

That's Bob Paisley, Reuben Bennett, Bill Shankly, Joe Fagan — and famous Anfield personalities have first bite at a new red and white striped rock with Liverpool F.C. running right through the middle. It's on sale from Barker and Dobson sellers around the ground and at the Daily Draw office, today and every match day.

*Anfield Review 11*

★ ANFIELD'S TV SPECTACULAR ★

Anfield Review 11

A picture taken from just behind the TV camera—that's it on the left—as David Coleman interviews Bill Shankly and Ronnie Yeats after the first Match of the Day in colour between Liverpool and West Ham. The television lights can be seen hanging from the boardroom ceiling and shining on the trophies in the background. See From us . . . to you (page 9).

Filming after the first Match of the Day in colour, at Anfield in 1969

CHRISTMAS SHOPPING—ANFIELD STYLE !

Anfield Review 11

If you are short on ideas for presents for Christmas, call into the Daily Draw office in the car park as Roger, Ian and Gerry did this week. They were impressed with the slippers made in football boot style in club colours, also diaries, ties, pens and other club souvenirs.

**British Rail**

Take a "Winterbreak"
**WEEK-END IN LONDON**
Two nights in a British Transport Hotel and return rail fare
from LIVERPOOL £9.12.6
Ask at your local station or travel agency.

**Snacks & Beverages** may be obtained at moderate prices from the quick service refreshment bars around the ground.

Players helped promote Christmas gifts on sale at Anfield in 1969

---

4   Anfield Review

# From us . . .

PRESIDENT: T. V. Williams
CHAIRMAN: H. E. Roberts   VICE-CHAIRMAN: Ald. A. B. Collins, M.B.E., J.P.
DIRECTORS: H. Cartwright      S. C. Reakes, J.P.      C. J. Hill
E. A. F. Sawyer      J. H. Smith, F.C.A.
MANAGER: Bill Shankly              SECRETARY: Peter Robinson

## . . . to you
# Farewell-and thanks Roger

ROGER HUNT, scorer of 245 League goals in over 400 games, has left Anfield after ten glorious years, with achievements and memories that give him a unique place in Liverpool history.

From his first game against Scunthorpe at Anfield on September 17, 1960, he was a model player. In a career spread over ten years he was booked only twice, for trivial matters, and that for a player in the thick of football's most hectic skirmishes in front of goal is a distinction few can claim.

All our scoring records are his—41 goals in 1961–62, club top scorer for eight successive seasons, and no Liverpool player can rival his 34 appearances for England.

Hunt was not only a great marksman; he was a great player too.

Modesty was one of his greatest qualities. Ask the youngsters. If Roger's name is not in every Liverpool fan's autograph book it can only be because the owner never asked for it. He never turned anybody away.

Compliment him on a wonderful career and his typical reaction is, "With such a wonderful bunch of colleagues my job was

Roger Hunt

made easy." Is it any wonder Hunt was such a favourite with everybody?

Good luck at Bolton, Roger, and thanks for being a member of our family for so long and so successfully.

🙵 The President, Chairman, Directors, Players and Staff wish all Supporters a very happy and prosperous New Year.

When Roger Hunt moved on in December 1969, tribute was paid in the Sheffield Wednesday programme

---

## Who goes into the next round ?

Considerable doubts have arisen over the experimental rule that in the case of a draw on aggregate for the two legs of the tie any away goals scored will count twice. So let us try to get it straight!

So far as tonight's game is concerned the effect of this rule is as follows:—

If at the end of 90 minutes play Liverpool are leading by a score of exactly 1-0, extra time will be played (30 minutes). If the score is then still exactly 1-0 the teams will toss for the right to into the next round of the competition.

If the score after 90 minutes (or 120 minutes) play is anything other than 1-0 for Liverpool the overall winner is decided. Quite simply Liverpool must then win tonight's game by at least two clear goals (2-0, 3-1, 4-2, 5-3 etc.) to go into the hat next time.

Snacks and Beverages may be obtained at moderate prices from the quick service refreshment bars around the ground.

The 'away-goals count double' rule was explained in the Juventus programme in October 1965

## Pen Pictures of the Visiting Stars

**BERT TRAUTMANN (Goalkeeper)**

It was in October, 1949, that Manchester City signed Bert Trautmann from St. Helens Town, and what a great capture the former ex-German prisoner-of-war has since proved to be! There is no more popular player in the Manchester City team, and for that matter few more popular throughout the country. Bert had the honour of being chosen as Footballer of the Year in 1956, and 24 hours after receiving his award showed amazing courage when continuing in the City goal for the last fifteen minutes of the Cup Final with a fractured bone in the neck. Bert's brilliant goalkeeping in the Eddie Spicer benefit match here is still remembered by all who saw it. He has played over 400 first-team matches for the Mancunians.

**JIMMY ARMFIELD (Right-back)**

This splendid full-back, who first began his career as an outside-right—after playing Rugby while at school—has risen to England International standard, first as an Under-23 player, then as a full-fledged senior internationalist. He played nine times for the Under-23 eleven, and has now figured in eight full internationals—with the likelihood of many more to come. Jimmy made his Football League debut in 1954-55 season, and eighteen months ago was voted the Young Footballer of the Year. At one time it was reported that he was considering going out of football and concentrating on another career. Fortunately for Blackpool he has taken a part-time job only, so that he can continue to delight football followers with his stylish play.

**JOE WALTON (Left-back)**

Like Billy Liddell, Joe Walton has been a regular in post-war football, and has run up a big total of appearances for Preston North End since he joined them from Manchester United, at a fee of around £10,000, in March, 1948. Prior to that Joe had had seven years on the staff of the Manchester club. He has played in over 450 League and Cup games for Preston, and still ranks among one of the finest backs in the country, bringing his years of experience to bear in the task of circumventing opposing wingers. A native of Manchester, Walton can play equally well in either full-back position, but despite his consistency an England cap has eluded him, though in his earlier years he throughly deserved one.

**MAURICE SETTERS (Right-half)**

Like Jimmy Armfield, Maurice Setters has been almost automatic choice for England's Under-23 side for some seasons. He played his first Under-23 game three years ago this week, and was chosen on sixteen consecutive occasions, being captain for the last seven matches. Tenacious and hard-working, Maurice is a native of Honiton (Devonshire), and played for Exeter City before West Bromwich Albion signed him in 1955. He was transferred to Manchester United in January last, at a fee reported to be around £30,000. He has played for England as a schoolboy and a Youth international as well as in Under-23 games, and looks a certainty for full international honours in the near future.

**JIMMY DUGDALE (Centre-half)**

A native of Liverpool, Jimmy Dugdale began his career with Harrowby, in the West Cheshire League, before he was spotted by West Bromwich Albion, for whom he first signed professional forms in May, 1952. He got a Cup winners' medal with the Throstles in 1954, playing for England's "B" team on three occasions the same season, as well as for the Football League. He was signed by Aston Villa in February, 1956, and has been one of the stalwarts of their defence ever since.

**DON REVIE (Left-half)**

A native of Middlesbrough, Don Revie first began to attract the attention of League club scouts when playing for Middlesbrough Swifts, but as so often happens, it was a club from a considerable distance away which gave him his first big chance. That was Leicester City, for whom he signed towards the end of the war. In November, 1949, Hull City paid £20,000 for his services, and two years later Manchester City signed him at an even greater figure. The "Revie plan" of a deep-lying centre-forward provided Manchester City with some spectacular victories, but after five seasons at Maine Road, Don moved on to Sunderland, again at a substantial fee. That was in November, 1956, and two years later he joined his present club, Leeds United. He has been Footballer of the Year (in 1955), has played for England "B" and the Football League, and also in six full internationals.

**STANLEY MATTHEWS (Outside-right)**

So much has been written of the magic of Stanley Matthews that there is nothing now to say that hasn't been said scores of times already. For years the football critics have been prophesying that this, that, or the other season would surely be Stanley's last, yet he has gone on delighting the public with his inimitable performances. Even nowadays, though naturally unable to sustain his endeavours to the same pitch as he did ten years ago, there are flashes of the old Matthews' brilliance to light up the game. We hope that will be the case again tonight. Next February Stanley will be 46 years of age. He has played in over 600 peace-time Football League games for Stoke City and Blackpool, to say nothing of his countless caps for England and scores of Cup and friendly matches. His League debut was as long ago as 1931-32 season!

**JIMMY McILROY (Inside-left)**

One of the very few signings Burnley have made from other professional clubs since the war, Jimmy McIlroy cost them around £9,000 when they secured his services from Glentoran in March, 1950. Not many clubs have the good fortune to get a player of McIlroy's calibre at such a bargain figure, for in the opinion of many good judges Jimmy is one of the three best inside-forwards in Great Britain today. He made his League debut on October 21, 1950, at the age of 19, and up to the end of last season had played in 345 League games for the Turf Moor club, scoring 85 goals. Since playing his first game for Ireland in October 1951, Jimmy has been automatic choice ever since, and has now played in no fewer than 38 consecutive international matches, a wonderful tribute to his consistency.

**NAT LOFTHOUSE (Centre-forward)**

Nat is the first of two players figuring in tonight's game whom most folks had not expected to see in action again. Last year the "Lion of Vienna", as Lofthouse will always be remembered, announced his retirement, following an ankle injury which refused to yield to treatment. But the long rest from Soccer had such beneficial effect that just before this season began Nat decided to try his luck again. So far he has been playing in Bolton's Central League side, but is hopeful eventually of getting back to complete fitness and having another crack in the First Division. We hope he makes it. Nat began his career with Bolton during the war, and scored 252 League goals for the Wanderers in post-war...

---

**THE OPPOSITION**

Pages dedicated to opponents tended to include written profiles like the ones (above) from Billy Liddell's testimonial and the Reykjavik game in 1964 (right)

## KNATTSPYRNUFELAG REYKJAVIKUR

**(REYKJAVIK FOOTBALL CLUB)**

A few years before the turn of the century, a Scottish printer was hired by the biggest printing shop in Reykjavik. His name was James B. Ferguson and he was from Glasgow. Soon after his arrival he started teaching youngsters the rudiments of football and athletics. Out of these training sessions in bare gravel fields in the western half of the then hamlet of 3,000 inhabitants originated the first football club of Iceland, Reykjavik F.C. The founders were youngsters from the "West Town, and the club has ever since drawn most of its support and members from that part of the town, a residential area today of about 30,000 inhabitants. All but one of the present team are born and brought up in this district.

After more clubs had been founded, regular competitions were started, and around 1910 a member of the club ordered from a friend in England the most popular jerseys of the time, and he got the Newcastle United colours, to which the club has adhered ever since.

After the First war the club took up more sports, swimming, athletics, tennis, skiing, gymnastics, boxing, handball, badminton and basketball. During the last 35 years the club has been the most prominent and stabilised sports club in Iceland, has supplied numerous participants in international events in various sports, chief among whom are European Champions in shotputting in 1946 and 1950, and in long jump in 1950. The club has also supplied a high proportion of the leading personalities in Reykjavik and Iceland sports associations, and has thus also in the administrative sphere done its best to further Icelandic sport.

After almost a complete change of its first team players 1957-1958 the club has been the leading club in Iceland, champions in 1959, 1961 and 1963, and cup-holders since 1960, when that competition was started. During that period the club has played vs. Bury (won 1-0), St. Mirren (0-0), Dundee (lost 1-3), and Middlesex Wanderers (3-3). When St. Mirren signed up the most promising and strongest forward of the club in 1961, Thorolf Beck, the side lost much of its bite.

Since 1912 the club has gained the championship title 18 times. The club runs annually 3 boys teams, 3 junior teams, 2 senior teams, and all the present players have been brought up through these ranks, not one is acquired from other clubs.

**HEIMIR GUDDJONSSON (Goal-keeper)**, 27 years old. Became a first team regular in 1957. Has been capped 5 times. An engineer by profession.

**GISLI THORKELSSON (Goal-keeper)**, 22 years old. Has been a solid and dependable reserve since 1959. Was chosen for the international vs. Finland in August this year. A chauffeur at the B.P. company.

**HREIDAR ARSÆLSSON (Right full-back)**, 34 years old. First team regular since 1952, has played 205 games for the club, and been capped 8 times. Printer.

**BJARNI FELIXSON (Left full-back)**, 27 years old. A regular since 1958. Capped 5 times. An accountant by profession.

**THORDUR JONSSON (Right half-back)**, 19 years old. Came into the first team last year, and was chosen this year for the 'B' international team. A grammar school student.

**HÖRDUR FELIXSON (Centre half-back)**, 32 years old. A first team player since 1949 and has played 240 games for the club. Has played 11 times for Iceland. In private life bureau chief.

**THORGEIR GUDMUNDSSON (Left half-back)**, 20 years old. Debuted this year as a centre half-back. Is an apprentice electrician.

**GUNNAR GUDMANNSSON (Outside-right)**, 34 years old, a regular since 1947 in the first team, and has played 282 matches, which is a club record Has been capped 9 times. A sports hall manager for the municipality.

**SVEINN JONSSON (Inside-right)**, 26 years old. A first team player since 1956, has gained 12 caps. A chartered accountant.

**GUNNAR FELIXSON (Centre-forward)**, one of three brothers in the team. He is 24 years old, a regular since 1960, 4 times capped. An insurance company representative.

**ELLERT SCHRAM (Inside-left)**, 24 years old, captain of the team. Debuted in 1957, has been capped 10 times. He is studying law at the University of Iceland.

**SIGURTHOR JAKOBSSON (Outside-left)**, 23 years old. Came into the team in 1962, has 4 caps and is a printer by profession.

**ARSÆLL KJARTANSSON (Full-back)**, 19 years old. Has been a reserve the last 2 years. A chauffeur and an apprentice air-pilot.

**JON SIGURDSSON (Inside-forward)**, 23 years old. A reserve since 1959 with 50 games to his credit. A carpenter.

# Liverpool FC 1964/65

## Welcome
### R.S.C. Anderlechtois

We extend a warm and sincere welcome to the Directors, Officials, Players and Supporters of the Anderlecht Club, on this, the first leg of the Eighth-Finals of the European Champion Clubs' Cup Competition.

The Royal Sporting Club of Anderlecht, formed in 1905, have been, in post war years, the outstanding Club in Belgium, and by virtue of their Championship successes, are experienced campaigners in Europe's premier competition.

In a recent visit to Belgium to watch our visitors of this evening play a home League match, our Manager, Mr. Shankly, was most impressed with their play, which confirmed the impression gained from the International Match, England v. Belgium, played at Wembley, last month, in which seven of the Anderlecht players participated. Mr. Shankly was also most appreciative of the hospitality and friendliness afforded him during his visit.

We have many happy memories of our game with Anderlecht in Belgium in 1950, and we trust that they will take back with them pleasant recollections of their visit to the City of Liverpool.

## Bienvenue
### R.S.C. Anderlechtois

Aux Directeurs, Officiers, Equipiers et Adhérents du Club Anderlecht, à l'occasion de cette première étape de ces Huitièmes Finales de Concours de Coupe des Clubs Champions d'Europe, nous faisons un accueil sincère et enthousiaste.

Le Club Sportif Royal d'Anderlecht, formé en 1905, s'est montré, au cours des années depuis la guerre, d'être le Club belge le plus éminent et, en vertu de ses réussites dans le Championnat, de vieux routiers du métier dans le premier concours d'Europe.

Au cours d'une visite récente en Belgique pour observer nos visiteurs de ce soir dans un match de championnat national, notre Directeur, M. Shankly, a trouvé leur jeu très impressionnant, ce qui a raffiné l'opinion déjà établie par leur match international, Angleterre c. Belgique, à Wembley au cours du mois dernier, où sept équipiers d'Anderlecht ont pris part. M. Shankly a aussi fait grand cas du bon accueil et de l'amitié manifestes envers lui au cours de cette visite.

Nous gardons beaucoup de très bons souvenirs de notre match contre Anderlecht en 1950, et nous osons espérer qu'ils rentreront chez eux avec des souvenirs aussi agréables de leur visite à la Ville de Liverpool.

# HELP TO SOLVE THE PARKING PROBLEM AT ANFIELD

## ... by following these useful tips

**THE SIZE OF THE PROBLEM**

For you, it's only as big as your car. But almost 10,000 other motorists would also like to find match-day parking near the ground.

TIP Don't insist on trying to park close to the ground. There just isn't room for everyone. By parking your car further from the ground, you'll have a much easier time, and get away quicker after the match.

**IF YOU ARRIVE EARLY AND DO PARK NEAR THE GROUND**

Remember that parking is authorised on one side only of certain streets.

TIP Comply with NO PARKING SIGNS and you won't be caught "off-side". And follow police directions: constables on duty know where space is available and direct traffic accordingly.

**PAUSE FOR BREATH**

Police regulations require vehicles parked in authorised streets to stay put for fifteen minutes—five minutes before and ten minutes after the end of a match. This is for your safety and the safety of pedestrians.

TIP Don't be impatient to get away. More haste—less speed! When it's your turn to get into gear you'll move much more smoothly—avoiding bumps and jams, and saving petrol!

**PENALTY SPOT**

Obstruction must be avoided so that other traffic—especially ambulances, fire engines and police vehicles can move freely. So, you can't expect the police to take a lenient view of traffic offences.

TIP Don't let the score go against you. Co-operate with the police and don't box other motorists in. And, if Anfield is your home ground, don't be hesitant about telling visiting motorists to park sensibly.

### GET THIS OFFICIAL LEAFLET

It contains a clear, keyed map of the area surrounding the ground. Also, full details of streets in which parking is authorised, and the main requirements of the Regulations for direction and control of match-day traffic.

Get your copy from: The Secretary, Liverpool F.C. Supporters Club, 212 Lower Breck Road, Liverpool 6.

There was a dual-language welcome for Anderlecht fans and officials in November 1964

## TEAMS

| LIVERPOOL (Canary-Yellow Jerseys) | | A.F.C. AJAX (Red & White Jerseys) |
|---|---|---|
| (1) LAWRENCE | Referee: Mr. Krnavek (Poland) | (1) BALS |
| (2) LAWLER | | (2) SUURBIER |
| (3) MILNE | | (3) PRONK |
| (4) SMITH | | (4) SURENDONK |
| (5) YEATS | | (5) VAN DUIVENBODE |
| (6) STEVENSON | | (6) MULLER |
| (7) CALLAGHAN | | (7) GROOT |
| (8) HUNT | Linesmen: | (8) SWART |
| (9) ST. JOHN | Mr. Hartmann (Poland) (Red Flag) | (9) CRUYFF |
| (10) STRONG | | (10) NUNINGA |
| (11) THOMPSON | Mr. Spotak (Poland) (Yellow Flag) | (11) KEIZER |

JACK SHARP SPORTS LIVERPOOL

Substitute:
**OGSTON**

Substitute:

Parking was such an issue in 1965 that the club issued advice to fans

Reds fans were used to the big names in their own squad in December 1966 but this Ajax line-up for the European Cup tie that season included a 19-year-old Dutchman called Johan Cruyff

## GUEST SPOT 'The Anfield Hoodoo'
### by Reg Drury News of the World

Maybe it's because I'm a Londoner ... that I fear Chelsea will return empty-handed from this afternoon's match and that the Kop chorus will be letting rip with their victory hymns by 4.40. All the vital statistics are loaded against Tommy Docherty's boys in blue.

I should really say the Shankly statistics, for it is a fantastic fact that since Bill left Huddersfield to become Liverpool's manager on December 1st, 1959, only a single League victory has been recorded by a London club at Anfield.

It is a remarkable record stretching over nearly eight years and a total of thirty-one League matches in the top two divisions. The Liverpool figures in full show twenty-three wins, seven draws, one defeat and a goal-average of 72-28.

West Ham were the notable exceptions with a 2-1 success at Anfield in 1963-64. Indeed, the "Hammers" can really hold their heads up high—as the only London lot to almost break even at Anfield since the "Greatest" came under the Shankly spell.

They have also managed a couple of draws (2-2 in 1964-65 and 1-1 in 1965-66) in their five trips, losing only twice.

On the other hand, of course, Liverpool have hit the high-spots at Upton Park on more than one occasion. Few of us present will forget their devastating display, to win 5-1, in a mid-week encounter a couple of seasons ago.

But let's return to the Anfield hoodoo which has demoralised all the capital clubs since December, 1959, and examine the team-by-team results.

Arsenal (five defeats, one draw, goal-average 5-16); Charlton (three defeats, goal-average 2-6); Chelsea (four defeats, goal-average 3-8); Fulham (four defeats, one draw, goal-average 5-11); Orient (two defeats, one draw, goal-average 3-13); Spurs (three defeats, two draws, goal-average 4-10); West Ham, bless their hearts (one win, two draws, two defeats, goal-average 6-8).

In the circumstances, it would hardly be surprising if every London team board a Liverpool-bound train suffering from the "Shankly shakes" ... though, in Spurs case, their lack of success at Anfield goes back to the days before Bill was born.

Believe it or not—and some Everton fans will find it hard after their two 1-0 wins at Goodison Park in the past six months—but Spurs haven't triumphed at Anfield for fifty-five years.

Liverpool, by contrast, have registered victories on all the First Division grounds in London in recent seasons. Though there have been occasional s[...]

### NEXT MATCHES AT ANFIELD
FOOTBALL LEAGUE C[...]
**LIVERPOOL v. BOLT[...]**
WEDNESDAY, 13th SEPTEMBER, 1967

CENTRAL L[...]
**LIVERPOOL v. HUDD[...]**
SATURDAY, 16th SEPTEMBER, 1967

13

## GUEST SPOT INTO EUROPE WITH LIVERPOOL
### by JAMES MOSSOP of the 'Sunday Express'

What would you give to be able to travel with your favourite team on one of their flights to a strange land to fight a European Cup battle?

To the fan who lives for every kick on a Saturday, gobbles up every word that is written in midweek and reckons to know his football inside-out, this would be a dream come true.

Let me give you a small insight on one of these trips—the recent 1,500 mile visit to Rumania for the second leg of the European Cup tie against Ploesti.

It is a long and arduous four day affair [...]

early for training at the stadium he played on twenty-eight years ago for Preston North End.

They take it quietly in the afternoon for the next day is match day and now all the training has been done. But for the officials and Pressmen the afternoon is the opportunity to inspect pitch and facilities at Ploesti—an oil town forty miles away.

Mr. Shankly likes the pitch. The sun is blazing badly into one goal. "Must remember that at the toss-up," he [...]

## GUEST SPOT

## "THE ANFIELD CLAN"
### by ERIC COOPER
of the 'Daily Express'

The Mersey Sound is international and the chants of the Spion Kop choir famous wherever they are copied. But if Scottish pipes were swirling out tribute to Bill Shankly and his merry warriors it wouldn't be entirely out of place.

Everybody knows, inside or outside of Merseyside, that Liverpool's football glory of the past five years has been spear-headed by a Scottish manager, a Scottish coach in Reuben Bennett, and four more Scots like big Ron Yeats, Ian St. John, Tommy Lawrence and Bill Stevenson.

There were eleven Scots in the party that went out to meet Petrolul Ploesti in the European Cup, eight of them players, and there must be a dozen or more Scots on the playing strength.

But this is nothing new. In fact, whackers, you might even say that the foundations of Liverpool's football progress were largely built with Scottish blood.

Perhaps ALL, because the very first Liverpool team, which owed its existence to a split with Everton as to the rental of the Anfield Road ground, was exclusively Scottish.

For that reason alone, it should not be surprising that Liverpool have always looked kindly on the kilted brigade and have produced probably as many Scottish as English internationals.

Often enough in those early days the Liverpool team played before empty benches, but it was not for lack of merit. They gained a Second Division place in the Football League in the second year of their existence and immediately con-founded the prophets by winning the championship with only one defeat in twenty-eight matches.

After a quick relegation and promo-tion again, they finished League runners-up to Aston Villa, who beat them in the last match of the season, and a couple of years later, in 1901, succeeded as League champions a Villa side that had won the title in four seasons out of five.

Fair-haired Alec Raisbeck is still remembered as one of these Liverpool stalwarts and one of the best half-backs of all time.

There were other stars, too, like Jimmy Hannah, the two McQueens, Jimmy Miller of Dumbarton, who also played for Sheffield Wednesday and Derby County. Wylie of Glasgow Rangers was another.

Later Kenny Campbell, Dunlop, McKinlay, McNab, Billy Liddell, Tommy Younger, and the tradition is carried on in the present team of Cup and championship winners.

Who knows but what we might soon be singing the praises of Bobby Graham, Ted McDougall and Ian Ross, among others.

Maybe, indeed, it is not merely a coincidence that the Scotland Road out of Liverpool city leads towards League Soccer.

Aye, eye, laddies ... Ron Yeats! ... St. John!

### ANFIELD GROUND FUND COMMITTEE
### EUROPEAN CUP IN AMSTERDAM
## A.F.C. AJAX (Amsterdam) v. LIVERPOOL F.C.

We will be having a Special Draw for this game. There will be four Prizes for two persons:

The Prizes will include:
**Travel · Hotel Accommodation · Match Tickets · Five Pounds Cash Prize**

The trip will take two days these being the 7th and 8th December. The Drawtickets will be 1/- each. Don't forget to get Yours, you could be a lucky winner of this exciting trip.

Tickets on sale after the match around the ground and also at the Daily Draw Office.

*'Guest Spot' was a chance for newspaper correspondents to provide an occasional column from their own press perspective. In November 1966 Eric Cooper of The Daily Express hailed LFC's Scottish roots: "Maybe, indeed, it is not merely a coincidence that the Scotland Road out of Liverpool city [centre] leads towards league soccer"*

## LIVERPOOL FOOTBALL CLUB
# SEASON TICKET RENEWALS
### SEASON 1962-63

I hereby make application to renew Season Ticket/s for All Football League and Central League matches to be played at Anfield during the 1962/63 Season, and enclose herewith remittance for £ : : , in payment thereof.

Name............................................................

Address.........................................................

.......................................................................

.......................................................................

(BLOCK LETTERS PLEASE)

#### Seats Occupied 1961/62

| Ticket No. | Stand | Row | Seat No. |
|---|---|---|---|
| | | | |
| | | | |
| | | | |
| | | | |
| | | | |

#### Charges — 1962/63

| | Reserved and Numbered Seat | Reserved but not Numbered Seat |
|---|---|---|
| | £ s. d. | £ s. d. |
| "D" Stand ... ... ... | 8 10 0 | 8 0 0 |
| "F" Stand ... ... ... | 7 10 0 | 7 0 0 |
| "C" Stand ... ... ... | 7 10 0 | 7 0 0 |
| "B" Stand ... ... ... | 7 0 0 | — |
| "K. Rd." Stand ... ... ... | 8 0 0 | 7 10 0 |

Reservation Fee — Shareholders' Privilege Tickets, £1.0.0

Application Forms duly completed together with appropriate remittance to be received at the Club Offices by **June 2nd, 1962.**

---

*Anfield Review* 9

## From us . . .

PRESIDENT: T. V. Williams
CHAIRMAN: H. E. Roberts   VICE-CHAIRMAN: Ald. A. B. Collins, M.B.E., J.P.
DIRECTORS: H. Cartwright   S. C. Reakes, J.P.   C. J. Hill
E. A. F. Sawyer   J. H. Smith, F.C.A.
MANAGER: Bill Shankly   SECRETARY: Peter Robinson

### . . . to you

We hand this page over to Horace Yates, Sports Editor of the Daily Post, to tell the story of Liverpool's part in the growth of televised football, culminating in the choice of Anfield for BBC TV's first colour Match of the Day.

## We complete a hat trick of TV firsts

NOT every club offered the same warm welcome and co-operative attitude to television as Liverpool.

From the outset they realised that TV had an important part to play in the game, and that so long as adequate safeguards were guaranteed, it could be a happy and profitable association.

So it has proved, and last Saturday Liverpool were proud to complete a hat-trick of television firsts.

The televising of the West Ham game was the first match to go out over the national network in colour.

Liverpool were also chosen to start the "Match of the Day" programme in 1964.

In 1950 Liverpool's F.A. Cup final with Arsenal marked the spread of TV coverage of the event beyond the London area.

Just how important a part television is now playing in our lives is shown by the fact that viewing audiences have increased from 1964's 20,000 for the B.B.C. 2 programme to 10,000,000 last Saturday.

I don't think it was mere sentiment that caused the BBC to come back to Anfield for their historic evening in soccer colour. It was that Anfield was the natural setting, with its colourful background provided by the Kop and the thrilling entertainment on the field.

The programme's producer, Alex Weeks, said, "We wanted a colourful place and Anfield seemed the obvious choice".

That the Liverpool-West Ham match should be chosen on a day that the Manchester "derby" was pulling in the biggest attendance of the afternoon was noteworthy.

Of course, Liverpool manager Bill Shankly has established himself as a popular favourite on the TV screens, because of his spontaneous humour and straight-from-the-shoulder talking. Not everybody is at home in front of the cameras, but they hardly seem to worry Bill.

British Rail   **26 and 29 NOVEMBER 1969**

Take a "Winter break"
## WEEK-END IN LONDON

Two nights in a British Transport Hotel and return rail fare from LIVERPOOL **£9.12.6**
Ask at your local station or travel agency.

---

Far left: a season ticket renewal page from April 1962.

Left: in 1969 we were told how the televising of a match in colour completed a 'hat-trick' of TV firsts

---

IN TRIBUTE

TO THE MEMORY OF

THE RIGHT HONOURABLE

SIR WINSTON CHURCHILL
K.G., O.M., C.H.

ONE MINUTE'S SILENCE

WILL BE OBSERVED

BEFORE THE KICK-OFF

---

Right: a notice in the Stockport programme of 1965 following the death of Winston Churchill

Far right: FA Cup final ticket details later that year

---

# F.A. CUP FINAL
### 1st May 1965
### TICKET ALLOCATION

**SHAREHOLDERS:**

| Holding | | |
|---|---|---|
| 1— 9 Shares | 1 Ticket at 7/6 | |
| 10—39 Shares | 1 Ticket at 25/- | |
| 40—59 Shares | 2 Tickets at 45/- | |
| 60—79 Shares | 2 Tickets at 63/- + 1 Ticket at 17/6 | |
| 80—99 Shares | 2 Tickets at 63/- + 2 Tickets at 17/6 | |
| 100 Shares and Over | 4 Tickets at 63/- + 2 Tickets at 17/6 | |

**SEASON TICKET HOLDERS:**

As the Total Number of Tickets received is only 15,000, all sections must share in a reduced allotment. The allotment possible to Season Ticket Holders, is equal only, in number, to half of the Season Tickets issued for the current Season.

It has been decided that only those Season Ticket Holders, whose Season Ticket Numbers (Not Seat Numbers) end in 1, 3, 5, 7 or 9, may apply for tickets as under:

| | |
|---|---|
| Kemlyn Road Stand, Blocks "G", "K" and "L" and Main Stand, Block "C" | Ticket at 45/- |
| Kemlyn Road Stand, Blocks "H" and "J" and Main Stand, Block "B" | Ticket at 25/- |
| Main Stand, Blocks "D" and "E" | Ticket at 17/6 |

**BALLOT TICKETS:**

With regard to the numbered tickets issued at the match v. Stoke City, at Anfield, on Saturday, 3rd April, 1965, to all paying spectators other than Season Ticket Holders, a Ballot has been made and the lucky numbers are as follows:

Tickets bearing only the numbers ... 5, 6, and 8

All Tickets with numbers ending ... 05, 06, 08, 18, 20, 32, 34, 36, 42, 43, 46, 53, 58, 69, 73, 89, 97 or 00.

**Holders of these Lucky Numbers may apply for Ticket at 7/6**

### THE ABOVE ALLOCATIONS WILL BE STRICTLY ENFORCED

---

#### METHOD OF APPLICATION

**Applications** from Shareholders, appropriate Season Ticket Holders, and Holders of Winning Ballot Tickets, must be made by POST ONLY (NO PERSONAL APPLICATIONS CAN BE ENTERTAINED) to reach the CLUB OFFICES, ANFIELD ROAD, LIVERPOOL, 4, not later than **Thursday, 22nd April, 1965**, and must be accompanied by Stamped Addressed Envelope and Correct Remittance.

Shareholders are required to quote number of Shares held.

Season Ticket Holders entitled to apply must enclose No. 11 Voucher duly completed.

Holders of Winning Ballot Tickets must enclose the Numbered Ticket with their name and address on the back thereof.

Envelopes addressed to the Club should be marked in top left corner—"Shareholder", "Season Ticket Holder" or "Ballot" according to category of applicant.

### ALL APPLICANTS ARE REQUESTED TO ENSURE THAT THEY COMPLY FULLY WITH THE INSTRUCTIONS GIVEN

**LIVERPOOL** (Red Jerseys)

Right             Left

LAWRENCE (1)

LAWLER (2)      BYRNE (3)

STRONG (4)    YEATS (5)    STEVENSON (6)

CALLAGHAN (7)   HUNT (8)   ST. JOHN (9)   SMITH (10)   THOMPSON (11)

Referee:
Mr. Karl Kainer (Austria)

Linesmen:
Mr. Benesch (Red Flag)
Mr. Zembsch (Yellow Flag)

CORSO (11)    SUAREZ (10)    PEIRO (9)    MAZZOLA (8)    JAIR (7)

PICCHI (6)      GUARNERI (5)      TAGNIN (4)

FACHETTI (3)        BURGNICH (2)

SARTI (1)

Left      **F.C. INTERNAZIONALE** (Blue & Black Striped Jerseys)      Right

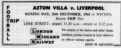

How team line-ups were displayed over two pages, including (top) the visit of European champions Internazionale in May 1965

---

European away-days were still quite a novelty in 1969 so the club described how they contact opponents and find the right team hotel

A BEA Comet, chartered by the club to take the players to Portugal for Wednesday's European Fairs Cup tie with Vitoria Setubal.

Anfield Review 3

## Europe again — and the work it involves

NEXT Tuesday our players set off to Portugal, one of the few countries we have not visited in European football.

The public is well aware of the planning that goes into the playing of these important games with clubs 'spying' and compiling dossiers on each other. What is less known is the arranging that goes on behind the scenes, starting as soon as the draw is made.

Contact has to be made between the clubs, and that's not always easy. One team we had to play did not write one letter to us, although they sent 24 telegrams. You either have to be very brief, or spend a lot of money, using that system to agree on dates, kick-off time and venue.

*Having thrashed that out we then have to decide on travel and accommodation. The decision whether to use service or charter planes hinges on many things.*

Is there a service route convenient for where you are going? Do the flight times coincide with the times you want to arrive and depart? Can you book seats for a party that may be 36 strong with directors, players, officials and Pressmen? What about the meals aboard the plane? Are they suitable for trained footballers travelling to play a big game?

Regarding hotels we have found from experience that those in the city are more suitable, even though they can be more noisy. The standard of service and food is invariably more reliable than at hotels well out of town.

But we also have to consider the distance from the hotel to the football ground and whether we can book for such a big party.

Trying to get a hotel that is satisfactory on all points is not always easy.

We have had that much trouble over training facilities that Mr. Shankly prefers the team to train at Melwood before flying out. Abroad it is not always possible to use the match ground and there are not always floodlights at the training pitch. If there are they have a habit of going out at the crucial moment!

One other point. If we are drawn against a team from a Communist country there is the problem of visas. We usually send a member of our office staff to the appropriate embassy in London to personally collect visas to avoid delay and risk of loss.

So you can see that European football involves more people than the players. It affects nearly everybody at the club.

# KICK OFF
## with
# BENT'S
# OLD TOM
## STRONG ALE
### THAT KEEPS OUT THE COLD!

---

## W. HUGHES (Garages) Ltd
### LORENZO DRIVE - LIVERPOOL 11

★

### Vauxhall and Bedford Agents
### Repair Specialists

★

### Telephones STAnley 1381/2

---

# PARK DRIVE

## for pleasure

**PLAIN 20 for 3/5**

**TIPPED 20 for 2/10**

GALLAHER'S
Park Drive
cigarettes

Manufactured by
GALLAHER LTD
VIRGINIA HOUSE
LONDON & BELFAST

## LEAGUE TABLES
*(Up to and including Tuesday, 24th April 1962)*

### LEAGUE—DIVISION I

| | P. | W. | D. | L. | F. | A. | Pts |
|---|---|---|---|---|---|---|---|
| Ipswich T. | 41 | 23 | 8 | 10 | 91 | 67 | 54 |
| Burnley | 40 | 21 | 10 | 9 | 100 | 62 | 52 |
| Tottenham | 40 | 19 | 10 | 11 | 82 | 65 | 48 |
| Everton | 40 | 19 | 10 | 11 | 82 | 65 | 48 |
| Sheffield U. | 40 | 18 | 11 | 11 | 77 | 49 | 47 |
| Aston Villa | 40 | 19 | 9 | 13 | 61 | 67 | 47 |
| West Ham | 40 | 18 | 7 | 15 | 63 | 52 | 43 |
| West Brom. | 40 | 16 | 10 | 14 | 72 | 79 | 42 |
| Blackpool | 41 | 15 | 11 | 15 | 69 | 68 | 41 |
| Arsenal | 41 | 15 | 11 | 15 | 69 | 68 | 41 |
| Sheffield W. | 39 | 17 | 6 | 16 | 63 | 56 | 40 |
| Bolton W. | 41 | 15 | 9 | 17 | 72 | 73 | 39 |
| Manchester U. | 41 | 15 | 10 | 16 | 61 | 66 | 40 |
| Blackburn | 40 | 14 | 11 | 15 | 49 | 53 | 39 |
| Manchester C. | 41 | 16 | 7 | 18 | 75 | 80 | 39 |
| Leicester | 40 | 16 | 6 | 18 | 68 | 67 | 38 |
| Birmingham | 41 | 14 | 10 | 17 | 63 | 78 | 38 |
| Wolves | 41 | 13 | 10 | 18 | 71 | 83 | 36 |
| Notts F. | 41 | 13 | 10 | 18 | 62 | 77 | 36 |
| Fulham | 40 | 12 | 7 | 21 | 62 | 70 | 31 |
| Cardiff | 40 | 9 | 13 | 18 | 45 | 71 | 31 |
| Chelsea | 41 | 9 | 9 | 23 | 62 | 93 | 27 |

### LEAGUE—DIVISION II

| | P. | W. | L. | D. | F. | A. | Pts |
|---|---|---|---|---|---|---|---|
| LIVERPOOL | 39 | 25 | 8 | 6 | 92 | 36 | 58 |
| Sunderland | 41 | 22 | 8 | 11 | 84 | 49 | 52 |
| Leyton O. | 41 | 21 | 10 | 10 | 67 | 40 | 52 |
| Scunthorpe | 41 | 21 | 7 | 13 | 85 | 67 | 49 |
| Plymouth A. | 41 | 19 | 8 | 14 | 73 | 72 | 46 |
| Huddersfield | 41 | 16 | 12 | 13 | 67 | 56 | 44 |
| Southampton | 41 | 17 | 9 | 15 | 72 | 61 | 43 |
| Stoke C. | 41 | 17 | 8 | 16 | 54 | 52 | 42 |
| Newcastle | 41 | 15 | 9 | 17 | 64 | 55 | 39 |
| Charlton A. | 40 | 15 | 9 | 16 | 68 | 71 | 39 |
| Rotherham | 41 | 15 | 9 | 17 | 67 | 76 | 39 |
| Norwich | 41 | 14 | 11 | 16 | 60 | 68 | 39 |
| Bury | 41 | 17 | 5 | 19 | 52 | 74 | 39 |
| Preston N.E. | 41 | 14 | 10 | 17 | 53 | 57 | 38 |
| Middlesbro' | 41 | 15 | 7 | 19 | 74 | 71 | 37 |
| Luton T. | 41 | 16 | 5 | 20 | 67 | 71 | 37 |
| Walsall | 41 | 13 | 11 | 17 | 66 | 74 | 37 |
| Derby C. | 41 | 13 | 11 | 17 | 66 | 74 | 37 |
| Leeds U. | 41 | 11 | 12 | 18 | 47 | 61 | 34 |
| Swansea | 40 | 11 | 11 | 18 | 56 | 60 | 33 |
| Bristol R. | 41 | 13 | 7 | 21 | 53 | 79 | 33 |
| Brighton | 41 | 10 | 11 | 20 | 42 | 84 | 31 |

*Anfield Review* **15**

---

LIVERPOOL F.C.
STANDO KOP for the CUP

*At a time like this... there's only one drink—*
*Mackeson!*

# TRUMANNS —
# D. T. BROWN
## FOR STEEL IN
# LIVERPOOL

**D. T. BROWN (STEEL) LTD.**
132 VAUXHALL ROAD,
LIVERPOOL 3

Phone 051-236 8384 (4 lines)

**TRUMANNS (STEEL)**
MOSS LANE, WALK[...]
MANCHESTER

Phone 061-790 4511 [...]

---

# ITS A WINNER!
## Liverpool F.C. Supporters Club holdalls

**EXCLUSIVE TO MILLETTS 28!**
## ONLY 22/6

Officially approved by the Supporters Club and only available at 25, Church Street! Get yours today! There's a great range of other gear available too—including supporters scarves and bob caps, a full range of football kit and the largest selection of warm and weather-proof clothing! Call in and see for yourself the finest value in the country.

LIVERPOOL FOOTBALL CLUB

**Milletts 28**
THE NAME TO VALUE

25, Church Street, Liverpool.

---

# Lesley (DECORATORS) LTD.
"SPECIALISTS TO THE TRADE"

## 60a ALLERTON ROAD,
## WOOLTON,
## LIVERPOOL 25

051-428 4096

Painting Contractors to:—
Liverpool F.C., Ltd.
Ministry of Works
North Western Gas Board
Hospital Management Board
Etc.

12

---

## 1960s ADVERTS
Products and services advertised included cigarettes, holdalls, steel, several varieties of beer, a car garage and a decorator

# CHAPTER 4

# 1970s

From Shankly to Paisley, Keegan to Dalglish...
The matchday programme was there to
chronicle this decade of personnel change but
prevailing dominance for the Reds

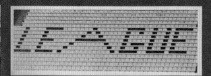

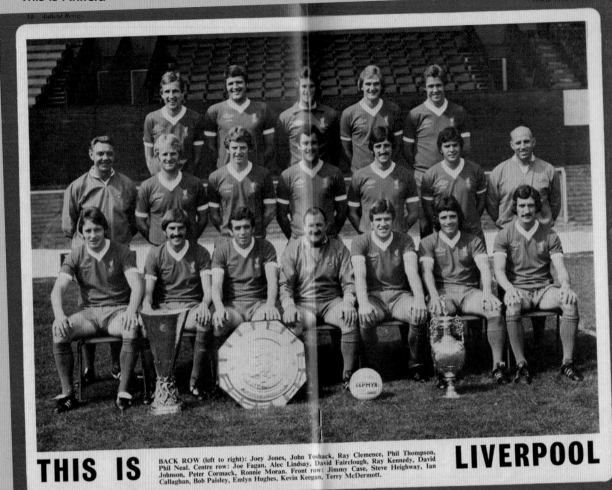

**THIS IS**

BACK ROW (left to right): Joey Jones, John Toshack, Ray Clemence, Phil Thompson, Phil Neal. Centre row: Joe Fagan, Alec Lindsay, David Fairclough, Ray Kennedy, David Johnson, Peter Cormack, Ronnie Moran. Front row: Jimmy Case, Steve Heighway, Ian Callaghan, Bob Paisley, Emlyn Hughes, Kevin Keegan, Terry McDermott.

**LIVERPOOL**

O n football's global stage the Seventies were kick-started by Brazil's brilliant World Cup win in Mexico, while at home Liverpool continued to compete for domestic honours first with Bill Shankly's second great side then with Bob Paisley's all-conquering team.

The matchday programme evolved too, with players featuring more regularly alongside messages from the manager and the established tranche of opposition profiles, fixtures and results, and games and goals.

In 1970-71 the Reds finished fifth in the League and reached the last four of the European Fairs Cup (the precursor to the UEFA Cup and Europa League), but there was FA Cup final heartache as they lost to Arsenal in extra-time. Having beaten Everton 2-1 in the Maine Road semi-final, Liverpool went down by the same score at Wembley. At the next day's homecoming Shankly proclaimed: "Yesterday at Wembley we lost, but you the people have won everything."

The following season started with a bang – new signing Kevin Keegan scoring on his Anfield debut versus Nottingham Forest – but it ended with last-gasp title disappointment as Brian Clough's Derby County were crowned champions.

Liverpool made amends by clinching an eighth title following a goalless draw at home to Leicester City on 28 April 1973. Three weeks later there was a first European trophy with Borussia Moenchengladbach beaten 3-2 on aggregate in the two-legged UEFA Cup final. Shankly told the *Liverpool Echo*: "The people on the Continent are beginning to get frightened of Liverpool – [Borussia striker] Günter Netzer told me so tonight."

Season 1973-74's trophy was the FA Cup, claimed with a one-sided 3-0 victory over Newcastle United in the final. In the League the Reds finished runners-up to Don Revie's Leeds United and lost to Red Star Belgrade in the early stages of the European Cup.

Two months after the FA Cup final came a bombshell: "It has not been a decision taken quickly, it has been on my mind for the last twelve months," said Shankly at a midday press conference at Anfield on Friday 12 July 1974 of his retirement as Reds boss aged just 60. "I feel it is time I had a rest from the game." With a city and the football world in shock he then headed to Melwood to complete the signing of Ray Kennedy from Arsenal. A fortnight later Bob Paisley reluctantly agreed to succeed him as manager.

In his first season as manager Paisley guided the team to runners-up spot behind Derby County in the League and they exited the Cup Winners' Cup to Ferencvaros. But in 1975-76 there was another League and UEFA Cup double: a ninth top-flight title

Bobby Graham allows a camera into his home to witness his recuperation in 1970

# 'PIC' OF THE WEEK

*By courtesy of Mercury Press*

It is two weeks since Bobby Graham broke his ankle and here he is at home smiling and confident he will be playing again before Christmas. All the strain in the Graham household is being taken by three-year-old Robert—on his head.

Bobby says, "The leg feels fine with no pain at all. I would like to thank all the fans who have sympathised and sent their good wishes. They bucked me up a lot and I'm looking forward to showing my appreciation where it matters —on the pitch. I believe I will be doing that a lot sooner than we thought when the accident happened."

A 'Q&A' with Emlyn Hughes in 1971 reveals scampi as his favourite meal and Barrow as his holiday resort of choice

won with high drama away to Wolves, with Kevin Keegan and John Toshack again the dynamic duo upfront, and FC Bruges beaten over two legs in the European finale.

Elsewhere, the first half of the decade had seen Ajax lift their third European Cup (1973), ABBA win the Eurovision Song Contest with *Waterloo* (1974), Alf Ramsey sacked as England manager and West Germany's World Cup triumph (1974), Kirkby boxer John Conteh taking WBC light-heavyweight title and *Jaws* released in cinemas (1975).

Although Liverpool narrowly lost in the 1977 FA Cup final to Manchester United, they won their 10th League title and lifted the European Cup in Rome with a 3-1 victory over Borussia Moenchengladbach. As far as Anfield nights go, the quarter-final second leg against St Etienne was up there with Inter Milan in 1965, and in recent years only Chelsea in the Champions League (2005), Borussia Dortmund in the Europa League (2016) and Barcelona in the Champions League (2019) have matched it for sheer tension and drama. To possess the matchday programmes for all five is to be a happy fan.

With *Stars Wars* in the cinemas, out went Keegan for a new adventure in Germany, and on 10 August 1977 in came a replacement number seven from Celtic, the one-and-only Kenny Dalglish, for a Liverpool love-affair with the Kop. Alan Hansen had just preceded him and they were followed by Graeme Souness.

With Dalglish in irresistible form in 1977-78, top-scoring for the Reds with 31 goals in all competitions, a second European Cup was won with the Scot grabbing the winner against FC Bruges in the Wembley final, but back home Liverpool were runners-up to surprise champions Nottingham Forest while long-server Ian Callaghan retired.

Following Argentina's World Cup win, normal service was resumed in the League in 1978-79 as the Reds accumulated a record 68 points (under the old two-points-for-a-win system) and established a record for conceding the fewest goals, 16, by a top-flight side. The season also saw one of Anfield's finest performances: a 7-0 victory over Tottenham Hotspur on Saturday 2 September 1978 described by the *Daily Post* newspaper as "the greatest moment even in Liverpool's long history of greatest moments – the locked-out thousands will never believe their bad luck. Only the lucky 50,705 can listen to the stories and know that there is no exaggeration."

Title no12 was delivered in 1979-80 with victory over Aston Villa at Anfield. But there was FA Cup semi-final heartache at the hands of Arsenal – after a third replay!

# THE ANFIELD REVIEW

1913/14 1949/50 1970/71 Football League Champions Division 1 1900/01 1905/06 1921/22 1922/23 1946/47 1963/64 1965/66 FA Challenge Cup Winners 1964/65 Finalists

**FOOTBALL LEAGUE—DIVISION 1**

# LIVERPOOL

v.

# LEEDS UNITED

SATURDAY, 1st JANUARY, 1972

Kick-off 3.00 p.m.

Two Reviews for the
price of one . . . . 5p

FOOTBALL LEAGUE CUP

Fourth Round Replay

**LIVERPOOL**
*versus*
**HULL CITY**

TUESDAY 4th DECEMBER, 1973
Kick-off 1.30 p.m.

A League Cup tie in December 1973

"There is only one direct link between club and supporters – the programme", club secretary Peter Robinson wrote. And he recognised the value, after actively working to produce a "better, brighter and more informative" publication. It paid off, the club sold a quarter-of-a-million copies, close to 25,000 per match, in the 1970-71 season.

Liverpool made a point of re-designing the cover after each season. It wasn't the only thing that required refreshing. With so much success on the pitch, the honours panel on the front had to be continually updated. Such was the club's domination across the Seventies, there was no choice but to move the ever-expanding list of trophies to the inside cover.

It wasn't long before the club recognised the potential of souvenir 'special' programmes, increasing the page-count – predominantly with match-action photos – with a slight increase in price to cover it. They tended to appear towards the end of the season as the team closed in on another final.

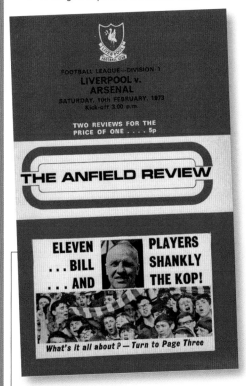

A Shankly teaser on the cover in 1973

A league encounter with Tottenham in 1974

The cover for the 1977-78 season had a drop-cap 'L' in the masthead (right) and trophies galore on show – this was a special issue ahead of the European Cup final v FC Bruges at Wembley six days later. Plenty of content teasers too

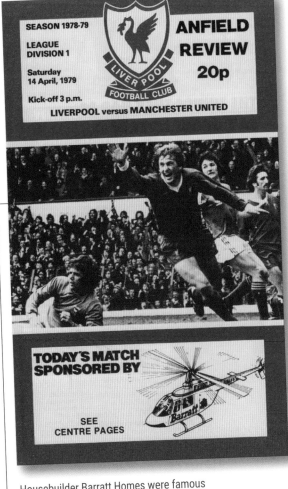

Housebuilder Barratt Homes were famous in the late 1970s for their helicopter TV commercial and here the chopper gets on the cover of the Manchester United programme

Collector's item siren: the cover of the programme from one of Anfield's most famous nights, the European Cup quarter-final second leg against St Etienne in 1977

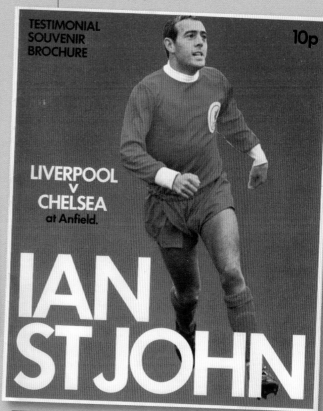

A simple but striking full-colour cover for Ian St John's testimonial programme in 1973

The Borussia Moenchengladbach match was abandoned after 27 minutes in 1973 due to heavy rainfall. It took place the following day with the same programme on sale at Anfield

Fans were the focus on the cover of the programme for the home leg of the 1976 UEFA Cup final

An FA Cup replay against Coventry City provided the opportunity for the first Anfield programme of the 1970s on Monday 12 January

## STRAIGHT FROM BILL SHANKLY

NOBODY needs to tell us that Liverpool will be the team they're all trying to beat—at home, and in Europe—this season. That's the price you have to pay for achieving success on the scale that we did, last spring. The title and the U.E.F.A. Cup—they went well together; but they're just facts in the record books now.

What we have done has been recognised, very generously, by people throughout the game. But they will be watching now for what we do this season—and our opponents, in the League, the European Cup, the F.A. Cup and the League Cup, will all be trying to take us down a peg. If they master us, or even match us, it will be a matter for pride, so far as they are concerned.

So we know that every game we play will be hard, and competitive. Yet, at the same time, I believe we shall bring two new and powerful reinforcements to our own armoury: the knowledge that we are striving to repeat what we have already proved can be done—win the title and a European trophy; and the added confidence and experience we have gained from succeeding through no fewer than 66 gruelling games last season.

The average age of our team is around 24—and ALL the players will have gained from their experience of last season's battles. We may well find that the tension has been lifted, also, to some extent.

Somehow, I get the feeling that we shall enjoy playing more, now that the boys have ended the hard struggle to win a major honour. They will have increased in stature, I hope, because they now have something tangible, something real, to show for their efforts.

They have won the big prize, the League championship; and they have won a trophy in Europe, where they played a dozen games against good teams. Our U.E.F.A. Cup final against Borussia Mönchengladbach produced the two best matches I have ever seen in European football.

## I'D LIKE US TO BE T-H-E CHAMPIONS!

But we are committed to not one, but four competitions: the League, the European Cup, the F.A. Cup and the Football League Cup. I make no apology for saying that we would have preferred three; we feel four is too much of an involvement.

At the same time, we shall be going for everything again, as we have done in the past. We're not the sort of club, not the sort of team that sacrifices one thing purely to succeed elsewhere.

Winning the title in successive seasons would be a tremendous feat. We have now won the championship of the First Division eight times, and I would like Liverpool to win it for a ninth time, to make them the champions of champions. But the main thing is to start off well in the League . . . and then we'll take it from there.

In late August 1974, in his second home match as manager, Bob Paisley used his programme notes to assure fans he could handle the job: "I hope and believe I can shoulder the responsibility." Ronnie Moran and Joe Fagan were able assistants

Managers' columns were not as resolutely established in matchday programmes as they are these days. The early 70s were a busy time for Bill Shankly as he built a second great team to challenge for honours and his own page was an occasional affair. At the start of 1973-74 (left) he praised his League title and UEFA Cup winners, admitted the League Cup was an inconvenience but vowed: "We shall be going for everything again." A second FA Cup at the end of the season was ample reward.

It was a similar story as Bob Paisley eased himself into the manager's role. His 'Team Talk' column would come and go. Maintaining continuity, promoting from within and a promise to bring continued success were key messages as he took charge of team affairs.

In 1975 Bob was reminiscing about a record home crowd for a 1952 cup tie with Wolves – recorded as 61,905

**EUROPEAN CUP WINNERS**
Seasons 1976-77 and 1977-78

**U.E.F.A. CUP WINNERS**
Seasons 1972-73 and 1975-76

**LEAGUE CHAMPIONS**
Seasons 1900-01, 1905-06, 1921-22 1922-23, 1946-47, 1963-64 1965-66, 1972-73, 1975-76 1976-77

**F.A. CUP WINNERS**
Seasons 1964-65 and 1973-74

## FORTY YEARS ON . . .

### SO MAKE IT A S-P-E-C-I-A-L CHEER

GIVE Liverpool team-manager Bob Paisley a SPECIAL cheer tonight . . . for it's the 40th anniversary of his arrival at Liverpool. It was on 8th May, 1939, that he joined the club as a player, and during this 40-year span he has graduated via the backroom side to be the man at the helm, AND contributed so much to the club's success.

BOB has seen it all happen at Anfield . . . relegation, promotion, League championships, European Cup, U.E.F.A. Cup, F.A. Cup . . . and, typically, his 40th anniversary has been a working day for him, just as it was when, in November, 1977, he went to Buckingham Palace to receive the O.B.E. Then, he hurried back for the Coventry game—and tonight it's Villa, with the Anfield climax in Liverpool's bid to make an 11th League Championship a fitting anniversary gift for manager Bob Paisley.

### LIVERPOOL CHAIRMAN MR. JOHN W. SMITH SAYS . .

THIS is a memorable occasion, not only for Bob Paisley, but for Liverpool Football Club, because we are able to pay a deserved tribute to one of the finest managers this club has ever had. And it is true to say that Bob is the epitome of everything a manager should be.

He has worked his way up from the bottom to the top, and his behaviour and attitude to the game have set a wonderful example for up-and-coming managers throughout football.

He sets an example which is first-class in every respect, and we count ourselves fortunate not only that he joined us, 40 years ago, but that through all the years he

### THE EPITOME OF WHAT A MANAGER SHOULD BE . . .

has given such exemplary service to great club.

There can be no argument that Paisley has been one of the reasons the success Liverpool have achieved home and abroad, right the way through and we sincerely hope he will remain with us for many years to come.

*YOU WILL NEVER WALK ALONE, IF YOU BECOME A MEMBER OF THE*
**LIVERPOOL F.C. SUPPORTERS' CLUB**
(Register open for a limited period)
Apply to Mr. T. Hodgson (Hon. Sec.), 212 Lower Breck Road, Liverpool L6
(Please send stamped, addressed envelope for postal replies)

CHAIRMAN John W. Smith, J.P.
TEAM MANAGER Bob Paisley
GENERAL SECRETARY Peter Robinson

DIRECTORS H. Cartwright, S. C. Reakes, J.P., C. J. Hill, J. T. Cross, W. D. Corkish, F.C.A.

2 Anfield Review

The Aston Villa programme from May 1979 marked the 40th anniversary of Bob Paisley's arrival at Anfield – and he celebrated the occasion by helping the Reds clinch the title with a 3-0 win

In March 1979, Paisley used the league programme against Ipswich Town to outline his dream of winning the FA Cup as a manager

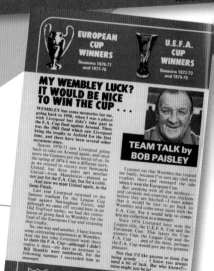

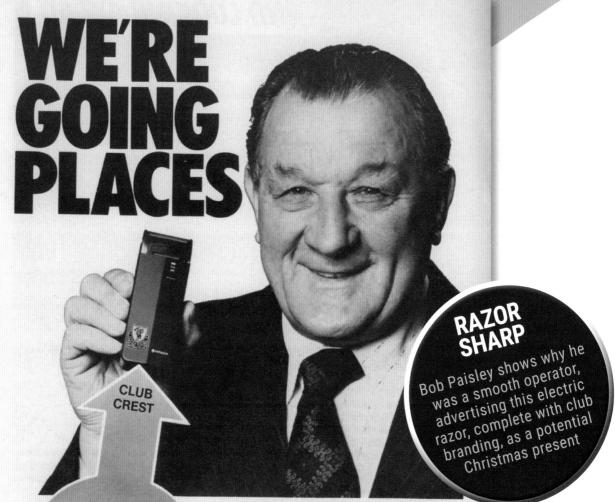

# WE'RE GOING PLACES

CLUB CREST

**RAZOR SHARP**

Bob Paisley shows why he was a smooth operator, advertising this electric razor, complete with club branding, as a potential Christmas present

## AND KEEPING TRIM AT HOME OR AWAY..

... with Hitachi's BM-31 pocket-sized shaver, complete with batteries and proudly featuring the Liverpool Crest. From the Club Shop now.

Or send cheque/P.O. (includes P & P) to Rees Electrics and we'll add your own name to the case along with Liverpool's *(mail order only)*. At no extra cost.

**What a gift for Christmas!**

Allow 21 days for delivery. Money back if not delighted.

**Rees Electrics, Ace Works, Cumberland Avenue, Park Royal, London N.W.10.**

LIVERPOOL F.C.
YOUR NAME
HITACHI

## PRICE ONLY
# £12·95

20 **Anfield Review**

## HUNG OUT TO DRY

Players were quite receptive to cheesy photo opportunities in the 1970s – as Ray Clemence is proving here by hanging his clean-sheets out at Anfield in 1979

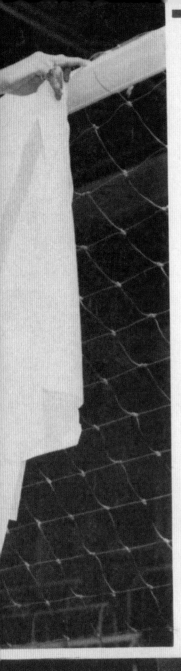

# RAY'S LOOKING FOR MORE CLEAN SHEETS!

**THERE** can never be enough clean sheets for Ray Clemence—because his aim is to keep one every time he plays for Liverpool and England. Last season Ray kept the 300th clean sheet of his career in the 0-0 draw against Nottingham Forest—and he's aiming to stop the goals going past him again this term, especially as it's his testimonial season. "I don't keep records," says Ray, "so I have to go by what people tell me." But if he doesn't keep records, he certainly sets them!

# . . . AND A TIMELY TRIBUTE TO BOB

**BOB PAISLEY** received a timely tribute, when the Northern Football Writers' Association played host to Liverpool and their manager at a dinner. Bob's Manager of the Year trophy was on show, and the sportswriters marked his 40 years' service at Anfield by presenting him with a wall clock. Pictured in this Liverpool Daily Post and Echo photograph are (left to right): Ronnie Crowther (Northern F.W.A. chairman), Don Evans, Dick Bott, Bob Paisley, Norman Wynne, national F.W.A. chairman Mike Langley, Tony Derry (sales director, Bell's Scotch Whisky), Dennis Lowe and Mike Charters.

TV cameras and crews became a regular occurrence at Anfield, not just to film proceedings on the pitch. In late 1977 there was a piece for long-running BBC sport show *Grandstand*, previewing a World Cup qualifier between Wales and Scotland with players from both nations 'refereed' by England's Emlyn Hughes– with the League championship trophy and European Cup in the foreground, and the matchday programme on hand to capture the moment.

One of those players, John Toshack of Liverpool and Wales, had composed his own book of football-related poetry the year before, and the programme advised readers that it was on sale "in all leading Liverpool bookshops and of course our own Souvenir Shop."

Tosh and Ray Clemence also hosted their own early Sunday-evening local radio shows.

## GOSH it's TOSH
### John Toshack
#### Poems and Pictures
foreword by Kevin Keegan

GOSH, IT'S TOSH . . . Yes, the Liverpool striker has broken into print with a book of poems, and—not surprisingly—the accent is on football. The book comprises more than 60 photographs illustrating the career of "Tosh" at Liverpool, and coupled with those are 17 poems relating to events in his career.

There is the Wales-England centenary match, The Injury (how the thigh injury occurred, and how it was later to affect his whole outlook on the game, as well as cancel his prospective move to Leicester).

The book, a Duckworth-Elmswood publication (price £2·25), and distributed by Gerald Duckworth & Co., The Old Piano Factory, 43 Gloucester Crescent, London NW1, will be on sale in all leading Liverpool bookshops . . . and, of course, it will be on sale at our own Souvenir Shop.

"Tosh" recalls: "I did a little piece on the centenary game, one on the injury, and one on the U.E.F.A. Cup final, and it snowballed from there. Once I get started, I enjoy doing these poems. Most of it is tongue in cheek . . . the people who know me as a person will know it's me talking . . . every word in it is my own.

"Possibly people who don't know me would take some of the things the wrong way, if they wanted to, and think I'm being pig-headed; but that isn't the case— those who know me will laugh, and accept it as being 'Tosh'."

"In many ways, the book is a souvenir of last season—the U.E.F.A. Cup, the championship, the Nations Cup with Wales. It was a tremendous season for me, a season when everything happened, and no one can take it away from me."

The 'Likely Lads' feature from the 1975-76 season highlighted some of the players' other interests, from Steve Heighway flying planes...

# THE LIKELY LADS

## STEVE GETS A BIG KICK OUT OF FLYING IN LITTLE PLANES

WHILE elder brother John pilots jumbo-jets for British Airways, Steve Heighway takes every opportunity possible to sample the delights of flying in light aircraft. "I've always been nuts on planes," says Steve.

He has a friend who is an air-taxi operator from Manchester airport, and from the age of around 12 to 18, Steve used to go along on Sundays and take bookings and collect the money from the customers. Sometimes he was able to go along for the ride himself.

had to drop the aircraft hobby for a bit, but after a year or so, I found I could fit in trips to aerodromes on a Sunday. At home, I have a VHF set which enables me to listen to the airwaves and pick up any interesting aircraft which may be coming in or going out.

"I haven't got a pilot's licence—if I ever became affluent enough and had the time, I'd consider going for one—but I've logged a lot of hours flying in light aircraft.

★ HERE'S another of our picture specials, in which HARRY ORMESHER features the Liverpool players in different roles. Today's "Likely Lad" is Steve Heighway, who gets a kick out of flying . . . not the jumbo-jets, like his elder brother, but light aircraft. Steve has gone from train-spotter to plane-spotter, as well.

★ HERE WE go, with a new series which spotlights the Liverpool stars in a different role. You see them in action in the red jersey—but what about their hobbies? This series, with pictures by HARRY ORMESHER, kicks off with a look at midfield man PETER CORMACK . . . and you'll see him in a new, and probably unexpected light.

# THE LIKELY LADS

## A PASTIME FOR PETER—BUT IT MIGHT HAVE BEEN A CAREER

THE PICTURE in the top right-hand corner shows Peter Cormack in an all-action role for Liverpool—if his flying header had counted, he would have been a first-minute marksman against West Ham at Anfield. But the Hammers' goalkeeper, Mervyn Day, pulled off a brilliant save . . .

The picture on the opposite page shows Peter Cormack in another, and far more leisurely role . . . that of artist. And you see him painting in watercolours in the garden of his home.

In fact, Peter might well never have become a professional footballer, had he been able to achieve a boyhood ambition, for he says: "I had a bit of a talent for art when I was at school—I won a prize or two—and I started trying my hand at cartoons.

"I tried to land a job drawing cartoons, but there wasn't anything going, at the time." So Soccer eventually claimed . . . in top . . .

In his spare time as a family man, however, Peter has done cartoons of animals which have decorated the walls in the children's room. Some of the animals have featured television and film-cartoon favourites, others have been the product of Peter's own mind's eye.

"Somehow, I always seem to finish up drawing or painting an animal—it might be an elephant, a tiger, a sheep-dog. I reckon it takes me 20 minutes to half an hour to complete a picture, though sometimes I pencil it in before doing the painting, and then it takes longer."

Peter isn't interested in doing "still life" pictures, and he doesn't "dabble in oils." He has done a couple of oil paintings, "but I wasn't too impressed with them," he says.

Does he fancy taking up art seriously, when his career as a footballer comes to a close?—"I don't think so . . . I think of it as a hobby now, not as a possible . . .

...to Peter Cormack's love of painting...

★ HERE'S another picture special in our series on the Liverpool players featuring them in different roles. On the opposite page, Ian is giving his usual, non-stop display on the park . . . but below, HARRY ORMESHER has captured him in a totally relaxed mood. It's Ian Callaghan, back home . . . and involved with his hobby, which is gardening.

# THE LIKELY LADS

## SO EVERYTHING IS 'COMING UP ROSES' IN IAN'S FRONT GARDEN

IT'S hardly surprising to learn that the quiet man of Anfield has an utterly relaxing hobby — gardening. Ian Callaghan, who has played well over 700 first-team games for Liverpool, may be a perpetual-motion man in midfield, but away from the action, he settles for the quiet life.

And the picture below shows Ian tending to the roses which give him the greatest pleasure from his garden. Ian admits that he wasn't responsible in the first

place, for the beautiful show of roses which decorate his front garden—"It's thanks, really, to the people who owned the house before we moved in, six years ago," he says with a smile.

"They really loved roses, and so when we moved in, we found we had a fabulous show—and I've made sure ever since that the roses have bloomed each year.

"The Queen Elizabeth roses—they're pale pink, and the bushes grow to six or seven feet tall—form a sort of hedge round the front garden, and people often stop to admire the display during the summer. I must say that the Queen Elizabeths are my favourites, too."

Some people will tell you that roses are tender plants, that they should be pruned only once a year, and then only at certain times. Ian says: "They are tougher than many people think, although they do need a bit of attention. But they're worth it.

"I feed the roses, and make sure they are pruned a bit towards the back-end of the year, when they're fading, and then I give them another and more thorough pruning as spring is coming. I don't know if I've got 'green fingers,' but I've been lucky in that nothing I've planted has died on me!

"Apart from football, my life centres around my home and family, and the gardening is just about my only hobby. I don't claim to be an expert, even on

roses, but I get tremendous pleasure out of the garden, and we've had some smashing displays of roses over the past few years.

"We've changed the garden quite a bit, and we have various plants and flowers growing—red-hot pokers, conifers, rhododendrons and so on—but we've made sure that the rose bushes remained where they were.

"And I suppose we owe a debt of thanks to the former occupants for making sure that we inherited such beautiful roses. I've made sure they haven't been allowed to fade away."

...to Ian Callaghan's interest in gardening

### The Captains look back

# MY FAVOURITE DERBY GAME MEMORY!

## What a day!

### says Tommy Smith

### LIVERPOOL 5 EVERTON 0

WHEN Everton came to Anfield in September 1965 it was only 12 months after they had beaten Liverpool 4-0, so we were particularly keen to do well.

Our fans had taken some stick since that match and I suppose it needed something like a 5-0 win to wipe out the memory.

The way we played in the first half we should have been able to send our fans home happy at the interval. We gave Everton as big a roasting as any side has had at Anfield. We hit both posts in the first minute, Brian Harris cleared a shot from Roger Hunt off the line and Tommy Wright hooked the ball away from Ian St. John as he was about to put it in the net.

Yet at half-time we were only one up—and I got it, with a header. I think it's the only one I've ever scored!

But within seven minutes of the start of the second half Roger and Willie Stevenson made it 3-0, Roger made it four later on and in the last minute Ian St. John gave the Kop the fifth goal they wanted.

Fabulous. What a day! Every derby game we win is great, but I doubt if any could better the way I felt that afternoon.

## What a night!

### says Alan Ball

### EVERTON 1 LIVERPOOL 0

ALL derbies generate a fantastic atmosphere, yet the city can never have been so wrapped up in one as the fifth round F.A. Cup-tie in March 1967.

So many people wanted to see it that close-circuit television was used to relay the match to Anfield where 40,000 fans saw it on huge screens in addition to the near-65,000 at Goodison.

Maybe it was because we were aware of the big crowd across the park that made the game at Everton even more tense than usual. Undoubtedly the fact that it was a vital Cup-tie had a lot to do with it. But that derby was certainly a bit special to play in, which made it a bit special to win.

Victory went to Everton with what I still regard as the goal of my life. Both teams know scoring chances don't come often in derbies, and when the ball ran loose off Tommy Lawrence and Jimmy Husband I knew there was one in sight.

I got to the ball just as Tommy Smith, Ronnie Yeats and Lawrence closed in and hooked it into the net.

It was one of the great moments of my career and is undoubtedly one of the reasons I love playing in derbies. The tension and pressures can be almost unbearable, but what an atmosphere!

A focus on 1977 star signing Kenny Dalglish with the departing Kevin Keegan admitting "Liverpool have come up with a ready-made replacement"

## GET LOST? – HE'S THE MAN WHO CAN LOSE YOU! SAYS SKIPPER HUGHES

**Focus on our record signing, Kenny Dalglish**

THE BARE facts of the story alone made headlines . . . Liverpool's record-equalled signing of Scotland international Kenny Dalglish from Glasgow Celtic. It followed a day of drama, in which Liverpool team-manager Bob Paisley and chairman Mr. John W. Smith sped to Glasgow by car, after Celtic had given word that their skipper was for sale.

Kenny Dalglish, aged 26, capped 47 times by Scotland, and a player who would do his job equally well from midfield or as a striker, would have been snapped up by half a dozen of the top clubs—but Liverpool landed him. And the news brought reaction from around the world of Soccer.

Lou Macari, who was a team-mate of Kenny's at Celtic, conceded that he never thought he would be allowed to leave", and added the significant comment: "He would have been great for Manchester United." Macari and Kenny Dalglish formed a fine partnership in their days together at Parkhead.

Manchester City manager Tony Book, whose £300,000 swoop for striker Mick Channon had caused a stir, admitted: "When we signed Mick, I believed he tipped the scales in our favour, but now things have balanced out again."

And Kevin Keegan, the man Kenny was signed to replace: "Kenny Dalglish

has been the best Scottish player for the last four years. He is such a good player he would fit in anywhere."

Kevin also said: "Liverpool have come up with a ready-made replacement. The Liverpool fans will like him. We are completely different, with different qualities and strengths—what we have in common is a desire to see the ball in the back of the net, whether we put it there or help one of our team-mates to do the job."

And Kenny himself confessed that, having sought a new challenge, he could think of no club better than Liverpool to offer it. "I'm not trying to take over from Kevin—I'll just try to be my own man. At Celtic I got into the habit of collecting silverware, and it's one I want to continue."

The size of the fee, Kenny stressed, did not worry him. "I don't have to carry a price tag on my back—just play to the best of my ability." Team-

manager Bob Paisley made the point: "There's no doubt about Kenny's ability . . . by signing him, we have got one of the best players—if not the best player—in Britain. He has so much ability, and he can play in any position, as all good players can."

Liverpool skipper Emlyn Hughes knows a thing or two about switching positions, for he has done this successfully—and he knows what it's like to play for England against Kenny Dalglish.

● One hand on the European Cup, and hoping to help us retain it . . . that's Kenny Dalglish, our new signing. Picture: Daily Mail.

Emlyn says: "He's a world-class player, and possibly he and Trevor Francis are the only two who could have come here and replaced Kevin Keegan.

"Kenny seems to 'get lost'—you think you've held on to him, and the

(continued on page 20)

The stars of 1979 show off their recently-captured trophies, pictured in the Bolton programme that August

**AND THE TEAM OF THE YEAR**

'Accent on the Action' gave us a peek at how pre-season looked in 1975 while (right) in 1976 there was a picture tribute to the indomitable Tommy Smith

## IT'S THE NEW LOOK AT LIVERPOOL

YOU'LL recognise the track-suited figure, even from the back view . . . but there's a special reason why the photographers are making sure they get their shots on target. On the right, you see the result, as Phil Thompson and Toni Byrne "model" the new-look Liverpool jersey with the Hitachi motif.

12 Anfield Review

Anfield Review 13

The photographers were out in force to picture Phil Thompson modelling in the new Liverpool kit – complete with Hitachi sponsor – in 1979. There have been more glamorous locations!

**Two matches** in four days . . . then back to the reserves

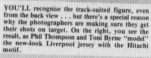
CAREER STORY . . . STEVE OGRIZOVIC

PETER McDONNELL, who is now with Oldham, waited more than three years to play in Liverpool's first team—and in vain: Steve Ogrizovic, who followed in his footsteps, played twice within four days—against Derby County and Leeds United—a matter of months after arriving at Anfield as understudy to Ray Clemence.

Needless to say, Ray was injured when Steve got his chance . . . and since then, it's been back to the reserves and a waiting game for the 6 ft. 3 in.-tall 'keeper who joined Liverpool from Chesterfield. With luck, though, Steve can wind up with a Central League-championship medal this spring.

Arthur Cox, manager of Chesterfield, still keeps a fatherly eye on Steve's progress from a distance, and he says: "Whenever I ask about him at Liverpool, they tell me he's living up to expectations and doing well. I'm sure he'll make it to the top."

Steve himself was under no illusions as to the situation when he signed for Liverpool in November, 1977, and his tally of three first-team appearances to date indicates how difficult it is when England's No. 1 'keeper is the man in possession. But Steve was prepared to wait, and life with Liverpool has been a whole new experience for him.

And goalkeeping was a new experience for him, too, at one time—because "Oggy" was a schoolboy centre-forward. But he always fancied trying his hand at stopping people from scoring goals, and he switched to being the last line of defence in his final year at school.

## THE ONE-TIME 'COPPER' HAS TO PLAY A WAITING GAME

Having taken "O" levels, he was studying for his "A" levels when he decided to become a police cadet, and for six months he worked as an apprentice on the force before passing out as a constable and alternating between footslogging on the beat and being a Panda patrol-man.

It was while he was playing in goal for a youth club—he was still in the police—that Steve was recommended to Chesterfield, and he remained a "copper" while playing as an amateur with the Saltergate club. Then Arthur Cox persuaded Steve to turn professional, and football became his career.

After Chesterfield had drawn a League Cup-tie, Steve was promoted for the replay, and he kept his place. He learned of Liverpool's interest in him when he read a newspaper, played in his 18th League game for Chesterfield the next day—and the same night heard from his manager that an offer had been made. On the Monday, Steve arrived at Anfield, and signed the forms that made him a Liverpool player.

The 'Career Story' feature focused on goalkeeper Steve Ogrizovic in the Norwich programme in February 1979

## A MAN AND HIS MEDALS...

Extreme left: Ian Callaghan had so many medals by the time of his testimonial in 1977 that a key was needed to list them all!

Left: By October 1978, Ray Clemence was not only a top goalkeeper but a radio star too!

18 Anfield Review / Anfield Review 19

# THIS IS LIVERPOOL

BACK ROW: (left to right): Joey Jones, Phil Thompson, Ray Clemence, Alan Hansen, John Toshack.
CENTRE ROW: Joe Fagan (coach), Alec Lindsay, David Fairclough, Ray Kennedy, David Johnson, Phil Neal, Ronnie Moran (trainer).
FRONT ROW: Jimmy Case, Ian Callaghan, Tommy Smith, Bob Paisley (team manager), Emlyn Hughes (captain), Steve Heighway, Terry McDermott.

## and the new boy

OUR NEW signing Kenny Dalglish (inset) sums up his hopes for the future like this: "I'm not here for personal glory . . . so long as Liverpool are successful and let me share in the glory, that will do for me. I can only give of my best.

"I do like to get keyed up a bit before a game—it's good to get the adrenalin flowing. And I'm really looking forward to the atmosphere, each time we play at Anfield!"

# LIVERPOOL, CHAMPIONS OF EUROPE...

THAT'S THE title of a book, just published, which is the players' own official story of last season's double triumph. It covers Liverpool's excursion into Europe from the day they first played Reykjavik in the European Cup, back in 1964, and it brings you bang up to date with the triumph in Rome.

There is a foreword by Ian Callaghan, a reminder of the 1965 European Cup-tie against Inter-Milan, stories about the European safari from Northern Ireland to Turkey, and great games—such as the one against St. Etienne—relived.

One chapter (naturally) is headed: "The Glory of Rome?"

There are also many pictures in colour, full statistics of Liverpool's European ties and, in all, a 62-page souvenir of stirring Soccer deeds. The book (price £2.95) is on sale at the Souvenir Shop.

In the West Brom programme in August 1977 the boys had a few trophies to show off

# THE GOALS WE SCORED AGAINST HIBERNIAN

In addition to the magnificent Steve Heighway goal on the front cover of this Review, our games with Hibernian produced two other memorable goals.

The one that completed our 2-0 victory in the home leg was scored by Phil Boersma, a chip from a position on the right wing deceiving Hibs' goalkeeper, dropping over his head and under the bar (see picture on left).

Below is the goal John Toshack scored in the away leg which gave us a 1-0 win. The picture shows him turning away after heading the ball into the net from a centre by Heighway.

*Daily Post and Echo pictures*

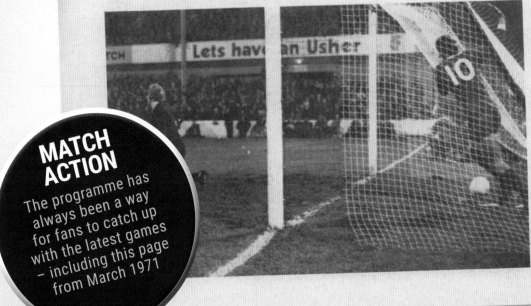

**MATCH ACTION**

The programme has always been a way for fans to catch up with the latest games – including this page from March 1971

The trophy may have been won three months earlier but in August 1977 it wasn't too late to revel in the glory of the club's first European Cup win

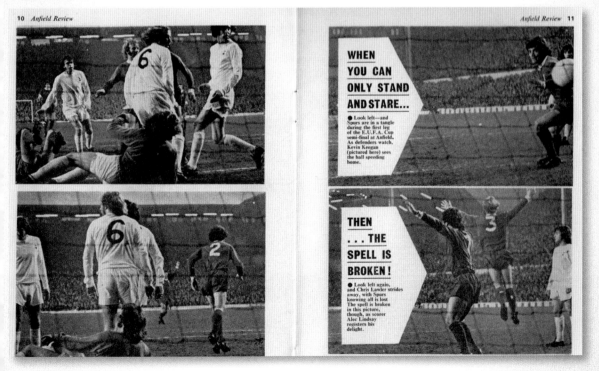

The programme for the home leg of the UEFA Cup final against Borussia Moenchengladbach in 1973 gave the chance to look back on Alec Lindsay's semi-final winner against Spurs

## THE HEIGHWAY ROUTE TO GOAL

MUNICIPAL DE SAN SEBASTIAN

● THE Heighway patrol—and danger signals loom for Real Sociedad.

● DOWN goes the 'keeper, and a defender is left trailing.

● THE final touch, and the ball is speeding towards goal.

● THAT'S IT . . . and Liverpool are one up against Real Sociedad.

Goals from the 3-1 UEFA Cup second-round away win at Real Sociedad in 1975 featured in the programme for the second leg at Anfield – which the Reds won 6-0

● Terry McDermott led Liverpool's six-shooters with a hat-trick in the Super Cup triumph over SV Hamburg, and his first and third goals are pictured here. Terry also won a trophy as man of the match over both legs of the tie, to make it a great birthday celebration for him. Pictures: Harry Ormesher.

## PHIL ROUNDS OFF THE EVENING

● BY THE time this picture was taken, Ian Callaghan had made it two for Liverpool, but the Reds weren't quite finished yet. Phil Thompson, who normally is concerned with stopping goals, gets into the attacking act, and he soars aloft to head home No. 3 for Liverpool.

**Tetley**

**You car**

Anfield Review 5

ERMAC HEADS LIVERPOOL'S SIX-SHOOTERS IN THE SUPER CUP

Terry Mac was the toast of Anfield as his hat-trick blew Hamburg away in the 6-0 UEFA Super Cup win in December 1977. This picture special featured in the QPR programme 11 days later

# SOME MEMORABLE EUROPEAN GOALS AT ANFIELD

Roger Hunt's against Inter Milan

Alun Evans's against Setubal

Ian St. John's against Anderlecht

Roger Hunt's against Setubal

Ian Callaghan's against Petrolul

Geoff Strong's against Celtic

Pictures by courtesy of Liverpool Daily Post and Echo,

## ST. JOHN AMBULANCE BRIGADE

The First Aid Services on this ground are provided by No. 5 Area of the St. John Ambulance Brigade whose members work entirely Voluntarily. New recruits—Men, Nurses, Boy and Girl Cadets (from 11 years) are very welcome.

Apply in the first instance to:
THE AREA SECRETARY, 31 Renville Road, Liverpool 14.

In the Dynamo Bucharest programme of October 1970, there was a gallery of some of Anfield's most memorable European goals

This picture of Alun Evans, against Ferencvaros in 1970, was lauded for the striker's athleticism – and the clarity of the image!

# The Anfield Review 'Pic' of the Week

Probably the best action picture we have seen this season. Alun Evans suspended in mid-air as he leaps between four Ferencvaros defenders. The picture is of unusual clarity for a night match, another advantage of our new lighting system.

**Goal Pictures by Harry Ormesher**

# Accent on the ACTION!

## 'HEADS I WIN' —EVERY TIME

★ Below: John gets airborne while another John—John Brownlie—can only watch as this picture header brings Liverpool's striker goal No. 2.

## The picture goals that took 'Tosh' to 150 . . .

★ LIVERPOOL'S Welsh international star, John Toshack, scored his first-ever hat-trick for the club in the U.E.F.A. Cup-tie against Hibernian at Anfield, and his three goals took us into tonight's second-round tie. The goals also saw John notch a career total of 150, so it was an occasion for celebration all round.

★ **Above:** It's Toshack versus McArthur, and the Hibs 'keeper is beaten by a header, which registers Liverpool's first goal.

★ **Bottom right:** Seven . . . that's Kevin Keegan . . . eight, nine, 10 . . . and that's JOHN TOSHACK, climbing well above the Hibs defence to make sure that Liverpool took their place in the draw for the second round of the U.E.F.A. Cup. The ball sped goalwards to make it Liverpool 3, Hibernian 1—and a hat-trick for John.

John Toshack's first Liverpool hat-trick – in a 3-1 win against Hibernian – was celebrated in the Real Sociedad programme in November 1975

## GOAL THAT KEPT THE EUROPEAN CUP AT ANFIELD

THE scene was Wembley, last May— but this was the goal that kept the European Cup in Liverpool's possession at Anfield, and this remarkable sequence of pictures (there are more on pages 16 and 17) show exactly how canny Kenny Dalglish brought Bruges to their knees in the final.

He latched on to a pass from Graeme Souness, looked up to see how the land lay, and then began his deadly work of destruction. Behind him, a Bruges defender is already stranded; ahead of him, the Bruges 'keeper is committed . . . and so Kenny picks his moment to strike.

As the 'keeper goes down, Kenny chips the ball diagonally towards the target area, while the defender looks on, powerless to do anything about it. The 'keeper does manage to get to his knees, but there's a look of despair about him as all three players watch the flight of the ball towards the gaping net. And if you turn to pages 16 and 17, you'll see exactly how the final job of demolition was completed.

*Picture sequence by* **HARRY ORMESHER**

The Reds kicked off their European adventure in September 1978 by remembering how Kenny Dalglish had inspired victory in the European Cup final a few months earlier

Here's Steve Heighway in 1976 talking about his favourite goals – with a fantastic shot of him scoring against Tottenham, taken by the club's official photographer Harry Ormesher. Harry later hung up his camera and went on to breed racehorses, including a Derby winner in 2006.

Journalists were also keen to appear in the programme with their own tales of travel to far, foreign lands with the team. On the right, James Mossop of the Sunday Express re-lives a Fairs Cup flight back from Bucharest in November 1970!

Below is how an opposition section looked in 1972.

## The Goal of My Life

### by STEVE HEIGHWAY

STEVE HEIGHWAY has made a habit of scoring goals against Spurs—the latest is pictured alongside, as he puts his best foot forward and hammers the ball past 'keeper Pat Jennings in our last match at Anfield. It was Steve's second goal this season, and the 54th of his career.

"I've scored seven or eight goals against Tottenham now, and I always enjoy playing against them, because they ae one of those teams prepared to make a game of it," says Steve.

There's no doubt in his mind, either, about the most important goal he's scored for Liverpool; it was the one which took us into the final of the U.E.F.A. Cup, in 1973. Tottenham had played the first leg of the semi-final at Anfield, and left trailing by the only goal of the game. So the scene was set for a thriller in the White Hart lane return.

Tottenham didn't disappoint their fans, either, because they scored two goals that night. But they weren't enough—because Steve Heighway slotted home a goal which meant the tie finished 2–2 on aggregate . . . and Liverpool went through to the final on the rule that away goals count double.

Steve recollects: "The ball came over from the right, and while the Spurs defenders were keeping watch on another Liverpool player, he let the ball come through to me. I was close to goal, and I hooked the ball in."

But if that goal, as Steve says, was probably the most important he's scored for Liverpool, the one which gave him the greatest personal satisfaction was scored on a May afternoon at Wembley one year later.

"The move started when Ray Clemence kicked the ball upfield; then John Toshack got his head to the ball, and nodded it on; I ran on to the ball, took it round a defender, and clipped it past the 'keeper into the corner of the net."

The game, of course, was the 1974 F.A. Cup final against Newcastle United. The goal was sandwiched between two scored by Kevin Keegan. But for Steve, it was the most satisfying moment, "because I'd scored and finished on the losing side in the 1971 final, and this time, finish on the winning team".

● Picture by Harry Ormesher

---

4 Anfield Review

## LIVERPOOL F.C. WELCOMES

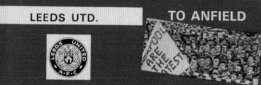

LEEDS UTD. TO ANFIELD

Anfield Review 5

**PRESIDENT:** T. V. Williams
**CHAIRMAN:** H. E. Roberts
**DIRECTORS:** H. Cartwright, S. C. Reakes, J.P., C. J. Hill, E. A. F. Sawyer, J. W. Smith J.P., J. T. Cross
**MANAGER:** Bill Shankly
**SECRETARY:** Peter Robinson

# A CLASH OF TWO OF ENGLAND'S TOP CUP TEAMS!

TODAY'S tie brings together two of the most successful Cup sides of the past decade.

Though Leeds last season lost in remarkable fashion to Fourth Division Colchester in the fifth round, they have appeared in two F.A. Cup finals plus two more semi-finals over the past seven years.

In addition Leeds have reached three Fairs Cup finals, winning the trophy twice; they have won the League Cup and were semi-finalists in the European Champions Cup.

Our last two home defeats were both inflicted by Leeds so we have much to try and avenge this afternoon. And, in one sense, tradition is on our side—Leeds United have never beaten us in an F.A. Cup tie.

We have met only twice in this tournament, beating Leeds 3–0 in the first round of 1924-25 and 2–1 in the 1965 Wembley final.

We may see as many as ten survivors of that Wembley epic on the park today—Liverpool's Lawler, Callaghan, Smith and Thompson with Sprake, Reaney, Bremner, Charlton, Hunter and Giles of Leeds.

Paul Reaney, though an England international, is no longer a regular member of the Leeds side. And Jack Charlton, a hero of over 600 games for the club, missed the League match at Anfield last month because of injury

### Memories of 1965 Wembley meeting

and had to leave the field in their next game at Ipswich.

The others will almost certainly be on parade. **Gary Sprake** has played well over 350 League games for the club since his debut, at the age of 16, in 1962, and now has 23 Welsh caps.

**Billy Bremner,** such an inspiring captain, still has that youthful look although he's played more than 400 games for the club and has been picked for Scotland on 28 occasions.

**Norman Hunter,** like all his regular colleagues, is an international player. He has 15 England caps.

**Johnny Giles,** the former Manchester United player, has battled for the Republic of Ireland on numerous occa-

★JOHNNY GILES who has played in three F.A. Cup finals.

sions. Johnny has played in three F.A. Cup finals—for Manchester United in 1963 and Leeds in 1965 and 1970.

England full-back **Terry Cooper** started as a left-winger, which is one of the reasons why he is today one of the finest overlapping full-backs in the business.

Versatile **Paul Madeley** is now operating at right-back though he won one of his four England caps as a midfield player.

### LANCASHIRE SENIOR CUP
● On 15th February we visit Turf Moor to play Burnley in the semi-final of the Lancashire Senior Cup (kick-off 7.30).

Scottish international **Peter Lorimer** is top scorer with 19 goals but **Allan Clarke** and **Mick Jones,** who have both suffered injury-enforced absences, haven't been on the mark as consistently as usual this season.

Both are £100,000 players and England caps, Jones netting Sheffield United a six-figure fee four years ago while Clarke broke British records with a £150,000 move from Fulham to Leicester and a £165,000 transfer to Leeds. He started with Walsall.

**Eddie Gray,** one of Leeds' midfield schemers, earned his eighth Scottish cap this season.

# The Anfield Cabaret—all the way from Bucharest

THE success of Liverpool's last flight into Europe, to Bucharest, could have far-reaching repercussions. Can you imagine Bill Shankly weighing up the possibility of a new signing and asking: "Does he sing, dance or tell monologues?"

Maybe you can't. But if you had been among the privileged few on an unforgettable flight back from Rumania, maybe you could.

I can. And there will be another valid question next time we clamber aboard for a flight home: "What time does the Ronnie Yeats show start?"

Forgive me for dwelling on the after-football which, I suppose, should remain a secret of the Aer Lingus Boeing 737 that brought us home. Yet I feel "The Ronnie Yeats Show" typified the new spirit of this growing Liverpool side.

It all started soon after dinner on the four-hour night flight home. Yeats, with impeccable timing and sense of fun, took over the in-flight loudspeaker and announced: "Gentlemen, this is your ex-captain speaking . . ."

He rocked us with a monologue, and pleaded that he was merely reading from a slip of paper handed him by Tommy Smith. Then sheer nostalgia forced him through "The Northern Lights of Old Aberdeen". By this time the show was well and truly on the road.

A Brian Hall solo, a song (or was it a gargle?) from Larry Lloyd, crooning from director Ces Hill, a speech from Bill Shankly, supporting acts from a variety of turns and a crashing climax the Kop would have been proud of in "You'll never walk alone".

The show was such a success that one of the Irish stewardesses sang "The Golden Bracelet" beautifully. And, never forget it, the Press did their share of entertaining, too.

I have travelled far and wide with many clubs but this was one of those occasions

JAMES MOSSOP, *of the "Sunday Express", lets you into a secret of Liverpool's last venture into Europe—the spontaneous entertainment on the journey home that typifies the spirit among the players.*

that will be stored in the memory box for ever.

Looking round the plane, as Bill Shankly must have done, brought confirmation that the transition from the magnificent side of the 'sixties to this new one on the threshold of the 'seventies, had been done without acrimony.

Ronnie Yeats and Tommy Lawrence were as important to this scene as were John McLaughlin and Phil Boersma.

Yeats, since he was deposed, has done nothing but encourage the youngsters who have taken over. His part in that memorable, spirit-binding trip home was vital.

The final cameo occurred as we were back over England not far from Speke. A BBC man with a tape recorder called for a final chorus that he could put out on a late night programme.

Bill Shankly, coca-cola in his fist, led the supreme belting at "You'll never walk alone".

That moment of instant magic stands frozen in time.

*Anfield Review*

**M**EET the Hughes family—which means Liverpool captain Emlyn, his wife, Barbara, and daughter Emma, who is now 16 months old. Like Emlyn, Barbara comes from Barrow—that was where she met Emlyn.

"It was during the close season, just after he had signed for Liverpool, and he invited me to a party," she says. That was about seven years ago, and Barbara and Emlyn were married two years ago last month.

Is she a football fan?—"Let's say that I'm interested in football generally—but that I'm a fan of Liverpool and Emlyn Hughes!" she laughs. "I enjoy going to watch Liverpool play, and up to Emma being born, I had hardly missed a match.

"I still try to go, whenever possible, and when I can't get to the game, I've got two radio programmes and the television on, so that I don't miss the news as to how they're making out."

When Emlyn isn't playing at Anfield, or travelling with Liverpool around the country or abroad, there's nothing he likes better than to sample real home cooking.

"He doesn't like fancy food," says Barbara. "He won't eat onions—in fact, he doesn't like vegetables, except for peas. It's got to be something plain, like steak, or steak and kidney pie. His favourite is steak, chips and peas."

Emlyn's "diet" of home cooking doesn't seem to have done him any harm, either, judging by the tremendous energy he puts into every game—and he's played more than 400 for Liverpool now, since he was signed from Blackpool in 1967.

It's a safe bet that Barbara never dreamed, the day she married him, that she was becoming the wife of a man who was to skipper not only Liverpool, but England.

● *Picture by Harry Ormesher.*

## BACK HOME

**A** ROUND Kirkby way, the name of Thompson is a household word when it comes to talking football. And not just because Phil is a Liverpool player. For Phil's younger brother, 14-year-old Ian, is following in his footsteps by playing for Kirkby Boys . . . and, again like Phil, he can slot into the back-four line or play in midfield.

Pictured here are Phil, Ian, twin sisters June and May, who are 13 years old, and Mum and Dad. That leaves 18-year-old Denise, Linda (25), who is married, and Owen, who is also married.

Phil's Mum and Dad—Owen and June—go to watch Liverpool in action, home and away. As for Ian, Dad reckons he's going to be even taller than Phil, and maybe a little bit heftier.

Phil, of course, has been out of the action for several weeks because of a cartilage operation. But after playing last week he hopes soon to be bidding for a return to First Division football. "He can't get back soon enough," says Phil's Dad.

When football isn't taking up his time—and that's not often—Phil enjoys being a do-it-yourself mechanic, and he keeps his car on the top line. Elder brother Owen is a motor mechanic, and between them, they give the car expert attention.

Phil's lean frame belies his strength—Emlyn Hughes says he's "strong as a lion"—and he can eat anything without worrying about putting on weight. But he doesn't like chips—when he has his favourite home-cooked meal of steak, it's got to be mashed potatoes.

● **Picture by Harry Ormesher.**

The 1974-75 season programmes contained the 'Back Home' feature where fans found out a bit more about the home lives of the stars they watched every week – for example discovering that Phil Thompson didn't like eating chips, while the only vegetables Emlyn Hughes ate were peas!

## LIVERPOOL    TOTTENHAM

**HOW THEY LINE UP**

(Red Shirts)
1 Ray CLEMENCE
2 Phil NEAL
3 Alan KENNEDY
4 Phil THOMPSON
5 Ray KENNEDY
6 Emlyn HUGHES (Capt.)
7 Kenny DALGLISH
8 Jimmy CASE
9 Steve HEIGHWAY
10 Terry McDERMOTT
11 Graeme SOUNESS
Substitute:

**REFEREE**
Mr. G. E. Flint (Kirkby-in-Ashfield)

**LINESMEN**
Mr. S. Leaver (Red Flag)
Mr. A. Robinson (Orange Flag)

(White Shirts)
1 Barry DAINES
2 Don McALLISTER
3 John GORMAN
4 Glenn HODDLE
5 John LACY
6 Steve PERRYMAN (Capt.)
7 Ricardo VILLA
8 Osvaldo ARDILES
9 Gerry ARMSTRONG
10 John DUNCAN
11 Neil McNAB
Substitute:

## HALF-TIME SCOREBOARD

| | FIRST DIVISION | | | SECOND DIVISION | |
|---|---|---|---|---|---|
| A | Manchester U. v. Everton | ....... | K | Blackburn R. v. Orient | ....... |
| B | Arsenal v. Q.P.R. | ....... | L | Burnley v. Notts. Co. | ....... |
| C | Aston Villa v. Southampton | ....... | M | Oldham A. v. Stoke C. | ....... |
| D | Bolton W. v. Birmingham C. | ....... | N | Sunderland v. Preston N.E. | ....... |
| E | Chelsea v. Leeds U. | ....... | O | Wrexham v. Leicester C. | ....... |
| F | Derby Co. v. Coventry C. | ....... | | THIRD DIVISION | |
| G | Middlesbrough v. Ipswich T. | ....... | P | Hull C. v. Chester | ....... |
| H | Norwich C. v. Manchester C. | ....... | Q | Peterboro' v. Tranmere R. | ....... |
| I | Nottingham F. v. West Brom. A. | ....... | | CENTRAL LEAGUE | |
| J | Wolves v. Bristol C. | ....... | R | Man. City Res. v. Liverpool Res. | ....... |

JACK SHARP SPORTS LIVERPOOL

Printed by Seel House Press Ltd., Seel Street, Liverpool L1 4AY

## The Who's Who of Liverpool's playing staff: Season 1978-79

| | DATE SIGNED | PREVIOUS CLUB | BIRTH-PLACE | HEIGHT ft in | WEIGHT st lb |
|---|---|---|---|---|---|
| **GOALKEEPERS** | | | | | |
| Ray Clemence | 12.6.67 | Scunthorpe Utd. | Skegness | 6 0 | 12 9 |
| Steve Ogrizovic | 7.11.77 | Chesterfield | Mansfield | 6 3 | 14 7 |
| Peter McDonnell | 29.7.74 | Bury | Bury | 6 1 | 13 0 |
| **DEFENDERS** | | | | | |
| Jeff. Ainsworth | 14.7.75 | Apprentice | Liverpool | 5 9 | 11 7 |
| Derek Carroll | 25.4.78 | Dundalk | Dublin | 5 5¾ | 9 12 |
| Alan Hansen | 5.5.77 | Partick Thistle | Alloa | 6 1 | 13 0 |
| Alan Harper | 17.9.75 | Apprentice | Liverpool | 5 8 | 9 7 |
| Emlyn Hughes | 28.2.67 | Blackpool | Barrow | 5 10½ | 12 9 |
| Colin Irwin | 5.12.74 | Amateur | Liverpool | 6 0 | 12 6 |
| Joey Jones | 14.7.75 | Wrexham | Llandudno | 5 11 | 11 7 |
| Brian Kettle | 7.5.73 | Apprentice | Prescot | 5 9 | 12 13 |
| Phil Neal | 9.10.74 | Northampton T. | Irchester | 5 11 | 12 2 |
| Tommy Smith | 5.4.62 | Schoolboy | Liverpool | 5 10½ | 13 5 |
| Phil Thompson | 22.1.71 | Schoolboy | Liverpool | 6 0 | 11 8 |
| Alan Kennedy | 14.8.78 | Newcastle United | Sunderland | 5 9½ | 11 10 |
| **MIDFIELD** | | | | | |
| Synan Braddish | 25.4.78 | Dundalk | Dublin | 5 7 | 10 11 |
| Ian Callaghan | 28.3.60 | Schoolboy | Liverpool | 5 7 | 11 11 |
| Jimmy Case | 2.5.73 | Amateur | Liverpool | 5 9 | 12 7 |
| Ray Kennedy | 12.7.74 | Arsenal | Seaton Delaval | 5 11 | 13 3 |
| Sammy Lee | 7.4.76 | Apprentice | Liverpool | 5 7 | 10 1 |
| Terry McDermott | 13.11.74 | Newcastle Utd. | Liverpool | 5 9 | 12 13 |
| Kevin Sheedy | 30.6.78 | Hereford Utd. | Builth Wells | 5 8½ | 10 10 |
| Graeme Souness | 10.1.78 | Middlesbrough | Edinburgh | 5 11 | 12 13 |
| **FORWARDS** | | | | | |
| Trevor Birch | 8.12.75 | Apprentice | Ormskirk | 5 11 | 11 13 |
| Kenny Dalglish | 10.8.77 | Glasgow Celtic | Glasgow | 5 8 | 11 13 |
| Brian Duff | 25.4.78 | Dundalk | Dublin | 5 10 | 10 12 |
| David Fairclough | 9.1.74 | Apprentice | Liverpool | 5 11 | 11 1 |
| Howard Gayle | 23.11.77 | Apprentice | Liverpool | 5 10½ | 10 9 |
| Steve Heighway | 19.5.70 | Amateur | Dublin | 5 10½ | 11 2 |
| David Johnson | 12.8.76 | Ipswich T. | Liverpool | 5 10 | 12 4 |
| Gary McCartney | 23.8.78 | Apprentice | Belfast | 5 9 | 10 2 |
| Colin Russell | 22.4.78 | Apprentice | Liverpool | 5 10 | 10 7 |
| Robert Savage | 9.1.78 | Apprentice | Liverpool | 5 7 | 11 1 |
| Jimmy Williams | 22.4.78 | Apprentice | Liverpool | 5 6½ | 9 2 |

Player stats (above) from the Spurs game in September 1978 and the 'Half-time Scoreboard' (left) on the back-page. The capital letters matched ones in front of the Kemlyn Road stand where the scores were shown on cards – 70s technology!

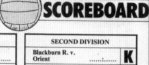

## Liverpool's 53rd Eurotrip...

**BILL SHANKLY** was sitting in the lounge of the Aperghi Hotel holding an impromptu Press conference on characters he had known in the game when some exiled Merseyider now living in Greece made the mistake of asking him whether he and his players were going to see the sights of Athens.

"We're not here for a holiday," snorted the Liverpool boss. "We're here to do a job of work."

The League's most experienced European campaigners were in Athens for the second leg of their U.E.F.A. Cup game against A.E.K. Athens. The fact that they were in a city where modern civilisation began, that their hotel stood within a few miles of the Acropolis did not make a scrap of difference. For Shankly and his men were there for a match and the fact that it was in Athens rather than Aldershot or Alaska was irrelevant.

The nearest Liverpool's players came to seeing the sights was on the 20-minute coach ride from the airport to their hotel nestling in the hills some 15 kilometres from the capital.

The modern footballer may travel to the world's most exotic cities but if he's a Liverpool player he's unlikely to see much further than his hotel front door. For Liverpool, the name of the game is winning . . . and everything is geared to that end.

Less than 48 hours after convincingly beating Chelsea at Anfield on a wet and windy afternoon, Liverpool flew off into Manchester's Ringway Airport into the Greek sun . . . 16 players, five club officials, three directors and a party of 11 Pressmen. League Football went with them.

The players had already trained at their Melwood training ground. With the match scheduled to kick off an three the following afternoon, there would not be any more time for training.

Shankly does not particularly care for Europe or Europeans. He does not say so openly but he does not spend any longer than necessary abroad and certainly does not trust foreign food. With meals served during the flights to and from Greece, he intended making sure that his men sampled as little Greek cuisine as possible. Tea and toast before bed—a similar short snack in the morning before the game.

Liverpool have learned from experience the problems of Europe. They know to be wary of foreign food, hotels situated in the centre of foreign cities, long delays at airports. Everything is aimed at making the trips as undemanding as possible for the players.

SHANKLY does not like flying—the only member of the club who dislikes air travel. Ron Yeats was a notoriously bad traveller but the present side have no qualms. The BAC one-eleven was jetting south east at 29,000 feet over Germany when Shankly began to lose his nervousness and gave a run down on the places to avoid in Europe.

"Germany, Holland and Belgium are the best for hotels, food and organisation. Eastern Europe is bad, Rumania the worst of the lot. Dirty hotels, bad food, bad water. When we last played in Bucharest the temperature was in the 90s. Hungary? I went there as a player with Preston in 1938 and it was the bright city of Europe. Now? I don't think it's had a coat of paint since." Players and Press nodded in agreement . . . Rumania was a country to avoid if possible.

Tommy Smith and Ian Callaghan, two of Liverpool's most experienced travellers sat at the back of the plane reading. Emlyn Hughes, John Toshack and reserve 'keeper Frankie Lane were involved in one of several card schools while Hughes and Toshack ribbed each other about English and Welsh international football.

It was just before eight p.m., Greek time, when the plane landed at Athens airport and the invasion by the Greek Press and well-wishers began. "Meester Shankiee" screamed the local news hounds, 'weed you defend?' The Liverpool boss was short but courteous. Outside the airport someone was playing 'You'll never walk alone' on a cassette tape recorder. The cassette belonged to Fred Devereaux who claimed he had once lived opposite Ian Callaghan before emigrating to America where he was enlisted in the U.S. air force and posted to Greece.

The coach trip to the hotel at Kifisia took the players past some of the more modern sights of the city . . . the American Embassy, the Athens Hilton, and the tallest building in Greece. The Greek Press prepared for their next assault on an English side . . . Tottenham Hotspur were due to land ten minutes after Liverpool for their match in the same competition against Olympiakos.

*Opposite . . . Liverpool's Steve Heighway and Brian Hall outside their Athens' hotel before the U.E.F.A. Cup game.*

15

Programme readers in the Seventies were treated to a colour 'League Football' insert which now and again had a Liverpool feature like this one, reporting on the trip to AEK Athens for a UEFA Cup second round second leg in November 1972. "We're not here for a holiday," growled Shanks. "We're here to do a job of work." The Reds won 3-1.

**BRIGHT FUTURE**
The club were very proud of their new floodlights in 1970 and this article in the Manchester United programme in September shone a light on why...

## Throwing some light on our new lights

# You won't see better than this!

UNTIL a couple of weeks ago Real Madrid's famous San Bernabeu stadium was the brightest lit football ground in Europe. Today our new floodlights make Anfield just as bright—and probably as bright as any in the world.

When our supporters saw them for the first time during the game with Crystal Palace few can have known they were watching soccer under lights 10 times more powerful than on most other First Division grounds.

The experience prompted a lot of admiration, comment and questions. Today we shall answer some of the questions and add a few more interesting items of information about the lights.

The basic facts are: The new system—costing around £50,000—provides a white light of about 504,000 watts. It is made up of 42 massive 10 kilowatt lamps specially developed for colour television. Each lamp is equivalent to almost 900 domestic 100 watt tungsten lamps.

The new system—with lights along the main stands and in the gantries—does away with the traditional four pylons. This means there are no long shadows and it provides a uniform spread of light.

Apart from acquiring one of the best lit stadiums in the world, we now have one of the few grounds in this country to meet the B.B.C.'s optimum standards for satisfactory transmission of colour television.

This means that all outside colour broadcasts from Anfield will achieve a quality that until now has been reserved solely for the studios. The high level of lighting enables the camera crews to take close-up views in colour, which is only possible if the lighting is designed at a high level.

Any level below that of Anfield limits the producers of sports programmes in their use of different lenses, which means that most soccer matches are covered by the use of a wider viewing angle than is normal with black and white transmission.

The installation was supplied and designed by Philips, and their 10 kW mercury halide lamp is the largest of its type in production in the world today. The effect on the ground is 200 times as bright as Liverpool's Lime Street.

Early programmes in the 1974-75 season gave us the chance to meet new boys Phil Neal, Terry McDermott and Ray Kennedy

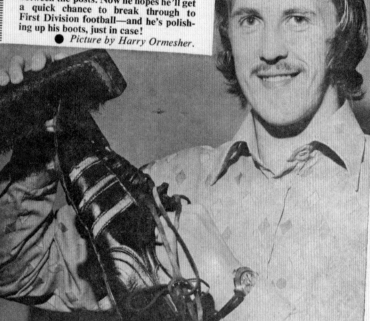

Anfield Review 3

## MEET ANOTHER NEW BOY

MEET the new boy from Northampton, Phil Neal—a player for any position, as his previous club record shows. Phil joined Northampton straight from school, and made his debut as a 16-year-old, while still an apprentice.

And he played in EVERY position for his old club, including goal. Twice, when the 'keeper was injured, Phil went between the posts. Now he hopes he'll get a quick chance to break through to First Division football—and he's polishing up his boots, just in case!

● *Picture by Harry Ormesher.*

...eld Review

## ...ME — BY A ROUNDABOUT ROUTE

THIS IS IT . . . Ray Kennedy, who hails from the North-East and arrived at ...rpool via Arsenal, welcomes Terry McDermott, Liverpool born and bred, who ...ed at Anfield via Bury and Newcastle United. Once, Terry stood on the Kop . . . ...he's at the heart of the action.

## The Anfield Review 'Pic' of the Week

*Mercury Press*

You won't see two happier invalids than these. Here are our latest casualties, Alec Lindsay and Peter Thompson, side by side in hospital listening to last week's F.A. Cup draw. The looks on their faces answer the questions we have been receiving about them.

This 'Pic of the Week' from January 1971 shows Alec Lindsay and Peter Thompson listening to the FA Cup draw while in hospital – both recovered well enough to be involved in the final that May

6  *Anfield Review*

# 'BILL SHANKLY .. THIS IS YOUR LIFE'

**and secretary PETER ROBINSON reveals**

## *HOW WE KEPT THE SECRET*

FOR two months, three people at Anfield kept the secret . . . that Liverpool manager Bill Shankly was to be the subject of the television programme, "This Is Your Life". The men in the know: Liverpool chairman Eric Roberts, secretary Peter Robinson, and Bill's right-hand man, Bob Paisley.

Peter Robinson takes up the story of the secret which was kept from the man most closely concerned until the moment Bill Shankly stepped off the train at Euston station, London, when the team went to play West Ham.

Peter says: "There were several ideas about the programme. One was to lure Bill to Anfield for a bogus board meeting, then rush him to Manchester. But they couldn't do the programme in Manchester. So, finally, it was decided to catch Bill when the team went to London. And THAT caused problems . . .

"We were ringing Mrs. Shankly when we knew Bill was at the training ground; we were sweating that word wouldn't get out; the day before the team went to London, we were in a bit of a flap, because the Liverpool-London trains were delayed . . . but fortunately, on the Friday, the timetable worked out right.

"Bill was a bit suspicious when he got home Friday afternoon and found a note from his wife saying she was out shopping —he knew she didn't normally go shopping at that time. Then he wondered a bit when he met the players for the trip south, and saw them all dressed up— normally, they wear casual clothes for travelling.

"We had brought Tommy Smith into it, as club captain, and two days before the programme he told the rest of the players. It was real M.I.5 stuff. We even arranged with British Rail that the team should be in the first coach, so that Bill would be the first to step off the train at Euston, and the cameras were sited for this. But the train pulled further into the station than we thought, and the cameras finished up focusing on the third carriage.

"Bill had spotted the cameras, and told Bob Paisley he reckoned there must be a film star on the train or something. As Bill got off the train, Bob stuck to him and suggested that it must be a fire, and that they'd better go and have a look . . . and so he got Bill to the right spot for the cameras.

"We were a bit concerned, too, about the players, for Bill likes to get them settled into the routine on away trips, without delay, but it all panned out. They usually have honey, toast and tea in their hotel at 10 p.m. . . . this time, the food was laid on at the T.V. theatre, and the players were back in the hotel and ready for bed at 10.30. And the whole show had been kept as a complete surprise from Bill until the last possible second."

In fact, the man who was most disappointed of all was . . . Peter Robinson. For his plans to travel with the team and keep an eye on things were rudely shattered by a three-letter word—'flu. So Peter had to retire home to bed, instead of taking the train to London. But, like millions of others, he caught the T.V. show that paid such a glowing tribute to Bil Shankly, the indomitable manager of Liverpool.

---

### THE BRIAN LABONE TESTIMONIAL MATCH
### EVERTON v. LIVERPOOL

Goodison Park—TUESDAY MARCH 13, 1973
(kick-off 7.30)

Tickets available as follows:

STAND (inclusive of Donation and Testimonial Programme)
85p and 75p

GROUND 40p

PADDOCK 45p

CALL AT THE EVERTON BOX OFFICE (ANY TIME) BULLENS ROAD

---

Bill Shankly was the subject of hit TV show *This Is Your Life* in 1973 and club secretary Peter Robinson used the Derby County programme to explain how they kept it a secret from the boss

## Record Season for the Anfield Review

*Anfield Review* 11

THIS is the 31st and final *Anfield Review* of a season which has proved its most successful ever.

As with everything else at Anfield the success of our programme is based on teamwork. You, the fans, have played your customary part by buying nearly three-quarters of a million copies to give us a record sale.

When the club decided two years ago to have a better, brighter and more informative programme it involved nearly everybody at the club. They have all helped out and it might surprise you to know the number of people who have been called on to fill 31 issues.

**Bill Shankly**, in possibly the busiest season of his managerial career, has contributed articles when he has felt there has been something to say.

**His players** have done their bit with the Star Choice feature and expressing opinions on significant matches.

Secretary **Peter Robinson and his staff** have been heavily committed in the administrative work involved, writing letters, requesting and returning photographs, producing records and statistics etc.

*Peter Robinson*

**Joe Fagan** and **Ronnie Moran** have provided all the gossip, opinion and latest news for the ABC feature which has proved to be popular.

### CLUB TEAMWORK PAYS OFF WITH ¼ MILLION SALE

Journalists throughout the country have produced articles, sometimes without much notice, in time to meet the printer's deadline, and their newspapers have loaned us some very good photographs. The *Daily Express*, *Daily Mirror*, *Daily Mail* and *Mercury Press*, a local agency, have been particularly helpful.

**The directors** have taken a great interest in the *Review* and have chipped in with opinion and advice.

For such a compact programme it is amazing the number of people involved in producing it—not forgetting the printers.

It is inevitable in the publishing business that there is the occasional crisis, the odd panic, the race to beat the deadline, the last-minute snag. But every issue came out on time, if only just. And you showed your appreciation by supporting it.

We have some new ideas for next season's *Review*. If there are any you would like to be considered drop them on a postcard to "The Editor", Anfield Review, Liverpool F.C., Anfield Road, Liverpool L4 0TH.

## 800 UP – AND EMLYN AND RAY BRING THE TOTAL TO 1,750

NO NEED to identify the three Liverpool players pictured above - every Anfield fan knows who they are. And we're spotlighting them for a very good reason, indeed—because each has just clocked up another milestone in his career with the club.

Ian Callaghan must take pride of place, for when we played Manchester United at Old Trafford in mid-week, "Cally" took his total of appearances for Liverpool to 799. So he'll doubtless be given a special cheer when he goes out today for the game that brings his carreer total to 800.

Skipper Emlyn Hughes played his 550th game for Liverpool when we met United at Old Trafford on Wednesday, and Ray Clemence completed 400 games for the club when we played at Norwich. And, as if to emphasise that they intend to keep right on going, all three figure among Liverpool's ever-presents this season.

So, too, does Steve Heighway, who should celebrate his 350th game for Liverpool when we tackle St. Etienne in the European Cup on March 2. And for Joey Jones, next Saturday's match marks his half-century in the colours of Liverpool.

This afternoon's match sees Kevin Keegan complete 300 appearances for Liverpool, and Phil Thompson hopes to celebrate his 200th game for us when we play Newcastle United here next month.

The Southampton programme in May 1971 celebrated reaching around 750,000 sales for the season, while the landmarks in February 1977 were reached by the players – Ian Callaghan, Emlyn Hughes and Ray Clemence hitting appearance milestones

Long-standing Anfield DJ George Sephton was in the spotlight in the Hamburg programme in 1977

*Anfield Review* 7

**GEORGE SEPHTON** was, to use his own phrase, "a Koppite of long standing." But now he sees Liverpool from another angle, for the man who has been "a Liverpool fan ever since I was old enough to go to a football match", is our resident match-day D.J.

After 10 years of being a Koppite he acquired a paddock season ticket. Then he wrote to the club offering his services as a D.J., and Liverpool took him up on the offer. That was more than six years ago.

"Apart from the records—I link up with the hospitals for almost an hour before the game— I'm in touch with the police room on a 'hot line'.

"I try to be careful not to leave the 'mike' on when there's a sudden panic. Touch wood, nothing disastrous has happened so far . . ."

● MEET THE face behind the voice . . . Anfield commentator George Sephton, who keeps you up to date with team news, and doubles as our resident DJ at home matches.

## GEORGE IS OUR MAN BEHIND THE 'MIKE'

There was news of long-term contracts for Bob Paisley and Peter Robinson in the Crystal Palace programme in 1977

European adventures in Dresden and Barcelona featured in the UEFA Cup final programme in April 1976

The West Ham edition in December 1973 pictured Roger Hunt handing Emlyn Hughes a Golden Boots award

Ray Clemence was pictured in the cockpit of the plane *en route* to Stromsgodset in Norway in 1974

# WE HOPE YOU HAD A GOOD TIME TOO!

*Mercury Press Photo.*

*Anfield Review 7*

For once Bill Shankly and Norman Wisdom weren't the stars of the show. They met at the Christmas party the club held at Anfield for the players' children and here they are trying to cope with the entertainment. Norman Wisdom took time off from rehearsals from his Robinson Crusoe pantomime at the Empire Theatre in order to be present.

The Leeds United programme on New Year's Day 1972 featured the meeting of two huge characters – Bill Shankly and entertainer Norman Wisdom – at the club Christmas party

The match sponsor of the QPR game in August 1978 got a full page to advertise, while Norwegian humour after Stomsgodset's 11-0 loss to the Reds in 1974 was shown in cartoon form in the Ferencvaros programme in 1974

# CHAPTER 5

# 1980s

A decade of almost complete dominance on the pitch – with players
and trophies making a regular appearance on the front cover of the
matchday programme – but with two terrible tragedies off it

Once the major transatlantic port of the British Empire, the city of Liverpool was at an economic low ebb in the Eighties. But the Reds remained a source of local pride with their python-like grip upon English football, and at the end of the previous decade the club had become the first in the UK to exploit the commercial potential of shirt sponsorship.

Accompanied by a burst of colour in the programme – check out those pinks, yellows and greens among the pin-stripe reds – LFC's dominance reached new heights, challenged occasionally by Everton and other sides eager to gatecrash the party. There was tragedy, also, on two awful occasions.

From season to season the programme underwent changes to its appearance – some cosmetic, some more substantial – and the decade also saw the introduction of full-colour action photography from recent Anfield fixtures.

In 1980-81 the Reds finished fifth in the League and were knocked out of the FA Cup by Everton, but ample consolation came in the form of a first League Cup success, over West Ham in a Villa Park replay, and a third European Cup, won in Paris.

In the next campaign, title no13 was won in May 1982 with triumph against a Tottenham side featuring Liverpool old boy Ray Clemence in goal as a rapturous Spion Kop saluted goals by Mark Lawrenson, Kenny Dalglish and Ronnie Whelan. There was another League Cup triumph, too, with Whelan and rookie striker Ian Rush scoring in a 3-1 victory over Spurs in the final.

Manager Bob Paisley admitted: "The toughest part of this job is producing new players at the right time. You've always got people telling you what you should do. They tell you to bring in new players but it isn't as easy as that. There comes a point when you have to say to the youngsters: 'You've had your education – now go through with it'."

In the wider world in the early part of the decade, Ronald Reagan became US President, Britain and Argentina went to war over the Falkland Islands, and Apple unveiled its Macintosh PC.

Back in English football the news had a familiar feel to it. Season 1982-83 – champions again. Liverpool finished eleven points clear of Graham Taylor's Watford, having stayed top since the end of October. And when the Reds beat Manchester United to win a third League Cup earlier in March, the team insisted that retiring manager Paisley collect the trophy.

At the end of the next season, fans on the Kop stayed behind for 40 minutes after the final home game, against Norwich, to hail their title-winning heroes, one of whom, Ian Rush, had scored 47 goals in all competitions. It was Liverpool's third championship in a row – they became the only club to achieve this since the war. A fortnight later, with a fourth League Cup long since in the bag, Joe Fagan rounded off his first term as boss with the European Cup, won in Rome again, to make it a trophy treble.

In late May 1985, having finished as runners-up to Everton in the League, the Reds were set to contest a fifth European Cup final when tragedy struck at the Heysel Stadium in Brussels before the match with Juventus – 39 spectators were killed after fighting broke out on the terraces. It seems strange now that, only a matter of weeks later, Live Aid took place at Wembley and the JFK Stadium in Philadelphia.

The first matchday programme of season 1985-86 struck a sombre note while previewing the new campaign. Banned

The back-page of the programme for the 1981 clash with CSKA Sofia

'Home Ground' was a popular feature in the 1985-86 programmes in which readers were invited into the players' homes

## THE LIVERPOOL LOOK—SEASON 1984-85

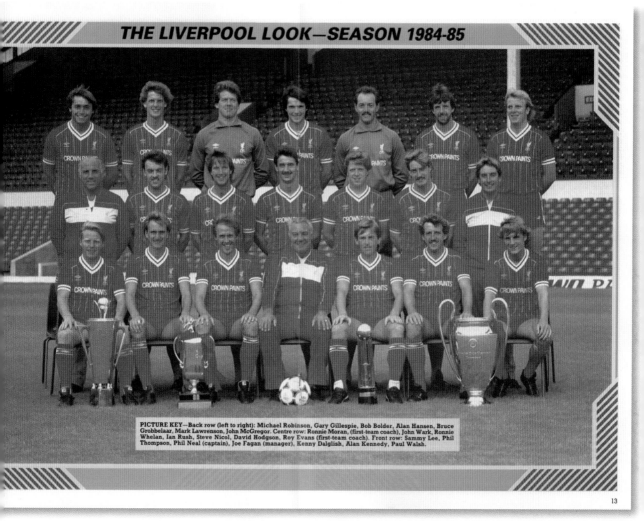

PICTURE KEY—Back row (left to right): Michael Robinson, Gary Gillespie, Bob Bolder, Alan Hansen, Bruce Grobbelaar, Mark Lawrenson, John McGregor. Centre row: Ronnie Moran, (first-team coach), John Wark, Ronnie Whelan, Ian Rush, Steve Nicol, David Hodgson, Roy Evans (first-team coach). Front row: Sammy Lee, Phil Thompson, Phil Neal (captain), Joe Fagan (manager), Kenny Dalglish, Alan Kennedy, Paul Walsh.

13

om European competition, Liverpool would ultimately clinch first League-and-FA-Cup double under player-manager enny Dalglish in a thrilling finale to the season, besting their ighbours across the park to both trophies. In the summertime ego Maradona's Argentina won the World Cup.

It was Everton's turn to win the title in 1986-87 with the Reds cond, while defeat to Arsenal in the League Cup final was the st time Liverpool had lost when Ian Rush had scored – in 146 mes!

But it was business as usual in 1987-88, and then some. In eason of scintillating football Liverpool finished nine points ear of Manchester United. The 17th title win in LFC history w John Aldridge, Peter Beardsley and John Barnes share 56 als and a major highlight was the 5-0 win over Nottingham rest at Anfield in April 1988, a week after the teams had met the FA Cup semi-final. Another Double, though, was thwarted Wimbledon in the FA Cup final at Wembley.

Saturday 15 April 1989. The darkest hour. Ninety-five rerpool fans (later rising to 97) lost their lives at the FA Cup mi-final against Forest at Hillsborough. In the immediate termath the city united as bereaved families and the club tried to come to terms with the tragedy. Anfield officials opened the ground for fans to pay their respects and leave countless tributes at the Kop end.

Football did resume that season, Liverpool beating Forest in a rescheduled semi-final at Old Trafford before prevailing 3-2 over Everton in an emotional Wembley final.

Three days later, the Reds beat West Ham 5-1 at Anfield in the League; a further 72 hours later they lost at home to Arsenal in a Friday-night title decider, thus finishing second in the table to the Gunners on goal-difference. It was an agonising way to lose – the all-important second goal coming in the last minute of the match – but many in the home crowd stayed behind to applaud the victors.

The final season of the decade saw the Reds regain the title – their 18th – by nine points from Aston Villa. A win over QPR confirmed top spot and on Tuesday 1 May 1990, after a 1-0 victory over Derby County featuring an 18-minute cameo by player-manager Dalglish, the trophy was handed over.

Somehow, though, Liverpool lost an FA Cup semi-final 4-3 to Crystal Palace whom they'd hammered 9-0 at Anfield earlier in the season.

The first home programme following the Hillsborough disaster in 1989 was a chance to reflect and mourn together.

The Manchester City programme in May 1981 was heavily influenced by the European Cup final coming up just days later

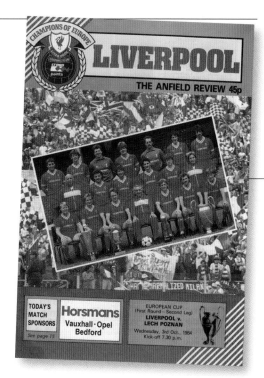

Proudly displaying an array of trophies, this team photo was used on the covers of the 1984-85 programmes

The first cover of the 1989-90 season, against Manchester City, gave the club a chance to show off its latest silverware

By the time Joe Fagan took over the manager's reins in 1983, the club had dispensed with its red-white-and-black programme palette and moved to a full-colour cover and centre pages with a refreshed design. And as Kenny Dalglish's side secured the League-and-FA-Cup double in 1986, there would be an upgrade to an all-colour issue.

Between 1982 and 1988 the club crest on the front cover incorporated the logo of shirt sponsor Crown Paints. A first for Liverpool, it demonstrated a sign of the times – major sponsorship deals were becoming integral to the financial stability of football clubs. Sponsors were here to stay – on the cover and in adverts inside.

In 1983 photographic giants Canon negotiated a three-year deal to be first to sponsor the English Football League which hence became the Canon League on the front of the LFC programme. A different action photo appeared on the cover of each issue as sponsorship of the League transferred to the *Today* newspaper (1986-87) then Barclays (1987-88). The cover's masthead or title alternated from red-and-white to yellow-red-and-grey.

This cover from April 1984 featured photos of the stars of the day like Ian Rush, Phil Neal, Graeme Souness, Bruce Grobbelaar and Kenny Dalglish

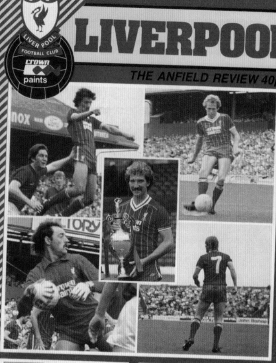

The Merseyside derby in November 1981 seemed like a good opportunity to display a picture of a Scouser lifting the European Cup!

This image was so popular it was used over and over again on the cover of 1985-86 programmes

LIVERPOOL

THE ANFIELD REVIEW 35p

MILK CUP 2nd ROUND 2nd LEG
**LIVERPOOL v.
IPSWICH TOWN**
Tuesday, 26th October, 1982
Kick-off 7.30 p.m.

INSIDE
TONIGHT'S
ISSUE

● The Cat and the Milk
Cup . . . story on page 3
● Double trouble!—Spotlight
on Ian Rush
● Focus on Europe . . . S.V.
Hamburg's Allan Hansen,
and the "Golden Boy" of
Juventus.

Moglet the Anfield cat heard there was milk around in October 1982 but could only find the Milk Cup

This was the cover on show the night the Reds were 'better than the Brazilians' in a 5-0 win against Nottingham Forest in April 1988

The Anfield Review 60p

BARCLAYS LEAGUE DIVISION 1
**LIVERPOOL v. NOTTINGHAM FOREST**
Wednesday, 13th April, 1988 Kick-off 7.30 p.m.

LIVERPOOL

TONIGHT'S MATCH SPONSORS
*Liverpool ECHO*
SEE PAGE 23

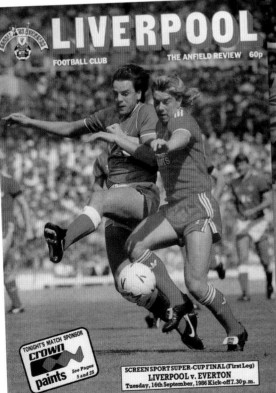

LIVERPOOL
FOOTBALL CLUB          THE ANFIELD REVIEW 60p

TONIGHT'S MATCH SPONSOR

crown
paints   *See Pages 5 and 25*

SCREEN SPORT SUPER-CUP FINAL (First Leg)
**LIVERPOOL v. EVERTON**
Tuesday, 16th September, 1986 Kick-off 7.30 p.m.

It's derby time again – this time in the final of the Screen Sport Super Cup in September 1986

# THE FINAL TEAM TALK

by

*Bob Paisley*

I EXPECT I shall have mixed emotions as the final whistle blows this afternoon, for it will signal not only the end of our last League game here this season, but my last appearance at Anfield in charge of team affairs. I've tried to imagine just how I shall feel, as I walk into the dressing-room after the match . . . but I'll know for certain when that moment comes.

In the meantime, I have no doubts about one thing: so many people have made this job easier for me to do, at various times during the past nine years, that I wonder now why I ever hesitated in taking it on. In fact, I have come to realise that the easiest thing about the job was the way that people went out of their way to be of genuine assistance.

As for the hardest thing during my time as manager . . . that's an easy one to answer. Quite simply, it was reaching a decision to pack the job in! But, having made that decision, I also accepted that everything—good and bad—has to come to an end sooner or later.

You cannot please all of the people all of the time, and I know that I haven't always suited everyone in this city, or even at this club; but, having conceded this, let me just add that fortunately, the people who from time to time have been critical of my actions turned out to be very much in a minority. And I'd like to think that I've never reached the stage where the critics and I were never going to be on speaking terms again!

I was asked this week what being a freeman of the city of Liverpool involved, and I answered—jokingly—that it meant, in my case, being given a free transfer! Seriously, I am very sensible of all the honours which have come my way while I have lived and worked in Liverpool, and I am not merely paying lip service to this club when I say that I regard most of the honours as being for Liverpool F.C. as well as for myself.

Now and again, there are odd things which annoy or frustrate you—I'm only human, like everyone else—but I can honestly say that never once have I regretted taking the managerial job, diffident though I might have been when I was asked to follow Bill Shankly.

I said at the outset that I hoped the team would do the talking for me, and I think I can fairly claim that, right the way through, the players who have worn Liverpool's colours during my spell as manager have done just that. Equally, I would be the first to pay tribute to the backing I have had not only from the players, but from everyone on the staff.

There have been times when I have felt, sincerely, that the players and the staff were making the job look ridiculously easy for me . . . and I must say, also, that the Liverpool supporters have been of tremendous help. I've had so many messages of goodwill from our fans that it would be impossible to reply personally to them all . . . so, please, take this as a heartfelt thank-you from me . . . to everyone.

> WE print without further need for comment a letter from a Watford fan, Mrs. Cathy Purrington. "I look forward to our match against Liverpool on May 14—I know it will be a marvellous game—and I am sure the Watford supporters will give Mr. Paisley as good a send-off as the Liverpool supporters. He is greatly admired, and I wish him all the best when he retires as manager."

11

Columns from managers and team captains, traditionally found near the front of an issue, have been a staple of matchday programmes for decades. Personalities, like management and playing styles, are all different and it's fair to say some have relished the writing requirement more than others, penning their notes themselves as opposed to dictating their thoughts to a club journalist or member of the press office to write up later.

Bob Paisley was famously a man of few words, the opposite of his more loquacious predecessor Bill Shankly, whereas skipper Alan Hansen was famously razor-witted in the Anfield dressing room.

In the Eighties, 'Team Talk by Bob Paisley' was followed by 'Joe Fagan's View' then 'Kick-Off with Kenny Dalglish' – all written in collaboration with editor Stan Liversedge.

Bob Paisley used his column in November 1981 to talk about derbies of the past

Kenny Dalglish used his first column as player-manager in August 1985 to thank everyone "for all the messages of goodwill"

# KICK·OFF with

**THIS IS** a season with a difference, in many ways, but we're looking forward to it – not least, because it will give us all the chance to become totally involved again and, in that respect, get the legacy of Brussels out of our system.

If ever there was a time when we needed the support of the true Liverpool fans, it is now; and I want to emphasise that the players do rely on the fans to rally round. Your support can help the team to succeed, just as much as the efforts of the backroom staff and the players themselves, who will always respond to encouragement from fans. So we're looking for the right kind of atmosphere around Anfield.

You might say I'm an old hand in a new job, this time out, for the managerial side is a new experience. But it's been a boost that the backroom staff have pledged their support, that Bob Paisley has taken on the role of team consultant, and that the likes of Ian Rush, Gary Gillespie and Craig Johnston are ready to stay at Anfield.

In pre-season games we have blooded players such as Ken de Mange, Wayne Harrison and Mark Seagraves. That was their reward for having done well in the reserves last term and in closed-door matches during recent weeks. What counts now, of course, is whether they can sustain their form – if so, it's good for them and the club, since it adds to our all-round strength.

Finally, let me just add my thanks for all the messages of goodwill. You can be sure they have been genuinely appreciated.

## A NEW LOOK ALL ROUND

**LIVERPOOL** line up in a new-look strip this afternoon . . . and our extended sponsorship deal adds a gloss to things. We have signed a four-year agreement with the world's leading sportswear company, adidas, and concluded a further three-year deal with Crown Paints.

This means that the Lancashire paint firm will be associated with Liverpool FC until at least the end of season 1987-88 – a total of six years' continuous sponsorship – and part of the fresh agreement is linked to the team's performances. So there is every incentive for us to succeed.

The Crown Paints package includes perimeter and programme advertising, tickets, entertaining facilities and the Crown name on the famous red shirts, while a new clause means that bonuses can be won, should Liverpool clinch major Cup competitions and/or the Canon League championship. Crown Paints chairman Peter Burns says of the new deal: "The club welcomes it – Liverpool are geared to results."

The adidas agreement is for the supply of team playing strip and other related products, and all garments feature exclusive adidas designs – adidas are producing replica garments, and the new range is available in retail outlets now.

**WELCOME BACK** to Anfield for the big kick-off – and [An]field Review has a new look again this season. [becau]se of increased production costs, we have had to [raise t]he price of your match-day magazine to 50p, but [we be]lieve you will agree that this still represents [excell]ent value for the money.

[This] time out, we have not only maintained the number [of page]s in full colour, but we have added colour on many [other p]ages . . . and we are also introducing several new [feature]s which, we believe, will inform and entertain, [while at] the same time keeping our supporters fully in [the pic]ture as to what's happening at Liverpool and [elsewh]ere. In fact, as the weeks go by, you will be able [to pick] up the issues so that the various articles and [features/]specials become a complete series.

[Incident]ally, the Anfield Review is on sale at the [Souvenir] Shop, as well as at the various selling points [around th]e ground, and it will pay you to get your copy [early. ] So make sure you're not disappointed!

constantly altering as the season changes its course.

The biggest problem we have—and I'm referring to the successful clubs—is that we are committed to too many matches at top level and that includes international games, as well as European and Cup competitions. All things considered, I think we deserve credit for staying the course for so long in so many tournaments—and when we win one, we do English football a service.

Team Talk
by [signature]

**ONE BY ONE**, the tournaments which could have brought several trophies to Anfield have come and gone, and I must confess that it was a disappointment not to be looking forward to a return to Wembley this season in the F.A. Cup and to a fourth final appearance in the European Cup. But you can't have everything . . . and I would not want people to think I was being greedy!

Now the Milk Cup final is behind us, and the remaining matches give us a chance to nail down the League championship; so, one way or another, we'll have made certain of qualifying for Europe again next season. And that, right at the start of a campaign, is always the priority.

Since Liverpool and Aston Villa went out of the European Cup, a great deal has been written and said about the quality of the opposition from the Continent, and what we call the English style of football has come in for considerable criticism. Frankly, I don't go along with all that.

No matter what may be wrong with our game, the facts speak for themselves—and the facts are that English clubs have dominated the European Cup for the past half-dozen seasons. If our football had been so lacking in quality, surely we would never have carried off the European Cup three times? And surely Nottingham Forest and Aston Villa wouldn't have won the 'trophy', either?

We can blame ourselves for having lost the quarter-final tie against Widzew Lodz; but, by the same token, the crack Continental clubs which fell to Liverpool, Forest and Villa in the various finals—and in the rounds preceding the finals—must have been asking themselves why they failed.

The answer must be that, on the night, their English opponents proved to be better at taking their chances and tucking the ball away into the net. And so, no matter whether the Continentals are more skilled than our players, the English style of football turned out to be successful.

Different countries have different climates, and teams play the kind of football for which they are best suited. We haven't got bone-hard grounds here right through the season; we don't take a mid-winter break; we DO have a variety of conditions to which we have to adapt.

I venture to suggest that, no matter what our so-called failings might be, we have the most varied game of all, simply because the conditions are

### MY THANKS

THIS is an appropriate moment to thank every one who helped to make our Milk Cup week-end in London such a success. Liverpool came off best against Manchester United, and collected three awards at the P.F.A. dinner . . . and, to cap it all, I went up for the cup!

This was one of Bob Paisley's final columns as Reds manager in April 1983 but he was able to reflect on success in the League Cup final when "I went up for the cup!"

CHAIRMAN
John W. Smith, C.B.E., J.P.
TEAM MANAGER
Joe Fagan
CHIEF EXECUTIVE/
GENERAL SECRETARY
Peter Robinson
DIRECTORS
H. Cartwright      S. C. Reakes, J.P.
C. J. Hill         W. D. Corkish, F.C.A.
J. T. Cross        S. T. Moss, J.P., C.C.
R. Paisley, O.B.E., M.Sc.(hon.)

## LEAGUE CHAMPIONS

Seasons
1900-01, 1905-06, 1921,22
1922-23, 1946-47, 1963-64
1965-66, 1972-73, 1975-76
1976-77, 1978-79, 1979-80
1981-82, 1982-83

## EUROPEAN CUP WINNERS

Seasons 1976-77
1977-78 and 1980-81

## U.E.F.A. CUP WINNERS

Seasons 1972-73
and 1975-76

## F.A. CUP WINNERS

Seasons 1964-65
and 1973-74

## LEAGUE CUP WINNERS

Seasons 1980-81
and 1981-82

## MILK CUP WINNERS

Seasons 1981-82
and 1982-83

## JOE FAGAN SIGNS IN...

I'M under no illusions about the size of the job I have taken on, in following Bob Paisley as team manager of Liverpool, so right at the outset let me give you, the supporters, just one guarantee. I promise that I shall give 100 per cent. in the effort to bring more success to this great club.

I realise that now, it rests with me to get the best out of the players, as Bob Paisley did before me; and I believe that I can get the best out of them because they know I want success . . . and so do they.

There is another, perhaps more personal factor: so many people have wished me good fortune in my new role that I feel Liverpool supporters are simply willing things to go well for myself and the club. And that also gives us all a tremendous incentive.

Basically, we still have the same backroom team—and I believe it's proved to be the best in the business. Now we are reinforced by a former Liverpool favourite, Chris Lawler, who has returned as reserve-team coach after four years of management in Norway. He has gained good experience, and he knows how we do things at Anfield.

We also have some new players—Michael Robinson, Gary Gillespie, Bob Bolder, to name but three—and I consider that we have strengthened our senior squad by adding to the competition for places. I have been delighted with the way players have said they're prepared to battle for places.

I realise that I shall not be able to satisfy everyone, but I can only say that I shall try to do the job my way—which means the way that I think is best for this club. You can believe me when I say that I never considered I should succeed Bob Paisley, as a right . . . but now that I have done, I reckon I know the score.

I know the players, and they know me. I know the guidelines set down by my predecessors. So everything is familiar—and one thing, above all, hasn't changed. Like the people who have gone before us, the players and myself are still hungry for success.

2

## BILL SHANKLY...

# THE

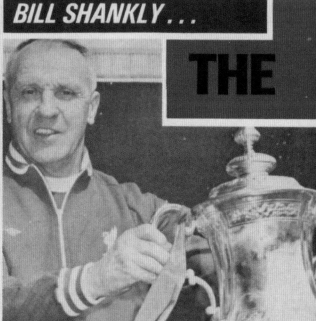

**GOODBYE, SHANKS**

Anfield Review editor Stan Liversedge paid a heartfelt tribute to Bill Shankly in the first league programme following the legend's death in 1981

## 'NO-ONE CAN EVER FORGET...'

"IT IS a loss that is irreparable. He has done so much for the club over the years. No-one can ever forget what he has done ..." Those words, spoken by Liverpool chairman Mr. John W. Smith in tribute to Bill Shankly, summed up the feelings of many more people about the man who became a legend in his own lifetime.

Mr. Smith said: "It is hard to find words to tell just how sad all of us at Liverpool must be. It must be the greatest shock we have ever had as a club. Bill was the greatest charismatic figure of football. We owe an incredible amount to him for what he did for us at Anfield."

Manager Bob Paisley reflected: "I ser under him for 15 unforgettable years. W success I have had as a manager reflect. much on him. He made a tremendous contr tion to everything that has happened at club—both while he was the manager after he retired because of the foundation had laid.

"We thought he was indestructible...we now left to mourn the loss of one of greatest figures the game has ever knowr

General secretary Peter Robinson agr adding: "I had the privilege and pleasur working with Bill for 10 years. The experie was unforgettable. I don't think many pee know just what he did for this club."

# ...DOMITABLE MAN

...LL SHANKLY would surely have been at ...nfield in the flesh this afternoon, had life ...ne according to plan. It didn't . . . but, even ..., his spirit will be with us, and no doubt there ...uld have been a brief smile on those craggy ...atures as he anticipated this particular duel. ...For it was Shanks who brought John ...oshack to Anfield—"an essential in modern-...y fitba'"', he once described the former ...verpool striker—and it would have appealed ... Bill's own fighting spirit that "Tosh" now ...turns with his First Division newcomers ...ho do battle with the old masters.

...Bill would have wished John Toshack well ... but he would certainly have wanted a Liver-...ol victory. As usual!

...The stories surrounding Bill Shankly are ...merous, but the theme running through ...em never varied. For always in evidence was ...e strength of his loyalty to Liverpool.

...One sportswriter who did a piece about the ...ub met him soon afterwards and was ...easantly surprised to be commended for ...at he had written. You didn't often expect ...aise from Shanks. But there had to be a ...nchline, and it was this: "Aye, you wrote ...out the honours we've won, but you missed ...e thing—we won the Charity Shield, as ...ell!''

...On another occasion, Bill was asked for his ...ews after an Anfield game in which (it was ...e of those very rare occasions) things had ...t gone well for Liverpool. The corridor ...tside the dressing-room was crowded with ...essmen, as Bill emerged and surveyed his ...oes.

That was another thing you remember about him . . . you could almost see yourself in the reflection of his shoes, for he always was meticulous about such matters.

But back to the Pressmen, and the one who had had the temerity to suggest that Liverpool were having problems . . . Bill looked up, and gave his answer: "Don't lean on that wall . . . it's been newly painted and we don't want to get it dirty!"

And so the stories went on . . . and they will continue to go on, maintained by those who witnessed Shanks in verbal action. For he was never stuck for an answer.

But at the end of the day, we shall remember him simply for being what he was: the indomitable man. The man who refused to surrender, and who imbued his team with that same spirit.

He had a close affinity with the fans, so it is appropriate that one of them should have the final say about Bill Shankly: "He was a Liverpudlian at heart. The people's man, too. I didn't know him well, but I met him less than a week before he died, and he made me realise anew what he had meant to this city. He was loved by many people, and everyone is upset by his untimely death. But one thing is for sure . . . we'll all remember him."

STAN LIVERSEDGE,
Editor, Anfield Review.

## GOOD-BYE, CLEM ... HELLO, BRUCE

### GROBBELAAR

### He's the 'keeper who scored from the penalty spot

ON THE day that Ray Clemence was signing for Tottenham Hotspur and ending a 14-year association with Liverpool, Bruce Grobbelaar was eagerly awaiting his First Division debut and hoping to follow in Ray's footsteps as our long-term, first-choice 'keeper.

Bruce has the right kind of background, too—because both his father AND his mother were goalkeepers! Bruce explains: "My Dad played for a team in Rhodesia and had one game for the national side, while my mother was the 'keeper in a hockey team. I used to watch them play, and I've played in goal since I was a youngster. I always wanted to be a footballer."

Now he's a Zimbabwe international, and getting a crack with the top club in this country ... something which seemed unlikely at one time. Bruce recalls: "When I was 15, I was supposed to go with another lad to Derby County and, hopefully, sign as an apprentice; but the whole thing fell through. After that, though, I was determined to get here somehow.

"In 1977 I came out of the Army and moved to South African football for just under a year. While I was playing in Durban, someone who had contacts with West Brom saw me, and in 1978 I spent five months with Albion. But I couldn't get a work permit.

"I went to Bournemouth for two weeks, but returned to Albion still unable to get that permit. Then, on the day I was due to go back home, I was told to take my boots to Derby's training ground, where Vancouver Whitecaps boss Tony Waiters wanted to see me.

"I went through an hour's training session, and Tony asked me if I fancied going to Canada. I explained that I was due to return to Africa that day, said I didn't know what decision to make; so it was agreed that I'd travel home the following day and Tony would contact me in Zimbabwe. He did, and arranged for me to go to Vancouver."

"I played one full game for the Whitecaps in my first season, and 30 in my second spell with them. Between times, I came back to England to play on loan with Crewe, and I got in 24 games with them. Tony reckoned that my spell in English football would make or break, and while with Crewe I had a couple of training sessions with Gary Bailey at Manchester United and Peter Shilton at Nottingham Forest.

"The day came when Tony Waiters rang and said he wanted me back in Vancouver, and I signed off with Crewe by scoring a penalty in my final game, against York. I'd been made captain for the day, and was told that if we got a spot-kick I could take it.

"When I went upfield the York 'keeper asked me where I reckoned I'd put the ball. I told him I'd shoot to his right—but as I reminded him after I'd blasted the ball into the roof of the net, I hadn't said whether I'd be shooting high or low!"

The rest of the story is history. Bruce recalls: "I know that Liverpool watched me more than once while I was with Crewe, and other clubs were said to be keen on me, Bob Paisley was the only manager interested enough to fly to Vancouver to see me there, and Liverpool were the only club which persisted in trying to

solve the work-permit problem. So now I'm here."

Ray Clemence once let in seven goals during his early days at Scunthorpe; Bruce once let in six goals while playing in South Africa against a side which wound up as league champions. "We were drawing 2-2 at half-time, had two

**CONTINUED ON PAGE 8**

### JIMMY SAYS 'YES'

TWO more players in our first-team squad were involved in transfer talks on the eve of the new season. Brighton wanted Jimmy Case, and promoted Swansea City moved in for Colin Irwin.

Jimmy, who found himself in and out of the side last season, after Sammy Lee had nailed down a regular place, spent a few days making up his mind. Finally, he decided to leave Anfield.

Colin, who had his longest-ever run in our first team last term, flew out to join Swansea on their pre-season Yugoslav tour, then signed ... and became skipper.

**Goes down great**

# Stones
## Best Bitter
### from
## Bass North West

Stones Best Bitter

---

*Departures, new arrivals and personal accolades and milestones for current players were invariably celebrated by the matchday programme.*

*'Home Ground' revealed how they relaxed away from the pitch with shots by photographer Harry Ormesher, while another feature quizzed them about their 'Sporting Heroes'.*

*Meanwhile, 'Backroom Man' in season 1989-90 focused on former players employed in new roles at the club. Phil Thompson, Roy Evans, Ron Yeats and Steve Heighway were among those covered.*

♦ Kenny Dalglish receives his King of the Kop award from Crown Paints managing director Mr. George Campbell, before the game against West Ham.

### KING OF THE KOP AND PLAYER OF THE YEAR —THAT'S KENNY DALGLISH

LIVERPOOL scooped the pool, when the winners of the Professional Footballers' Association annual awards were made known at the post-Milk Cupfinal dinner in London last Sunday night. With four players in the top six for the Player of the Year award, and two in the top six for the Young Player of the Year award, Liverpool really hogged the limelight.

Kenny Dalglish, skipper Graeme Souness, Mark Lawrenson, Sammy Lee and Ian Rush were all candidates for one or other of the awards ... and Ian was in the running for both the Player of the Year award ... a tribute indeed to his marksmanship during the course of the season.

Kenny Dalglish had already collected a recent sponsor's man-of-the-match award at Anfield and followed up by being presented with his Crown Paints-sponsored King of the Kop award, so being in line for the top players' award put him on a hat-trick.

And while Graeme Souness and Mark Lawrenson were his rivals, along with Manchester United's Bryan Robson and Arsenal's John Hollins, Sammy Lee was challenging Ian Rush, Norman Whiteside (United), Mark Chamberlain (Stoke), Gary Mabbutt (Spurs) and Paul Walsh (Luton) for the Young Player of the Year award.

In the end, it turned out to be a Liverpool-Manchester United affair, just as it had been in the Milk Cup final the previous afternoon. And when the names of the winners were announced, this was how the players' poll had finished.

**Player of the Year:** KENNY DALGLISH.
Runner-up: Bryan Robson.
Third: Ian Rush.

**Young Player of the Year:** IAN RUSH.
Runner-up: Norman Whiteside.

Bob Paisley presented Kenny with his award and stepped up to receive a presentation himself. This was the merit award for outstanding services to football and, appropriately, it was presented to him by another former Anfield hero, Roger Hunt. Bob follows in the footsteps of previous winners Bill Shankly, Sir Matt Busby, Tom Finney and Bobby Charlton.

### AND IAN COLLECTS THE YOUNG PLAYER OF THE YEAR AWARD ...

---

Transfer news in 1981 told us Ray Clemence, Jimmy Case and Colin Irwin were moving on – with a focus on the new man between the sticks, Bruce Grobbelaar

In 1983 Kenny Dalglish and Ian Rush won the PFA Player and Young Player of the Year awards

The 'new boys on parade' in September 1981 were Bruce Grobbelaar, Mark Lawrenson and Craig Johnston

**NEW BOYS ON PARADE**

...selves with Liverpool this ...der Mark Lawrenson and ...a taste of the action in quick ...Ray Clemence moved to ...pre-season trip to Ireland ...ing, like Mark, has shown ...For all three players, also, ... European Cup comp... ...e hoping that they and ...ome the end of the season.

---

### He needs just one medal to complete the set

RAY KENNEDY didn't realise it, until he was told . . . when he played against his old club, Arsenal, in the replay of the League Cup fourth-round tie, he was making the 600th appearance of his career.

"I've never been one to keep tally on my appearances and that sort of thing," he admits, "although someone did point out to me that I'd just played my 50th European tie for Liverpool.

He's also just scored his 50th League goal for the club, and is fast heading for 400 games with us.

Ray's remarkable record with Liverpool and Arsenal means that he needs only one medal to complete a unique full set. Capped 17 times by England, at club level he has claimed five League-championship medals.

### 600 UP FOR RAY

three European Cup medals, a U.E.F.A. Cup medal, a Fairs Cup medal, a League Cup medal and an F.A. Cup medal.

All he needs now is a winner's medal in the European Cup-winners Cup . . . and he sighs and smiles at the same time as he reflects: "The trouble is, every time I've a chance of doing something about it, it seems that my club also qualifies for another, bigger competition!

"In 1971, when Arsenal won the F.A. Cup, they al... ...into the ...after 1... 1974, 1... winning... Europe...

"Ho... time le... and it ... of med...

**Despite his name** having been linked with other clubs, Ray currently has his sights on a first-team place again, after his enforced absence through suspension.

He says: "The competition here has always been tremendous, and I reckon that once a man is in possession of a place, he's so determined to keep it that the fellow trying to replace him finds it harder than ever.

"This season we've seen several new faces in the side, and I think it will become even harder to get back into the team, as the younger players make their presence felt even more.

"The senior players have seen all the glamour, and the newcomers want a taste of it. But it's still a case of making sure you do your stuff to get in and stay in. And, as I say, I reckon the man in possession has the best chance."

Looking back over some vital goals and some equally vital games, Ray still feels that one result gave him the most satisfying moment of his career—and that takes some doing in a career which has been studded with success.

"Yes, the night we won the European Cup in Rome, back in 1977, still stands out in my mind. It was the first occasion we'd taken the coveted trophy . . . and it remains the best."

Ray has also enjoyed the experience of skippering Liverpool, after an in-and-out start to his career in the early days when he had arrived from Highbury. That was back in the summer of 1974. Now he's totalled close on 300 League games for us, has scored more than 70 goals for us, and needs only a handful to chalk up a career total of 150 goals.

In January 1982 the programme celebrated Ray Kennedy's 600th game, pointing out he only needed a European Cup Winners' Cup medal to complete his personal set

---

In May 1983 Bob Paisley was given a fitting send-off as he stepped down from his role as Liverpool manager

**THE FINAL SALUTE...**

"My ultimate ambition is to take over from Bob Paisley and Liverpool as undisputed masters of the English game and, subsequently, Europe. In terms of his record, Bob is the greatest manager of all time. He took over a superb club and team, but he has taken them forward to even greater achievements. I realise I'm setting myself a hell of a target in wanting to take over, but that is the only way I can think . . ."
Manchester United manager RON ATKINSON, on the eve of the Milk Cup final.

"I watched Liverpool beating Manchester United at Wembley, and even from those televised highlights it was clear to see what a great and complete team they are . . . The record of their manager, Bob Paisley, is second to none; he has swept up the honours at home and abroad with a string of achievements that will be almost impossible to beat."
Manchester City manager JOHN BENSON, on the day Liverpool won 4-0 at Maine Road.

SCRAP METAL
MERCHANTS AND PROCESSORS
IRON · STEEL · COPPER
BRASS · LEAD · ZINC · ETC.

WESTMINSTER ROAD

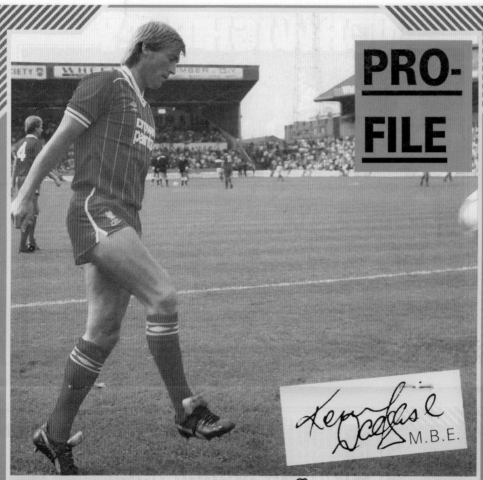

PRO-FILE

M.B.E.

LIVERPOOL'S 300-goal man, Kenny Dalglish, lets his feet do the talking for him, on the field of play. And away from the game, you rarely read quotes from the Scot whose Glaswegian accent is spiced with a dry kind of humour.

For him, this New Year began more auspiciously than did 1984, when he suffered a fractured cheekbone which put him out of the action for long weeks. The start of 1985 saw his name in the headlines again – as the recipient of an MBE in the New Year's honours list. And people in football agreed that the honour was deserved.

Kenny himself says: "It was a pleasant surprise, an honour for myself and for my family. It's also something which reflects credit on everyone who has helped me throughout my career, not least at this club.

"Liverpudlians have been great to me ever since I arrived on Merseyside, and I'll never forget the reception the fans gave me when I came back after my injury last year and went on as substitute in the European Cup-tie against Benfica.

"Equally, this is a great club – one where nobody think he's bigger than the club. Everybody works for each other, and if we haven't been on top of the world so far this season, it's not been for the want of trying."

Many people admire the scoring feats of Kenny Dalglish. He has hit 100 League goals for Liverpool, a distinction he had already achieved with his first club, Glasgow Celtic. He overtook a Dennis Law record to

> Nobody knows Kenny's qualities better than I do. We joined Celtic at the same time, played in the reserves and graduated to the senior side together. Kenny is the perfect team man—never flashy, but always working hard for everybody around him. He won't be spectacular for Liverpool. That's not his style. But he will be consistent and effective. He'll play anywhere, score goals, never stop grafting.
> —LOU MACARI, the day Kenny Dalglish signed for Liverpool in August, 1977.

become the leading British marksman in the history of the European Cup. He equalled Law's 30-goal record for Scotland in the victory over Spain last November, and he is right on course for his 100th international cap.

Away from Anfield, Kenny enjoys a game of golf – he's a 12-handicap man – and "getting home to the family." The latest addition is a German shepherd dog named Scully who arrived in the Dalglish household at the age of three weeks and is now something over seven months old.

Ask Kenny if there's one person he admires in sport, and back comes the clipped, direct answer: "I admire anyone at the top of their profession. It may seem glamorous, at times, but most of the people who reach the top make sacrifices to achieve such a position."

Ask him who he would like to have been, other than Kenny Dalglish, professional footballer, and he answers instantly: "Nobody." Then explains: "I've been very fortunate . . . I would probably have ended up otherwise being a joiner. I started out sweeping up shavings, when I was an apprentice at the trade."

Signed on August 10, 1977, for a British-record fee, Kenny has totalled close on 750 games (420 of them for Liverpool) and divided his 320 goals almost equally between Celtic and this club. They say you can make statistics tell almost any story you want; but in the case of Kenny Dalglish, the figures speak for themselves.

> Kenny Dalglish has been the No. 1 footballer for me since the day he arrived at Anfield from Glasgow Celtic . . . and at that time I was still just a nipper, going on 10. I admire him for his all-round play but what I like most is the way he manages to create space inside the 18-yard box, which gives him the time to do things. For me, that's the hallmark of a great player, and time and again Kenny Dalglish has shown that he is one.
> —Liverpool's newest recruit, WAYNE HARRISON, this week.

This 'Pro-File' feature in January 1985 focused on Kenny Dalglish, with tributes from team-mates past and present

'Candid Camera' captured the many faces of goalkeeper Bruce Grobbelaar in 1989

Steve McMahon's 'Sporting Heroes' had a strong Everton influence in 1987

'Signing in' in 1987 was John Barnes, who had already made a big impression by the Oxford United programme in September

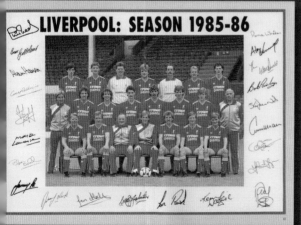

A team photo of the squad that would go on to win the double in 1986, while Ian Rush didn't quite re-sign in time to make the 1988-89 version

HOME GROUND for **Craig Johnston** means being with his family—his wife, Jenny, and daughter Chelsea, who will be a year old on October 11. Jenny is an Australian, and she was just 13 when she first met Craig. Now she's been in England seven years, and says: "It's like a second home, though I've got to admit I prefer Australia, because that IS home."

The rest of the family comprises two Border collie dogs, and apart from walking the dogs Craig enjoys his spare-time hobbies of photography and playing the guitar.

Jenny says: "Craig spends around five hours a day practising the guitar, and for someone who's self-taught, he plays it very well. He's not a TV fan, though he watches Top of the Pops and football, plus educational programmes, and he's not a do-it-yourself man, although he has done a fair bit of decorating in the house".

Craig isn't faddy about food, either, though the Johnstons are into health foods right now. But if he has a pet hate, it's queuing . . . Jenny says: "Craig won't queue for anything."

● Continued on Page 14

## HOME GROUND

★ THE first in a sparkling new series of candid-camera shots and stories featuring Liverpool players away from the match action, and on home ground. Here we put the spotlight on Craig Johnston, his wife, Jenny, and their 11-month-old daughter, Chelsea.

● Pictures by Harry Ormesher.

● Continued from Page 11

If there's one person he idolises, it's singer Bruce Springsteen, and Jenny says: "Craig went to three of his concerts during the summer, when he was supposed to be staying home."

If he hadn't been a professional footballer, is there some other sport Craig would have chosen?—Jenny chuckles and says: "Well, Craig's mother always wanted him to be a doctor—she still does, for that matter, according to the letters we get from her. But while Craig likes watching all kinds of sport, I think he would have liked to be a Rugby League player in Australia—he really loves watching the game."

What is he likely to do, when his footballing days are over?—"Well, he was pretty clever at school—he got nine O levels—and was top of his form in nearly every subject. But I don't think he'll start studying to be a doctor!

"Seriously, we'll probably go back to Australia,

● Craig Johnston pictured in the dark re[...] he has fitted up at home.

and I reckon that Craig will then try h[...] making a living from his photography[...]

One final question: why the choice o[...] for their daughter's name?—"Well, i[...] popular name, these days . . . th[...] American singer, Chelsea Brown, and [...] 'On Golden Pond' Jane Fonda w[...] Chelsea. More to the point, we chose a[...] we thought it sounded nice." And you[...] fairer than that.

ALL being well, Craig Johnston pl[...] 100th League game for Liverpool a[...] and he can look forward to many [...] because he has just signed a contrac[...] will keep him at Anfield for two more[...]

11
14

The 'Home Ground' feature in the 1985-86 season found out more about the home lives of the players, in this edition discovering Craig Johnston hates queuing but might become a photographer!

THE FIRST goal Jan Molby scored for Liverpool was against Chelsea at Stamford Bridge on December 1, 1984. In fact, it was his only goal in 13 games that season. Since then, however, he's made his name as a marksman, especially from the penalty spot, and he was ticking away a spot-kick against Chelsea here just over a year ago, on November 30, 1985.

Last season, indeed, Jan scored 10 goals from the penalty spot, after he had indicated his readiness to have a go, if called upon. Now he's the recognised penalty taker, and he's netted from the spot in all the major domestic competitions. He started out with TWO penalty goals against Tottenham Hotspur in September, 1985, his second set up by beating the 'keeper's left at Chelsea, Manchester United (in the Milk Cup), West Ham, York City (FA Cup), Watford (FA Cup), Oxford United, Birmingham and Norwich City (Screen Sport Super-Cup).

This time out he's taken his tally to nine already with penalties against Fulham, Arsenal, Charlton Athletic, Oxford United, Luton Town and, of course, FOUR in two games against Coventry City, as he shot his way into the Liverpool record books.

And goalkeepers in English football can anticipate more of the Molby brand of marksmanship, because he's pledged himself to Liverpool for four more years.

JAN MOLBY started out as a penalty marksman with a brace of goals against Spurs (here's one of them, above), and since then he's shown that he can send the 'keeper one way or the other. Below, last season's spot-kick against Chelsea.

**SPOT-ON!**

After he signed a new contract, the programme in 1986 focused on Jan Molby's expertise from the penalty spot after the Dane had notched nine already by December that season

Other 'Home Ground' subjects were snooker-playing Mark Lawrenson, Steve Nicol (who had a family portrait taken by Craig Johnston), Bruce Grobbelaar, who was happy to go back in time for his family photo, Sammy Lee, who showed off the house he was doing up, and record-playing Jim Beglin revealed how he almost ended up working for Aer Lingus

I DIDN'T need much persuading to come back . . . I spent seven years here, and I missed it a bit because of the fans and the people around the club. Juventus are a great club, and I don't regret going there—I think I'm a lot better off for the experience, though I don't know if it will make me a better player. We'll have to wait and see. Juventus looked after me well—the only problem was the language. It was a good career move, not a step backwards. But I'm happy. If I go anywhere again from Liverpool, it will be a step downwards . . . so, hopefully, I will be here to stay.

"**T**HE LIVERPOOL fans have been great to me, and I'm thankful to the club for giving me my big chance by signing me from Chester. I like to think I've repaid Liverpool's faith and that we part on even terms, as it were. I reckon I've been lucky, because I've had a lot more good times than bad, and that means I'll take with me plenty of happy memories."

That was Ian Rush talking, and his words appeared in the last issue of the Anfield Review for season 1986-87. It was the day we played Watford, and more than 40,000 fans made it an emotional afternoon as they turned up to give "Rushy" a tremendous send-off as he prepared to join Italian giants Juventus.

So the Liverpool faithful paid their tribute, with Ian repaying the compliment and responding in style by scoring the winning goal. And now the Welsh-international striker is back—in fact, it's almost as though he had never been away. His return has sparked off tremendous interest throughout the world of football, and Liverpool's coup in re-signing him upstaged all that had gone before in a close season of exceptional spending by the top clubs.

The Ian Rush story started at Chester, of course, where he first made his mark as a striker. He got his first-team chance after Ian Edwards had been sold to Wrexham, scored 14 goals in 34 League games, and signed for Liverpool eight years ago last April. His last goals for Chester—two against Colchester United on April 12, 1980—ensured that his side won 2-1, and they also snuffed out Colchester's hopes of snatching a promotion place.

Ian's boss at Chester then was Alan Oakes, who said of his transfer to Liverpool: "I reckon he can go all the way to the top." Which he did . . . an automatic choice for his country, as well as his club, and goals

galore. He claimed his first medal with Liverpool after playing in the 1981 League Cup-final replay against West Ham, scored the first senior hat-trick of his career in 18 minutes against Notts. County at Meadow Lane in January, 1982 . . . and carried on from there.

In season 1982-83 Ian rattled in four goals against Everton in a Goodison Park derby game, and thus equalled a record which had stood for 47 years. His first hat-trick in the FA Cup came in March, 1985, when he stole the headlines as we beat Barnsley—and his display prompted defender Paul Futcher to say: "Short of getting a double-barrelled shotgun and blowing off his head, I don't think he can be stopped!"

By the time he left Liverpool for Juventus, Ian had totalled 11 hat-tricks in his senior career and scored more than 220 goals. And when he returned for a couple of matches in this country, after his first season with Juventus, he showed that he had lost none of his ability, even if goals had been more difficult to come by in Italy.

Ian confessed that he had been touched by the reception he received when he appeared at Anfield last May in Alan Hansen's testimonial match. "I was happy to see the fans here still wanted me," he said. And when he played at Leeds in the John Charles-Bobby Collins testimonial game, he earned praise for the way he slotted into the English style of Soccer again.

Now he's back, and every Liverpool supporter will wish him well as he starts his career here for the second time around. Not so long ago we were saying: "Thanks for the memories, Rushy" . . . and now we're saying: "It's great to have you back where you belong."

**FACTS & FIGURES**

IAN RUSH was Liverpool's leading marksman for five seasons out of six before he moved to Juventus—and now that he's back, he'll get the chance to reply to the invitation team-boss Kenny Dalglish issued to him 16 months ago, when he said: "We're sorry to see him go—but he'll always be welcome to come back and beat Dixie Dean's record!"

It was in what seemed to be his final derby-game appearance against Everton that he scored twice, as we won 3-1, and those goals put him level with Dean, who had hit 19 in derby games. Now "Rushy" gets his chance to go at least one better.

This is how Ian Rush has scored goals for Liverpool in League games since he was signed from Chester: Season 1981-82—17; season 1982-83—24; season 1983-84—32; season 1984-85—14; season 1985-86—22; season 1986-87—30. It adds up to more than a century of goals in the First Division, 207 for Liverpool altogether in 331 appearances.

16

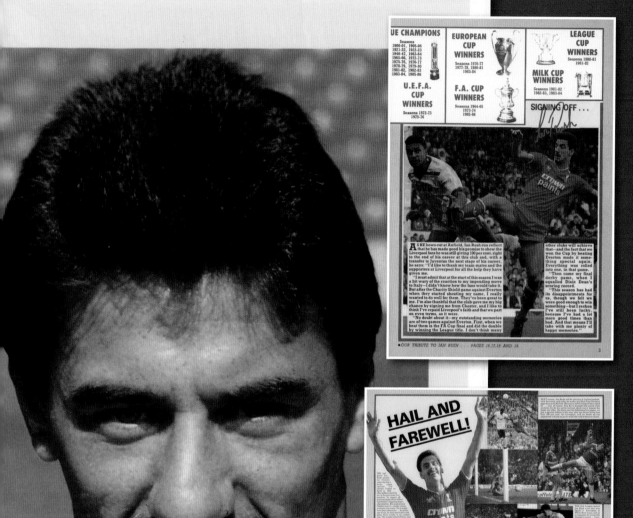

# E RUSH
# ACTION

RPOOL'S rivals were quick to react to the return of Ian Rush. Aston Villa manager **Graham Taylor** d the signing as "great news for English football . . . I don't believe it's a body blow for the of the First Division, but more of an inspiration to all of us." rmer Manchester United manager **Ron Atkinson**, now at West Brom: "A sensational coup, by standards." And Sheffield Wednesday team-boss **Howard Wilkinson**: "Any injection of quality only be in the better interests of the game . . . it's good news for British football." ddlesbrough skipper **Tony Mowbray**: "I've tried to picture playing against all the centre-forwards e First Division, but I never dreamed of Ian Rush." And Newcastle United captain **Glenn Roeder**: great for the game that he's returning."

## GOODBYE AND HELLO

Considering his impact on the pitch and the high-profile nature of his move to Juventus, the Ian Rush saga was well-covered in the programme

17

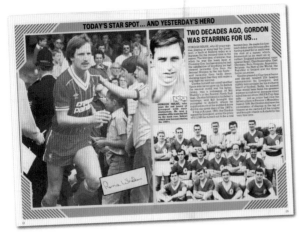

'Star Spot and Yesterday's Hero' in 1983 focused on Ronnie Whelan and Gordon Milne

'Backroom Man' Phil Thompson was in charge of the reserves in 1989

Behind-the-scenes photos of the players on a coach trip to London in 1983

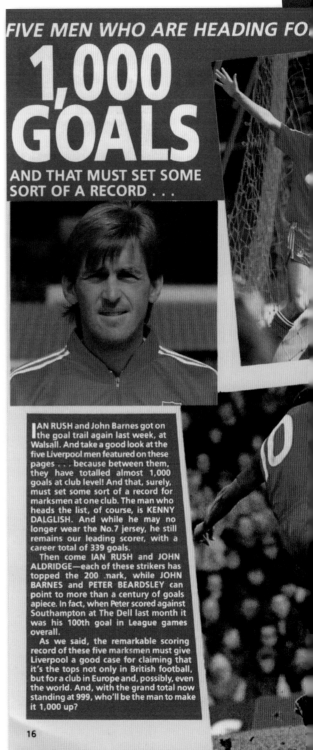

## FIVE MEN WHO ARE HEADING FO

# 1,000 GOALS

### AND THAT MUST SET SOME SORT OF A RECORD . . .

IAN RUSH and John Barnes got on the goal trail again last week, at Walsall. And take a good look at the five Liverpool men featured on these pages . . . because between them, they have totalled almost 1,000 goals at club level! And that, surely, must set some sort of a record for marksmen at one club. The man who heads the list, of course, is KENNY DALGLISH. And while he may no longer wear the No.7 jersey, he still remains our leading scorer, with a career total of 339 goals.

Then come IAN RUSH and JOHN ALDRIDGE—each of these strikers has topped the 200 mark, while JOHN BARNES and PETER BEARDSLEY can point to more than a century of goals apiece. In fact, when Peter scored against Southampton at The Dell last month it was his 100th goal in League games overall.

As we said, the remarkable scoring record of these five marksmen must give Liverpool a good case for claiming that it's the tops not only in British football, but for a club in Europe and, possibly, even the world. And, with the grand total now standing at 999, who'll be the man to make it 1,000 up?

16

17

In October 1988 Liverpool had five players – Kenny Dalglish, Ian Rush, John Aldridge, John Barnes and Peter Beardsley – who had 999 goals between them

Advertisers were clamouring to bask in Liverpool FC's reflected glory as a procession of domestic and European honours arrived in the Anfield trophy cabinets. The advertisements were something of an eclectic mix: from travel agents, hotel chains and airlines to car-dealerships and scrap-metal merchants, banks and breweries.

Remember Higson Ales with their cleverly-named matchgoers? Among them, Rock Ferry with his gold chain and quiff poised to sip his pint; the flat-capped old-timer, Albert Dock; and Ann Field, the Reds fanatic with the shaggy hairstyle, long red-and-white scarf and rosette, platform shoes and a frothy pint in hand.

Shirt sponsor Candy, most famous for washing machines and dishwashers, reminded us of the return of striker Ian Rush from Juventus with the line 'The two best imports from Italy in a long time'.

KP showed us a bag of dry roasted peanuts holding aloft a scarf with the words 'More of a mouthful than Borussia Münchengladbach'; a little later came 'More tantalising than Kenny's swerves'.

There was even space for the Manchester Programme Shop to place an advert offering LFC programme subscriptions and big matches involving the Reds.

As the 1980s drew to a close, the club's own newly-opened programme shop also featured.

British TELECOM
*Seen in all the best places.*

# 'When you've roared your throat raw, kop a pint of Higsons!'

Says Old Higsonian **Ann Field**

# WHAT A RESULT

## ARROW SIGNED UP BY LIVERPOOL

The Stars
of Anfield Road.

The Stars
of Paradise Street.

Holiday Inn LIVERPOOL
*A better place to be*

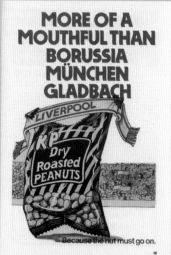

# MORE OF A MOUTHFUL THAN BORUSSIA MÜNCHEN GLADBACH

Because the nut must go on.

*Guess who'll be on top again this season?*

Candy
COOLING · LAUNDRY · DISHWASHING · COOKING

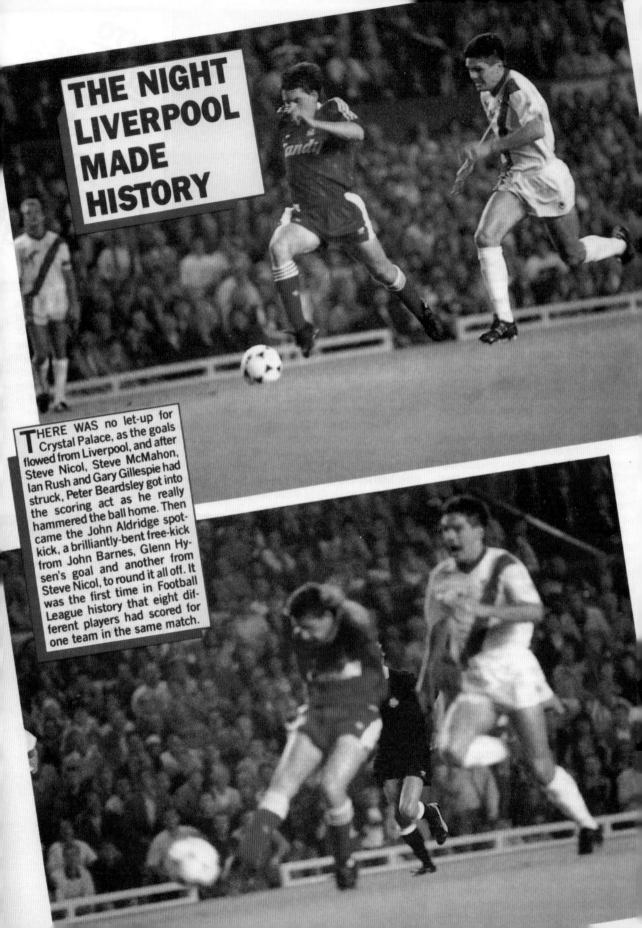

# THE NIGHT LIVERPOOL MADE HISTORY

**T**HERE WAS no let-up for Crystal Palace, as the goals flowed from Liverpool, and after Steve Nicol, Steve McMahon, Ian Rush and Gary Gillespie had struck, Peter Beardsley got into the scoring act as he really hammered the ball home. Then came the John Aldridge spot-kick, a brilliantly-bent free-kick from John Barnes, Glenn Hysen's goal and another from Steve Nicol, to round it all off. It was the first time in Football League history that eight different players had scored for one team in the same match.

# REWRITING THE RECORD BOOKS!

## AND JOHN ALDRIDGE SIGNS OFF WITH A GOAL . . .

THE TEAM that stuck nine goals past Crystal Palace without reply rewrote the Liverpool record books, because this was the club's biggest victory in First Division football, and the margin equalled our all-time record in the League – a 10-1 hammering of Rotherham Town in our Second Division days, back in 1896. And these pictures are especially memorable, because they show marksman John Aldridge stepping up to score the final goal of his career as a Liverpool player, as he strikes from the penalty spot to make it Liverpool 6, Palace 0.

## A TRIBUTE FROM KENNY DALGLISH . . .

I HAVE already commented briefly in the Anfield Review about Liverpool's decision to allow John Aldridge to move to Real Sociedad, but tonight I would like to enlarge upon this and, at the same time, pay a very real personal tribute to a player who, without any question, was popular both on and off the park.

The Liverpool fans took Aldo to their hearts, because they knew he was one of their own; and the players all had a high regard for him, both as a professional and as a person. When he went on as substitute in the game against Crystal Palace, any of his team-mates would have been happy to step aside for the occasion. And that's a measure of his all-round popularity. It was an emotional night all round, and I must admit I got a bit of a lump in my throat, so I could imagine what John Aldridge was feeling. The goals he scored for this club speak for themselves – his record as a marksman has been tremendous right through his career, and he showed he could do his stuff at every level of the game. It was a matter of very real regret to me that, in the end, we couldn't give Aldo what he deserved – a regular first-team spot. So, rather than keep him hanging on, as it were, we agreed to let him go.

It was a difficult decision to make, because here was a fellow whose heart and soul were in the club, and he was always prepared to make a contribution as a team man, rather than as an individual. But in the end, it became a question of doing what was best for everyone in the circumstances, and there were no hard feelings about it.

While John Aldridge was sorry to be going, I know that he looks upon this new chapter in his career as a challenge and – knowing him as I do – I'm sure he'll give the same kind of commitment to Real Sociedad that he gave to Liverpool. He wouldn't know how to go out there and not try 100 per cent.

I was delighted he got the chance to get into the action against Crystal Palace, and that he was also able to tuck away one final goal. He bowed out at Anfield as he had started here, and now everyone at this club wishes him every success in Spain. He can be sure there will always be a warm welcome, whenever he wants to come and pay us a visit.

## JOHN ALDRIDGE TALKS ABOUT A LOVE AFFAIR WITH LIVERPOOL:
### Pages 12 and 13

● PICTURE BY JOHN COCKS

7

---

THIS WAS quite a moment for Glenn Hysen, because he'd just scored his first goal for Liverpool – and what a header he powered into the Crystal Palace net! No wonder our Swedish international defender felt like saying: "Now how about that!"

## 9-0
Who could blame the editor of the programme in 1989 for making the most of a record-breaking 9-0 League win over Crystal Palace?

IT'S "Well done" from him and "Well done" from him, as two of Liverpool's marksmen enjoy yet another goal in the scoring spree against Crystal Palace. And here's Ian Rush congratulating Steve Nicol, who beat Palace 'keeper Perry Suckling twice on the night.

22    23

## THE TALE OF TWO 'KEEPERS

TWO PICTURES which illustrate vividly the contrasting fortunes of the two 'keepers when we played West Brom at The Hawthorns. On the right, Tony Godden sees the ball zip past him as Kenny Dalglish makes it 2-0, after Steve Nicol had opened the scoring. In all, Godden picked the ball from the net five times. Bottom right, Bruce Grobbelaar is tested ... and pulls off a spectacular save from a Derek Statham penalty. And below, you can see what Alan Kennedy thinks about Kenny's brilliant goal. More goal pictures on Pages 6 and 7.

4

5

The contrasting fortunes of goalkeepers Bruce Grobbelaar and Tony Godden were highlighted in April 1985 following the Reds' 5-0 win at West Brom the previous month

## WE'RE ON OUR WAY . . . TO WEMBLEY!

A few days before the 1986 FA Cup final, Ian Rush's semi-final double against Southampton got fans in the party mood

## ACTION REPLAY
SOME FRIENDS DROPPING IN FOR PHIL'S GAME...

MERSEYSIDE ...UNITED!

Phil Neal's testimonial in 1985 was a friendly affair as neighbours Everton provided the opposition

THE Today League game against Luton Town at Anfield needed some serious ground work before it could get under way . . . and the top picture shows the Anfield staff clearing snow from the pitch. When the action began, Ian Rush was soon in the thick of it, and causing problems for 'keeper Les Sealey.

THE run-up to our first goal as Jan Molby is about to hammer the ball home from the penalty spot, and (inset) he signals his delight as he beats Luton 'keeper Les Sealey.

The orange ball was out at an icy Anfield for the visit of Luton Town in 1987

THE second round of the Littlewoods Challenge Cup produced more than 170 goals, and clubs from the First Division scored more than 100 of them. There were some big scores by teams and some outstanding individual performances, too, with Liverpool taking pride of place by scoring 13 goals in the tie against Fulham.

That result went down in the record books, because it beat the 12-2 aggregate score by which West Ham defeated Bury three years ago, and our 10-0 result in the first leg also equalled the Hammers' success in their home leg against Bury.

The first leg against Fulham, in fact, brought us our biggest-ever victory in domestic football, and it was a personal triumph for Steve McMahon, who struck four of our goals. Here are the first half-dozen, with Ian Rush (top left picture) opening the scoring, John Wark hitting goal No.2 (centre picture), Ronnie Whelan cracking home goal No.3 (bottom left), Steve McMahon notching No.4 (top right), John Wark heading No.5 (centre) and Steve McMahon making it six (bottom right).

There were big scores by other First Division clubs in the second round, too. Sheffield Wednesday hit Jimmy Melia's Stockport County team for 10 goals without reply altogether, while Everton rattled in an aggregate nine against Newport, Tottenham Hotspur blasted Barnsley for eight, Oxford United stuck seven past Gillingham, Manchester United did the same to Port Vale, and Leicester City hit Swansea City for six.

Over the two legs Steve McMahon and Everton striker Paul Wilkinson each managed a nap hand of goals. Oxford's John Aldridge totalled four, and Tony Cottee (West Ham) and Colin Walker (Sheffield Wednesday) were hat-trick men.

6

7

There were lots of pictures of goals to choose from as a record-breaking 10-0 win against Fulham in what was then known as the Littlewoods Cup was celebrated in 1986

# CHARITY BEGINS AT HOME!

LIVERPOOL players are used to playing at Wembley Stadium . . . so used to going there, in fact, that they refer to Wembley as Anfield South. So they felt quite at home when they played Tottenham Hotspur there in the pre-season Charity Shield game. And as our three Scots — Kenny Dalglish, Alan Hansen and skipper Graeme Souness demonstrate — Charity begins at home!

A 'Jock shot' from 1982 as Liverpool's three legendary Scots, Kenny Dalglish, Alan Hansen and Graeme Souness, paraded the Charity Shield

John Wark was the scourge of Lech Poznan in 1984, scoring in the European Cup first round away leg, then following up with a hat-trick

Kenny Dalglish led the way with a hat-trick in a 5-2 win against Manchester City in December 1982, Phil Neal and Ian Rush grabbing the others

THE ANATOMY OF A GOAL . . .

In January 1985 (below) there were shots from the previous month's World Club Championship match with Independiente in Tokyo

The Norwich City issue of August 1980 carried a typical action-spread of sequential shots by club snapper Harry Ormesher, showing Kenny Dalglish scoring against Crystal Palace in the previous home game

The programme for the title decider against Arsenal in May 1989 looked back at the FA Cup final success six days earlier

**MARKING A MILESTONE**
Marathon man Phil Neal chalked up his 800th career appearance in December 1984 and made a few more before leaving the club a year later

# 800 UP!

## And Phil is still as keen as ever to add to his list of honours

ALL being well, Liverpool captain Phil Neal will make the year-end a time for celebration in a Soccer sense, because it will mark another major milestone for him . . . since he will be chalking up the 800th appearance of his two-club career.

**And that's not bad for a footballer who, 10 years ago, arrived at Anfield from Northampton Town as a virtual unknown!**

Bob Paisley's first signing—and modestly priced at around £60,000—Phil made his debut for Liverpool on November 16, 1974, in a Goodison derby game against Everton; and after missing the next three first-team matches, he was back for the Anfield game against Luton Town . . . who, as it happens, are our next opponents here, in the final Canon League game of 1984.

As Phil looks back, he can reflect on the day he made his first-team debut for Northampton as a stripling of 16, and on the time when he came close to going part-time with Kettering. Which just goes to show that in football, things can change very suddenly . . . because after Liverpool had snapped him up, his career really took off.

Some of Phil's team-mates reckon he's the biggest eater on the Anfield playing staff . . . and certainly he's had a voracious appetite for the game of football, because rarely has he missed a match since he arrived at Liverpool. The first time he was an absentee was in October, 1976, when we played a European Cup-tie against Trabzonspor; and by the start of this campaign he had totalled 400 League games for Liverpool.

Phil took his career total of appearances to 700 in April, 1983, and 12 months later,

as we headed for yet another championship, Milk Cup and European Cup success, he was being described by one of the critics as "the model player". By then, he had collected 53 caps with England, and won just about every honour going.

The departure of Graeme Souness for Italy meant that Liverpool had to find a new captain, and manager Joe Fagan looked no further than Phil Neal. As he viewed this new challenge, Phil recalled his first day at Anfield, when he was getting changed next to Ian Callaghan. "It came home to me what a model professional he was, and I determined then to follow his example," said Phil.

He equalled Phil Thompson's all-time record by claiming a seventh League-championship medal, has played in four European and four League—Milk Cup—winning sides, as well as the one which won the UEFA Cup in 1976.

What this season still holds for Liverpool is anyone's guess, but with the FA Cup and the European Cup still in our sights—not to mention the second half of the League campaign—this much is certain: Phil Neal will be as keen as ever to add to the list of honours he has achieved with this club . . . and who's to say he won't succeed?

## SPOTLIGHT ON THE NEW BOY . . . PAGES 12 AND 13

11

TODAY'S the day Bob Paisley collects his Manager of the Month award for March. And when he receives his gallon bottle of Bell's Scotch Whisky from northern sales manager David Salmon, he will chalk up a new record in the awards scheme, because it's the 17th time Bob has been a Bell's winner.

Each award has been worth a gallon bottle of Scotch, and the record number of 17 awards is broken down like this: Manager of the Year in 1976, 1977, 1979 and 1980; nine overall Manager of the Month awards; two Divisional awards; and two Special Awards in 1978 and 1981.

Sadly for us, the European Cup goes back this time . . . but the Football

**YES, THIS IS A RECORD . . .**

League Cup stays at Anfield . . . and we're all hoping that the championship of the Football League will follow.

In that case, Bob would be a front runner for the Manager of the Year award again. Meantime, he'll settle for his second award in three months, which earns him a £250 cheque to go with that gallon bottle of Scotch.

In May 1982 Bob Paisley is pictured with his record 17th Bell's manager award

# GREAT SCOTT!

★ ON THE day that Bruce Grobbelaar, the latest in a long line of goalkeepers who have made their names with Liverpool, plays his 100th game for the club, we turn the clock back 70 years and recall the signing of Elisha Scott, whom many old-timers rate the daddy of them all. He kept goal for this club from 1913 to 1934.

★ IT WAS mainly due to the great ability and service of Scott that the directors of the day decided that Liverpool's telegraphic address should be "Goalkeeper". And it's interesting to note that Scott himself—who, at 5ft. 9½in. tall, never weighed more than 10st. 3lb.—related how he might never have joined the club.

## ELISHA RECEIVED £1 . . . FOR SIGNING FOR THE SEASON

BIBLICAL names were popular when Elisha Scott was born, and he was named after his grandfather, a County Antrim farmer. At 14, he was signed by Linfield, but was deemed too small and too young, so he went to a junior club, Broadway United—and from them to Liverpool.

Even so, he might have joined Everton, to whom he was recommended by his brother, Billy (who had played for the Goodison club and who kept goal for Ireland for 10 years). But, as Elisha said later: "Everton reckoned I was too young (he was 17), the officials turned me down . . . so Billy next mentioned me to Mr. McKenna, of Liverpool, who sent a deputation (Tom Watson was one) to see me play. To my surprise, I was signed on the spot.

"Liverpool, of course, had thought I was an amateur; but Broadway put in a claim for a transfer fee on the grounds that I was a professional, and Liverpool, after making inquiries, gave them to settle the matter as much money as properly equipped their ground (known as Bog Meadow) with palings etc.

"This was Liverpool's decent way out of any possible difficulties but, had they liked to fight over it, they would possibly have got off without giving any fee, for I had an understanding with Broadway that I was to have a free transfer from them when I wanted it. "Oddly, as Elisha says, he got no wages for being a professional . . . "I merely got £1 for signing for the season."

Injury to Kenny Campbell meant Elisha made his debut at Newcastle. "I remember gazing at

IN MY early days, there was more rough play than we see in the modern game. Sometimes there were fierce fights and disputes. Rioting among spectators was not unknown. And the poor, harassed referee often had to run for his life after the match.

Now that rough and brutal play has been practically eliminated, League teams should be playing better football than ever before. But I sometimes wonder whether the game has really improved. We hear rather too much about science and speed, these days. Never forget that football is a game.
—Quote by ELISHA SCOTT.

**CONTINUED ON PAGE 12**

11

HERE'S a toast to Liverpool and success again in the European Cup . . . and it comes from arguably the club's oldest supporter. For Mrs. Nellie Arnall celebrated her 100th birthday a couple of weeks ago and this lifelong Liverpool fan attended the game against Nottingham Forest as our guest. Mrs. Arnall didn't have far to travel, either, because she lives fairly close to Anfield. So one way and another, she felt perfectly at home.

**100 UP . . . AND HERE'S A TOAST!**

Above: Harry McKeever (Littlewoods) and host Bill Cotton, sales director of Leemacochac, our sponsors for the Nottingham Forest game.

23

100-year-old Nellie Arnall celebrated her big birthday with a trip to Anfield in March 1985

In March 1983 goalkeeping great Elisha Scott was remembered

**MEET MOGLET**

MOGLET arrived at Anfield as an abandoned waif . . . but today, as stadium-manager Bert Johnson explains, she's a universal favourite. Bert says: "She was thrown under the gate as a kitten, and we took pity on her. Now she's six, has had two litters . . . and people came from all over to say they would give the kittens good homes . . . even though they were in Newcastle United's colours of black-and-white stripes." Appropriately tonight, Moglet is featured with the Milk Cup on our front cover.

Moglet, who was abandoned at Anfield as a kitten, starred in the Ipswich programme of October 1982

The first home programme of 1987-88 (below) told fans how the ground had been improved, including a new visitor centre

# A NEW VISION FOR ANFIELD

## BACK HOME
### . . . and Anfield has had a facelift

ANFIELD could become an all-seater stadium, with a capacity of 40,000 spectators, over the next couple of years or so, as Liverpool look at plans which could involve the club in a massive £6M facelift. The Kop could be replaced by a seated area before the start of season 1990-91.

Architects have already visited Anfield, and Liverpool's chief executive, Peter Robinson, says: "We hope to have the plans in front of us very soon. Safety has to be paramount, and seating is the only way to ensure that another incident such as happened at Hillsborough does not occur again."

The Kop has long been the most famous terrace in football, and there is standing room at the other end of the ground for visiting supporters. Already standing capacity has been reduced for the remainder of this season.

There are also moves to extend the Kemlyn Road stand and install up to 5,000 more seats, and the club had set itself the target of financing that for Liverpool's centenary year in 1992. Now the question is whether or not the plans can be advanced.

In the meantime, and in response to pleas from supporters of both clubs, Liverpool and Everton agreed to remove the perimeter fences at Anfield and Goodison Park. And while support expressed their approval, there have also been expressions of appreciation from families who were bereaved, and from people who became casualties, concerning the efforts of the Liverpool players and their wives to help.

Liverpool's players, and those of Nottingham Forest, visited hospitals in Sheffield, while the wives of Liverpool players, along with social workers and Salvation Army officers, were among volunteers who offered comfort to bereaved families at Anfield. Players have also attended the funerals of Hillsborough victims.

Within days of the Hillsborough disaster, the club announced plans to make Anfield all-seater. "Safety has to be paramount," insisted chief executive Peter Robinson

### OUR NEW-LOOK LINE-UP WITH CANDY

LIVERPOOL have entered into a £3M sponsorship deal with Candy, a leading Italian domestic appliance manufacturer whose UK headquarters are at Bromborough, Wirral, where most of the 600-strong, Candy-group workforce in the UK is employed. The sponsorship agreement is for three years, and starts next season.

Liverpool chairman Mr. John W. Smith, who thanked Crown Paints for their support over six years, says of the new sponsorship deal: "We look forward to a mutually-prosperous future . . . our sponsors are based on Merseyside, and the association of Liverpool and Candy can only be beneficial to the area.

"It is particularly pleasing that this sponsorship offers us all the opportunity to strengthen the links between Merseyside and Italy, where Liverpool FC already enjoys a very warm relationship

with Juventus Football Club."

Liverpool team-manager Kenny Dalglish points out that many of Candy's employees are also Liverpool supporters, and says: "It is exciting and satisfying that a Merseyside company is supporting us as we try to do our best for Merseyside. We will be pleased and proud to wear the Candy name on our shirts each time we play during the next three years."

Candy managing director Mr. David Del Seronne left says the sponsors are "thrilled to be involved with the greatest team in Europe in this way . . . we are aligning ourselves with the best in football, a club with an enormous reputation, and a by-word for integrity in sport. Equally important, Liverpool is also our local team. We are pleased to be able to make the most of the chance to bring Merseyside and Italy closer together."

Candy's sponsorship of Liverpool began in 1988, with stars of the day lining up in a new kit

In August 1985, in the aftermath of Heysel, chairman John Smith was very clear in his view that the season ahead "must mark a return to sanity"

## THE CLEAN-UP STARTS NOW!

LAST SEASON was a disaster for English football—and tragic for many innocent fans who died attending their favourite sport.

Last season must be the last of its kind—English Soccer simply cannot go through another season like it, if it is to survive as a sport.

Soccer must make itself safe and rid itself of the minority who have brought violence, hooliganism, intimidation and disgrace to far too many matches.

This season must mark the return to sanity in our sport and, with it, our eventual return to free competition with clubs abroad.

Accordingly I, and my fellow directors, want to serve notice on all who would cause trouble on or around our ground. This club has resolutely set its

### THE CHAIRMAN

face against hooligans. We are determined to stamp them out, and to this end we have taken various measures which will result in safety and public order.

In addition, we have informed the Chief Officers of Police that they have our full backing in taking firm action against anyone who steps out of line.

We give due notice that we shall fully support a determined and thorough policy of prosecution, and if those tried are found

guilty, we hope the courts will hand out heavy punishments.

As one single illustration of this, we have asked the police to eject from the ground anyone who goes on the pitch without specific authority.

No hooligan can expect any quarter on or around this ground from the club, the police and, I hope, the vast mass of decent fans who want to enjoy the game in peace, comfort and security. That is what we aim to provide for our fans. They deserve no less.

We shall, of course, expect the highest standards of conduct from our players so that they set a good example, on behalf of the club, to all on the terraces.

So, to summarise: the game we all love has got to be cleaned up. We have

### WRITES . . .

got to give every family who would like to come and enjoy themselves watching their favourite team the confidence to do so.

If we don't, it is no exaggeration to say that Soccer will simply go down the drain and cease to exist as a serious sport. THE CLEAN-UP STARTS NOW.

J. W. SMITH
CHAIRMAN

*No hooligan can expect any quarter on or around this ground . . . we have to give every family who would like to come and enjoy watching their favourite team the confidence to do so.*

# FACTS AND FIGURES 1982-1983

| | | Fixtures | Att. | Res. | 1 | 2 | 3 | 4 | 5 | 6 | 7 | 8 | 9 | 10 | 11 | 12 |
|---|---|---|---|---|---|---|---|---|---|---|---|---|---|---|---|---|
| 1982 | | | | | | | | | | | | | | | | |
| Aug | 28 | **West Bromwich A.** | 35,652 | 2-0 | Grobbelaar | **Neal** | Kennedy | Thompson | Whelan | Lawrenson | Dalglish | **Lee** | Rush | Hodgson | Souness | **Johnston** |
| | 31 | Birmingham City | 20,176 | 0-0 | Grobbelaar | Nicol | Kennedy | Thompson | Whelan | Neal | Dalglish | Lee | Rush | Hodgson | Souness | Johnston |
| Sept | 4 | Arsenal | 36,429 | 2-0 | Grobbelaar | **Neal** | Kennedy | Thompson | Lawrenson | Whelan | Dalglish | Lee | Rush | **Hodgson** | Souness | Johnston |
| | 7 | **Nottingham Forest** | 27,145 | 4-3 | Grobbelaar | Neal | Kennedy | Thompson | Lawrenson | Whelan | Dalglish | Lee | **Rush** | **Hodgson**(2) | **Souness** | Johnston |
| | 11 | **Luton Town** | 33,694 | 3-3 | Grobbelaar | Neal | Kennedy | Thompson | Lawrenson | Whelan | Dalglish | Lee | **Rush** | Hodgson | **Souness** | **Johnston** |
| | 14 | Dundalk Euro C 1 (1L) | 16,500 | 4-1 | Grobbelaar | Neal | Kennedy | Thompson | **Whelan**(2) | Hansen | Dalglish | Lee | **Rush** | **Hodgson** | Souness | — |
| | 18 | Swansea City | 20,322 | 3-0 | Grobbelaar | Neal | Kennedy | Thompson | Lawrenson | **Johnston** | Dalglish | Lee | **Rush**(2) | Hodgson | Souness | **McDermott** |
| | 25 | **Southampton** | 32,996 | 5-0 | Grobbelaar | Neal | Kennedy | Thompson | **Whelan**(2) | **Lawrenson**(2) | Dalglish | Lee | Rush | Johnston | **Souness** | **McDermott** |
| | 28 | **Dundalk Euro C.1 (2L)** | 12,021 | 1-0 | Grobbelaar | Neal | Kennedy | Thompson | **Whelan** | Hansen | Dalglish | Lee | Johnston | McDermott | Souness | — |
| Oct | 2 | Ipswich Town | 24,342 | 0-1 | Grobbelaar | Neal | Kennedy | Thompson | Whelan | Hansen | Dalglish | Lee | Johnston | Lawrenson | Souness | **Fairclough** |
| | 5 | Ipswich T Milk Cup 2 (1L) | 19,329 | 2-1 | Grobbelaar | Neal | Kennedy | Thompson | Whelan | Hansen | Dalglish | Lee | **Rush**(2) | Lawrenson | Souness | Johnston |
| | 9 | West Ham United | 32,500 | 1-3 | Grobbelaar | Neal | Kennedy | Thompson | Whelan | Hansen | Dalglish | Lee | Rush | Lawrenson | **Souness** | **Johnston** |
| | 16 | **Manchester United** | 40,853 | 0-0 | Grobbelaar | Neal | Kennedy | Thompson | Whelan | Hansen | Dalglish | Lee | Rush | Lawrenson | Souness | Johnston |
| | 19 | J K Helsinki Euro C 2 (1L) | 5,722 | 0-1 | Grobbelaar | Neal | Kennedy | Thompson | Whelan | Hansen | Dalglish | Lee | Rush | Hodgson | Souness | — |
| | 23 | Stoke City | 29,411 | 1-1 | Grobbelaar | Neal | Kennedy | Thompson | Whelan | Hansen | Dalglish | Lee | Rush | **Lawrenson** | Souness | Hodgson |
| | 26 | **Ipswich T. Milk Cup 2 (2L)** | 17,698 | 2-0 | Grobbelaar | Neal | Kennedy | Thompson | **Whelan** | Hansen | Dalglish | Lee | Rush | **Lawrenson** | Souness | **Hodgson** |
| | 30 | **Brighton & Hove A.** | 27,929 | 3-1 | Grobbelaar | Neal | Kennedy | Thompson | Whelan | Hansen | **Dalglish**(2) | Lee | Rush | **Lawrenson** | Souness | Hodgson |
| Nov | 2 | **J. K. Helsinki Euro C.2 (2L)** | 16,434 | 5-0 | Grobbelaar | **Neal** | **Kennedy**(2) | Thompson | **Johnston** | Hansen | **Dalglish** | Lee | Rush | Lawrenson | Souness | **Hodgson** |
| | 6 | Everton | 52,741 | 5-0 | Grobbelaar | Neal | Kennedy | Thompson | Johnston | Hansen | Dalglish | Lee | **Rush**(4) | **Lawrenson** | Souness | **Hodgson** |
| | 10 | **Rotherham Utd. Milk Cup 3** | 20,412 | 1-0 | Grobbelaar | Neal | Kennedy | Thompson | **Johnston** | Hansen | Hodgson | Lee | Rush | Lawrenson | Souness | Fairclough |
| | 13 | **Coventry City** | 27,890 | 4-0 | Grobbelaar | Neal | Kennedy | Thompson | Johnston | Hansen | **Dalglish** | Lee | **Rush**(3) | Lawrenson | Souness | Hodgson |
| | 20 | Notts County (F.A 1) | 16,914 | 2-1 | Grobbelaar | Neal | Kennedy | Thompson | **Johnston** | Hansen | **Dalglish** | Lee | Rush | Lawrenson | Souness | Fairclough |
| | 27 | **Tottenham H.** | 40,691 | 3-0 | Grobbelaar | **Neal** | Kennedy | Thompson | Johnston | Hansen | **Dalglish**(2) | Lee | Rush | Lawrenson | Souness | Fairclough |
| | 30 | **Norwich City Milk Cup 4** | 13,235 | 2-0 | Grobbelaar | Neal | Kennedy | Thompson | Johnston | Hansen | Dalglish | Lee | Rush | **Lawrenson** | Souness | **Fairclough**(1) |
| Dec | 4 | Norwich City | 22,909 | 0-1 | Grobbelaar | Neal | Kennedy | Thompson | Johnston | Hansen | Dalglish | Lee | Rush | Lawrenson | Souness | Whelan |
| | 11 | **Watford** (F.A 2) | 36,690 | 3-1 | Grobbelaar | **Neal**(2) | Kennedy | Thompson | Whelan | Hansen | Dalglish | Lee | **Rush** | Johnston | Souness | **Fairclough** |
| | 18 | Aston Villa | 34,568 | 4-2 | Grobbelaar | Neal | **Kennedy** | Lawrenson | Whelan | Hansen | **Dalglish** | Lee | **Rush** | **Hodgson** | Souness | Fairclough |
| | 27 | **Manchester City** | 44,664 | 5-2 | Grobbelaar | **Neal** | Kennedy | Lawrenson | Whelan | Hansen | **Dalglish**(3) | Lee | **Rush** | Hodgson | Souness | **Fairclough** |
| | 28 | Sunderland | 35,041 | 0-0 | Grobbelaar | Neal | Kennedy | Lawrenson | Nicol | Hansen | Dalglish | Lee | Rush | Hodgson | Souness | Fairclough |
| 1983 | | | | | | | | | | | | | | | | |
| Jan | 1 | **Notts County** | 33,643 | 5-1 | Grobbelaar | Neal | Kennedy | Lawrenson | Johnston | Hansen | **Dalglish**(2) | Lee | **Rush**(3) | Hodgson | Souness | Fairclough |
| | 3 | **Arsenal** | 37,713 | 3-1 | Grobbelaar | Neal | Kennedy | Lawrenson | Johnston | Hansen | **Dalglish** | Lee | **Rush** | Hodgson | **Souness** | Fairclough |
| | 8 | Blackburn R (F A 3) | 21,967 | 2-1 | Grobbelaar | Neal | Kennedy | Lawrenson | Johnston | Hansen | Dalglish | Lee | **Rush** | **Hodgson** | Souness | Fairclough |
| | 15 | West Bromwich A | 24,560 | 1-0 | Grobbelaar | Neal | Kennedy | Lawrenson | Johnston | Hansen | Dalglish | Lee | **Rush** | Hodgson | Souness | Whelan |
| | 18 | **West Ham Milk Cup 5** | 23,953 | 2-1 | Grobbelaar | Neal | Kennedy | Lawrenson | Johnston | Hansen | Dalglish | Lee | Rush | **Hodgson** | **Souness** | **Whelan** |
| | 22 | **Birmingham City** | 30,986 | 1-0 | Grobbelaar | **Neal** | Kennedy | Lawrenson | Whelan | Hansen | Dalglish | Lee | Johnston | Hodgson | Souness | Fairclough |
| | 29 | **Stoke City (F.A.4)** | 36,666 | 2-0 | Grobbelaar | Neal | Kennedy | Lawrenson | Johnston | Hansen | **Dalglish** | Lee | **Rush** | Hodgson | Souness | Whelan |
| Feb | 5 | Luton Town | 18,434 | 3-1 | Grobbelaar | Neal | **Kennedy** | Lawrenson | Johnston | Hansen | Dalglish | Lee | **Rush** | Hodgson | **Souness** | **Whelan** |
| | 8 | **Burnley Milk Cup S.F. (1L)** | 33,520 | 3-0 | Grobbelaar | **Neal** | Kennedy | Lawrenson | Johnston | Hansen | Dalglish | Lee | Rush | **Hodgson** | **Souness** | **Whelan** |
| | 12 | **Ipswich Town** | 34,976 | 1-0 | Grobbelaar | Neal | Kennedy | Lawrenson | Johnston | Hansen | **Dalglish** | Lee | Rush | Hodgson | Souness | **Whelan** |
| | 15 | Burnley Milk Cup S.F (2L) | 20,000 | 0-1 | Grobbelaar | Neal | Kennedy | Lawrenson | Johnston | Hansen | Dalglish | Lee | Rush | Hodgson | Souness | **Whelan** |
| | 20 | **Brighton (F.A.5)** | 44,868 | 1-2 | Grobbelaar | Neal | Kennedy | Lawrenson | Whelan | Hansen | Dalglish | Lee | Rush | Hodgson | Souness | **Johnston**(1) |
| | 26 | Manchester United | 57,397 | 1-1 | Grobbelaar | Neal | Kennedy | Thompson | Whelan | Lawrenson | **Dalglish** | Lee | Rush | Johnston | Souness | Hodgson |
| Mar | 2 | Widzew Lodz Eur C 3 (1L) | 45,531 | 0-2 | Grobbelaar | Neal | Kennedy | Lawrenson | Whelan | Hansen | Dalglish | Lee | Rush | Johnston | Souness | **Hodgson** |
| | 5 | **Stoke City** | 30,020 | 5-1 | Grobbelaar | **Neal** | Kennedy | Lawrenson | Whelan | Hansen | **Dalglish**(2) | Lee | Rush | **Johnston** | **Souness** | Hodgson |
| | 12 | **West Ham** | 28,511 | 3-0 | Grobbelaar | Neal | Kennedy | Lawrenson | Whelan | Hansen | Dalglish | **Lee** | **Rush** | Johnston | Souness | Hodgson |
| | 16 | **Widzew Lodz Eur. C. 3 (2L)** | 44,494 | 3-2 | Grobbelaar | **Neal** | Kennedy | Lawrenson | Whelan | Hansen | **Hodgson** | Lee | **Rush** | Johnston | Souness | F'clough/Th'son |
| | 19 | **Everton** | 44,737 | 0-0 | Grobbelaar | Neal | Kennedy | Lawrenson | Whelan | Hansen | Dalglish | Lee | Rush | Johnston | Souness | Hodgson |
| | 22 | Brighton & Hove A | 25,030 | 2-2 | Grobbelaar | Neal | Kennedy | Thompson | Whelan | Hansen | Dalglish | Lee | **Rush**(2) | Johnston | Lawrenson | Fairclough |
| | 26 | Man. Utd (M C F Wem) | 100,000 | 2-1 | Grobbelaar | Neal | **Kennedy** | Lawrenson | **Whelan** | Hansen | Dalglish | Lee | Rush | Johnston | Souness | Fairclough |
| Apr | 2 | **Sunderland** | 35,821 | 1-0 | Grobbelaar | Neal | Kennedy | Lawrenson | Whelan | Hansen | Dalglish | Lee | Fairclough | Johnston | **Souness** | Nicol |
| | 4 | Manchester City | 35,647 | 4-0 | Grobbelaar | Neal | **Kennedy** | Lawrenson | Whelan | Hansen | Dalglish | Lee | **Fairclough**(2) | Johnston | **Souness** | Nicol |
| | 9 | **Swansea City** | 30,010 | 3-0 | Grobbelaar | Neal | Kennedy | Lawrenson | Whelan | Hansen | Dalglish | **Lee** | **Rush** | Johnston | Souness | **Fairclough**(1) |
| | 12 | Coventry City | 14,821 | 0-0 | Grobbelaar | Neal | Kennedy | Lawrenson | Whelan | Hansen | Dalglish | Lee | Rush | Johnston | Souness | Fairclough |
| | 16 | Southampton (F A S F) | 25,578 | 2-3 | Grobbelaar | Neal | Kennedy | Lawrenson | Whelan | Hansen | **Dalglish** | Lee | Fairclough | **Johnston** | Souness | **Hodgson** |
| | 23 | **Norwich City** | 37,022 | 0-2 | Grobbelaar | Neal | Kennedy | Lawrenson | Whelan | Hansen | Dalglish | Lee | Hodgson | Johnston | Souness | Fairclough |
| | 30 | Tottenham Hotspur | 44,907 | 0-2 | Grobbelaar | Neal | Kennedy | Thompson | Lawrenson | Hansen | Dalglish | Johnston | Rush | Hodgson | Souness | Nicol |
| May | 2 | Nottingham Forest | 25,107 | 0-1 | Grobbelaar | Neal | Kennedy | Thompson | Lawrenson | Hansen | Dalglish | Johnston | Rush | Hodgson | Souness | **Nicol** |
| | 7 | **Aston Villa** | | | | | | | | | | | | | | |
| | 14 | Watford | | | | | | | | | | | | | | |
| | 21 | F A Cup Final | | | | | | | | | | | | | | |

Home matches in **bold** type  Goalscorers in **bold** type  Substitute in **bold** type when called on

Fixtures copyright Football League Limited and must not be reproduced without permission of Football League Limited

**Average home league gate: 34,581**
**Aggregate home league gate: 691,623**

## DIVISION 1 TABLE

(Up to and including Monday, 2nd May, 1983)

| | P. | W. | D. | L. | Goals F. | Goals A. | Pts |
|---|---|---|---|---|---|---|---|
| LIVERPOOL | 40 | 24 | 9 | 7 | 85 | 34 | 81 |
| Watford | 40 | 21 | 5 | 14 | 71 | 53 | 68 |
| Nottingham Forest | 40 | 19 | 8 | 13 | 57 | 48 | 65 |
| Manchester United | 38 | 17 | 13 | 8 | 49 | 32 | 64 |
| Aston Villa | 39 | 20 | 4 | 15 | 58 | 46 | 64 |
| Everton | 40 | 17 | 9 | 14 | 60 | 46 | 60 |
| Tottenham H. | 38 | 17 | 9 | 12 | 57 | 46 | 60 |
| Southampton | 39 | 15 | 12 | 12 | 53 | 54 | 57 |
| Stoke City | 40 | 16 | 9 | 15 | 52 | 57 | 57 |
| West Ham United | 38 | 17 | 4 | 17 | 59 | 56 | 55 |
| Arsenal | 39 | 15 | 10 | 14 | 54 | 52 | 55 |
| Ipswich Town | 39 | 14 | 12 | 13 | 59 | 46 | 54 |
| West Brom. A. | 40 | 14 | 11 | 15 | 49 | 48 | 53 |
| Norwich City | 40 | 13 | 11 | 16 | 48 | 55 | 50 |
| Notts. County | 40 | 14 | 7 | 19 | 52 | 67 | 49 |
| Luton Town | 39 | 11 | 13 | 15 | 63 | 76 | 46 |
| Sunderland | 40 | 11 | 13 | 16 | 46 | 60 | 46 |
| Coventry City | 40 | 12 | 9 | 19 | 43 | 55 | 45 |
| Birmingham City | 40 | 10 | 14 | 16 | 37 | 55 | 44 |
| Manchester City | 40 | 12 | 8 | 20 | 46 | 69 | 44 |
| Brighton | 40 | 9 | 13 | 18 | 37 | 65 | 40 |
| Swansea City | 39 | 9 | 11 | 19 | 48 | 63 | 38 |

## CENTRAL LEAGUE TABLE

(Up to and including Monday, 2nd May, 1983)

| | P. | W. | D. | L. | Goals F. | Goals A. | Pts |
|---|---|---|---|---|---|---|---|
| Everton | 28 | 16 | 7 | 5 | 43 | 18 | 39 |
| West Brom. A. | 27 | 16 | 6 | 5 | 42 | 16 | 38 |
| Aston Villa | 25 | 16 | 3 | 6 | 60 | 28 | 35 |
| Manchester Utd. | 25 | 15 | 4 | 6 | 50 | 23 | 34 |
| Stoke City | 27 | 13 | 6 | 8 | 48 | 47 | 32 |
| LIVERPOOL | 26 | 13 | 5 | 8 | 50 | 32 | 31 |
| Sheffield Wed. | 24 | 13 | 4 | 7 | 46 | 31 | 30 |
| Blackburn Rovers | 27 | 12 | 4 | 11 | 47 | 49 | 28 |
| Newcastle United | 24 | 9 | 7 | 8 | 33 | 29 | 25 |
| Sheffield United | 25 | 10 | 5 | 10 | 32 | 39 | 25 |
| Leeds United | 23 | 5 | 9 | 9 | 22 | 35 | 19 |
| Bury | 25 | 7 | 5 | 13 | 35 | 51 | 19 |
| Coventry City | 26 | 6 | 4 | 16 | 27 | 52 | 16 |
| Blackpool | 26 | 7 | 1 | 18 | 33 | 63 | 15 |
| Huddersfield T. | 27 | 5 | 4 | 18 | 28 | 48 | 14 |
| Wolves | 27 | 3 | 6 | 18 | 18 | 54 | 12 |

## GAMES AND GOALS AT A GLANCE...

### Season 1982-83

| | League games | League goals | Other games | Other goals |
|---|---|---|---|---|
| Bruce Grobbelaar | 40 | — | 17 | — |
| Phil Neal | 40 | 8 | 17 | 3 |
| Mark Lawrenson | 38 | 5 | 14 | 2 |
| Steve Nicol | 3 | — | — | — |
| Phil Thompson | 22 | — | 9 | — |
| Alan Hansen | 32 | — | 17 | — |
| Alan Kennedy | 40 | 3 | 17 | 3 |
| Terry McDermott | 2 | — | 1 | — |
| Graeme Souness | 39 | 9 | 17 | 2 |
| Ronnie Whelan | 28 | 2 | 12 | 5 |
| Sammy Lee | 38 | 3 | 17 | — |
| Craig Johnston | 30 | 5 | 13 | 3 |
| Kenny Dalglish | 40 | 18 | 15 | 2 |
| Ian Rush | 34 | 24 | 16 | 6 |
| David Hodgson | 21 | 4 | 13 | 5 |
| David Fairclough | 8 | 3 | 3 | 1 |

## CENTRAL LEAGUE GAMES AND GOALS

### Appearances Season 1982-83

Wardle 26, Halsall 20; Kelly 19; Savage 4; McGregor 26; Harper 25; McDermott 1; King 25; Russel 2; Jewell 24; Gayle 8; Nicol 20; Kilshaw 7; Fairclough 16; Foley 18; Hodgson 7; Johnston 2, Seagraves 15, Bleasdale 6; Warriner 1; Rodon 2; Wharton 3; Whelan 1, Thompson 6; McLean 3; Leather 2; Ablett 3; West 3, Beglin 1.

### Goals

McDermott 1, Jewel 9; Gayle 3, Fairclough 15; Hodgson 4; McGregor 2, Bleasdale 2; Halsall 3; Rodon 2; Wharton 1; Foley 3, Harper 2; Nicol 1; West 1, Thompson 1.

● **The Top Twenty records played on this ground are loaned by Robert Crease Music Stores, 14 County Road, Liverpool 4.**

## CAREER DETAILS

| | League games | League goals | F.A Cup games | F.A Cup goals | League Cup games | League Cup goals | European games | European goals | For Liverpool Total games | Liverpool Total goals | Career Totals games | Career Totals goals |
|---|---|---|---|---|---|---|---|---|---|---|---|---|
| Grobbelaar | 82 | 0 | 6 | 0 | 18 | 0 | 12 | 0 | 118 | 0 | 142 | 1 |
| | *24* | *1* | | | | | | | | | | |
| Kennedy | 167 | 12 | 14 | 0 | 29 | 2 | 20 | 3 | 230 | 17 | 426 | 28 |
| | *158* | *9* | *21* | | *17* | *2* | *2* | | | | | |
| Neal | 357 | 35 | 36 | 2 | 49 | 3 | 56 | 10 | 498 | 50 | 706 | 81 |
| | *188* | *29* | *11* | *1* | *9* | *1* | | | | | | |
| Lawrenson | 77 | 7 | 6 | 1 | 18 | 2 | 9 | 1 | 110 | 11 | 364 | 20 |
| | *225* | *7* | *12* | *1* | *17* | *1* | | | | | | |
| Thompson | 338 | 8 | 36 | 0 | 43 | 1 | 50 | 5 | 467 | 14 | 467 | 14 |
| Hansen | 193 | 6 | 21 | 2 | 32 | 1 | 27 | 3 | 273 | 12 | 381 | 19 |
| | *86* | *6* | *4* | | *18* | *1* | | | | | | |
| Souness | 208 | 31 | 22 | 2 | 33 | 4 | 29 | 6 | 292 | 43 | 497 | 65 |
| | *176* | *22* | *13* | | *15* | | *1* | | | | | |
| Lee | 121 | 10 | 11 | 0 | 21 | 2 | 20 | 3 | 173 | 15 | 173 | 15 |
| Dalglish | 242 | 96 | 24 | 12 | 42 | 22 | 35 | 8 | 343 | 138 | 667 | 305 |
| | *204* | *112* | *31* | *11* | *60* | *35* | *29* | *9* | | | | |
| Johnston | 49 | 11 | 4 | 1 | 8 | 2 | 5 | 1 | 66 | 15 | 143 | 31 |
| | *64* | *16* | *6* | *0* | *6* | *0* | | | | | | |
| Rush | 73 | 41 | 6 | 5 | 19 | 10 | 10 | 4 | 108 | 60 | 147 | 77 |
| | *34* | *14* | *5* | *3* | *0* | *0* | *0* | *0* | | | | |
| Whelan | 61 | 13 | 4 | 0 | 14 | 5 | 9 | 4 | 88 | 22 | 88 | 22 |
| Fairclough | 98 | 34 | 15 | 4 | 21 | 10 | 19 | 7 | 153 | 55 | 153 | 55 |
| Hodgson | 21 | 4 | 3 | 1 | 5 | 2 | 5 | 2 | 34 | 9 | 174 | 29 |
| | *125* | *16* | *9* | *4* | *6* | *0* | *0* | *0* | | | | |

*Italic figures indicate statistics with other clubs*

## CENTRAL LEAGUE

### FIXTURES 1982/83

DIVISION 1

| | | | | F. | A. |
|---|---|---|---|---|---|
| 1982 | | | | | |
| Sept. | 4 | Aston Villa | a | 3 | 1 |
| | 18 | **West Brom. A.** | h | 1 | 1 |
| | 30 | Newcastle Utd | a | 1 | 2 |
| Oct. | 9 | **Stoke City** | h | 3 | 0 |
| | 27 | Stoke City | a | 2 | 2 |
| | 30 | Everton | a | 0 | 0 |
| Nov. | 6 | Manchester Utd. | a | 1 | 6 |
| | 10 | Sheffield Utd. | a | 1 | 0 |
| | 20 | **Blackburn R.** | h | 3 | 1 |
| | 23 | Sheffield Wed. | a | 0 | 1 |
| Dec | 14 | Coventry C. | a | 3 | 2 |
| | 18 | **Aston Villa** | h | 1 | 2 |
| 1983 | | | | | |
| Jan | 11 | **Blackpool** | h | 3 | 1 |
| | 15 | **Manchester Utd.** | h | 1 | 2 |
| | 24 | **Wolverhampton W.** | h | 2 | 0 |
| | 27 | Leeds Utd | a | 4 | 1 |
| Feb | 1 | **Huddersfield T.** | h | 2 | 1 |
| | 14 | **Sheffield Utd.** | h | 4 | 0 |
| | 26 | **Everton** | h | 0 | 1 |
| Mar | 14 | Wolverhampton W. | a | 7 | 1 |
| | 30 | Blackburn R. | a | 0 | 1 |
| Apr. | 11 | **Bury** | h | 3 | 0 |
| | 13 | Bury | a | 1 | 1 |
| | 15 | West Brom. A. | a | 1 | 3 |
| | 19 | **Sheffield Wed.** | h | 3 | 2 |
| | 26 | **Leeds Utd.** | h | 0 | 0 |
| May | 3 | **Coventry City** | h | | |
| | 11 | Blackpool | a | | |
| | 14 | **Newcastle Utd.** | h | | |
| | 17 | Huddersfield T. | a | | |

## FINAL MATCH AT ANFIELD

**CENTRAL LEAGUE**

**LIVERPOOL v. NEWCASTLE UTD.**

**Saturday, 14th May, 1983**
**Kick-off 2 p.m.**

How the opposition pages looked for the visit of Everton in October 1984

The big threats from Tottenham Hotspur were picked out in September 1985

The BBC's John Motson interviews Ray Clemence in 1980, nine years after his first commentary at Anfield

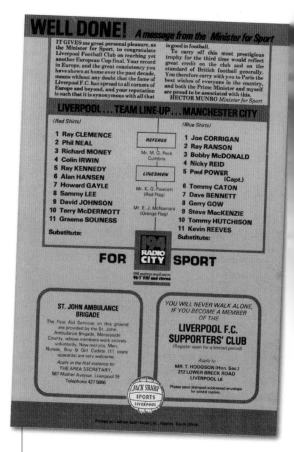

The Minister for Sport passed on his congratulations after the Reds reached the 1981 European Cup final

*Giovanni Trapattoni . . . under pressure, but he delivered the goods.*

# SPOTLIGHT ON OUR SUPER-CUP RIVALS

## WILL IT BECOME JUVENTUS A FOUR-TIME AFFAIR?

LIVERPOOL and Italian champions Juventus could be meeting FOUR times during the course of this season—in home-and-away legs of the Super Cup . . . and twice again, if their paths should cross in the European Champions' Cup. For "Juve", one of the great clubs of Italian football, replaced AS Roma as entrants into the European Cup this season.

Having won the Cup-winners Cup last spring, and thus qualified to meet Liverpool in the Super Cup, Juventus will be especially keen to avenge Roma's defeat in the final of the Champions' Cup—not because they are great allies, but because Juventus themselves are still striving to claim the European Cup for the first time . . . although they have carried off the Italian League title eight times in the past 11 years, and a record 21 times altogether.

Juventus have competed on the European circuit on two dozen occasions, but from this lengthy involvement they can point to only two successes—the UEFA Cup in 1977 and the Cup-winners Cup last spring. They were losing finalists to Ajax in the European Cup (1973), and in the Fairs Cup to Leeds United (1971) and Ferencvaros (1965).

Oddly enough, there is a strong English connection with Juventus, because in the first place they got their nickname of "The Zebras" from their famous black-and-white striped shirts . . . yet the original strip was taken to Italy by one of the players who, while visiting Nottingham, was struck by the colours worn by Notts. County.

The balance of power in Italian football has swung between Turin and Milan, with Torino, Inter-Milan and AC Milan being the great rivals of Juventus. After the second world war, it was Torino who dominated the Italian championship scene for four years; then came the Superga air crash which decimated the Torino team, and "Juve" became top dogs again.

During that spell, they were coached by an Englishman, Jesse Carver. Then came a Welshman who was to be an idol of the Juventus fans during the late 1950's . . . the legendary John Charles. He starred with the Argentinian ace, Enrico Omar Sivori, and an Italian named Giampiero Boniperti . . . who later became president of the club.

Juventus, of course, have the backing of the wealthy Agnelli family, who own the Fiat motor corporation, and they have splashed money around like water, at times. It was "Juve" who signed Liam Brady from Arsenal; then he moved to Sampdoria as the Turin club added two more foreign names to an illustrious list of home-based players.

Six of them—Dino Zoff, Claudio Gentile, Antonio Cabrini, Gaetano Scirea, Marco Tardelli and Paolo Rossi—had starred for Italy in the 1982 World Cup in Spain; yet "Juve" still went out and spent £2M on French star Michel Platini and the Polish flyer, Zbigniew Boniek.

Not surprisingly, there was tremendous pressure last season on coach Giovanni Trapattoni to produce the goods, in the shape of the Cup-winners Cup. And he duly obliged.

Now Juventus, having claimed the UEFA Cup and the Cup-winners Cup, and having failed in one final of the Champions' Cup, want to make up for that omission by carrying off the European Cup to make it a hat-trick . . . and, for good measure, to get the better of Liverpool in the Super Cup, so that they can claim to be the No. 1 club not merely in Italy, but in Europe.

### TROPHY TIME FOR JOE

**JOE FAGAN takes a bow at Anfield today as he officially receives his Manager of the Year trophy, and we are sure all our supporters will give him a special cheer. Joe came top of the poll when the name of the Manager of the Year was announced at the star-studded function in Glasgow last May, and he received his cheque from Mr. Raymond Miquel, chairman and managing director of Bell's Scotch whisky, who will also make the presentation today. Now the Manager of the Year trophy goes on show at Anfield alongside the European Cup, the Canon League-championship trophy, the Milk Cup and the Central League-championship trophy.**

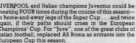

*Paolo Rossi . . . one of six Juventus players who starred for Italy in the 1982 World Cup.*

*Michel Platini (above right) and Zbigniew Boniek (centre) . . . they cost a cool £2M.*

12 13

The QPR programme from September 1984 speculated that the Reds could meet Juventus four times that season and focused on some star players – but it turned out being twice, in the European Super Cup and the European Cup final

SEASON 1892-93 LANCASHIRE LEAGUE

LIVERPOOL 8 HIGHER WALTON 0

# The Years of Glory . . .

★ *HERE'S a new, four-page series which makes compelling reading for every Liverpool supporter, because it spotlights the years of success . . . going right back to season 1892-93, when we finished as champions of the Lancashire League.*

★ *IN EACH issue of the Anfield Review we shall feature a season or seasons in which Liverpool won a major trophy—sometimes several trophies. And it will build up into a dossier which will be well worth keeping. So don't miss it!*

**LIVERPOOL have long been recognised as one of the biggest names in football . . . yet there was a time when we couldn't command sufficient support to claim a place in the League! Our application to join the newly-formed Second Division was turned down, and so we became members of the Lancashire League.**

It wasn't long, however, before Liverpool were making the powers-that-be sit up and take notice, for by the end of that first season (1892-93) in the Lancashire League we had finished as champions and, for good measure, carried off the Liverpool District Cup. The title success was achieved at the expense of Blackpool, who had to settle for second place on goal average.

Liverpool still had a price to pay for their success, though, because after both trophies had been stolen (shades of the FA Cup and the World Cup!) the club had to fork out £130 to replace them.

Liverpool kicked off by winning seven of the first eight games in the Lancashire League during season 1892-93, starting with an 8-0 home victory over Higher Walton—in front of a crowd of just 200! For the visit of Bury the gate shot up to 4,000, and Liverpool obliged by scoring four goals without reply.

Malcolm McVean . . . he was Liverpool's first ever League marksman when he scored against Middlesbrough Ironopolis on September 2, 1893.

There were some homely names among the opposition . . . West Manchester, Fleetwood, Rossendale, South Shore, Heywood Central, Fairfield, Nelson, Blackpool and Southport, while Liverpool's team was laced with Scottish names such as McQue, McVean, McQueen, McCartney and Hannah.

Joe McQue was signed from Celtic, Malcolm McVean from Third Lanark; Matt McQueen and his brother, Hugh, arrived from Leith Athletic; and John McCartney came from Paisley St. Mirren, while Andrew Hannah had played in three Scottish Cup finals for Renton.

In 22 matches Liverpool scored 66 goals, and McVean was a regular marksman, as were two other players, Wyllie and Miller, who hit three goals in a 5-0 win at Higher Walton and five at home against Fleetwood, while Wyllie and Miller each hit hat-tricks in qualifying rounds of the FA Cup, against Newtown and Nantwich, respectively. Miller, indeed totalled 27 goals in 28 appearances, and Wyllie scored 16 overall.

In League games on home ground, Liverpool scored 44 goals and conceded only seven, as we won 10 games and lost only to Blackpool, while away we won seven, drew two and lost two matches, which meant that we finished up with 36 points and a better goal average than Blackpool—who, ironically, did the double over us.

Hannah, McLean and Wyllie were ever-presents, and McVean, McBride, Miller, McQue and McCartney missed only a handful of games, while the McQueen brothers each totalled 16 appearances.

So there was a definite tartan flavour about that first championship success, and it carried over to the following season when the League's Second Division was extended and Liverpool gained admission at the expense of Bootle.

Season 1893-94 was a repeat of the previous term, in that Liverpool wound up as champions again, this time claiming a place in the top flight of the Football League, and the Scottish clan was well in evidence throughout the 28-match campaign.

It was a remarkable season, by any standards, because we never lost a match—our record read like this: Played 28, won 22, drawn 6. All 14 home games ended in victory for Liverpool, who scored 46 goals and conceded a miserly half-dozen, while away the goals tally was 31 to 12. So we totalled 50 points and finished at the top of the Second Division.

McLean was the only ever-present, though the McQueen brothers each missed only one game, and McQue, Hannah, McBride and McVean also totalled more than a score of appearances apiece, while McOwen—a goalkeeper who had played just one League match the previous season—was first choice on 23 occasions this time out.

In the Lancashire League, gates had ranged from 150 (away against Higher Walton) to 8,000 (at Bury), though the average was around 2,000. In the Second Division, the attendance figures illustrated the increased interest in Liverpool with 8,000 against Small Heath, home and away, and similar-sized crowds against Newcastle United, Notts. County and Burton Swifts, while other gates varied between 3,000 and 6,000.

Clubs then in the Second Division included Arsenal (beaten 5-0 away), Ardwick, Lincoln City, Burton Swifts, Walsall Town, Crewe Alexandra, Northwich Victoria, Grimsby Town and Burslem Port Vale, who were one of the few clubs to manage even a draw with us.

The first Liverpool marksmen of the League campaign were McVean and McQue, while Stott hit a hat-trick in our best win of the season—6-0 against Middlesbrough—and McVean scored all three goals against Walsall. Stott was Liverpool's leading marksman, with 14 goals, while Hugh McQueen totalled 11 and a newcomer, Henderson, hit 10.

### SEASON 1892-93 LANCASHIRE LEAGUE

Blackpool (h) 0-2, (a) 0-3
Bury (h) 4-0, (a) 0-3
Fairfield (h) 5-0, (a) 4-1
Fleetwood (h) 7-0, (a) 4-1
Heywood Central (h) 6-2, (a) 2-1
Higher Walton (h) 8-0, (a) 5-0
Nelson (h) 3-0, (a) 3-2
Rossendale United (h) 2-1, (a) 2-0
Southport (h) 2-0, (a) 1-1
South Shore (h) 4-1, (a) 1-0
West Manchester (h) 3-1, (a) 0-0

**• Liverpool finished as champions**

### WE'RE LOOKING FOR A BIT OF HISTORY

LIVERPOOL Football Club is looking for slices of history to go on display in the **ANFIELD VISITOR CENTRE**, due to be opened later this year. The Centre, to be housed in a first-floor suite currently under construction as part of a development scheme within the Main Stand, will trace our history since the club's *formation* in 1892.

We now wish to appeal to supporters of the club and followers of football in general with a request for any unusual or significant souvenirs and items of memorabilia associated with the club.

Mr. Peter Robinson, Chief Executive of Liverpool Football Club, says: "We would be most interested to hear from anyone prepared to donate or loan items to the Visitor Centre. Naturally it will contain many of the trophies we have won over the years, but it is our aim to make the Centre as interesting and varied as possible. I feel sure there must be many items tucked away in cupboards or attics whose owners would be happy to see them enjoyed by a wider public."

Mr. Robinson requests any fans who can help to send written details only to Liverpool F.C. (Visitor Centre), Anfield Road, Liverpool L4 0TH . . . but NOT to send items themselves, at this stage.

6 7

'The Years of Glory' feature in 1987 homed in on the campaigns when the Reds won silverware, starting with the 1892-93 season, when the Lancashire League title was claimed

# FROM HILLSBOROUGH

### IT'S BACK TO BUSINESS
#### IN THE BARCLAYS LEAGUE . . .

LIVERPOOL got back to business in the Barclays League with a derby game against Everton at Goodison Park, and while the result was important, more important still was the fact that the fans of both teams showed they could remain united, even though they retained the traditional, friendly rivalry. These pictures by John Cocks capture the scene, and the mood.

**THE KOP THANKS YOU ALL  WE NEVER WALKED ALONE**

LIKE thousands of Liverpool
*Anfield Review* photogra
John Cocks travelled to
borough for the FA Cup semi
against Nottingham Forest, he
to see us win – and record a v
on film. Instead, after the first
flurry of match action, he f
himself taking pictures he had

**STANDING STRONG**

While the programme captures moments of joy, it also has the sad duty of reflecting moments of despair, as it did after the Hillsborough disaster of 1989

expected to take. Once home, still numbed by what he had seen, he was saying: "I don't even know what I've got in the camera."

He did recall seeing Liverpool fans helping to save lives as they hauled people to safety, and he recalled the ambulance wheels churning across the green grass of the Hillsborough pitch.

On the Sunday, instinct impelled him to go to Anfield . . . to find that the fans had had the same idea. They made their way to the ground and started to pay their homage to the dead by leaving flowers, scarves and other favours. And 72 hours after the disaster, John Cocks was at Anfield again, to record the scene. "The goalmouth had been turned into a kind of shrine," he said simply. "People just never stopped coming, to pay their last respects."

# CHAPTER 6

# 1990s

A decade of huge change saw fluctuating fortunes on the pitch
and a matchday programme that had many identities

**T**he Nineties changed the game of football forever. Commissioned in the aftermath of Hillsborough, the Taylor Report recommended the implementation of all-seater stadia. The 14th FIFA World Cup finals, otherwise known as Italia 90, spawned a new generation of magazines, fanzines and TV shows. And along came the Premier League.

LFC's matchday programme also changed and even toyed with a 'landscape' format – as if turned on its side – at the start of the decade only to revert to the traditional 'portrait'.

It was variously entitled 'LIVERPOOL' then 'REDS' and combined colour photography throughout with a graphical blend of reds, yellows and greens and predominantly black-on-white typography.

At the end of 1990-91 the Reds finished runners-up to Arsenal in a season of three LFC managers: Kenny Dalglish, Ronnie Moran (as caretaker) and Graeme Souness. Two days after an FA Cup fifth-round replay at Everton had finished 4-4, Dalglish resigned and Moran oversaw first-team duties until the appointment of Souness in April 1991.

Liverpool were sixth at the end of 1991-92 – their lowest position since 1964-65 – but there was an FA Cup final triumph over Sunderland at Wembley with Souness back in the dugout four weeks after heart surgery. The goals were scored by Michael Thomas, a Souness signing, and Ian Rush with his fifth in three final appearances.

At the start of the following season – the first in the newly-formed Premier League – Anfield's new Centenary Stand was officially opened as LFC celebrated its 100th birthday. The Reds again had to settle for sixth place in the league, lost domestic cup-tie replays to Crystal Palace and Bolton Wanderers and went out of the European Cup Winners' Cup against Spartak Moscow.

Season 1993-94 brought an eighth-place finish, exits from the League Cup and FA Cup after replays against Wimbledon and Bristol City, and Souness ultimately replaced as boss by Roy Evans. But there were brighter moments too: in September teenage striker Robbie Fowler scored on his debut, against Fulham in the League Cup, and in January the Reds roared back from three down to draw with Manchester United at Anfield, with Nigel Clough scoring two goals.

The season's end saw the 'Kop's Last Stand' as it made way for a new all-seater structure, with Norwich City's 1-0 win doing little to spoil the celebrations on Saturday 30 April 1994.

Within 12 months Evans had struck silver: Liverpool beat Bolton in the Coca-Cola Cup final in April 1995 with Steve McManaman on target twice. His team then finished fourth as Kenny Dalglish's Blackburn Rovers pipped Manchester United to the title, while Fowler was LFC's top-scorer with 31 goals in all competitions.

Ahead of the 1994-95 season, with football and music sharing the limelight, rival bands Oasis and Blur released singles on the same day in what was dubbed 'The Battle of Britpop'. The staging of the European Championships in England the following summer – to a soundtrack by Frank Skinner, David Baddiel and Lightning Seeds frontman (and Reds fan) Ian Brodie – would only fuel the game's popularity.

Spearheaded by new signing Stan Collymore and goal-machine Fowler, the Reds played some thrilling football in

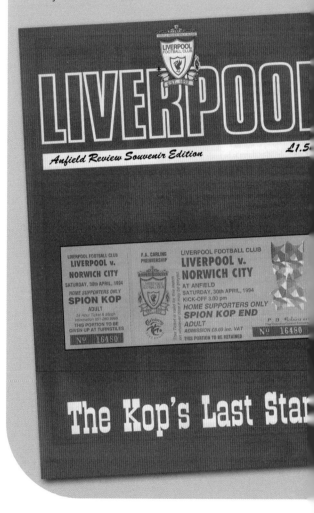

This was the unique cover produced to mark the last home game in front of the standing Kop in April 1994 when Norwic City were the visitors

1995-96, finishing third and narrowly losing in the FA Cup fina April featured one of the greatest games in Premier League history: Liverpool 4 Newcastle United 3, settled by Collymore': last-gasp strike in front of the Kop.

Less than a year on, history repeated itself, this time Fowle rescuing the Reds after the Magpies – by then with Kenny Dalglish in charge – had come back from three down. Liverpc were fourth in the 1996-97 table and reached the last four of the Cup Winners' Cup where at Anfield they almost overturn a 3-0 first-leg deficit against Paris St-Germain.

In 1997 the matchday programme also paid tribute to the late Stan Liversedge, its editor for 20 years until his retiremer in 1991.

Meanwhile, a new striking sensation was taking football by storm: Michael Owen. In 1997-98 he'd find the net 18 times in the league for third-placed Liverpool and would score a

## The Premier Leaguers

PAUL STEWART, Liverpool's £2.5million signing (inset) arrived too late to be included on the official team group for the launch of the FA Premier League. This is how they line up:

Back Row, left to right; Jan Molby, Nicky Tanner, Mike Hooper, David Burrows, Bruce Grobbelaar, Mark Walters, Rob Jones.

Middle Row, left to right; Ronnie Moran, David Burrows, Michael Thomas, Istvan Kozma, Barry Venison (now with Newcastle United), Ronny Rosenthal, Ray Houghton (now with Aston Villa), Steve McManaman, Phil Boersma, Roy Evans.

Front Row, left to right: Mike Marsh, Dean Saunders, Steve Nicol, Graeme Souness (manager), Mark Wright (captain), Ian Rush, Ronnie Whelan.

Picture: JOHN COCKS

ANFIELD REVIEW

## Fond farewell to old favourites

FORMER favourites Ray Houghton and Barry Venison were the two big-name transfers from Anfield in the close season.

Ray joined Aston Villa and manager Ron Atkinson for £900,000 and Barry went to Kevin Keegan at Newcastle United for £250,000.

Liverpool will soon be facing wily Ray in his new claret and sky-blue shirt. They play at Aston Villa on September 19.

For Barry, North-East born, it meant a sentimental journey home, although he had played previously for Newcastle's great rivals, Sunderland, and captained them in a Milk Cup Final against Norwich City in 1984-85 season at the age of 21. His main objective is to help the well-supported Geordies into the Premier League.

Both will be fondly remembered at Anfield and the club wishes them well in their new ventures.

CLUBCALL

17

6

Following his death two weeks earlier, one of the club's greatest-ever servants, Bob Paisley, was on the cover of the Charlton programme in February 1996

wonder-goal against Argentina at the 1998 World Cup finals, scorching through their defence to fire home.

Back at Anfield a statue of Bill Shankly was unveiled in December 1997, in front of Bill's widow Nessie, and in April 1999 it was Bob Paisley who was honoured with a new 'Gateway' featuring three European Cups.

The Reds had slipped to seventh in the 1998-99 season which saw French coach Gerard Houllier made joint-boss with Roy Evans. Their managers' notes in the matchday programme were diplomatically called 'Evans & Houllier: In Discussion'. Mixed results led to the former standing down with Houllier now in sole charge.

A new name commanded the headlines after Liverpool's 4-1 home victory over Sheffield Wednesday in the Premier League in December 1999: midfielder and local lad Steven Gerrard, who scored his debut goal for LFC.

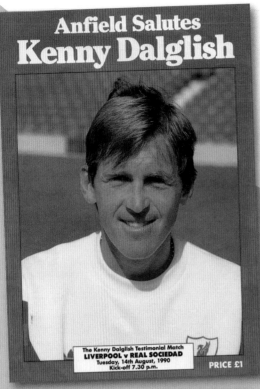

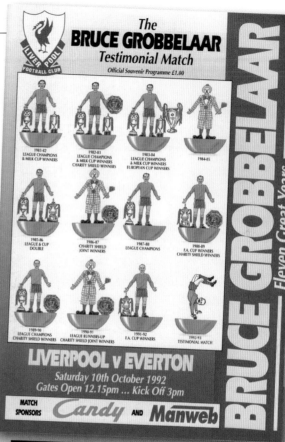

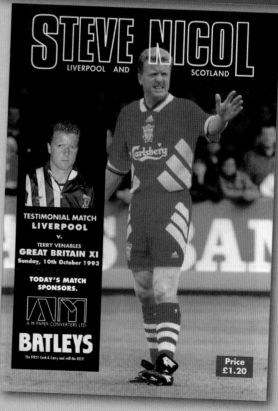

Big names with testimonials at Anfield in the 1990s included Kenny Dalglish, Bruce Grobbelaar, Ronnie Whelan and Steve Nicol

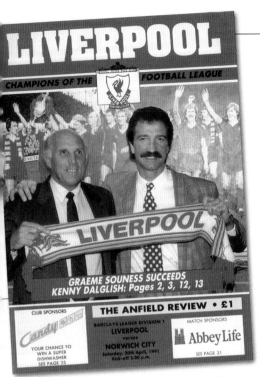

A delighted Graeme Souness was on the cover of the Norwich programme in April 1991, having succeeded Kenny Dalglish as Liverpool manager

The first programme of 1992, against Sheffield United, was a chance to celebrate Liverpool's centenary year using a black-and-white image of the pioneers of the club

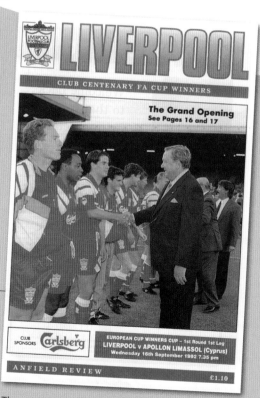

The cover image of the Apollon Limassol programme featured UEFA president Lennart Johansson, who'd been at Anfield to officially open the Centenary Stand

*Production issues in the early part of the 1990-91 season saw the short-lived landscape format replaced in late November with the more familiar portrait version. It came with a slight name-change: from 'Anfield Review' to 'The Anfield Review'.*

*The following season, 1991-92, the pin-stripe cover lasted till October when it was replaced with three distinctive stripes to reflect the new Adidas shirt worn by the players, while at the start of 1992 a new LFC crest appeared on the cover to mark the start of the club's centenary year.*

*Programme line-ups on the back cover changed with the new era of the Premier League; gone were the straightforward listings of 1 to 11 and substitute and in came squad numbers and tick-boxes for fans at the match to note the starting XI.*

*Great club stalwarts received testimonials during this era. Programmes for these matches had a different look and feel as they were not produced by the usual programme team.*

The 1994-95 covers had the word 'REDS' overlaying a full-page image − and this one from April used a picture of Ian Rush lifting the newly-acquired Coca-Cola Cup

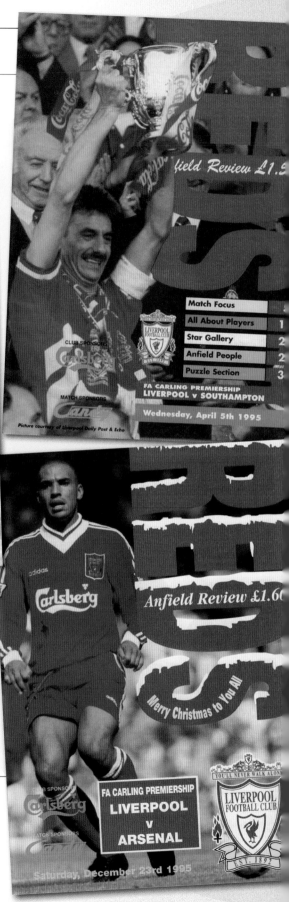

Roy Evans and Mike Walker were pictured ahead of their first Merseyside derby as managers − and it was the Liverpool boss who had bragging rights after a 2-1 win in March 1994

This pre-Christmas cover in December 1995 for the visit of Arsenal featured Stan Collymore and a smattering of snow!

Bob Paisley's wife Jessie was on the cover of the Aston Villa programme following the unveiling of the Paisley Gateway in April 1999

Phil Babb was wearing the famed ecru-coloured away shirt on the cover of the derby programme in October 1996

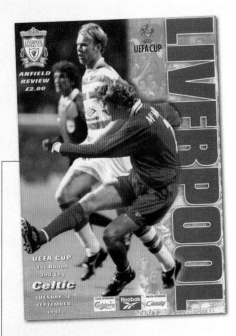

Steve McManaman was in action on the cover of the UEFA Cup programme as the Reds faced Celtic in the first round in September 1997

Shanks was the cover star when the Reds hosted Coventry City in December 1999, 40 years after his first game in charge

*No fewer than four Liverpool managers plus a 'caretaker' provided the manager's notes during the decade. Programme editor Stan Liversedge, at the last minute, 'guested' as the full impact of Kenny Dalglish's resignation was noted in 1991 and when the programme announced that Ronnie Moran had "been confirmed as the man in charge of Liverpool team affairs until the end of the season," the column was temporarily replaced with 'Barclays League Scene'.*

*'The Graeme Souness Verdict' was introduced upon the appointment of the former Reds midfielder as boss, followed three years later by 'Manager's View' with Roy Evans.*

*Then a major restructure of managerial duties during the close-season of 1998 brought the first joint-manager column between Evans and Gerard Houllier. It was short-lived and the latter ultimately imparted his sole views under his own name.*

★ *THE FOLLOWING is a statement from the chairman of Liverpool Football Club, Mr NOEL WHITE, concerning the resignation of Kenny Dalglish as team manager. The message is addressed primarily to all Liverpool supporters and it conveys the feelings of everyone at the club.*

IT WAS with very real regret that we learned of the decision by Kenny Dalglish to resign as team manager, and let me say straight away that I know all our supporters will share this regret with us. I would like to assure our supporters that we did everything in our power to try to persuade him to change his mind, and to continue to do the job which he had done with such conspicuous success during the last five years or so.

However, he made it clear – and I know he would tell you this himself – that he was determined to give up active participation in professional football, and he has also assured us that we could do nothing to alter his decision to resign.

I cannot emphasise too strongly to our supporters that we had no wish to see Kenny Dalglish leave the club he has served so long and so loyally – in fact, I rate myself as one of his greatest fans. But, at the end of the day, there was only one thing that we could do, and that was to respect his wishes and accept his decision as being irrevocable.

This being so, it remains only for us at Liverpool to wish him every success in the future, and I know that in saying this I am speaking for every Liverpool fan. Liverpool Football Club and Kenny Dalglish have parted on the most amicable terms, and I can say without hesitation that there will always be a warm welcome for him here at Anfield.

As a player, he gave this club outstanding service, and as team manager his contribution has been no less noteworthy. As I said when announcing the news of his departure, Ronnie Moran has taken over as acting manager, and there are few people who know more about the workings of this club. Ronnie has served Liverpool in one capacity or another for close on 40 years, and he has been first-team coach for the past eight years. As he undertakes his new responsibility, I know that you will wish him well.

**SCENE 1**

GRAEME SOUNESS has succeeded Kenny Dalglish as the team manager of Liverpool Football Club – and in doing so, he renews an association which began when he moved from Middlesbrough to Anfield in January, 1978.

As Graeme Souness orchestrated the moves from midfield – remember the goal he created for Kenny Dalglish in the 1978 European Cup final against FC Bruges at Wembley? – so Liverpool collected the silverware. There were five League championships, including a hat-trick from 1982 to 1984. The European Cup came to Anfield three times, the League-Milk Cup, as it was then, four times in a row ... and when we beat Everton in a Maine Road-final replay, it was a Graeme Souness goal that was the match-winner.

He also scored one of our penalty goals in the famous European Cup-final shoot-out against AS Roma in 1984, and then he made his departure after 352 appearances and 56 goals for Liverpool, as he took up a new challenge by joining Italian-club Sampdoria. Two years later he was back in British football as he took over as team boss of Glasgow Rangers, whom he has steered to three League titles (with a fourth looking probable) and four Skol League Cup successes.

The Rangers manager – 38 next month – said when he signed in at Anfield in 1978: "Any player would give his right arm to play for Liverpool." Three years later, he was wearing the captain's armband and saying: "It is the biggest honour I have had in my career." While with Liverpool, Graeme Souness became a regular visitor to Wembley, and his career as a Scotland international also flourished ... and now he is back at Anfield, to take up the challenge of leading Liverpool on to new glories. Every Liverpool fan will wish him well.

**THE GLORY YEARS: PAGES 12 & 13**

Chairman Noel White made a statement in the Arsenal programme in 1991 regarding the surprise resignation of Kenny Dalglish

By the time the Reds played Norwich in April 1991, the club were ready to announce the appointment of Graeme Souness as manager

# BARCLAYS LEAGUE

## SPOTLIGHT ON THE MANAGERS
### AND GRAEME SOUNESS says . . .

I CANNOT put into words the feelings that I have had in the last week. I could come out with many old clichés but I just want to say IT'S GREAT TO BE BACK.

As I am sure you have read, it is not my intention to make big changes. There is a wealth of experience here in Ronnie Moran, Roy Evans and the rest of the staff, which I intend to call upon when required. Why change a formula which has been the most successful in the history of British Football.

My philosophy is very simple. I demand that my players give 100% to Liverpool Football Club every time they cross that white line We all know it is impossible for us to play well every game, but if I get that 100% commitment I can ask for no more.

The players here have got to realise what an honour it is to play for this Football Club – the most famous and the most successful Football Club in the world.

You can never make any promises in Football, but what I can say is that every effort will be made to maintain the standards this Club has set in the past.

As a player here I fully understood and accepted the disciplines and responsibilities that go with being a Liverpool player and I fully expect that those who follow will also be equally committed to the cause.

Our immediate aim is to win the League Championship and, whilst matters are not entirely in our own hands, we will strive to achieve our objective. In football anything can happen and in my book there is not such a thing as a lost cause.

2   *Anfield Review*

## HE'S BACK AND THIS TIME AS 'THE BOSS'

Liverpool supporters are regarded throughout Europe as the most passionate and knowledgeable spectators in the game. When I played here the support was vital to our performances. A player never means to make a bad pass or to make what appears to be an obvious mistake. I know it is hard to contain criticism at that particular time, because you the supporter some-

times becomes frustrated, but at the end of the day we all want the same thing – continued success for Liverpool Football Club. I would ask you to please get behind the team, especially in the run-in to the Championship. Your very special kind of support is vital!

Graeme Souness addresses the fans and asks for their support ahead of the Crystal Palace match on 23 April 1991

# Liverpool Football Club

# EVANS & HOULLIER

## IN DISCUSSION

**G**OOD evening and welcome to Anfield for our prestigious Pirelli Cup clash with Inter Milan.

The pre-season preparations so far have been really pleasing. The lads have looked sharp and lively in the training sessions, while the match fitness has improved game by game. We have one more match after this one, against Celtic at Parkhead this weekend, and that will undoubtedly be another stern test for us which is exactly what we need.

There have been a few additions to the squad since last season. Steve Staunton needs no introduction to Liverpool fans following his previous spell with the club, Sean Dundee has settled in really well and has looked lively in training, while Vegard Heggem has also quickly made himself at home.

We are still looking to strengthen and it is no secret that we would like to bring in another defender before the start of the season. It's difficult to get players in of the quality we demand, but we will keep persevering and hope we can further improve our squad in the near future.

Of course there has been a major change to the management structure since last season and this is our first opportunity, as joint team managers, to explain the thinking behind the new appointment which was announced in July.

Finishing third last season in the Premiership table wasn't a bad performance overall, but it could have been better. It was felt that an addition to the management team would strengthen the club and help us take the next step which is lifting the championship.

We know the idea of joint managers is new in the English game, but it isn't considered unusual at all in Europe and we believe this is a partnership to relish, not one to fear.

For this partnership to be successful, and for it to get the desired results, then of course we need to be able to work together and bounce ideas off each other. The important thing is that we share the same philosophies on how the game should be played and we have already built up a good relationship in the few months we have been in contact. We both feel this can work.

Neither of us has an ego and any decisions taken will be in the best interests of Liverpool Football Club. Of course there are going to be times when we have different opinions - that is only natural because we can't agree on everything - and when those times arise we will sit down

## *'Decisions taken will be in the best interests of the Club'*

and talk through the situation before coming to a joint decision.

There are people who have been sceptical about this partnership, and of course we understand the concerns. But we are convinced it can be successful and so let's all be positive about what lies ahead.

We are looking to the future and we firmly believe this is the way forward. Liverpool has always been a forward thinking club and that has again been demonstrated by this decision to appoint joint managers.

As always, the important thing is going to be what happens on the field over the course of the season. We are the team behind the team and we believe we have a squad of players capable of going all the way this season.

**LIVERPOOL CLUB CALL 0891 121 184 - FIND OUT WHAT'S GOING ON!** 3

*Calls cost 50p per minute at all times*

The first joint-manager column produced by Roy Evans and Gerard Houllier came in August 1998

# Gerard Houllier

**G**OOD afternoon and welcome to Anfield for our Premiership clash with Leeds United. The last couple of days have been very emotional for everybody connected with the club and I am particularly sad that my joint managerial partnership with Roy Evans wasn't the success we hoped it would be.

We tried our very best to make it work but in the end we had to accept that it wasn't working as we had anticipated. I would have liked Roy to have stayed longer, but at the same time I respect his decision to leave.

My relationship with him was fine and he is a truly wonderful man. His integrity, commitment and concern for the club was tremendous.

The message he left with me was: "Gerard, tell the players to keep their heads up, and tell them to keep working their socks off for Liverpool Football Club."

After being appointed team manager, I wanted an assistant who had a Liverpool heart. Phil Thompson was recommended to me and I am delighted to welcome him back to the club.

As a successful former player and coach, I'm sure he will be a valuable addition to the backroom team.

We know the situation at the moment is not ideal. We have had some poor results and under-achieved. The fans are unhappy and I understand their frustrations.

Our objective is get back on a winning track as soon as possible and that will only happen with lots of effort and total commitment.

We need new players and have been assured by the

0891 121 184    Liverpool Club Ca

Roy Evans left his role as joint-manager and in November 1998 Gerard Houllier explained the new approach

Things were a lot different in February 1994 as Evans described his joy and pride at taking his place in the Anfield hotseat

## MANAGER'S VIEW          By ROY EVANS

**T**ODAY'S game against Coventry City is my first at Anfield as manager and the pride I feel is almost indescribable.

I am a Liverpool lad. I stood on the Kop as a youngster and understand the football expectations of all our supporters.

Let me say here and now, though, that I appreciated the efforts of my predecessor, Graeme Souness, and am sorry that things did not work out for him.

His dedication to the job could never be questioned. He wanted the Club to win everything in sight. The staff wish him well and we hope that he enjoys success in his next venture.

The major team responsibility is now mine, however, and our army of followers will be asking what Roy Evans can offer. Well, I have been in the game too long to make reckless promises, but I will demand 100 per cent effort from every player who wears the red shirt.

High standards we have known will be the yardstick for the future and Liverpool will always be investigating the top end of the transfer market, squad strengthening is never out of

# I demand 100 per cent from everyone who wears the red shirt

our minds, but I will be sensible with money.

It was almost 30 years ago when I was presented to manager Bill Shankly as a 15-year-old prospect and the respect I had for that man was ultimate.

"You are joining the greatest club in the world" he told me in his office. I believed him then, and I believe it now. We have the best supporters, too, and I hope that a new and very

happy marriage has begun.

The job holds no fears for me. Good and experienced men are around me at all levels and I recognise the magnitude of the task. But I am in charge of my own destiny and have come to terms with the demands of the job.

I know the feelings of the people who support us. Like them, I have experienced the triumphs and the heartbreaks at Anfield.

I came from a similar background to a lot of our supporters and we have a common bond – success for the Club. We must aim to win every remaining game this season and, at the same time, make our assessments in readiness for the one to follow.

Our 2–2 draw at Norwich City was well earned, but we let ourselves down at Southampton and Leeds. We did not defend well at The Dell and let ourselves chasing a 4–0 deficit. At Elland Road we paid dearly for two mistakes.

I extend a warm welcome to Coventry City today and their manager, our former player, Phil Neal. He won a sackful of medals with Liverpool and will know we hunger for more.

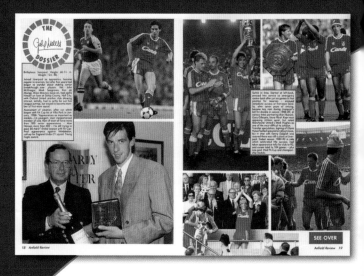

'The Dossier', usually over four pages, covered a different member of the first-team squad in each issue: a gallery of images with a brief career history and quotes from those in the game. Its replacement, 'Centre Stage', ran for two seasons – a double-page revealing a player's favourite meal, hobby, actress, TV show etc. Later, 'Star Gallery' delved into their horoscopes.

Ex-players weren't neglected, with 'Reds to Remember' a series in which Ronnie Moran recounted some of the stars he'd worked with. Kevin Keegan, he said, "oozed enthusiasm and determination." Craig Johnston "had strength and pace – he could whip crosses over for Kenny Dalglish and Ian Rush and also score goals." Alan Kennedy "maintained top fitness, he had a good turn of speed and could certainly strike a ball." Joey Jones "had a hatred of losing and would have played for Liverpool for nothing."

Another 'Dossier' featured Glenn Hysen and focused on his career, including his first Reds goal – against Crystal Palace

# in person

**NEWCOMER** Steven Gerrard began the season hoping to play as many games as possible for Liverpool's youth teams – but now his sights are set much higher.

A crop of injuries and suspensions forced boss Gerard Houllier to hand the youngster his first taste of senior action, and eighteen year old Gerrard confirmed his undoubted promise with performances which offer much encouragement for the future.

He says: "The manager has given me my chance in the side, and I am really pleased that it has come so early. I am training on a full time basis with the boys now and I can only improve as a result.

"I can't pretend I expected to be in the first team squad so soon but I have done my best in the games I have played so far and I think the manager has been pleased with me. I don't think I have looked out of place in the first team."

> ❝ I have been a Liverpool fan all my life and have always dreamt of playing at Anfield ❞

Gerrard made his debut in the last couple of minutes of Liverpool's recent Anfield clash with Blackburn before being named in the starting line-up for the following games against Tottenham and Celta Vigo.

His display against the Spanish side in the second leg of the UEFA Cup tie earned him the man of the match award and left him revelling in the fact that he had realised a boyhood dream. He says: "I have been a Liverpool fan all my life and have always dreamt of playing at Anfield. The good thing about this club is that they do give youngsters a chance in the side, even though they have the money to spend millions of pounds on new players.

"I only played a couple of minutes against Blackburn but it was still a great experience for me. The game against Celta Vigo was just amazing and from a personal point of view I enjoyed the game immensely.

"It was a pity we couldn't get the result we wanted but we did our best and gave it everything we had.

"Some people said I was the best player on the night which was obviously nice to hear.

"Everything has happened really quickly for me this season but I am loving every minute of it. It's a great buzz to walk around the city and to be recognised by the supporters.

"I'm still just a young lad though and I know that when the boss has everyone fit I probably won't be in the side, but he knows what I am capable of doing and at the moment that is the important thing for me."

**STEVE GERRARD . . . Man of the Match against Celta Vigo**

Gerrard has been on Liverpool's books since the age of nine and is the latest in a long line of players to successfully come through the club's Centre of Excellence and make the step up into the first team.

At the age of sixteen he sustained a foot injury which sidelined him from the game for the best part of twelve months, but he has recovered from that set-back and has since earned international recognition with England at youth level.

He says: "I love the club and I would like to stay here for the rest of my career.

"I started this season playing in the Academy League and I just wanted to get as many games under my belt as I could.

"I then started playing in some of the reserve games and it was nice to make that step-up. It is hard to believe that I have since also gone into the first team.

"Playing in the first team is a great experience and now that I have sampled what it is all about I want to do it again and again.

"I have just tried my best in all the matches to far and that is all I can do. I am certainly at the best place to learn about the game."

Gerrard is competing for a position in the centre of midfield with players of the calibre of England stars Paul Ince and Jamie Redknapp, and he admits he is fortunate to have such players around to help him learn.

He says: "At the moment I am just finding my feet at first team level. It is all new to me and so I am thankful that I can work alongside top class players every day to try and improve my game.

"The competition for places in the midfield is very strong and I realise that when everyone is fit I probably won't be included in the starting line-up.

"There are internationals all over the place such as Ince, Redknapp, McManaman and Berger, along with plenty of other players who aren't in the side at the moment.

"It is a tough job getting into the team, but my aim between now and the end of the season is to play as many games as possible, to carry on improving and to steer clear of injuries.

"I am going to keep my feet on the ground because I am not the sort of person to get big headed about anything that has happened. I will take things one game at a time and work as hard as I can to impress the manager." ■

**NEW KID ON THE BLOCK**

A young Steven Gerrard was interviewed in December 1998 and admitted the "buzz" of fans recognising him around the city

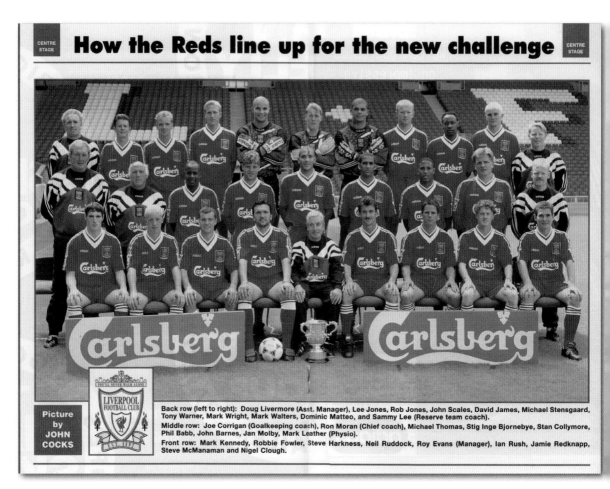

CENTRE STAGE

# How the Reds line up for the new challenge

Picture by JOHN COCKS

Back row (left to right): Doug Livermore (Asst. Manager), Lee Jones, Rob Jones, John Scales, David James, Michael Stensgaard, Tony Warner, Mark Wright, Mark Walters, Dominic Matteo, and Sammy Lee (Reserve team coach).

Middle row: Joe Corrigan (Goalkeeping coach), Ron Moran (Chief coach), Michael Thomas, Stig Inge Bjornebye, Stan Collymore, Phil Babb, John Barnes, Jan Molby, Mark Leather (Physio).

Front row: Mark Kennedy, Robbie Fowler, Steve Harkness, Neil Ruddock, Roy Evans (Manager), Ian Rush, Jamie Redknapp, Steve McManaman and Nigel Clough.

The team photo at the start of the 1995-96 season featured the League Cup that had been captured a few months earlier while the 'Star Gallery' item in 1994-95 focused on the likes of Steve McManaman, David James and John Barnes

**STAR GALLERY**

**Steve McManaman**
Birth date: 11.02.72
Birth sign: Aquarius

■ You may have to face some fears and misunderstandings in January as you pursue your ambitions for 1995, but the Aquarian New Moon may light the way ahead before the month is out. You should spend some time revising long-term aims. Chances of making progress will arise, but may take a form that will come as a surprise.
Picture by Clive Brunskill/ALLSPORT

**STAR GALLERY**

**David James**
Birth date: 1.08.70
Birth sign: Leo

■ You ought to be on Cloud 9. Recent events have given you a free hand to prove your talents. This is your moment of truth and, as your feelings of security grow stronger, you will find there is more to be enjoyed from facing life's risks than in comfortable inactivity.
Picture by MARK LEECH

**STAR GALLERY**

**John Barnes**
Birth date: 07.11.63
Birth sign: Scorpio

■ This is a big year for you. A full moon on your birthday suggest that it could contain your moment of truth. You must face your problems head-on rather than trying to evade difficult issues. Even when the going is tough you can turn the situation to your advantage.
Picture by MARK LEECH

### Anfield People

#### Bruce tells the fans: You made my day

BRUCE Grobbelaar's fans will never forget the testimonial day he laid on at Anfield. And he will never forget the day they gave him.

More than 20,000 turned up in tribute to one of the game's great characters and they were rewarded with a show that was pure Bruce.

Quite apart from the serious business of a full-scale Liverpool-Everton match, drawn 2-2, there was a six-a-side tournament which brought back old stars and golden memories.

George Best turned up to play alongside Frank Worthington and Gordon Banks. Former Reds like Alan Hansen and Alan Kennedy turned back the clock . . . even Ronnie Moran, a club servant for 40 years, pictured opposite with Everton manager Howard Kendall.

Gerry Marsden and Bruce raised the rafters by leading the crowd in singing You'll Never Walk Alone, Sten Boardman raised the laughs. And the courage of some of the special-needs children joining in the fun raised a few tears.

Just to be on the safe side Bruce had a witch doctor to cast out evil spirits at Anfield. It worked on the day, anyway.

Afterwards he said: "I want to thank every supporter who came along. I was moved by the atmosphere they created and hope that families will come back to Anfield for our club games.

"One of my biggest surprises came from the Jersey branch of the Supporters Club. They presented me with a beautiful certificate to congratulate me on my Testimonial in the Club's Centenary Year."

ANFIELD REVIEW — CLUBCALL 0898 12 11 84 TICKETCALL 0898 12 15 84 — 18

### Centre Stage

## Kings of the mountains
### PROVING THAT YOU HAVE TO WEAR A HAT TO GET AHEAD

THE old advertising slogan used to insist: You have to wear a hat to get ahead.

Well it certainly didn't do Liverpool any harm when they posed for this picture outside their luxury hotel in the Alps on the morning of their first-leg UEFA Cup game against Swarovski Tirol.

There was much laughing and mickey-taking when Graeme Souness led his squad out for a spot of relaxation in the mountain sunshine.

The traditional Tyrolean hats and a short outbreak of snowballing helped to settle a few nerves before the big match.

Some players were them Wild West style. Others, perhaps more appropriately, adopted the fashion favoured by Ken Dodd's Diddymen.

No doubt it was all good publicity for the hotel, appropriately named the Alpenkönig, which translates as Alpine King. And, of course the Reds finished well ahead.

Pictures by TED BLACKMOW of the Daily Mail.

Page 16 — CLUBCALL 0898 12-11-84 TICKETCALL 0898 12-13-84 — CLUBCALL 0898 12-11-84 TICKETCALL 0898 12-15-84 — Page 17

In October 1992 Bruce Grobbelaar thanked the fans for their support at his colourful testimonial

Graeme Souness and his players were pictured in Tyrolean hats on their visit to Austria to play Swarovski Tirol in the UEFA Cup in 1991

---

### Lucky Stars

# The signs that all point to success

THE new year has plenty on offer for Liverpool players according to a local amateur astrologer's of horoscopes!

For the youngsters who made the big breakthrough this season . . . for the established men who have already shaped their careers. There is good news, largely, for them all.

It says so in the stars. And here, we show their birth signs and dates with some light-hearted forecasts for the New Year . . .

**Taurus (21.4 to 21.5)**

Graeme Souness, Don Hutchinson and Torben Piechnik.

This is a splendid year to establish yourselves in the area of your choice, one for exhibiting your talents and strengths.

Believe in yourselves and you will benefit from self assurance, be positive in everything you do.

It is a year for sticking rigidly to your beliefs and you will be wiser and more contented for it. Look for the sunny side of life rather than the darkness and you will have no regrets.

Last year was not the best, but better times are on the way. New opportunities will arise to prove how capable and accomplished you are.

■ BURNDEN GLOOM . . . but better times were on the way

**Sagittarius (23.11 to 21.12)**

Steve Nicol, Istvan Kozma and Stig Inge Bjornebye.

Recent problems should be resolved in the immediate future and do not take past achievements lightly.

You should enjoy change and development and bear in mind the talents you have been blessed with.

It is a time for examining old habits and making changes where you feel it would help.

Do not be afraid to ask for assistance when the need arises and correct decisions will bring you enormous benefits.

**Leo (24.7 to 23.8)**

Mark Wright   David James

A number of problems lie ahead and they must be met fairly and honestly. The New Year will offer good opportunities to solve these problems and it is well within you to succeed.

Believe in your strengths, your fears will prove to be unnecessary at times. Change should be met with conviction.

**Libra (24.9 to 23.10)**

Ronnie Whelan, Ronny Rosenthal, Ian Rush, Paul Stewart and Bruce Grobbelaar.

The year of 1993 presents a good variety of special opportunities and you should make positive strides in important areas.

Enjoy your triumphs and do not dwell on troubles from last year. Errors are inevitable but do not brood on such happenings – remain logical about them and feel good in these happy days. You should treasure all previous achievements and maintain high standards. A wonderful year is taking shape, remember that.

**Aquarius (21.1 to 19.2)**

Mike Hooper and Steve McManaman.

You can dispose of and exasperate those who have let you down in terms of trust in the past. Your hopes may have been dashed at the end of last year and left you puzzled . . . but 1993 should provide better things. You will learn a lot in the next twelve months. Events in February should lift your morale and the year should be progressive and exciting.

**Gemini (22.5 to 21.6)**

Nicky Tanner, Mark Walters and Lee Jones.

Train your mind to meet relevant matters only and you will know a year of sound achievements, good experiences and worthy challenges.

Your initial aim for 1993 is to stay fit and healthy and allow your feelings to unfold naturally. Your special kind of enthusiasm and affection should rub off on others around you.

**Cancer (22.6 to 23.7)**

Mike Marsh, Jan Molby and Jamie Redknapp.

December saw the start of a new era and forthcoming changes should be to your advantage. You must stamp your own personality on events this year and remember what you learned from 1992.

The result of decision-making will give you more assurances for the future and you must express feelings from the heart.

**Virgo (24.8 to 23.9)**

Michael Thomas and Steve Harkness.

The new year should be better than the one you have just left behind. It will offer marvellous opportunities to touch new peaks and you must square up to the events of 1993 with self honesty.

Better news lies ahead and you must aim for the top and forget mishaps of the past.

## Helping the most important people in football

Football is much more than a game of 90 minutes. Every day clubs throughout Britain are providing recreational and sporting opportunities for their local communities.

Much of this has been achieved with the help of the Football Trust. As part of its commitment to Football, The Trust has granted £4M to set up the National Football and Community Development Scheme.

Bringing club and community together, Trust-backed initiatives have provided a variety of local amenities, including:

● Artificial pitches for local teams
● Coaching for youngsters
● Support for women's football
● Facilities for people with disabilities

The Football Trust is helping the game at all levels.

**THE FOOTBALL TRUST**
*Helping the game*

20 — ANFIELD REVIEW — CLUBCALL 0898 12 11 84 TICKETCALL 0898 12 15 84 — 21

As 1993 began, the programme came over all astrological to find out what was in store for players in the future, with Leos like Mark Wright and David James told that 'problems lie ahead and they must be met fairly and honestly'

# Putting on the style of 1892

WHAT an impression they would have made 100 years ago, these stars of Liverpool 1992.

They tried dressing in the style of the men who took the field for the club's first competitive match...in the Lancashire League against Higher Walton on September 3, 1892.

Their boots look fit for service on a building site. Those thick shirts and long, long shorts could surely withstand the coldest winter's day, but how they must have suffered when the sun shone.

Mark Wright and his men are wearing the most important feature of all for any team group of the late 19th Century...a grim, uncompromising expression. Their faces tell you everything.

No mistaking the danger man. That has to be Ian Rush, looking positively dastardly behind that bounder's moustache as he holds the leather ball. That haughty figure sitting next to him (Dean Saunders) just has to be another goalscorer.

And for sheer arrogance, can you beat that goalkeeper with the strange sounding name for the time, Bruce Grobbelaar!

The picture was taken towards the end of last season by MIKE MALONEY of The Sunday People, who are to present a framed enlargement to the club. Appropriately, it will be displayed in one of the lounges of the new Centenary Stand.

**STEP BACK IN TIME**

At the start of the centenary season of 1992-93, the squad were pictured dressed as the heroes of 1892, with shiny boots and stern expressions!

## It really was Robbie's year

### 100 GOALS

Pictures by JOHN COCKS

■ Of all the match balls that Robbie Fowler has stuffed up his shirt for safekeeping when leaving the pitch with a hat-trick or better to his name, this one is very special.

It marks the day the former pupil of Ian Rush provided the most striking evidence yet that he is a master in his own right.

Not that there has ever been much doubt about his potential for greatness.

His Liverpool and England teammate Steve McManaman predicts: "He's so good that he can break every Anfield goalscoring record."

Robbie, who insists that he is not interested in records, took his latest achievement in his stride.

He insists: "Ian Rush has achieved everything in the game. If I have got half of what he has achieved at the end of my career, I will be well happy."

### SCORECARD OF A FIRST-CLASS CENTURY

| | | | Venue | | Score | Goals |
|---|---|---|---|---|---|---|
| **1993/94** | | | | | | |
| 23 | Sep | CC Cup | Fulham | A | Won | 3-1 | 1 |
| 6 | Oct | CC Cup | Fulham | H | Won | 5-0 | 5 |
| 17 | Oct | Premier | Oldham Athletic | H | Won | 2-1 | 1 |
| 30 | Oct | Premier | Southampton | A | Won | 4-2 | 3 |
| 28 | Nov | Premier | Aston Villa | H | Won | 2-1 | 1 |
| 4 | Dec | Premier | Sheffield Wednesday | A | Won | 3-3 | 1 |
| 18 | Dec | Premier | Tottenham Hotspur | A | Draw | 3-3 | 2 |
| 13 | Mar | Premier | Oldham Athletic | A | Won | 3-0 | 1 |
| 13 | Mar | Premier | Everton | H | Won | 2-1 | 1 |
| 23 | Apr | Premier | West Ham United | A | Won | 2-1 | 1 |
| 7 | May | Premier | Aston Villa | A | Lost | 1-2 | 1 |
| **1994/95** | | | | | | |
| 20 | Aug | Premier | Crystal Palace | A | Won | 6-1 | 1 |
| 28 | Aug | Premier | Arsenal | H | Won | 3-0 | 1 |
| 31 | Aug | Premier | Southampton | A | Won | 2-0 | 1 |
| 21 | Sep | CC Cup | Burnley | A | Won | 2-0 | 1 |
| 5 | Oct | CC Cup | Burnley | H | Won | 4-1 | 1 |
| 8 | Oct | Premier | Aston Villa | H | Won | 3-2 | 2 |
| 15 | Oct | Premier | Blackburn Rovers | A | Lost | 2-3 | 1 |
| 22 | Oct | Premier | Wimbledon | A | Won | 3-0 | 1 |
| 29 | Oct | Premier | Ipswich Town | A | Won | 3-1 | 2 |
| 9 | Nov | Premier | Chelsea | A | Won | 3-1 | 1 |
| 26 | Nov | Premier | Tottenham Hotspur | H | Draw | 1-1 | 1 |
| 26 | Dec | Premier | Leeds United | A | Won | 2-0 | 1 |
| 28 | Dec | Premier | Manchester City | H | Won | 2-0 | 1 |
| 31 | Dec | Premier | Leeds United | H | Won | 2-0 | 1 |
| 2 | Jan | Premier | Norwich City | H | Won | 4-1 | 1 |
| 4 | Feb | Premier | Nottingham Forest | A | Draw | 1-1 | 1 |
| 15 | Feb | Premier | Crystal Palace | H | Won | 1-0 | 1 |
| 19 | Feb | FA Cup | Wimbledon | H | Won | 2-0 | 1 |
| 4 | Mar | Premier | Newcastle United | A | Won | 2-0 | 1 |
| 8 | Mar | Premier | Crystal Palace | A | Won | 2-0 | 1 |
| 11 | Mar | FA Cup | Tottenham Hotspur | H | Won | 3-1 | 1 |
| 5 | Apr | Premier | Southampton | H | Won | 3-1 | 1 |
| 12 | Apr | Premier | Arsenal | A | Won | 1-0 | 1 |
| 17 | Apr | Premier | Leicester City | H | Won | 2-0 | 1 |
| **1995/96** | | | | | | |
| 26 | Aug | Premier | Tottenham Hotspur | A | Won | 3-1 | 1 |
| 16 | Sept | Premier | Blackburn Rovers | A | Won | 2-1 | 1 |
| 23 | Sept | Premier | Bolton Wanderers | H | Won | 5-2 | 4 |
| 1 | Oct | Premier | Manchester United | A | Draw | 2-2 | 2 |
| 4 | Oct | CC Cup | Sunderland | A | Won | 1-0 | 1 |
| 25 | Oct | CC Cup | Manchester City | H | Won | 4-0 | 2 |
| 21 | Oct | Premier | Manchester City | H | Won | 6-0 | 2 |
| 18 | Nov | Premier | Everton | H | Won | 1-2 | 1 |
| 17 | Dec | Premier | Manchester United | A | Lost | 0-2 | 1 |
| 23 | Dec | Premier | Arsenal | H | Won | 3-1 | 3 |
| 1 | Jan | Premier | Nottingham Forest | H | Won | 4-2 | 2 |
| 6 | Jan | FA Cup | Rochdale | A | Won | 7-0 | 1 |
| 20 | Jan | Premier | Leeds United | H | Won | 5-0 | 2 |
| 31 | Jan | Premier | Aston Villa | H | Won | 2-0 | 1 |
| 11 | Feb | Premier | Queens Park Rangers | A | Won | 2-1 | 1 |
| 18 | Feb | FA Cup | Shrewsbury Town | A | Won | 4-0 | 1 |
| 28 | Feb | FA Cup | Charlton Athletic | H | Won | 2-1 | 1 |
| 3 | Mar | Premier | Aston Villa | H | Won | 3-0 | 2 |
| 20 | Mar | FA Cup | Chelsea | N | Won | 2-0 | 1 |
| 20 | Mar | FA Cup | Leeds United | H | Won | 3-0 | 1 |
| 3 | Apr | Premier | Aston Villa | A | Won | 3-0 | 1 |
| 16 | Apr | Premier | Newcastle United | H | Won | 4-3 | 1 |
| 16 | Apr | Premier | Everton | A | Draw | 1-1 | 1 |
| **1996/97** | | | | | | |
| 17 | Aug | Premier | Middlesbrough | A | Draw | 3-3 | 1 |
| 21 | Sept | Premier | Chelsea | H | Won | 5-1 | 1 |
| 25 | Sept | ECW Cup | FC Sion | A | Won | 2-1 | 1 |
| 27 | Oct | Premier | Charlton Athletic | A | Draw | 1-1 | 1 |
| 31 | Oct | ECW Cup | Derby County | A | Won | 2-1 | 1 |
| 13 | Nov | ECW Cup | FC Sion | H | Won | 6-3 | 2 |
| 23 | Nov | Premier | Charlton Athletic | H | Won | 4-1 | 1 |
| 26 | Nov | CC Cup | Arsenal | H | Won | 4-2 | 2 |
| 14 | Dec | Premier | Middlesbrough | H | Won | 5-1 | 1 |

100 Goals scored in 165 matches. 102 in all with 4 against Middlesbrough.
Ian Rush scored 100 in 166 matches.

### 100 GOALS

■ Liverpool's latest centurion is also the current International Supporters Club Player of the Year and is pictured above with the Carlsberg Trophy which he received last month. Robbie succeeded Steve McManaman, who finished runner-up in the 1995-96 poll of ISC members in every part of the world. Our picture below shows him receiving the Man of the Match magnum after the Middlesbrough game from Carlsberg Chief Executive Ebbe Dinesen.

Just over three years after his debut, Robbie Fowler clocked up 100 goals for the Reds, a fact celebrated in December 1996

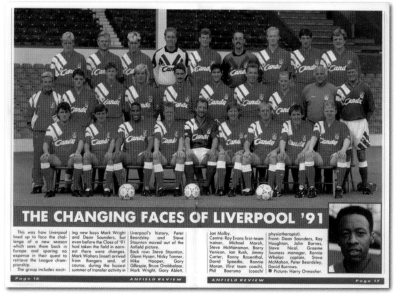

## THE CHANGING FACES OF LIVERPOOL '91

This was how Liverpool lined up to face the challenge of a new season which sees them back in Europe and sparing no expense in their quest to retrieve the League championship.

The group includes exciting new boys Mark Wright and Dean Saunders, but even before the Class of '91 had taken the field in earnest there were changes. Mark Walters (inset) arrived from Rangers and, of course, during the busiest summer of transfer activity in Liverpool's history, Peter Beardsley and Steve Staunton moved out of the Anfield picture.

Back row: Steve Staunton, Glenn Hysen, Nicky Tanner, Mike Hooper, Gary Gillespie, Bruce Grobbelaar, Mark Wright, Gary Ablett.

Jan Molby.

Centre: Roy Evans first-team trainer, Michael Marsh, Steve McManaman, Barry Venison, Ian Rush, Jimmy Carter, Ronny Rosenthal, David Speedie, Ronnie Moran, (first team coach), Phil Boersma (coach) physiotherapist).

Front: Dean Saunders, Ray Houghton, John Barnes, Steve Nicol, Graeme Souness manager, Ronnie Whelan captain, Steve McMahon, Peter Beardsley, David Burrows.

■ Picture: Harry Ormesher.

Page 16 — ANFIELD REVIEW / ANFIELD REVIEW — Page 17

### The game I remember

**Emlyn Hughes**

*Liverpool v Stromsgodset Drammen*
*Cup Winners' Cup Rd 1 - 1st leg Sept. 17, 1974*

It was the night the sledgehammer cracked a nut when Liverpool powered a record-breaking 11 goals without reply past Stromsgodset of Norway in the Cup Winners' Cup.

Only goalkeeper Ray Clemence and Brian Hall failed to score against the part-timers in an avalanche of goals at Anfield. It was also a record goals 'spread'.

"We just went out and played enjoyable football the fans loved and made sure we didn't get injured," recalls Emlyn (Mighty Em) Hughes, captain of the team.

"We never thought about taking our foot off the gas. It wasn't a case of wanting to make the Norwegians look humble. We had a job to do and we did it well and we enjoyed doing it.

"But I can't remember if my goal was a scrappy tap-in or an absolutely magnificent 35-yarder."

Norwegian football has developed hugely at club and national level since that September night in 1974 when Stromsgodset were swamped with goals by Alec Lindsay (pen), Phil Boersma (two), Phil Thompson (two), Steve Heighway, Peter Cormack, Hughes, Ian Callaghan, Tommy Smith and Ray Kennedy.

Advanced training techniques have enabled players from traditionally less gifted football nations to match the best.

"Our game then was control and pass and if you could do that you had a chance of being a footballer," says Emlyn.

"Now the game is a combination of sprint, speed and stamina, and the gap between teams at home and abroad has narrowed.

"I don't think there will ever be massive wins again. Some may be easier, but you don't get an easy game in Europe any more. Norwegian football has taken tremendous strides forward since then.

"In my ten years from losing the FA Cup Final 2-1 to Arsenal in 1971, then the years onward to Heysel, I don't think our supporters realised how good we were.

"I don't think even we realised what we were achieving. We were just better than the rest ... almost untouchable.

"We won the League every other year, six European trophies, FA Cups, League Cups and they gave us the Charity Shield every year. We were expected to be winners. But a spell of such domination will never be repeated."

Ferencvaros of Budapest beat Liverpool on the away goal rule in the second round, losing to Dinamo Kiev in the Final of the only European competition not to have been conquered by the Reds – up to now.

■ WINNER ... Emlyn Hughes with the 1974 Charity Shield ... one month later they hit 11 goals against Stromsgodset

**'Every year they gave us the Charity Shield'**

### THIRST QUENCHER! LUCOZADE SPORT

The team photo from August 1991 showed new faces while 'The game I remember' in March 1997 had Emlyn Hughes recalling the 11-0 thumping of Stromsgodset in 1974 – but one thing he couldn't remember was how he scored his goal!

# Centre Stage

DEAN SAUNDERS is now firmly embarked on a goalscoring career with Liverpool which he hopes will justify the record £2.9 million fees they paid for him this summer.

The Welsh international, whose transfer from relegated Derby County made him the most expensive player in British football, turned down both Nottingham Forest and Everton in the belief that his hunger for attacking medals could be better satisfied at Anfield.

Dean is the son of a former Liverpool player, Roy Saunders, and profited from hours spent with his father and a football when he was a small boy.

"He taught me a lot about the game," Dean recalls. "He showed me how to take up the right positions at the right time. He was a great enthusiast and I owe him a lot."

Here Dean answers questions about some of his favourite things...

**MEAL** — Silver side.

**HOBBY** Sport ... any sport.

**FILM** Fatal Attraction. It seemed so real.

**ACTOR** I haven't got one.

**ACTRESS** Same again.

**TV SHOW** Cheers. It has me laughing from start to finish.

**BOOK** Any sports biography.

**COLOUR** Red.

**DRINK** Wine of water.

**MEMORY** The arrival of our first daughters, Danielle.

**SPORTSMAN** Ian Botham. He is capable of performances in all aspects of his game. Others are not.

**PLAYER** John Barnes. He is the best in Britain.

**GROUND** Brighton. I was younger when I played there and enjoyed every exciting minute.

**MATCH** When Wales beat Belgium 3-1 at Cardiff and we were not expected to win.

# Centre Stage

MARK WALTERS achieved what so many ambitious schoolboy footballers set out to do ... play for the club he supported.

Although he attended match day Birmingham City, he knew deep down that Aston Villa would give him the fulfilment he wanted. "I supported them from being seven years old," he recalls.

He also remembers the time when lack of money meant that Villa matches lasted only ten minutes as far as he was concerned. He saw only the referee of games after the gates had been opened to let out earlier leavers.

Manager Tony Barton signed him as a professional at the age of 16 and his vision and his touch made him an outstanding player. But after six years over the Midlands ties with Villa weren't strong enough to retain him, and he moved to Liverpool.

Mark answers questions about his favourite things...

**MEAL** Nothing can tingle out. I'm easily satisfied.

**HOBBY** Squash in the summer. It's good for fitness and sharpness of the eye.

**FILM** Fatal Attraction. The plot kept me guessing.

**ACTOR** Dustin Hoffman. Every film he makes is good.

**ACTRESS** Meryl Streep. She is outstanding.

**TV SHOW** Cheers or Only Fools and Horses.

**COLOUR** Purple, would you believe.

**DRINK** Orange and lemonade.

**SPORTSMAN** Mike Tyson. He is in a way against one sport and the best in the world.

**PLAYER** Ceasar of Napoli. He has all the talent.

**GROUND** Brina Park. That is one very special stadium.

**GAME** That one is to come ... with Liverpool.

# Centre Stage

DAVID BURROWS was spotted as a schoolboy in Dudley and trained with West Bromwich Albion as a 14-year-old.

Two years later he became an apprentice, then signed professional forms at the age of 18. But his talent needed more scope when words and he was transferred for about £550,000.

David had never played at Anfield before his arrival in October, 1988. "I was soon in the thick. At first I was overawed because I couldn't understand the size of the place," he recalls. "All I remembered were the views of Anfield around the ground and coming through The Shankly Gates."

When stories of Liverpool's interest first reached his ears he was left in a state of disbelief. "Every young player wants to come here," he claims. "I did not believe it at first, but once I was convinced, this was a mistake.

"It is an awesome place on the first day right up to Road and made the goosebumps here. I would still have enjoyed the experience."

Here, he answers the questions about his favourite things...

**MEAL** A Chinese curry, preferably beef.

**DRINK** Diet coke during the week and a glass of sweet wine at the weekends.

**HOBBY** Driving in indoors me.

**FILM** One Rose Over the Cuckoo's Nest. It was both serious and humorous.

**ACTOR** Steve Martin. I enjoy comedy films and he is the best.

**ACTRESS** Julia Roberts. Her performance in "Pretty Woman" was excellent.

**TV SHOW** Phil Cool's. He is up to date with his marvellous impersonations.

**BOOK** Brian Clough's autobiography. I found it very moving.

**COLOUR** Black. Black clothes and black cars.

**MEMORY** Meeting with the 3.00 am sessions at Anfield before my defeat against Coventry City. The atmosphere and welcome were unforgettable.

**SPORTSMAN** Myself in the house, danger instead of opting for retirement. And he is British.

**GAME** It A-9 debut for West Bram at Aston Villa. The score was 5-3 at half-time and the game was played at 180mph.

**GROUND** Wembley. I feel sorry for those who have never played there. I want to go as often as possible.

**PLAYER** Former Liverpool captain Alan Hansen. I watched him on television and thought he was the most complete defender I had ever seen. Later, I was fortunate enough to play alongside him.

MARK WRIGHT was bought for about £2.2m from Derby County before this season opened, but was struck down with injury almost as soon as his Anfield career had begun.

The diagnosis of a "dead leg" later became an achilles tendon. It has meant a much longer lay-off than at first feared.

"This has been especially frustrating because I wanted to make an early impact with my new club," he says. "I wanted to be among the action."

Wright began his career with Oxford United, but was soon spotted by bigger clubs and moved on to Southampton before collecting his England caps.

He was later transferred to Derby County, but left for Liverpool at the same time as striker Dean Saunders.

Here he answers questions about his favourite things . . .

**MEAL**
Spaghetti Bolognese.

**HOBBY**
Tennis, but only in the summer.

**DRINK**
Whatever is served after I land my first medal with Liverpool.

**FILM**
Any Pink Panther movie.

**ACTOR**
Peter Sellers, who else?

**ACTRESS**
Kim Basinger. The reasons must be obvious.

**TV SHOW**
I have two, Cheers and L.A. Law.

**BOOK**
Anybody's autobiography, I like to know what people have done with their lives.

**COLOUR**
It is now Red.

**MEMORY**
The birth of my daughters, Lauren Emma and Hollie Louise, I am a family man.

**SPORTSMAN**
The relay team which was British and beat the best in the world in Tokyo.

**GAME**
The World Cup semi-final against West Germany in Italy. The feeling of being 90 minutes away from a final was unforgettable. I have not won anything yet.

**GROUND**
Anfield, even before I was transferred.

**PLAYER**
Franz Beckenbauer, a defender who could score goals and play almost anywhere, despite the quality of the opposition. I would like to have met him.

'Centre Stage' in the 1991-92 season found out Dean Saunders' favourite TV show was Cheers, Mark Walters was a big fan of Mike Tyson, and that David Burrows' playing inspiration was Alan Hansen – a man he got to eventually play alongside

All the Liverpool goals from the pulsating 4-4 draw with Everton in 1991 featured in the Arsenal programme the following month

A 7-1 win against a Derby County team featuring Dean Saunders and Mark Wright in March 1991 was deemed worthy of a double-page spread in the Coventry programme the following month

# Two shots of genius launch the celebration

■ The goals that launched an almighty celebration are pictured on the opposite page. Top: Bolton defenders look on aghast as Steve McManaman wriggles between them to squeeze the ball past goalkeeper Ian Branagan. Below: He cuts in from the left with a stunning dribble, then coolly slots the ball just inside the post past the keeper's fingertips. Jamie Redknapp, left, and Phil Babb, John Scales and Rob Jones, above, were among the players taking turns to pose with the trophy. And manager Roy Evans insisted on a line-up of the backroom staff, including the club doctor, Mark Waller, wearing the white shirt.

18

19

---

# The McManaman Final

■ GOOD RESULT . . . Steve McManaman with the trophies one shared and one all his own

■ GOOD LUCK . . . from Sir Stanley

THE mood was set for Steve McManaman's finest hour and a half by a handshake and a few words of encouragement from Sir Stanley Matthews.

The young winger went out to conquer Wembley, just as the old Wizard of Dribble had done so many times before.

His performance earned him the Coca-Cola man of the Match trophy as well as his share of the Coca-Cola Cup, raised so proudly by skipper Ian Rush.

Steve stood alongside Ian as he collected the Cup from 80-year-old Sir Stanley, who offered the matchwinner the ultimate compliment. "He told me he liked the way I dribble," said Steve. "Coming from him, that was quite a tribute. I just hope I can carry on playing as long as he did."

Sir Stanley, oldest player ever to appear in the First Division, retired at 50. In 1953 he helped Blackpool to win the FA Cup in a game which has been named The Matthews Final. This one could go down as The McManaman Final.

Manager Roy Evans was in a doze after joining the line of managers since Bill Shankly who have all won trophies. He has earned his place in Club history, for this was a record fifth League Cup win. Ian Rush is the only player to have five winner's medals.

"I'm delighted for the players because of the effort they have put in," said Roy, who has reorganised and revitalised the team in his first full season in charge. "Now we are back in Europe, which was always the priority."

He said of Macca, who took his tally for the season to a modest nine: "His goals were fantastic. He gets more kicks up the backside than praise in training, but he's been different class in a lot of games this season." Steve was a star when Liverpool won the FA Cup three years earlier, turning the game against Sunderland in the second half. "That was a great occasion," he recalled, "but this was even better because people had written us off at the start of the season."

Macca was also involved in a fine example of sportsmanship after the game, when Scouser Jason McAteer, who played his heart out against his favourite team, collapsed in tears after Bolton's defeat. Steve and Jason's Irish international teammate Phil Babb raced over to let him hold up the Cup.

Jason, subject of a £3million bid by Roy Evans before the season, exchanged shirts with his midfield rival Jamie Redknapp. He was wearing it when he paid this tribute: "Macca is the top man. If you give him space he will destroy you. That is what he did to us - twice."

## Two goals, two trophies and an unforgettable tribute from Sir Stanley

20

21

## *Wembley*

*Album*

CLUBCALL 0898 12 11 84 TICKETCALL 0898 12 13 84

# It isn't every day that Centenarians win the FA Cup

MAY 9, 1992 will always be remembered at Anfield as the day a bunch of Centenarians won the FA Cup.

It was a perfect day to celebrate the club's 100th anniversary at the end of a traumatic season. And celebrate they did in a joyful huddle on the Wembley turf.

Elsewhere there was a touching exchange of congratulations (left) between manager Greame Souness, allowed out of hospital after his heart operation, and Ronnie Moran, the faithful assistant who led the team out in his place.

Pride of place on the open-top bus when the team returned in triumph to Merseyside went to goalscorers Ian Rush and Michael Thomas. That's them holding the Cup on the opposite page.

Below Michael is shown delivering the mighty volley which put his team ahead early in the second half.

Pictured alongside is Ian Rush celebrating the second goal which killed off gallant Sunderland from the Second Division. Lifting him off his feet is, appropriately, Steve McManaman, a late choice after recovering from a semi-final injury. It was his skilful dribbling down the right flank which changed the game.

A memorable FA Cup win in May 1992 was captured in 'Wembley Album' in the Sheffield United issue in August of that year

*ANFIELD REVIEW*

8

'Crown Prince' Michael Owen starred in the Reds' 3-0 win at Crystal Palace in December 1997

The Reds may have gone out of the UEFA Cup to Genoa in March 1992, but it was still a night to remember for atmosphere and sportsmanship

Ian Rush's testimonial was in the Manchester City issue in December 1994, with the legend admitting he was a bag of nerves on the night

# Robbie races to his first century

■ Robbie Fowler is a stat man's dream. Just as an appetiser, he gave them the Premiership's fastest goal in the Premiership after 29 seconds of the 5-1 victory over a sorry Middlesbrough side.

Ironically, he owed it to a bulldozing run from Stan Collymore, who had clocked the previous fastest in 33 seconds against Wimbledon.

With 21-year-old Robbie's career total now on the 99 mark, we were left to wonder whether he would finish the game with a faster 100 than Ian Rush. But only for 27 minutes.

Stan, revelling in his recall to the side and with the crowd behind him, cut through Boro's ill-organised defence to thunder a shot against the post. In the blink of an eye Robbie had netted the rebound and Rushie's century had been overtaken with a game to spare.

Just on half-time keeper

Gary Walsh failed to hold another Collymore thunderbolt and Stig Bjornebye headed in.

There was an unwelcome interruption from Jan Aage Fjortoft, who headed in a goal from a Boro free-kick in the 75th minute, before Robbie moved on to his third four-goal haul since coming into the team as an 18-year-old.

**Top left:** Robbie nets goal No 99 and turns away to check the time.

**Bottom left:** The century-maker turns again to accept Anfield's salute and December 14, 1996 becomes a notable day in Club history.

**Above:** Yet another Fowler hat-trick is completed in the 77th minute after Steve McManaman is given possession by Robbie Mustoe.

The fourth Fowler goal was the best of all and is featured overleaf.

■ Middlesbrough have yielded Robbie Fowler five goals this season and a day he will never forget, but they will also live long in Stig Bjornebye's memory.

Stig, who made his debut in December 1992, had not scored a goal for the Reds until this season, but he broke his duck at the Boro's Riverside Stadium on opening day and the header he got against them at Anfield was his third goal for the Club.

His second goal came from a free-kick against FC Sion at Anfield at the end of October.

12 / 13

---

Robbie Fowler just kept on scoring during the mid-90s, and the day he reached his century against Middlesbrough in December 1996 was celebrated in the Leicester City programme on Boxing Day

The previous month's Charlton programme saw another pictorial salute to Fowler after a two-goal show in a 2-1 win against Derby

# Robbie heads back where he belongs

Pictures by JOHN COCKS

■ A header that would not have looked out of place in a collection by Tommy Lawton or one of the other great exponents lifted Robbie Fowler back to the heights at Anfield.

It also ensured that the Reds picked up three points against Derby County, taking full advantage of the defeats that had befallen great rivals Manchester United and Newcastle 24 hours earlier.

Robbie claimed both goals in Liverpool's 2-1 win, bringing his total for the season to six and restoring him as the team's top scorer. It was his third game since returning to the team after a three-week absence with an ankle injury and he had not failed to score in any of them.

His leaping header was the perfect finish to a fine cross from defender John Scales, who is picked on our Front Cover in the act of delivering the ball.

Such was the impetus and Robbie's delight - that he finished up in the back of the net to a ovation from fans behind the goal.

Derby scored a minute from time, but otherwise Liverpool were never threatened in a game they should have won more handsomely.

■ Robbie Fowler produced his usual salute after breaching Derby's packed defence for his first goal in the 47th minute, but played it down when he was interviewed afterwards.

"I just followed the ball in like any striker would," he declared after being asked to talk the TV audience through the moment he pounced at close range after goalkeeper Russell Hoult failed to hold a fierce drive from Patrik Berger, pictured below.

"Typical Robbie," commented Ian Rush back in the Sky Sport studio, making it clear that his protege's knack of being in the right spot was a gift given to only a few.

Derby's resistance crumbled after the second goal, three minutes later and Robbie was deprived of a hat-trick just 15 minutes from time when Hoult parried a drive at the near post.

12 / 13

## A Robbie dazzler

*Premier Action*

■ Robbie Fowler's knack of producing goals from nothing have earned him more than his share of headlines, but this was his most audacious scoring attempt to date. It almost earned Liverpool a win against all the odds after Southampton had taken a 1-0 lead in the 60th minute. Robbie was 45 yards from goal when he unleashed this outrageous floater which caught Dave Beasant off his line. The panic-stricken goalkeeper just managed to scramble the ball behind for a corner before ending up in the back of the net. Stan Collymore had scored a dramatic equaliser a few minutes earlier . . . see over.

**11**

### Approval from the Master

*Premier Action*

■ A typical piece of smash and grab by Robbie Fowler changed the game against Chelsea after Glenn Hoddle's team had taken a shock lead in the third minute.
It lasted just six minutes before Robbie snatched two goals in 50 seconds, bringing his total for the season to 16 in an astonishing 17 games. He even hit the crossbar five minutes later after Jamie Redknapp had shot against a post.
Robbie is pictured above delivering a deadly shot to finish off a great breakout and precision pass from Jan Molby. In our other picture his admiring mentor, Ian Rush, helps him celebrate the poacher's header which gave him his second.

**14**

Two goals in 50 seconds from Fowler turned a November 1994 match against Chelsea completely on its head

Left: It wasn't a goal this time but an audacious shot from 45 yards against Southampton in December 1995 almost brought the house down

# Michael's hat-trick caps devastating team display

Newcastle United 1
Liverpool 4

1/2. Paul Ince's shot proved too hot for Shay Given, with Michael firing in the rebound.

3/4. A precise through ball from Steve McManaman sets up goal number two.

5/6/7. Good work from Karlheinz Riedle presents the opportunity for a superb third.

8. That'll do nicely, as Incy and Macca celebrate a memorable hat-trick.

**12**  Liverpool ticket call and prize line  0891 121 584
Calls cost 50p per minute at all times

0891 121 184  Liverpool Club Call - find out what's going on  **13**
Calls cost 50p per minute at all times

Michael Owen grabbed the headlines when his spectacular hat-trick sank Newcastle in August 1998

'Anfield People' reported on everything from fans and players to club staff.

Vouchers were printed on the back cover of the programme at the start of 1994-95 and this continued for a further five seasons. Early issues from each season had voucher-cards inserted into the middle – collect them all and send off the completed card and you stood a chance of winning a season ticket in the prize draw.

The visit of Crystal Palace in April 1998 saw a first: for the only time in the programme's history, a four-page advertisement wraparound, for 'The New Astra from Vauxhall Motors'.

John Barnes is on-hand when the experience is all a bit too much for a four-year-old fan at the Anfield derby of March 1993

# The Evans Era starts here

THE midnight oil had been well and truly burned when Roy Evans arrived home from Selhurst Park with thoughts of Wembley still spinning through his brain.

Success in the Coca-Cola Cup semi-final had left him just one game away from a major trophy in his first full season as Liverpool manager. He was drained and hoped he could sleep.

That prospect vanished when his 20-year-old son Stephen came through the door. He, too, had been to London and applauded Robbie Fowler's winning goal.

"All he wanted to do was talk about the Liverpool fans," says Roy. "Mind you, they had been brilliant."

The Evans home has always been Red and open to football discussions. "I'm still a supporter," says Roy. "I have decisions to make and teams to choose, but I'm still a supporter. We share the same feelings.

"And this Wembley final against Bolton Wanderers is all about them and the players."

Another decision is about to be made . . . what will he wear to lead the team from the tunnel? "It may be a new suit. It may be the sports jacket and trousers I've worn in every round of the competition."

Whatever the outcome, he'll feel a deep sense of pride at Wembley in two weeks.

"I am genuinely delighted for our players," he insists. "At least they have a Wembley appearance to show for the work they have put into their season. They deserve such a reward for effort and persistence."

Roy looks back on his first full season in charge and remembers the early warnings he was given about management. "I was told that it would be a lonely job, but I haven't found it that way.

"I have confided in the staff and their loyalty has been given freely. They could not have been more helpful. We have known triumphs and disasters, but the good and bad days have been shared.

"Then there's the supporters, who have given us fantastic encouragement at home and away. I keep going back to them, but I make no apology for that."

Roy, 48, first went to Wembley with England Schoolboys and played in a 0-0 draw against Germany before a crowd of 97,000. "That was every boy's dream," he recalls.

His next visit was with Liverpool in the 1964-65 season, when goals from Roger Hunt and Ian St John earned them a 2-1 victory over Leeds United and Anfield's first FA Cup. "I was an apprentice professional and that was a very special day, too," he declares.

He was chosen for the squad of 16 when Liverpool beat Newcastle United 3-0 in the 1974 FA Cup Final. Kevin Keegan got two goals and Steve Heighway got the other. "I did not expect to play, but the experience was memorable," he says. Roy has been back frequently since then in his various capacities as reserve-team trainer, first-team trainer and assistant manager.

But Wembley 95 will have a meaning all its own. He's been there with previous managers Bill Shankly, Bob Paisley, Joe Fagan, Kenny Dalglish and Graeme Souness . . . this time, though, he's the man in charge.

Sentiment will not be confused with professionalism on possibly the biggest day of his football life. He will think long and hard about the opposition from the lower division.

"Bolton have played well enough this season to command the respect of any team in the land," he warns. "They have Premier League potential and we'll treat them as such. We will be involved in a difficult game."

'I'm still a supporter . . . this is all about them and the players'

## Best wishes from Ronnie

RONNIE Moran was the last man to lead out Liverpool at Wembley – against Sunderland in the 1992 FA Cup Final when manager Graeme Souness was recovering from heart surgery.

He's delighted the honour goes to Roy Evans now that the Reds are back there. Ronnie has known him for more than 30 years and recalls: "He was a 16 year-old apprentice when I was in the first team and I used to give him a lift in for training. He always kept me waiting, too!

"Roy came from my old team, Bootle Boys, and played left-back, the same position as myself. He was a hard worker and always wanted to succeed."

Ronnie believes that Roy has earned his Wembley honour because of the way he has run the playing side and worked in harmony with the staff. "It was a big job to take over, but he thought things out and made good decisions.

"I ended my playing days in the Reserves with Roy and his assistant, Doug Livermore, when they were only youngsters. They were good listeners, good learners and good workers."

## It's a Cup Final between friends

MANAGERS Roy Evans and Bolton's Bruce Rioch first met as teenagers at Lilleshall.

They were called into the England Youth squad for training and games almost 30 years ago. Rioch, who later won 24 caps with Scotland, remembers the days well. "I could see then that Roy had total dedication," he recalls.

"There was only a small group of us and, to be fair, we all ate, drank and slept football."

Rioch was included in an England squad because the rules stated that you could play for your country of birth. He was born in Aldershot.

"Roy and myself have been good pals ever since. I was at Everton as a player and our paths have crossed many times."

One such encounter was at Anfield two seasons ago, when Bolton dismissed Liverpool from the FA Cup. "They were going through a difficult period at that time," says the Bolton boss.

"I would say we caught them at a good time – I'm not sure whether we'll catch them again at a good time."

Roy Evans was wondering what to wear at Wembley after his side beat Crystal Palace to reach the Coca-Cola Cup final in 1995

# THE LIVERPOOL WAY AHEAD

LIVERPOOL Football Club have once again set the standards for others to follow, after unveiling their state of the art Soccer Academy – the biggest in Europe.

Liverpool's youth system has always been prosperous – as evidenced by the number of local players who have progressed to first-team level – but Chairman David Moores and Executive Vice-Chairman Peter Robinson gave one hundred per cent backing to Academy Director Steve Heighway back in 1996 when he advocated a way of improving the development process still further.

At an estimated cost of £10 million, stage one of the purpose built Academy – the first of its kind in Britain – is now complete offering youngsters of all ages the best possible opportunities of realising their dreams of succeeding in the professional game.

Situated in Kirkby, the Academy has 10 grass pitches, three of which are floodlit, all containing full drainage and irrigation systems. There is also a separate synthetic pitch – the most advanced of its kind in the country – which has its own floodlighting and spectator accommodation.

The Academy also houses an Operations Centre which contains all the players' changing facilities together with a state of the art physiotherapy and medical centre, administration offices, classes and dining facilities for all.

Steve Heighway, Liverpool's Academy Director, has been at the forefront of all the planning right from the outset and he is understandably delighted with the end product. He says: "Plans for the Academy were first discussed two and a half years ago when it became clear that Melwood wasn't big enough to cater for everybody. The first team needed the facilities at Melwood and we realised we needed to plan for the future ourselves.

"There are two differing sets of priorities between the first team and the youth sides. The first team is all about preparing the players to go out and win games on a Saturday afternoon whereas we are about nurturing young talent and preparing for the future. The functions of the two units are different and so it made sense for us to have a base of our own.

"The Board of Directors at the club were very receptive of my ideas and they offered nothing but total support all the way through. I think everyone is delighted with the Academy and it certainly is a dream come true for me to be involved in such a set-up.

"We went abroad to see academies that other clubs have built and we picked up some very good ideas from clubs such as Ajax and Auxerre. I believe we have the best of everything now in that we have encompassed some of the ideas we got from abroad and we have also included our own thoughts. It is a good mixture which we are confident is the best way forward for us."

The Academy took eighteen months to build and, over the course of the coming months, even more facilities will be added. Phase two of the development will see the construction of an indoor soccer hall which is scheduled for completion in August. The third phase of the project will see the building of a 30 bed residential lodge in order to provide accommodation for youngsters from within the UK, Ireland and Europe along with facilities for visiting foreign teams.

Says Steve: "We all have a massive responsibility now to ensure we continue developing these young boys into first team players. I am certainly aware of how big that responsibility is and I know the other coaches are as well.

"People talk about the young boys who come here and say they are getting great opportunities here. That is true but also it shouldn't be forgotten that all of the backroom staff, the coaches, physios, doctors and everyone else who works at the Academy feel this is a great opportunity for them as well. I don't think it is going too far to say I am enjoying this job now more than ever before. There is nothing like our Academy anywhere in the country and I believe we even have the best facilities in Europe."

## ACADEMY FACTS

■ The Academy provides two to three weekly coaching sessions of two hours each for boys in the Under-9's, Under-10's, Under-11's, Under-12's, Under-13's, Under-14's, Under-15's and Under-16's age categories.

■ Academy Scholarships are offered to boys in the 16-21 age groups, with their five day week containing three half-days at college or eventually participating in in-house educational sessions.

■ Over five tiers of grass seed was sown at the site and 12,500 metres of land drainage laid.

■ The club sought permission from the Environment Agency to sink two 300 feet boreholes at the Academy to provide its own source of water for irrigation purposes. The water is stored in a 21,000 gallon water tank.

■ Over 110 tons of steel were used in the perimeter fencing of the site alone.

■ The Academy was designed with local environmental needs in mind. All surface water from the site is stored in four underground storage tanks. Controlled pumping to Kirkby Brook can only take place when surrounding water levels have dropped to alleviate any danger of flooding the River Alt.

■ The Academy has two full time groundsmen, two full time physiotherapists together with a dedicated Academy doctor.

■ Layout of the 45 acre site.

A three-page fold-out in the Middlesbrough programme of February 1999 explained the progress of the club's new academy in Kirkby while (right) the opening edition of the 1994-95 season detailed how the new seated Kop Grandstand was coming along

# Stan's final tribute

## He edited the Review as Reds made history

FORMER Anfield Review editor Stan Liversedge, whose death was briefly reported in our last issue, had a deep and abiding love of football.

A large congregation was reminded of this earlier this month at a funeral service in St. Anne's Church, Sale, Cheshire, near the home he shared with his wife Hilda.

Stan was a native of Blackburn, but his football interests were widespread. As a journalist, he worked in Manchester as deputy sports editor with the Sunday People and later moved to Merseyside to join the Liverpool Daily Post and Echo.

Eventually, he became a freelance, reporting football and producing several books. He was editor of the Anfield Review for 20 years.

Even after his retirement some six years ago, he continued to research and write books about the Club.

Just hours before he went into hospital last month, he was putting the finishing touches to a book featuring Liverpool fans, whose fervour had always impressed him.

Peter Robinson, Vice-Chairman and Executive recalls: "Stan Liversedge was steeped in the history and traditions of Liverpool Football Club.

He developed a fund of information, first as a newspaper football journalist and then as editor of the Anfield Review for many years.

"He edited the Review during the Club's most successful period before he retired in 1991. Then he went on to produce the official history of 100 years of Liverpool FC for our 1992 Centenary Year.

"He had first-hand knowledge of many of the events and the people who helped to shape our achievements.

"Stan will be mourned by all who knew him at Anfield. We send our sincere condolences to his family."

## Gold Rush!

WHY THE REDS HAD TO FIND A NEW LOOK IN A HURRY

In 1997 there was a tribute to the former editor of the programme, Stan Liversedge, while (right) a gold strip was a big talking point in the 1993-94 season

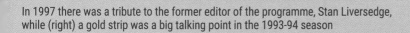

## My Kop Memories

### RON YEATS

■ *Liverpool's chief scout and the Sixties captain described by Bill Shankly as a colossus.*

' We beat Honved 1–0 in Hungary and Bill Shankly said we could all go out for a drink after such a good result.

We went to a club – probably the only one in Budapest in those days – and the lads pushed me onto the end of a dancing troupe. When we flew back home I told my family we'd had a quiet time . . . then television showed the pictures and there I was on screen kicking up my legs.

Was I in trouble!

But the Kop lads had seen those pictures too, and sang at our next home game 'Rowdy (my nickname) does the Twist!' The whole ground followed suit in song and I went the colour of my shirt.

Then there was the day we played Chelsea and thick fog was worsening at the Anfield end. The Kop knew we had scored, but didn't know the scorer. Visibility was that bad.

'Who scored the goal?' they sang . . . And the answer came back in melody: 'Tony Hateley, Tony Hateley.'

It was a great experience to play before the Kop and those fans warmed to everybody, friend or foe, who gave 100 per cent. '

### RONNIE MORAN

■ *The first-team coach and former player who has been employed by the Club for 44 years.*

' I stood on the Kop as a lad and the place was packed with humourists and enthusiasts – the right mix for football. Those fans had worked hard during the week and demanded the same effort from the players they supported. The noise they created was frightening, but players had nothing to fear provided they put 100 per cent into their game. '

### STEVE HEIGHWAY

■ *Liverpool's Director of Youth and former winger*

' My first experience of the Kop was in May, 1970, I was still a student at Warwick University, but had decided to sign professional for Liverpool on completing my Degree in June. As a student, I was quite surprised to be called by Mr. Bill Shankly, who invited me to play in Gerry Byrne's Testimonial for a Celebrity XI against the Liverpool side.

Not only was it my first visit to Anfield, but it was also at the age of 22 my first-ever visit to Liverpool itself. It was a filthy night with rain and sleet, but I recall that about 50,000 people were there.

The two teams walked side by side to the centre of the pitch and I stood next to an ex-Everton full-back who was playing in the Celebrity team. With total honesty and complete naivety, I quietly said to him: "Which end is the Kop"? He looked at me as if I had come from another planet, pointed to the bulging end rather than just the full end.

That was my first experience and, of course, there were many more opportunities to play in front of what was very obviously the fanatical end. I had good games and bad games through my eleven years, but I feel extremely fortunate that at no time did I ever feel animosity from the Kop.

I would have found that very difficult to live with and I am eternally grateful that the Kop always seemed to recognise that I was doing my best. '

### EMLYN HUGHES

■ *Former captain of Liverpool and England, one-time manager of Rotherham United and TV personality. Now director of a promotions company.*

' My special memory comes from the day we played Leeds United and a pass I intended for Peter Thompson went through to their keeper, Gary Sprake.

Gary collected the ball and I was annoyed with myself. I had to do something, so I ran across to their full-back and marked him for no apparent reason.

But Gary was about to throw the ball to him, saw me move and in changing his mind, finished up throwing the ball into his own net. Immediately the Kop gave me a tremendous ovation and chanted my name . . . they credited me with lightning thinking! Later the DJ put on the record 'Careless Hands' and the Kop joined in.

I found it natural, instinctive, to run to the Kop and give them a salute when we turned out. They were Liverpool. '

### TERRY McDERMOTT

■ *Assistant manager of Newcastle United under Kevin Keegan. Former England midfield man.*

' As a Kop supporter and a Liverpool player I was always astonished at the up-to-date wit and singing.

If a player or manager had been in mischief and the story appeared in the Saturday-morning papers, you could bet there would be a new, hilarious ditty the same afternoon. I'm sure somebody stood at the Kop turnstiles and handed out song sheets! '

### JOE FAGAN

■ *Succeeded Bob Paisley as manager and scored a unique treble of European Cup, League Championship and League Cup.*

' Kop support was above anything else and straight from the heart. Those supporters lifted players to undreamed heights. I have two personal memories from standing on the Kop as a lad before the war. Sunderland, in the days of Bobby Gurney and Raich Carter, were the smartest turned-out team I had ever seen. And I remember cracking my head on a barrier and seeing stars of a different kind! '

Known as the Oakfield Road Embankment,    it opened on September 1 in a heatwave

---

### Liverpool
*(Red shirts and shorts, white flashes)*
Manager: Roy Evans

| | | | |
|---|---|---|---|
| Bruce Grobbelaar | 1 | Bryan Gunn | |
| Rob Jones | 2 | Mark Bowen | |
| Julian Dicks | 3 | Rob Newman | |
| Steve Nicol | 4 | Ian Crook | |
| Mark Wright | 5 | Ian Culverhouse | |
| Don Hutchison | 6 | Neil Adams | |
| Nigel Clough | 7 | Efan Ekoku | |
| Paul Stewart | 8 | Colin Woodthorpe | |
| Ian Rush | 9 | Gary Megson | |
| John Barnes | 10 | John Polston | |
| Mark Walters | 11 | Jeremy Goss | |
| Ronnie Whelan | 12 | Mark Robins | |
| David James | 13 | Scott Howie | |
| Jan Molby | 14 | | |
| Jamie Redknapp | 15 | Daryl Sutch | |
| Michael Thomas | 16 | | |
| Steve McManaman | 17 | Ian Butterworth | |
| | 18 | Robert Ullathorne | |
| Torben Piechnik | 19 | Andy Johnson | |
| Stig Bjornebye | 20 | Darren Eadie | |
| Dominic Matteo | 21 | David Smith | |
| Steve Harkness | 22 | Chris Sutton | |
| Robbie Fowler | 23 | Deryn Brace | |
| Lee Jones | 24 | Andy Marshall | |
| Neil Ruddock | 25 | Jamie Cureton | |
| | 26 | Ade Akinbiyi | |
| | 27 | Spencer Prior | |

### Norwich City
*(Yellow shirts and green shorts)*
Manager: John Deehan

## My Kop Memories

### IAN RUSH

■ *Captain and all-time record goalscorer for the Reds and also for Wales. Still adding to his total.*

' I have lost count of the professional players who have asked me over the years: "What is it like to play in front of the Kop?"

I cannot imagine what my career would have been like without their support.

European nights and the sight of the Kop in full cry, the banners and the flags, will always be treasured by players and the atmosphere created for them.

My other vivid memory is from Alan Hansen's testimonial game when it was a Juventus player at Anfield. I thought those fans would be on a downer after losing to Wimbledon in the FA Cup Final, but they weren't.

Whenever I got near them they were asking me, one after another: 'When are you coming back to Liverpool?' They were talking to me all night, but I felt that would always be welcome.

The Kop fans will be seated next season, but the noise and encouragement for the team will always be the same. '

### RAY CLEMENCE

■ *Joined Barnet after parting company with Spurs. Goalkeeping great with the Reds and England.*

' When I first joined Liverpool I sat in the stand and marvelled at 20-odd thousand people singing and swaying together in the Kop.

Their fervour was incredible and topical. The singing of 'You'll Never Walk Alone' was another experience.

I look back on the derby games I enjoyed but the win over St Etienne is the one which stands out. It wasn't just the Kop which gave ultimate support that night, the whole stadium was gripped in a tremendous atmosphere.

My other memory is coming back to Anfield as a Spurs player for the first time. The reception I was given can only be described as a very emotional experience for myself.

But I have no individual memories because I closed my ears in order to concentrate on goalkeeping for 90 minutes. I heard the deafening roars but that's ok. '

### BRUCE GROBBELAAR

■ *Colourful veteran goalkeeper, 13 years at Anfield and revered by Zimbabweans after his World Cup exploits.*

' Those stories about the Kop making up their own original chants? I used to take them with a pinch of salt until I learned better.

They are terrific at composing instant words and music and the best heard came just after Freddie Laker had problems with an airline.

I kept high and collected a shot bound for the top corner of my goal and the immediate chant went up: 'Freddie Laker, Freddie Laker, Bruce is better in the air'.

The Kop fans, without fear of contradiction, are very knowledgeable on goalkeeping – more so that any other supporters at any club in the country. They produce quick lines when keepers make blunders but, let's be fair, they do make players smile. '

### KENNY DALGLISH

■ *Manager of Blackburn Rovers, former manager of Liverpool and one of the all-time great players with the Club and Scotland.*

' The memory which stays in my mind more than any other is walking through the Kop after the Hillsborough disaster and seeing the hundreds of tributes to those who had died.

I was with my son, Paul, and daughter, Kelly, on a Friday night after most of the people had left the ground.

That was the only time I faced the Kop. I will never forget it.

There were odd times when we were two goals behind and attacking the Kop end. Those supporters helped players all of the time, but they were invaluable when the team were trailing.

They knew we needed them and they realised their importance. So did we. '

### MIKE SUMMERBEE

■ *Businessman and former Manchester City and England forward, regarded as one of the game's jokers.*

' Manchester City were winning 2–1 with six minutes to go at Anfield and I took a corner at the Kop end.

They gave me some stick as I lowered my shorts. Minutes later they had gone 3–2 ahead through Roger Hunt and Ian St. John and the Kop chanted: 'Show us your backside, Summerbee' At least it sounded like that.

They were great fans, though, and fair to all visiting players who earned their respect. '

### JOEY JONES

■ *Coach at Wrexham and a hero of the Kop as the Reds' left-back.*

' I stood on the Kop as a kid and marvelled at the lively banter of the older supporters. My lasting memory, though, is of playing for Liverpool, raising my fist as I left the tunnel then hearing that deafening roar I got back from the Kop. '

### ALAN BALL

■ *Manager of Southampton, former midfield star with Everton and Arsenal, and youngest of England's 1966 World Cup Winners.*

' We were awarded a penalty while I played for Arsenal and picked up the ball at the Kop end and held up one finger to signify that I was about to put my team one goal in front. It was 0–0 at the time.

I scored . . . but thought about that gesture later on. Can you imagine the flak the Kop would have given me if I'd missed! I was a former Everton player.

But the Kop showed respect to players who put in their full lot and I believe I had their vote. They were wonderful people to play in front of and their power always turned me on.

I believed that I had to match the passion which they showed under that roof. Nothing less would have done for them. '

Stoke City were the visitors and a crowd of    30,000 saw Joe Hewitt give the Reds a 1–0 win

---

The Norwich City edition at the end of the 1993-94 season included memories from those who'd played in front of the famous terrace while Kop ticket-holders could win a unique memento from the day

Chief scout Ron Yeats, as one of the 'Anfield People', shared his account of the Reds' first trip to a European away game from his days as Liverpool captain. "We didn't know where Reykjavik was," he admitted

Robbie Fowler's PFA Young Player of the Year award was celebrated in May 1995

# LIVERPOOL: THE TITLE TRAIL OVER TWO DECADES

| Season | P | Home W | D | L | F | A | Away W | D | L | F | A | Pts | Final Position | Ever-Present | Leading Goalscorers | Average Attendance | Manager |
|---|---|---|---|---|---|---|---|---|---|---|---|---|---|---|---|---|---|
| 1970-71 | 42 | 11 | 10 | 0 | 30 | 10 | 6 | 7 | 8 | 12 | 14 | 51 | 5th | — | Alun Evans (10) | 38,948 | Bill Shankly |
| 1971-72 | 42 | 17 | 3 | 1 | 48 | 16 | 7 | 6 | 8 | 16 | 14 | 57 | 3rd | Ray Clemence, Chris Lawler, Emlyn Hughes | John Toshack (13) | 41,612 | Bill Shankly |
| 1972-73 | 42 | 17 | 3 | 1 | 45 | 19 | 8 | 7 | 6 | 27 | 23 | 60 | 1st | Chris Lawler, Larry Lloyd, Ian Callaghan | John Toshack } (13) Kevin Keegan | 48,127 | Bill Shankly |
| 1973-74 | 42 | 18 | 2 | 1 | 34 | 11 | 4 | 11 | 6 | 18 | 20 | 57 | 2nd | Ray Clemence, Emlyn Hughes, Kevin Keegan, Peter Cormack, Ian Callaghan | Kevin Keegan (12) | 42,332 | Bill Shankly |
| 1974-75 | 42 | 14 | 5 | 2 | 44 | 17 | 6 | 6 | 9 | 16 | 22 | 51 | 2nd | Ray Clemence, Emlyn Hughes | John Toshack (12) | 45,966 | Bob Paisley |
| 1975-76 | 42 | 14 | 5 | 2 | 41 | 21 | 9 | 9 | 3 | 25 | 10 | 60 | 1st | Ray Clemence, Phil Neal | John Toshack (16) | 41,623 | Bob Paisley |
| 1976-77 | 42 | 18 | 3 | 0 | 47 | 11 | 5 | 8 | 8 | 15 | 22 | 57 | 1st | Ray Clemence, Phil Neal, Emlyn Hughes | Kevin Keegan (12) | 47,220 | Bob Paisley |
| 1977-78 | 42 | 15 | 4 | 2 | 37 | 11 | 9 | 5 | 7 | 28 | 23 | 57 | 2nd | Phil Neal | Kenny Dalglish (20) | 45,540 | Bob Paisley |
| 1978-79 | 42 | 19 | 2 | 0 | 51 | 4 | 11 | 6 | 4 | 34 | 12 | 68 | 1st | Ray Clemence, Phil Neal, Ray Kennedy, Kenny Dalglish | Kenny Dalglish (21) | 46,406 | Bob Paisley |
| 1979-80 | 42 | 15 | 6 | 0 | 46 | 8 | 10 | 4 | 7 | 35 | 22 | 60 | 1st | Phil Neal, Phil Thompson, Kenny Dalglish | David Johnson (21) | 44,586 | Bob Paisley |
| 1980-81 | 42 | 13 | 5 | 3 | 38 | 15 | 4 | 12 | 5 | 24 | 27 | 51 | 5th | Phil Neal | Terry McDermott (13) | 37,547 | Bob Paisley |
| 1981-82 | 42 | 14 | 3 | 4 | 39 | 14 | 12 | 6 | 3 | 41 | 18 | 87 | 1st | Bruce Grobbelaar, Phil Neal, Kenny Dalglish | Ian Rush (17) | 35,060 | Bob Paisley |
| 1982-83 | 42 | 16 | 4 | 1 | 55 | 16 | 8 | 6 | 7 | 32 | 21 | 82 | 1st | Bruce Grobbelaar, Phil Neal, Ray Kennedy, Kenny Dalglish | Ian Rush (24) | 34,834 | Bob Paisley |
| 1983-84 | 42 | 14 | 5 | 2 | 50 | 12 | 8 | 9 | 4 | 23 | 20 | 80 | 1st | Bruce Grobbelaar, Alan Hansen, Alan Kennedy, Sammy Lee, Mark Lawrenson | Ian Rush (32) | 32,021 | Joe Fagan |
| 1984-85 | 42 | 12 | 4 | 5 | 36 | 19 | 10 | 7 | 4 | 32 | 16 | 77 | 2nd | Bruce Grobbelaar, Phil Neal | John Wark (18) | 34,465 | Joe Fagan |
| 1985-86 | 42 | 16 | 4 | 1 | 58 | 14 | 10 | 6 | 5 | 31 | 23 | 88 | 1st | Bruce Grobbelaar | Ian Rush (22) | 35,319 | Kenny Dalglish |
| 1986-87 | 42 | 15 | 3 | 3 | 43 | 16 | 8 | 5 | 8 | 29 | 26 | 77 | 2nd | Ian Rush | Ian Rush (30) | 36,284 | Kenny Dalglish |
| 1987-88 | 40 | 15 | 5 | 0 | 49 | 9 | 11 | 7 | 2 | 38 | 15 | 90 | 1st | Steve Nicol, Steve McMahon | John Aldridge (26) | 39,657 | Kenny Dalglish |
| 1988-89 | 38 | 11 | 5 | 3 | 33 | 11 | 11 | 5 | 3 | 32 | 17 | 76 | 2nd | Steve Nicol | John Aldridge (31) | 38,705 | Kenny Dalglish |
| 1989-90 | 38 | 13 | 5 | 1 | 38 | 15 | 10 | 5 | 4 | 40 | 22 | 79 | 1st | Bruce Grobbelaar | John Barnes (28) | 36,589 | Kenny Dalglish |
| Summary | 830 | 297 | 86 | 32 | 862 | 269 | 167 | 137 | 111 | 548 | 387 | 1365 | — | — | — | 40,142 average | — |

In the Aston Villa programme of September 1990, the Reds' record over the previous 20 years was laid bare, the club only finishing lower than second in the table once since 1971-72

18

**The Shankly Tribute**

# My Bill

BILL SHANKLY
He made the people happy

### Nessie remembers the great years

BILL Shankly, 5ft 6in in the flesh, 7ft 6in in bronze, was always larger than life. And no one appreciated that more than Nessie Shankly, the wife who supported him throughout his remarkable football career.

She is pictured gazing at the statue erected in his honour at Anfield earlier this month. It is another source of pride to add to the achievements she shared with the dynamic Scot who bestowed greatness to Liverpool Football Club after taking over as manager in December 1959.

At her request, the statue had been unveiled by Ron Yeats, now Liverpool's chief scout, who captained the team that climbed out of the Second Division in 1962 to begin a remorseless quest for trophies that has never been equalled by a British side. In fact he and John Smith arrived from Motherwell at the same time as Yeats from Dundee United. The Saint and Roger Hunt made a deadly strike pairing.

Ian Callaghan had already been blooded at the age of 17 and went on to complete 18 great seasons. Gerry Byrne took over at left-back from Ronnie Moran and wing-half Gordon Milne was recruited from Shankly's old club, Preston North End, to be followed by winger Peter Thompson.

In 1964 they won the Club's sixth League Championship and their first FA Cup was claimed a year later. In 1966 Liverpool took the title again, reached the final of the European Cup Winners' Cup and had three men – Hunt, Callaghan and Byrne – in the triumphant England World Cup squad.

UEFA Cup, in 1973. Shankly was named Manager of the Year.

In 1974 – just two months after an emphatic FA Cup Final win over Newcastle United – he told a press conference that he had signed Ray Kennedy from Arsenal. Then Liverpool's chairman, the late Sir John Smith announced to stunned reporters that Shankly had retired from League football. His reluctant successor was his assistant, Bob Paisley, who went on to break all records with his collection of silverware.

Bill Shankly died in Liverpool on September 29, 1981 after a short illness.

He was 68 and tributes flowed in from all over the world. His statue stands on the approaches to the new Visitor Centre at the Kop end, where he had a special affinity with the fans, who loved the man who gave them so much to celebrate. Appropriately the memorial bears this simple inscription

Bill Shankly
He made the people happy

**COVER STORY**

The bronze statue was commissioned by Liverpool FC sponsors Carlsberg and designed and crafted by the outstanding, Liverpool-born sculptor Tom Murphy, who is pictured on our front cover with his creation. It weighs three-quarters of a ton and stands on a plinth fashioned from Scottish granite.

Meanwhile, Shankly was planning his next team and in the late 60s and early 70s new names achieved fame ... like Tommy Smith, Chris Lawler, Emlyn Hughes, Steve Heighway, Ray Clemence, Brian Hall and, of course, Kevin Keegan. They won the title and the Club's first European trophy, the

Nessie Shankly admires the statue of her husband which was unveiled at Anfield in 1997

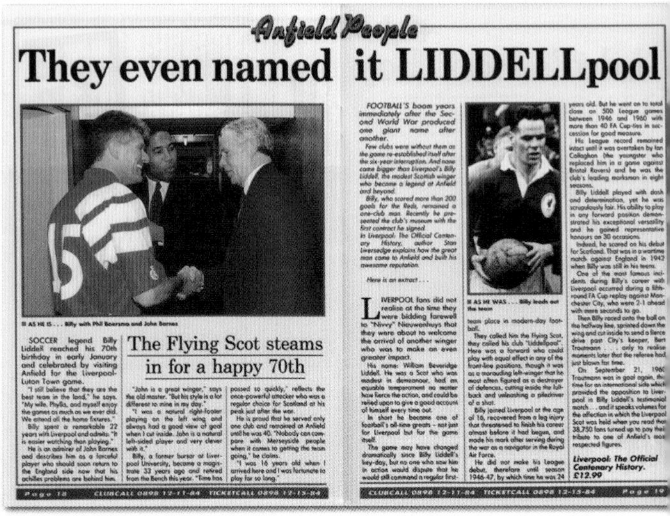

---

*Anfield People*

# They even named it LIDDELLpool

AS HE IS ... Billy with Phil Boersma and John Barnes

### The Flying Scot steams in for a happy 70th

SOCCER legend Billy Liddell reached his 70th birthday in early January and celebrated by visiting Anfield for the Liverpool-Luton Town game.

"I still believe that they are the best team in the land," he says. "My wife, Phyllis, and myself enjoy the games as much as we ever did. We attend all the home fixtures."

Billy spent a remarkable 22 years with Liverpool and admits: "It is easier watching than playing."

He is an admirer of John Barnes and describes him as a forceful player who should soon return to the England side now that his Achilles problems are behind him.

"John is a great winger," says the old master. "But his style is a lot different to mine in my day."

"It was a natural right-footer playing on the left wing and always had a good view of goal when I cut inside. John is a natural left-sided player and very clever with it."

Billy, a former bursar at Liverpool University, became a magistrate 32 years ago and retired from the Bench this year. "Time has

AS HE WAS ... Billy leads out the team

FOOTBALL'S boom years immediately after the Second World War produced one giant name after another.

Few clubs were without them as the game re-established itself after the six-year interruption. And none came bigger than Liverpool's Billy Liddell, the modest Scottish winger who became a legend at Anfield and beyond.

Billy, who scored more than 200 goals for the Reds, remained a one-club man. Recently he presented the club's museum with the first contract he signed in Liverpool. The Official Centenary History, author Stan Liversedge explains how the great man came to Anfield and built his awesome reputation.

Here is an extract:

LIVERPOOL fans did not realise at the time they were bidding farewell to "Nivvy" Nieuwenhuys that they were about to welcome the arrival of another winger who was to make an even greater impact.

His name: William Beveridge Liddell. He was a Scot who was modest in demeanour, had an equable temperament no matter how fierce the action, and could be relied upon to give a good account of himself every time out.

In short he became one of football's all-time greats – not just for Liverpool but for the game itself.

The game may have changed dramatically since Billy Liddell's hey-day, but no one who saw him in action would dispute that he would still command a regular first-

passed so quickly," reflects the once-powerful attacker who was a regular choice for Scotland at his peak just after the war.

He is proud that he served only one club and remained at Anfield until he was 40. "Nobody can compare with Merseyside people when it comes to getting the team going," he claims.

"I was 16 years old when I arrived here and I was fortunate to play for so long."

team place in modern-day football.

They called him the Flying Scot because he could play with equal effect in any of the front-line positions, though it was as a marauding left-winger that he most often figured as a destroyer of defences, cutting inside the full-back and unleashing a piledriver of a shot.

Billy joined Liverpool at the age of 16, recovered from a leg injury that threatened to finish his career almost before it had begun, and made his mark after serving during the war as a navigator in the Royal Air Force.

He did not make his League debut, therefore, until several years old. But he went on to total close on 500 League games between 1946 and 1960 with more than 40 FA Cup-ties in succession for good measure.

His League record remained intact until it was overtaken by Ian Callaghan (the youngster who replaced him in a game against Bristol Rovers) and he was the club's leading marksman in eight seasons.

Billy Liddell played with dash and determination, yet he was scrupulously fair. His ability to play in any forward position stamped his exceptional versatility and he gained representative honours on 30 occasions.

Indeed, he scored on his debut for Scotland. That was in a wartime match against England in 1942 when Billy was still in his teens.

One of the most famous incidents during Billy's career with Liverpool occurred during a fifth-round FA Cup replay against Manchester City, who were 2-1 ahead with men seconds to go.

Then Billy raced onto the ball as the half-time line, sprinted down the wing and cut inside to send a fierce drive past City's keeper, Bert Trautmann – only to realise moments later that the referee had just blown for time.

On September 21, 1960 Trautmann was in goal again, this time for an international side which provided the opposition to Liverpool at Billy Liddell's testimonial match ... and it speaks volumes for the affection in which the Liverpool Scot was held when you read that 38,750 fans turned up to pay their tribute to one of Anfield's most respected figures.

Liverpool: The Official Centenary History.
£12.99

Two more examples of the 'Anfield People' feature of the 1991-92 season see Billy Liddell explaining that he's a big fan of John Barnes, despite their wing styles being so different, while Tom Saunders remembered the days he was the club's 'Foreign Spy'

---

*Anfield People*

# Happy memoirs of the Red master-spy

TOM SAUNDERS ... noted the opposition secrets

LIVERPOOL'S return to European football has revived countless memories for former Youth Development Officer Tom Saunders.

He was the quiet, unassuming man who flew from city to city for almost a decade and gathered valuable information about the club's forthcoming opponents.

Tom, a Merseyside headmaster before he joined the Anfield staff in 1970, says modestly: "Anybody would have given their right arm for the same privilege. I was able to take in the whole spectrum of European football.

Such was the regularity of his trips in those golden years that he became known as "The Foreign Spy". His friends took him to some of the tastiest places in the football world.

But Tom, who still offers a helping hand at Anfield, emphasises that his brief was largely to build up a good relationship with the clubs Liverpool had drawn.

"That was point one and it was enjoyable. The different languages often posed problems, but football has a habit of bringing people together and getting along with each other regardless. I still receive Christmas cards from people I met."

He is delighted at Liverpool's return to Europe after a six-year

### I had to track down new contacts and make friends

absence. "I want them to do well again. I want to see those exciting nights back for everybody."

Among his duties were inspections of hotels. Quality of food and accommodation, plus assurances of undisturbed sleep, were essential. But Trabzon, in Turkey and near the Russian border, became a problem. "The place had only two hotels and their culture, their whole way of life, was different to ours," Tom recalls. "Some people carried out their business on the football while horses and carts rattled by. "When manager Bob Paisley

arrived with the players, he said that he had known better digs in the Western Desert."

"But the people were kind and generous. They gave Liverpool a marvellous welcome, even though we lost that European Cup game 1-0 before winning the second leg."

Tom's other duties included vetting the opposition for Bob and his successor, Joe Fagan. "We did not go too deeply into the techniques in those days," he explains. "I took a note of any dead-ball kicks which were different or might

ied some players who might have been causing a stir."

The Iron Curtain created problems. He was on his way to Poznan in Poland and became stranded in Warsaw because of a blizzard. Eventually he found a taxi and somewhere to stay, but he obliged to give away his club tie when it was recognised.

He made another trip to Dresden, to East Germany, via former coach Reuben Bennett and they passed through Checkpoint Charlie to catch their train.

"Reuben lit a cigarette in a non-smoking compartment and almost caused an international incident with the arguments he put up against the guards," says Tom, smiling at the memory.

---

AS YOU will see from today's programme, the Anfield Review has reverted to its previous shape and size, after production problems which, for reasons beyond our control, we have recently encountered. We hope and believe, though, that you will still consider your *Anfield Review* to be good value for the money...36 pages packed with stories and pictures, not to mention the chance for you to win prizes. And we can confidently assure all our supporters that we shall do our utmost to continue to inform, entertain...and make it well worth their while to carry on buying the *Anfield Review*.

Print problems were openly explained in the Manchester City programme of November 1990

## Caring in the Community

**Help me to build a dream in your city . . .**

**ROY CASTLE**, whose courage as a victim of lung cancer has inspired millions, takes over the Brian Hall Column to launch a special appeal at Anfield today

MY dream is to establish the world's first international Centre for Lung Cancer Research in Liverpool.

This unique £12m development will be sited opposite Liverpool University at the corner of Daulby Street and London Road.

The incidence of lung cancer is now very high.

It is already the most common form of cancer in men and becoming increasingly common in women. In some regions of the UK the figures for the disease are among the highest in the world.

That is why I am helping the Lung Cancer Fund and calling the campaign "Cause for Hope." The aim is to hasten the day when this scourge is removed from the community.

Great progress has already been made. Surgeons associated with the fund made medical history with new treatments and techniques in October 1991, when the first-ever keyhole operation for lung cancer was performed at the Cardiothoracic Centre in Liverpool.

The technique is less traumatic for the patient and leaves a much smaller scar than conventional surgery.

The Lung Cancer Fund has established a first-ever cancer counselling service which enables patients and relatives to talk to qualified staff about their worries and problems. But there is so much more to do.

We need to open smoking rehabilitation centres and more counselling clinics.

It is only through research, however; that a cure will be found. The Lung Cancer Fund is financing an intensive research programme into causes, prevention and treatment.

We can make lung cancer a thing of the past. That is why I extend a huge thank-you to all who contribute today towards the International Centre for Lung Cancer Research.

This centre will not be established in time to save my life, but it is an investment in the lives of our children and grandchildren.

CLUBCALL 0891 12 11 84 TICKETCALL 0891 12 15 84    25

Roy Castle appealed to Liverpool fans to help him raise money for the Lung Cancer Fund in 1994

---

**Liverpool Football Club – Season 1997/98**

# Rick's dream

FORMER Premier League supremo Rick Parry learns something new every day about the very different role of running a giant football club like Liverpool.

He could have no better instructor than Vice-Chairman Peter Robinson, who will one day hand over his other responsibilities as Chief Executive.

The man who rose from the position of Secretary to become recognised at home and abroad as an outstanding administrator has played a major part in keeping Liverpool FC at the forefront of football for more than 30 years.

One of the young fans he helped to make very happy as the trophies piled up at Anfield was Rick Parry, the Club's new Chief Executive designate. "Football has always been a big part of my life," he says. "I've loved the game since I was very young and I've always been a big Liverpool fan.

"Like most kids, I had dreams of becoming a professional footballer. I played in county schoolboy games and had trials with Liverpool and Everton. Going to Melwood and having a trial with Liverpool is a very special memory.

"I have vivid recollections of supporting Liverpool from about 1964. It was just at the time that the Liverpool success story was beginning. It was a terrific era in which to be a supporter."

Rick soon realised that he was not going to make the grade as a pro footballer, so directed his energies elsewhere and found new ways of making his mark on the game.

"Working on the setting-up of the Premier League was very exciting for me," he recalls and I loved every minute of my time there.

But I just couldn't refuse the chance to work for Liverpool. I'm here to learn from Peter Robinson to be ready for the day when he retires."

■ RICK PARRY . . . a fan since schooldays

## 'I just couldn't miss a job with Liverpool'

Liverpool's success during the glory years had a lot to do with continuity. They groomed people for management posts and that is what is happening here.

"Eventually, I will take over the reins, but at the moment I'm just trying to learn as much as I can about the day-to-day running of a football club.

I haven't been given a brief to change anything because the reality is that Liverpool have been the most successful club of all over the last 30 years."

LIVERPOOL CLUB CALL 0891 121 184 – FIND OUT WHAT'S GOING ON!    29

*Calls cost 50p per minute at all times*

Rick Parry spoke of his lifelong love of Liverpool FC when he became chief executive in 1997

---

**ANFIELD PEOPLE**

## The Big Macs

**Fan Fare**

Who better to promote the new McDonald's that was opened in the Kop in 1995 than a couple of Macs – McAteer and McManaman?

■ TWO of the biggest Macs around were happy to take first bite on the day Ronald McDonald moved into Anfield.

Jason McAteer (left) and Steve McManaman, stars with Liverpool and their respective countries Republic of Ireland and England – welcomed the official opening ten days ago of the McDonald's restaurant beneath the Kop Stand.

Liverpool are the first club in Europe to have a McDonald's inside their ground. It also caters for customers outside Anfield and service will be available seven days a week.

Manager Eddie Higdon says "We will be serving the full McDonald's menu, including breakfast and the new Vegetable Deluxe for non-meat eaters. We will be open normal McDonald's hours - from 8am until late at night.

Eddie is a Reds fan and his chances of watching the team will now be restricted. "I attended the Liverpool v Everton derby," he says "but I think that will be the last game I'll see for a while, even though I'll be working only a few yards away from the pitch."

McDonald's trade at more than 17,000 restaurants in 86 countries throughout the world and the new attraction beneath the famous Kop becomes the 632nd in the UK.

23

---

FOR ALL YOUR EXECUTIVE COACH REQUIREMENTS – CALL THE PROFESSIONALS – OFFICIAL CONTRACTORS TO LIVERPOOL F.C.

## ELLISON'S TRAVEL SERVICE

ST. HELENS' LEADING TRAVEL AGENTS
★
Telephone: St. Helens 22882/3 or 30505

ABTA

**THE WINNERS**

TWO winners of our end-of-season Picture-Puzzle competitions claimed tickets for matches at the start of this campaign, with Mr. Alan Jones, 3, Shand Street, Garston, Liverpool 19, having correctly identified one-time Southampton manager Ted Bates and Mr. Paul Stocks, 91, Henshaw Street, Stretford, Manchester, having named a former Manchester City and Scotland star, Willie Donachie, as the answer to the other puzzle. Both our winners claim their tickets for tonight's First Division clash at Anfield.

## FAMILIAR FACE, NEW COLOURS

LIVERPOOL fans saw a familiar face wearing new colours when they rolled up—more than 30,000 of them—for Kenny Dalglish's testimonial match, because the opposition from Real Sociedad included former Anfield favourite John Aldridge, who scored his last goal for this club almost exactly one year ago, when he bowed out by knocking in a spot-kick against Crystal Palace.

He has carried on scoring goals for his new club in Spain, as well, and now he's been joined by two other English players—Kevin Richardson, from Arsenal, and Dalian Atkinson, from Sheffield Wednesday. Real Sociedad obviously believe Aldo and their latest, £1.8M recruit, Atkinson, can forge a goal-den partnership.

However, when John Aldridge and his team-mates took on Liverpool at Anfield, it was a case of having to play second fiddle, because two goals from Ian Rush and one from Steve McMahon meant that Real lost 3-1. And—surprise, surprise—the man who laid on two of the Liverpool goals was . . . Kenny Dalglish.

22

John Aldridge's presence at Kenny Dalglish's testimonial as a Real Sociedad player was pictured in August 1990

## Reds to Remember

# The bin boy who became an idol!

■ THE MANAGER . . . greeting Newcastle fans

■ THE PLAYER . . . he captained England

THE player who became an outstanding England captain began his Anfield days seated on a dustbin.

That was Kevin Keegan . . . and first-team coach Ronnie Moran remembers him well.

"It was the backend of the 1970-71 season and our manager, Bill Shankly, was busying about and preparing for the FA Cup Final against Arsenal.

"Kevin perched himself on a dustbin and waited patiently until he was ready."

Ronnie was not especially surprised with the £35,000 signing of the dark-haired lad from Scunthorpe United.

"He was typical of the buys we made from the lower divisions in those days."

"There were very good reports about him, but he had it all to prove at Liverpool."

And Kevin, a miner's son with unmistakable ambitions, set about his monumental task the best way he could – with goals.

Ronnie recalls: "I had just taken charge of the Reserves and had him in my squad for three friendly games. He began in midfield, then I pushed him up front in pre-season games.

"The first team was abroad, but Peter Cormack was sent home with a knee injury and we were left with a problem to face. Bill Shankly arranged a practice match between the first and second teams at the training ground and Kevin completed a hat-trick against the Reserves.

"He was in . . . he played against Nottingham Forest at Anfield. We won 3–1 and he scored. There was no looking back for Kevin after that. We went from strength to strength."

His popularity with the fans, who admired his pace, skill and courage. He became a star attraction at every First Division ground in the land.

"Kevin oozed enthusiasm," says Ronnie. "He had good control, strength on the ball and a determination which kept him in the top flight here for about five years. He proved himself allover again with Hamburg, Southampton and Newcastle United.

"He learned our Liverpool ways quickly and added his own special talents to our style. We could all recognise the kind of person he was. Kevin was in a hurry with his career. He was a great lad too, and easy to work with."

Ronnie does remember, though, that Kevin ran with the ball in his early days at Liverpool –sometimes to excess. "But he soon worked it out. There was a time

to hold and a time to release the ball."

Kevin's first season in management, ended in a relegation fight at Newcastle United. But he and the Geordies survived and went to top the First Division last season.

"He has done very well there," adds Ronnie. "He is one that nobody can ever write off. He has confidence and has never shown a trace of big-headedness."

### RONNIE MORAN

■ Liverpool's long-serving first-team coach continues his series on the stars he has known at Anfield.

THE FIVE DO'S

1. **Do** keep fireworks in a closed box

THE FIVE DON'TS

1. **Don't** use a naked flame. Use a taper to light fireworks
2. **Don't** go back to a firework – once lit, it may go off in your face
3. **Don't** put fireworks in a pocket
4. **Don't** throw or fool with fireworks
5. **Don't** let pets outside

. . . but don't be blind to the dangers

### REDS TO REMEMBER

Featured in the 1993-94 programmes, Ronnie Moran spoke about legends, including "bin boy" Kevin Keegan and Joey Jones, who would "run all day"

Anfield Review

21

---

## behind the scenes

IVERPOOL head groundsman Reg Summers is reaping the reward of a considerable investment by the club who spent £400,000 in the summer relaying the Anfield pitch.

The pitch hadn't been draining as well as it should have been over recent seasons, and with Liverpool's proven commitment to providing the players with the best facilities available, the decision was taken to ensure the Anfield playing surface was as good as anything in the league. But, having been the head groundsman at Anfield for the last 28 years, Reg is experienced enough to know that on occasions you are in the lap of the gods as to how the pitch will play.

He says: "I do keep a regular eye on the weather forecast because we need to be prepared for all eventualities. We've had some drainage problems over the last couple of seasons which has made things a bit more difficult for us because the pitch always held wet for a couple of days after some heavy rain, making it hard for us to work with it.

"The club took the decision that we needed to relay the pitch and a contractor was brought in to do the work during the close season. We would have done it last season had it not been for

REG SUMMERS
Head Groundsman

between the date the pitch was seeded on June 26 and the day of our first game at Anfield this season against Inter Milan for it to bed in exactly as we would have liked it, but I think everyone is happy now with the way the pitch is playing."

A recent glut of home matches – today's game with Leeds is Liverpool's sixth Anfield fixture in less than a month - has ensured that Reg and his assistant Alan Webster have been working tirelessly to keep the pitch in top condition.

He says: "After a game we spend the next morning replacing every divot on the pitch, which can sometimes take quite a while. We then use the mower to flatten the pitch out in readiness for the next match. It's just a question of maintaining the pitch and ensuring it is ready for every game.

"If we got a bad weather forecast for the day of a game then we will mark the lines out the day before, and likewise if the forecast is bad the day before then we leave marking the lines until the day of the match.

"I have been here a long time now and I do take great satisfaction from my work. It is on display for everybody to see and I am confident that we won't have any major problems with the pitch this season."

### 'I do keep a regular eye on the weather forecast'

Head Groundsman Reg Summers on Anfield's newly installed pitch.

20

---

PLAYING THE GAME

## Club mourns Sir John

■ SIR JOHN SMITH . . . Golden era

SIR John Smith, the Kopite who went on to become the most successful Chairman in Liverpool's history, has died aged 74. He leaves a widow and a son.

The Club mourns his passing and looks back with gratitude on his 24 years of loyal and outstanding service as a Director and Chairman.

Sir John was knighted in 1989 for his contribution to the world of sport and industry, seven years earlier being awarded the CBE.

He succeeded Harold Smith as a Director in 1971, became Chairman in 1973 and - with managers Bill Shankly, Bob Paisley, Joe Fagan and Kenny Dalglish - led the Reds to one astonishing triumph after another. During his 17 years as Chairman, Liverpool won 22 major trophies, including four European Cups – a record which may never be equalled.

His willingness to stand aside and allow others to enjoy the great triumphs was part of his nature. However, he would speak proudly and passionately whenever he represented the Club. He worked in harmony with Chief Executive Peter Robinson and the Board.

Sir John served on the Football League Management Committee and in 1985 became Chairman of the Sports Council. He had been appointed to the Council five years earlier after presenting a report on the state of British tennis.

He was a magistrate, a Deputy Lieutenant, Deputy Chairman of the Merseyside Development Corporation and a member of the Chester Committee's local inquiry into football.

Sir John won the Merseyside Gold Medal as the area's outstanding personality. In his business life he was a Director of Tetley Walker Ltd for 11 years then joined First Castle Electronics in 1978.

Liverpool Chairman David Moores said: "He will be a tremendous loss to the Club. We valued his experience, his expert guidance and wise counsel."

Chief Executive Peter Robinson declared: "He was the outstanding chairman of his time. His record is unparalleled in football. He was a man of firm beliefs, but had a warm working relationship with managers and star players.

"Sir John was especially proud of the family atmosphere he helped to create and the continuity of managers from within the Club during his years of success."

### Tribute to Ken Addison

■ FORMER commercial manager Ken Addison has died at his home in Aughton. The Club offers its deepest sympathy to his wife Rusty and son Neil.

Ken, who was 67, pioneered the Development Association more than 30 years ago and retired in 1992. Wally Bennett, present Association manager, paid the following tribute: "His enthusiasm for Liverpool was infectious. He was a true professional and our staff will miss him.

"Ken still worked on match days and paid weekly visits to our office for a friendly chat with our agents. He was well respected throughout the game and other clubs came for his advice."

Players past and present made personal calls on Ken and he was proud of the fact that the Reds won 29 major trophies during his working years at

Anfield. He began as the Organiser of the Daily Draw Pool and his first office was a building site but next to the present Souvenir Shop.

Ken saw enormous changes over the years and said modestly at the time of his retirement: "I would like to think that I have contributed my little bit."

23

'Behind the scenes' in November 1998 featured head groundsman Reg Summers who told us about replacing all the pitch divots the day after a match while (left) the club mourned the death of Sir John Smith and Ken Addison in February 1995

## Reds to Remember

# Joey was always a fan

MANAGER Bob Paisley was strolling near the grounds of the team's country hotel in Holland and digesting an enjoyable evening meal.

It was pre-season and he and his lieutenants, Joe Fagan and Ronnie Moran, were discussing the fixtures which lay ahead at home and abroad. The serenity of that warm, summer evening was suddenly disturbed by a cyclist who hurtled through the trees of a nearby wood, singing at the top of his voice.

The figure who emerged with his feet perched high on the handlebars was defender Joey Jones. Paisley's strong reaction was predictable. He wasn't too pleased. And one sharp sentence in his choice North-East accent was enough to send the happy wanderer pedalling back to headquarters.

"That was Joey," says Ronnie. "He had energy to burn. Bikes had been lined up at the hotel door and he couldn't resist the exercise."

The same super-fit player won 72 caps for Wales and built up a very special relationship with the Kop and all Liverpool supporters. His style of play was infectious, his effort in games was always 100 per cent.

**RONNIE MORAN**
■ Liverpool's long-serving first-team coach continues his series on the stars he has known at Anfield.

Ronnie remembers him being signed from Wrexham after careful vetting by the Anfield scouts. Paisley studied their reports and made his move.

"Joey had a hatred of losing and would have played for Liverpool for nothing," says Ronnie.

He will always be remembered for his match-day salute to the Kop whenever the team emerged from the tunnel. The fist was clenched and the arm raised high as he galloped across the pitch.

"Visitors may have thought it was intimidating, but that was not the case," says Ronnie. "Joey had stood on the Kop as a boy. He was one of them and it was his way of releasing tension.

"Sometimes he would give his salute to all four corners of Anfield and the supporters would always respond to him. He was a genuinely good guy and the first to help anybody in trouble."

Many of his games were behind Ray Kennedy, the studious midfield player who had been a striker with Arsenal. Their styles were different, but the combination was highly successful.

"Ray was a cool customer with the better technique and vision," claims Ronnie. "But

'I think that he would have been happy to play for nothing'

■ JOEY the pal . . . lining up for Steve Nicol's testimonial match earlier this season alongside two of his old teammates, Tommy Smith and David Fairclough

Joey would run all day long and play with a high level of intelligence.

"His spirit was unbreakable and the two men blended together naturally.

"Ray and Joey were good for each other, different kinds of players who formed the right blend."

Joey was also an asset in the dressing-room, a constant joker who came out with a stream of one-liners.

He geed up players before kick-off and was always on the move in the nervous pre-match moments.

"He was a dream for us to work with," Ronnie reflects. "He feared nobody in the world when he stepped onto that grass.

"He roomed with David Fairclough, who liked to watch television until midnight on a Friday. That didn't always suit Joey, who liked his deep sleep.

'So he called David The Night Owl and would often make hooting noises over the breakfast table."

Ronnie liked the way Joey recovered from any blunder. Not even an own goal would affect his overall performance. "Because of his attitude he rarely played a bad game," he recalls.

"And the fame he earned with Liverpool never crossed his mind. I didn't see him sulk over anything. I was sorry when he left the Club."

Joey is now a coach at Wrexham and works with his former international team-mate, manager Bryan Flynn.

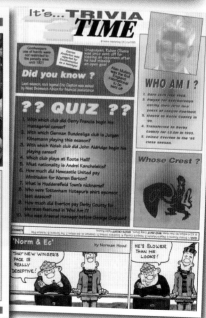

Interactive pages across the decade included crosswords, quizzes, cartoons and the chance to spot your face in the crowd

# The Last Picture Show

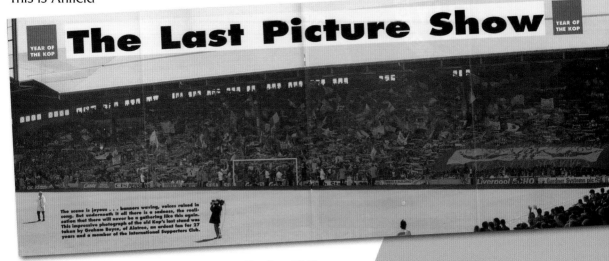

The scene is joyous . . . banners waving, voices raised in song. But underneath it all there is a sadness, the realisation that there will never be a gathering like this again. This impressive photograph of the old Kop's last stand was taken by Graham Boyce, of Aintree, an ardent fan for 27 years and a member of the International Supporters Club.

A four-page fold-out of the last match of the standing Kop was on show in the first issue of the 1994-95 season – what a sight

## TEAM CHECK

| LIVERPOOL (Red-and-white shirts) | | SOUTHAMPTON (White shirts) | |
|---|---|---|---|
| 1 | BRUCE GROBBELAAR | 1 | TIM FLOWERS |
| 2 | GLENN HYSEN | 2 | GLENN COCKERILL |
| 3 | DAVID BURROWS | 3 | MICKY ADAMS |
| 4 | STEVE NICOL | 4 | JIMMY CASE (Capt.) |
| 5 | RONNIE WHELAN (Capt.) | 5 | NEIL RUDDOCK |
| 6 | GARY GILLESPIE | 6 | RUSSELL OSMAN |
| 7 | PETER BEARDSLEY | 7 | MATTHEW LE TISSIER |
| 8 | RAY HOUGHTON | 8 | BARRY HORNE |
| 9 | IAN RUSH | 9 | ALAN SHEARER |
| 10 | JOHN BARNES | 10 | PAUL RIDEOUT |
| 11 | STEVE McMAHON | 11 | FRANCIS BENALI |
| Subs | | Subs | |

## SCORECHECK

| FIRST DIVISION | | SECOND DIVISION | |
|---|---|---|---|
| Norwich City v. Everton | | Barnsley v. West Ham Utd. | |
| Chelsea v. Coventry City | | Bristol Rovers v. Newcastle Utd. | |
| Manchester City v. Crystal Palace | | Charlton Athletic v. Hull City | |
| Sheffield Utd. v. Nottingham Forest | | Middlesbrough v. Blackburn Rovers | |
| Tottenham Hotspur v. Luton Town | | Notts. County v. Bristol City | |
| Wimbledon v. Manchester Utd. | | Oldham Ath. v. Plymouth Argyle | |
| TOMORROW: Aston Villa v. Arsenal (TV) | | Oxford Utd. v. Sheffield Wed. | |
| Derby County v. Queen's Park Rangers | | Port Vale v. Brighton & H.A. | |
| Sunderland v. Leeds Utd. | | Portsmouth v. Ipswich Town | |
| THIRD DIVISION | | Swindon Town v. West Bromwich. A. | |
| Chester City v. Southend United | | Wolverhampton W. v. Millwall | |
| | | TOMORROW: Leicester City v. Watford | |

REFEREE
Mr. R. A. Hart

LINESMEN
Mr. G. P. Davies (Yellow Trim)
Mr. K. Whittaker (Red Trim)

**SPORTS NEWS FIRST**
CITY 96.7 FM
CITY TALK 1548 AM 194m MW

How the back-page looked on the programmes of the 1990-91 season, this one being for the visit of Southampton in December 1990

## Anfield People

# In my heart I still remain No 1 fan...

By David Moores
Chairman
Liverpool FC

In 1991 self-confessed fan David Moores was still pinching himself after becoming chairman

DAVID·M·ROBINSON
Jewellers

THE WINNING TEAM

LONGINES

## The Grand Opening

# Mr Europe's Anfield fanfare

CROWD BEHAVIOUR WAS PERFECT SAYS LENNART JOHANSSON

The revamped Centenary Stand was officially opened by the UEFA president in August 1992

### Man for all seasons

*Anfield People*

**VICE-CHAIRMAN . . . another role for Peter Robinson**

'It's been my privilege to work with many talented managers'

Fans and ex-players celebrated the 40th anniversary of Bill Shankly's arrival at Anfield in December 1999, while Peter Robinson spoke about his service to the club in October 1996

**Back the Lady Reds**

*The Community*

# The Hillsborough Memorial Service

The club were encouraging fans to go along and watch Liverpool Ladies in action in November 1996, while the tenth anniversary Hillsborough Memorial Service was marked in April 1999

# The future face of Anfield

THIS IS HOW IT WILL LOOK NEXT SEASON

Your guide to watching the Reds in sheer luxury

**Regular Red at 86**

*Fan Fare*

In the Chelsea programme in February 1992 the club gave an insight into what the new-look Centenary Stand would be like, while an 86-year-old fan took centre stage in March 1995

A Reebok advert featuring Harry Enfield-type Scousers wearing the new yellow away top – with right-back Jason McAteer among the faces in the crowd, if you can spot him. Some fans felt it perpetuated stereotypes.

McDonald's took advantage of Liverpool having Patrik Berger in the squad (far-right, bottom) while Candy focused on LFC's 'clean up' of trophies and Carlsberg served up a series of witty ads.

The Times wanted everyone to know they had Steve McManaman on board as a columnist and Kick Sportswear showed off some rather colourful clobber!

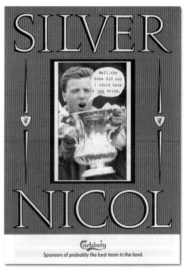

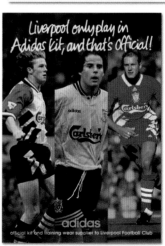

# CHAPTER 7

# INTO THE 2000s

European managers, European glory, and so many big moments on the pitch – there was plenty to read about within the pages of the programme in an exciting decade

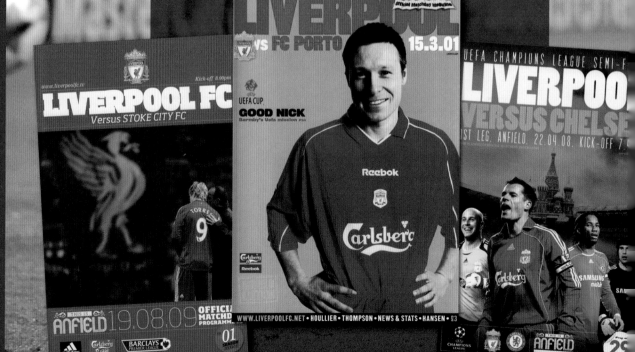

# This is Anfield

**T**he first decade of the new millennium began with Liverpool, as many fans put it, 'getting our pride back', under first Gerard Houllier and later Rafael Benitez as manager. As success returned to the pitch, for a while there was a radical new look to the matchday programme – published by Haymarket in a groundbreaking A4-sized format, combining the glossy look of a magazine with the playful tone of a fanzine while still respecting the club's traditions.

In the first of those two seasons, 2000-01, a side featuring Houllier signings Sander Westerveld, Sami Hyypia, Stephane Henchoz, Vladimir Smicer and Didi Hamann won a historic treble of League Cup, FA Cup (both at Cardiff's Millennium Stadium) and UEFA Cup (in Dortmund) as well as securing Champions League qualification with third place in the Premier League. But in October 2001 during a home game against Leeds United the manager was rushed to hospital to undergo emergency heart surgery.

Six months later Houllier returned for one of the great nights at Anfield as the Reds beat AS Roma 2-0 to reach the last eight of the Champions League. Previously the team had added the FA Community Shield and UEFA Super Cup to their trophy haul, and they'd finish runners-up to Arsenal in the Premier League.

The publishing honours were subsequently awarded to Sport Media, part of the same group which included the *Liverpool Echo* newspaper with its unrivalled archive of LFC material. Variously called 'THIS IS ANFIELD' then 'LIVERPOOL', the matchday programme sported colourful and eye-catching front covers with popular new features inside like 'The Kop & Goal Years'.

There was a seventh League Cup success in 2002-03 with victory over Manchester United but it was down to fifth in the Premier League and elimination from the Champions League then the UEFA Cup having lost to Celtic. The Reds were fourth the following season and enjoyed a third win at Old Trafford in four Premier League visits, but they were knocked out of the UEFA Cup by a Didier Drogba-inspired Marseille.

Who back then could have foreseen the climax to 2004-05? Champions of Europe! The semi-final second leg against Chelsea was an Anfield classic, then in the greatest European final of modern times Liverpool beat AC Milan on penalties in Istanbul after coming back from three goals down. Three-quarters-of-a-million people welcomed them home, with 300,000 gathered at the city's St George's Hall.

It meant the Reds could compete for the Super Cup, which they won by beating CSKA Moscow in Monaco, and the Club World Championship, which they somehow lost to Brazilian team Sao Paulo despite a dominant display, including three disallowed goals, in the Japanese city of Yokohama.

Five months later they were victorious in one of the best FA Cup finals ever, beating West Ham United on penalties after a 3-3 draw in Cardiff, with two stunning strikes by Steven Gerrard. They'd also finished third in the league.

That summer, Italy won the FIFA World Cup following an ill-tempered final against France in Berlin.

The following season, 2006-07, brought another third place, another Champions League semi-final win over Chelsea, this time on spot-kicks, and another final against AC Milan, this time in Athens but with a different outcome: the Reds lost 2-1.

It was all about new boy Fernando Torres in 2007-08, who'd arrived from Atletico Madrid. The explosive Spanish striker duly

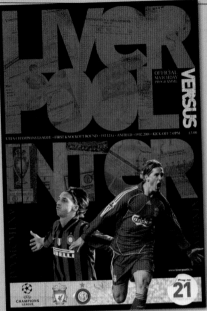

The visit of Inter Milan in 2008 warranted a special cover that had Fernando Torres and Zlatan Ibrahimovic pictured

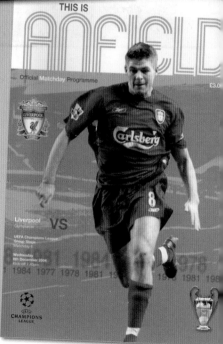

Fittingly, Steven Gerrard was on the cover of the programme for the Champions League visit of Olympiakos in 2004

set a new record for the most prolific foreign scorer in a debut season in England, with 33 goals as his side finished fourth an the city of Liverpool celebrated its European Capital of Culture status. But a third UCL last-four showdown with Chelsea ende in defeat.

The following campaign, 2008-09, Liverpool put four goals past both Real Madrid and Manchester United in the space of five days. Ultimately, though, they'd be runners-up in the Prem League to United and lose a Champions League quarter-final 1 Chelsea, 7-5 on aggregate.

The Benitez reign was brought to an end in the summer of 2010 after his team had finished seventh and reached the Europa League semi-finals, only to lose to Atletico Madrid on

LIVERPOOL VS WEST HAM UNITED 18.8.01

...ASS THE LIVERPOOL FIRST-TEAM SQUAD 2001/02

UNITED

LIVERPOOL VS WEST HAM UNITED 11

...way goals, in a season plagued by off-field uncertainty. ...Stability returned when Fenway Sports Group purchased ...C, but the appointment of Roy Hodgson as boss was short-...ed. When Kenny Dalglish returned to replace him in January ...11, one of his first tasks was to oversee the departure of ...rnando Torres and the arrival of Luis Suarez, who kicked off ... Anfield career with a goal on his debut against Stoke City. ...e Reds settled for sixth in the Premier League. ...Kenny soon waved the magic wand with a Carling Cup ...umph at Wembley over Cardiff City – Liverpool's first trophy ...r six years – in February 2012. There was a narrow defeat in ...e FA Cup final to Chelsea, before Dalglish was succeeded by ...endan Rodgers in the hot seat.

It's ours to keep . . .

UEFA CHAMPIONS LEAGUE • FINAL SIXTEEN • SECOND LEG • ANFIELD • 10.03.2009 • KICK-OFF 7.45PM

# Liverpool

## Real Madrid

*Official Matchday Programme £3.00*

Prog no:
**21**

www.liverpoolfc.tv

The 2000-01 season programmes had a version sold at the ground, but also a newsagent version

The first two full seasons of the Noughties saw the club produce a radically-different, large-format programme that the *Financial Times* newspaper described at the time as "a dramatic facelift which has attracted the attention of Premier League rivals and the Football Association, the game's governing body."

Publishers Haymarket had originally pitched to relaunch Liverpool FC's monthly magazine but Granada, which had recently bought a stake in the club to develop its media and commercial side, instead suggested an A4 glossy to be sold at each home game.

There was an 'Anfield Edition' on sale at the ground and a slightly more expensive version available from newsagents.

The *FT* added that the programme had been "identified as an under-exploited marketing tool offering scope for building brand loyalty" but was still "more in keeping with supporters than club directors, providing Liverpool with a credible vehicle to reach fans...

"It features specially commissioned photography and contributions from writers on broadsheet newspapers and magazines. The format also includes some of the irreverence of fanzines."

In March 2002 the programme was packed with content in a glossy magazine format

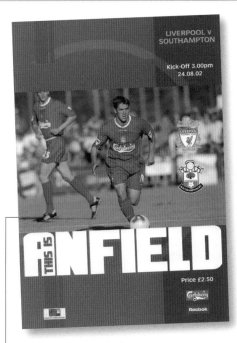

The first home game of the 2002-03 season featured a cover image of forward Michael Owen

John Arne Riise was the cover star of the Bolton Wanderers programme in December 2003

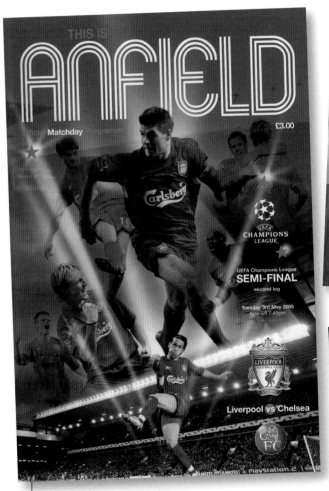

A fantastic night at Anfield deserved a fantastic cover – and that's what we got for the Chelsea Champions League semi-final in 2005

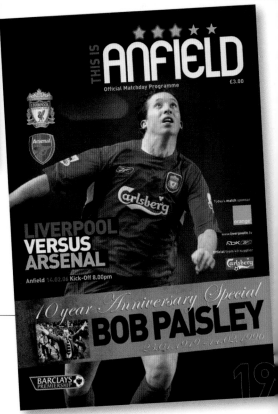

Three stars were glowing on the cover of the Arsenal programme in February 2006 to represent the three European Cups won by Bob Paisley as Liverpool manager as the club marked the 10-year anniversary of his death

New signing Craig Bellamy fronted up for the second league programme of 2006-07

Fernando Torres graced the cover and scored his first Anfield goal against Chelsea in August 2007

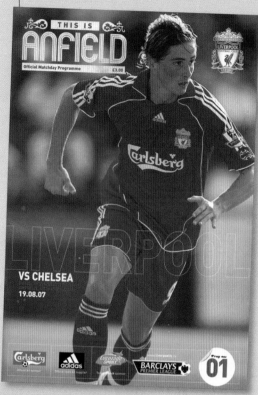

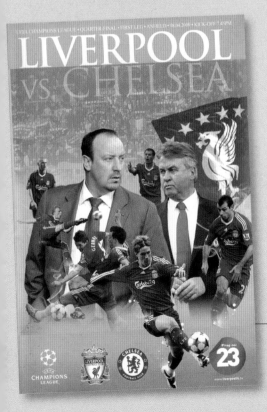

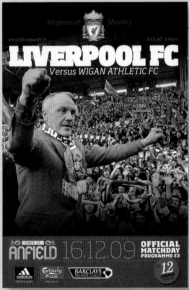

Fifty years after his arrival at Anfield, the club showed that Bill Shankly's immense contribution hadn't been forgotten as he featured on the Wigan cover

It seemed like the Reds were playing Chelsea every year in European competition and another special cover was designed for a Champions League quarter-final tie in 2009

# Rafael Benitez

**IT has been a strange season for us in many ways but it is good to be able to say it doesn't end today.**

To beat Chelsea and reach the Champions League final was a special moment for us all. I was very proud of the players and the supporters.

We could hear you all in the dressing room before the match; the atmosphere was fantastic. Talking with former players, they say it was the best they have ever experienced.

I like to play finals because I like to win things. AC Milan are a very big club, they were the best when I was starting to be a manager. They have always been a reference and to play against Milan in the final is a challenge.

I am disappointed with our performance away in the league, very disappointed. We have had 11 defeats. It's not normal to lose that many games; you can draw games if you play badly but we have lost them. Against Manchester City we lost in the last minute. These points we have lost add together and cost us.

I always think positively but we need to work in the summer to change things and prepare for next season.

The Carling Cup was fantastic - until the final. The FA Cup was another disappointing situation. I am frustrated because I want to give our supporters more to enjoy. Next year will be different. We will be stronger.

We have a clear idea - a big picture - of how to improve this club and we are working in different ways to do that.

We must be positive. We have been inconsistent in the league but I think we are improving for the future. We have a clear idea about what to do. We don't want to fight to be in the top four; we want to do more than that.

It would be nice to finish the Premiership season with a win today, which would put us in a positive mood for the next ten days.

We are thinking about the final, trying to play well, to win the game. We are watching videos and analysing AC Milan, as well as preparing the physical plan and the tactical plan. We have injured players from during the season who are improving and we need to prepare them.

It will be difficult. We know Milan have a lot of good players and a good manager. They have experience but we also have good players and we are hungry. It's just the same: 11 against 11. The atmosphere cannot be better than at Anfield but we have confidence and we believe.

**Honours**

**LEAGUE CHAMPIONS**

1900/01 1905/06 1921/22
1922/23 1946/47 1963/64
1965/66 1972/73 1975/76
1976/77 1978/79 1979/80
1981/82 1982/83 1983/84
1985/86 1987/88 1989/90

**EUROPEAN CUP WINNERS**

1976/77 1977/78
1980/81 1983/84

**EUROPEAN SUPER CUP WINNERS**

1977/78 2001/02

**UEFA CUP WINNERS**

1972/73 1975/76 2000/01

**FA CUP WINNERS**

1964/65 1973/74 1985/86
1988/89 1991/92 2000/01

**LEAGUE CUP WINNERS**

1980/81 1981/82 1982/83
1983/84 1994/95 2000/01
2002/03

**CHARITY SHIELD WINNERS**

1966 1974 1976 1979
1980 1982 1988 1989 2001

**CHAIRMAN**
DR Moores
**CHIEF EXECUTIVE**
RN Parry BSc FCA
**DIRECTORS**
N White FSCA, TD Smith,
KEB Clayton FCA, J Burns,
L Wheatley, JH Cresswell BSc ACA
**VICE PRESIDENTS**
HE Roberts, JT Cross
**TEAM MANAGER**
Rafael Benitez
**SECRETARY**
WB Morrison

### teven Gerrard

THE atmosphere might be a little bit strange going into today's game, largely because we have failed to qualify for the Champions League again next season through our league position and there's effectively nothing to play for today at least on paper.

This is Liverpool Football Club and there is always something to play for though - even if that's just professional pride and ensuring we finish the season with as many points as possible.

I'd like to think though that we will be going out onto the Anfield pitch today looking for a victory to say thank you to the fans who have given us the unbelievable level of support this season. I don't think there are a group of fans in world football who can match ours when they're in full voice.

We've not always turned in the performances their support has deserved this season, particularly away from home in the league but they've always backed us. For that reason alone it would be great to finish the season with a good victory.

I'm sure the fans will be out today in their numbers because they'll want to give us a send-off before we head for Istanbul and we'd like to end the league season on a high.

We'd be lying if we said that we weren't thinking a lot about Istanbul because it's such a tremendous opportunity to win the European Cup and it's going to be the biggest game of most of our lives but that won't deflect us today.

The manager is going to be watching us all closely in this game and in training between now and going to Istanbul because for the first time this year we have just about everyone fit and available for selection. That means there is going to be real competition not only for starting places against Milan but also for places on the bench.

The best way anyone can go about staking a claim for one of those places would be with a really good performance today against a well organised Villa team.

They've not had the best results in their last couple of games but they are always difficult to play against. Our games with them recently have never been very high scoring - there's normally just one goal between the teams. We'd like to change that today with a win and three points first and foremost but we'd really like to put on a show and build our confidence and belief ahead of May 25.

**LFC | 07**

### UP FRONT WITH GERARD HOULLIER

## "The plaudits must go to Phil Thompson, the boys and the team behind the team for the way they've responded in my absence"

LIVERPOOL HAS ALWAYS BEEN A family club and nothing has brought that home to me better than the way people have responded over the last three weeks. From the chairman to the technical team and players through to the administrative staff and fans I have been constantly encouraged by their affection, messages of support and genuine interest in my continuing recovery. I have felt a part of that extended family and I want to say a big thank you to everyone who has been by my side during this difficult period.

I've received absolutely first-class medical care at the cardiothoracic centre Liverpool NHS trust and I'd like to pay a special tribute to Mr Rashid and his team and thank all the nurses who have been fantastic. But I can also tell you what a marvellous boost it's been to me that the team has continued to win and has qualified for the next stage of the Champions League. I was very proud indeed of my players on Wednesday evening when we beat Dortmund and the plaudits must go to Phil Thompson, the boys and the team behind the team for the way they've responded during my absence.

Phil has done a wonderful job and has been keeping me in touch with everything that's going on within the camp and letting the lads know how I've been progressing. To me they've been the team of the month, though I hope that doesn't bring any sort of award and the inevitable jinx that accompanies it! The players have shown great resolve and that reflects the unity behind the scenes at Melwood.

I've been touched by the concern shown by many others from outside the club. I heard about the warm reception at Charlton and I can tell you five Premiership managers have also visited me in hospital. He wouldn't want me to say it, but I appreciated the fact my longstanding friend Alex Ferguson was one of those and despite the rivalry between the clubs it was a great boost to receive separate goodwill messages from the staff and players at Old Trafford.

United, like ourselves and Arsenal, have qualified for the next stage of the Champions League which means three English sides have again made it to the last 16 of Europe's elite club competition. I'd like to pass on my congratulations to them both, because coupled with the success last year of Leeds, it proves just how high the standard now is in the Premiership.

I was particularly pleased we finished unbeaten in our group as that demonstrated to me how much this side is developing in terms of strength, maturity and experience since we set out on the Uefa Cup trail just over a year ago. It's just left for me to wish the boys the best of luck today.

### A MESSAGE FROM PHIL THOMPSON

## "Qualifying will be the best get-well message"

EVERY SINGLE ONE OF US AT THE club knows how much this competition means to Gérard Houllier and how delighted he will be if we can break the jinx and progress to the second stage. That's the challenge tonight to make sure that when Gérard does return we've still something with the best in Europe.

As pleased as I am with the way the team has been performing, the real boost has been the way Gérard has continued to improve following his surgery. The treatment he's received at Broadgreen Hospital has been absolutely fantastic and I want to pay tribute to the efforts of everyone at the cardiothoracic unit.

I know, too, he's been very touched by the number of messages of goodwill and support he has received from Liverpool supporters and other fans as well as many people within the game itself. Thank you to everyone who has sent their best wishes.

My role is a clear one and that's to make sure we continue to adhere to the guidelines laid down by Gérard until he is able to take charge once again. Having worked with him for three years, I've a good idea what he's looking for and my job is to keep things going in the meantime.

I thought we did well at Boavista and should have won the game. We had some great chances to wrap it up but some good prizefighting discard us although I'm still proud of the way the boys performed.

We'll approach this game as any other with total respect for our opponents, but we do have home advantage and will be looking for the fans to make the difference with their backing from the off. So get behind the lads and help us send the best get-well message possible to Gérard Houllier by qualifying this evening.

---

**Between them, Liverpool's first two overseas managers were in charge for a dozen years, from 1998 to 2010, and their respective notes reflected their personalities and footballing cultures as well as their dexterity in communicating in a different language.**

**Gerard Houllier had spent time in the city of Liverpool as a teacher in the Sixties and was fluent in English, whereas Rafael Benitez had to learn on the job. Both were incredibly driven and disciplined.**

**When Houllier fell ill in the first half of the 2001-02 season, assistant Phil Thompson assumed duties in the dugout and on page 5, informing fans of the manager's progress as he recovered from heart surgery.**

**Houllier soon resumed his column and shown above are his notes for the game against Manchester United in late October 2000, in which he revealed that Alex Ferguson visited him in hospital.**

**The first season with Rafael Benitez in charge ended in the 'Miracle of Istanbul'.**

**On the left are his notes for the final home game of 2004-05, against Aston Villa, ten days before the Champions League final against AC Milan in Istanbul – along with Steven Gerrard's captain's column.**

**Rafa wrote: "It will be difficult... The atmosphere cannot be better than at Anfield, but we have confidence and we believe."**

The glory of...

The glory of...

### THE FILES OF ANFIELD ROAD

For several years in the 2000s, the history features were brought together in a section called 'The Files of Anfield Road'

# THE FILES OF ANFIELD RD

Hunting for goals . . . Roger Hunt is denied by Chelsea keeper Peter Bonetti but the Reds went on to win 2-1 at Anfield in November 1968 thanks to goals from Ian Callaghan and Tommy Smith (penalty)

**Digging deep into the Liverpool Football Club vaults to bring you history and mystery surrounding the men who gave us dreams and songs to sing...**

'Oh Campione' featured during the 2007-08 season and looked back – one at a time – at the Reds' 18 league championships to date

Thirty years after a stand-out title-winning season, the programme relived the 1978-79 campaign in great detail

A classic European tie against Anderlecht was celebrated during the 2005-06 season, including what was on TV, in the pop charts, at the movies and happening in the news back in 1964

# Dortmund uncovered

Where were you on 16 May? Sheltering from a Wagnerian downpour in an Irish bar? Rocking in the town square? This lot were...

**Bord Thoresen**
Norway's number one Red recalls the party in this square and an all-night celebration

*(magazine article reproduced within image)*

---

Think that fan-park parties with live music ahead of major European finals are a modern thing? Think again. Back in 2001-02 the programme told the fans' stories behind the recent UEFA Cup triumph in Dortmund. They included testimony from Phil Hayes, a Liverpool supporter and at the time manager of The Picket music venue in Liverpool, describing how the party got started.

He'd flown over on the morning of the match with club officials and local musicians Peter Wylie and John Power from the band Cast – both of whom would play a set before the big game – and from the airport they headed for the Alter Markt, the historic main square of Dortmund.

"You could feel this huge, joyous atmosphere and there were loads of Scousers at the side of the stage wanting to get on," recalled Phil.

"People were throwing flags and scarves on to the stage. It was a really special atmosphere."

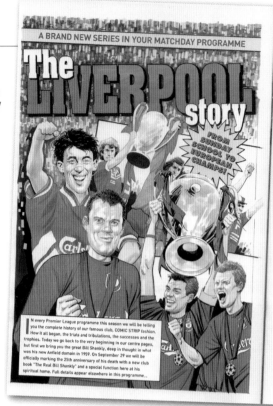

Season 2006-07 had a regular cartoon strip devised by Bob Bond and Ed Chatelier

by Bob Bond and Ed Chatelier

In 2009-10 'Class Of' was a chance to put offbeat questions to the squad's current stars – in this case Pepe Reina talked about roast dinners, dogs and Las Vegas

207

# THE BIG LEAGUE

## Come backstage as Anfield gets all dressed up for an historic European summit meeting...

If you think playing in the UEFA Champions League places increased demands on the Liverpool team, you should see what it does to the Anfield ground staff.

There is a strict code that every club must adhere to, and the men who make sure Liverpool do are UEFA venue director, Didier Andrist and David Sim of TEAM Marketing, the Swiss company responsible for the competition's format and overseeing its implementation.

The man who has to pull it all together at Anfield is Ged Poynton, Liverpool's stadium manager and safety-certificate holder. Even before Liverpool had played their qualifying games against Haka and made sure of their place in the league stages, TEAM Marketing and UEFA representatives visited Anfield, as they do for all participating clubs, to check out the existing commercial, catering and media facilities. Then three days before the home game against Boavista, there was another meeting.

"TEAM and UEFA personnel stayed with us until noon the day after the game."

### BEHIND THE SCENES
An in-depth feature in 2001 gave fans an insight into how the club's staff – including stadium manager Ged Poynton – had to prepare for big European nights

says Ged. "The same individuals are assigned to the club for the duration of our participation in the competition. "But, we've had a lot of experience with the international games at Anfield in recent seasons, so we're used to changes to the infrastructure on matchdays.

"The additional measures for every UEFA Champions League game don't compromise our existing safety plans at all. Our staff really are excellent and the external companies we bring in are also very good." >

## LIVE AND EXCLUSIVE

It takes 20 cameramen, 10 soundmen and one Des Lynam to bring the UEFA Champions League into the nation's living rooms, as Chris Hughes discovers.

The 'Kop 'n' Goal Years' debuted in 2003-04 – and this one from August 2003 focused on April 1966

# KOP "n" GOAL YEARS '66

Sunday, April 24 – Saturday, April 30, 1966

LIVERPOOL v CHELSEA

## Roger is back in the hunt for goals

### Liverpool striker to make his comeback

ROGER Hunt, the Liverpool forward who has been out of the team for some weeks with an ankle injury, returns to first team duty tomorrow at Anfield where Liverpool's second league championship win in three seasons is likely to be clinched. Hunt's return means that Geoff Strong is omitted.

A point from Chelsea will settle the championship.

The Anfield gates are being opened at 12.30.

John Dunn and Tommy Robson step into the Chelsea team. Dunn replaces Peter Bonetti, who injured an arm in the midweek Fairs Cup match in Barcelona, and Robson is on the left wing, allowing Tambling to move inside in place of Venables.

One other change involves the substitution of a forward, Bert Murray, for a defender, Alan Young, from the defensive line-up fielded in Spain.

On Thursday Liverpool will take to Glasgow the biggest following in the history of football in this city. Sixteen thousand tickets have already been sold at Anfield, and the estimate is that more than 20,000 Liverpudlians will be at Hampden Park for the European Cup Winners' Cup Final with Borussia Dortmund.

Thousands of private cars, special trains, coaches and planes will move this army of fans to Scotland on the day.

Friday, April 29, 1966

Roger Hunt . . . who has fully recovered from his ankle injury

>> **Last day title decider • Hillman Imp • Champion The Wonder Horse • Alfie • Twister "sex-in-a-box" scandal • Roger Hunt interview**

Elements of the 'Kop 'n' Goal Years' included memorable match reports, archive interviews, facts and stats

2009-10 had a series homing in on the seasons Bill Shankly was in charge of the Reds, and for the visit of Manchester City in November of that season the focus was the 1964-65 FA Cup-winning campaign

# This is what it's all about...

No-one needs reminding what our last game in Europe was. But we thought you might enjoy seeing some more images from that famous night in Istanbul when Liverpool were crowned Champions of Europe for the fifth time

## ONE NIGHT IN ISTANBUL

For the first few programmes of the 2005-06 season, the events that led to and followed the club's fifth European Cup win were still on everyone's minds

LFC | 25

## Thierry Henry

One of the best strikers in world football, Henry landed both the PFA and Football Writers player of the year awards last season after some stunning displays. He scored 24 Premiership goals and contributed a record breaking 20 assists, making the £10.5 million Arsene Wenger paid Juventus for him look as cheap as chips. Liverpool have only beaten Juve once in our history when we recorded a 2-0 win over them in the European Cup-Winners-Cup in 1965. The winner that night was **SCORED BY...**

## Geoff Strong

Strong is remembered by Kopites as a hugely versatile player who had a happy habit of popping up with crucial goals in big games. His headed winner in the 1966 European Cup Winners' Cup semi-final against Celtic remains his most famous of the 32 he scored for the Reds. Strong had previously scored 69 goals in 125 games for Arsenal and was snapped up by Bill Shankly for £40,000 in 1964, which was also the year when the charts were **TOPPED BY...**

## Cilla Black

Our Cilla from Scottie Road had a lorra, lorra hits in the swinging sixties and made it to number one twice that year with 'Anyone Who Had a Heart' and 'You're My World'. She launched her career as a TV personality on Surprise, Surprise 20 years later before going on to present Blind Date. Cilla has achieved a lot in her career and one of her personal favourite memories was the time when she sung a duet with her close friend, the late Dusty Springfield, who shared a surname with the town **LIVED IN BY...**

## Homer Simpson

Arguably the funniest character on TV, Homer is a Duff beer-drinking, donut-munching, nuclear power plant safety inspector. From getting committed to a mental institute and working as a Monorail driver to becoming an astronaut and almost causing several nuclear meltdowns, Homer has lived an eventful life in the public eye. He once decided to give up going to church much to the disgust of local reverend Timothy Lovejoy who shouldn't be confused with the bloke of the same name **WHO PRESENTS...**

## Stadio Olimpico

The Eternal City's Olympic Stadium will always hold a special place in the hearts of Liverpool supporters. Our first European Cup win in 1977 saw over 25,000 Kopites make the pilgrimage to Rome and many returned in 1984. More recently, Michael Owen conquered the Colloseum when his double-strike gave us a 2-0 UEFA Cup win in Italy. Arsenal also have happy memories of the stadium due to their 3-1 Champions League win there last season thanks to a brilliant **HAT-TRICK FROM...**

## Alan Kennedy

Known affectionately as 'Barney Rubble' by the Kop, left-back Kennedy scored 15 goals in his Liverpool career including two European Cup final winners. His first came in Paris against Real Madrid in 1981 and his second was the penalty shoot-out winner in the 1984 final when we beat Roma in their own back-yard **AT THE...**

## Soccer AM

Chelsea fan Lovejoy, who is reminded by Gooners' fans regularly that his side have only ever won one league title, joined Soccer AM in 1996 after working for MTV and as a producer on the Big Breakfast. With Torquay United die-hard Helen Chamberlain alongside him on the orange sofa and features such as the Soccerette, Showboat and the Third Eye, the Saturday morning show has developed a cult-following. The also have their own football team, the 'Badgers', who have fielded many ex-footballers including former **LIVERPOOL STAR...**

'Full Circle' in the Arsenal issue of October 2003 showed how Alan Kennedy was linked to Homer Simpson – d'oh!

The May 2007 Chelsea Champions League programme was a chance to look back at big semi-finals of the past

The Leeds issue of October 2001 saw the programme travel with the fans to the Newcastle away game

**PICTURE POWER**

Capturing goal and trophy celebrations is a programme priority – as these shots of the 2003 Worthington Cup final and the 2007 win in Barcelona show

of the storm

ALWAYS IN OUR THOUGHTS

Thousands of people gathered to remember the 96...

**SNOW PATROL**

Sometimes pictures are the most powerful way to tell a story and the memorial service to mark the 20th anniversary of the Hillsborough disaster was illustrated beautifully in April 2009

Javier Mascherano, Fernando Torres and the rest of the Reds squad were pictured in a 2009-10 programme having a snowball fight!

# A-Z
## Boot Room Boys

Let's drink to our success. Kenny Dalglish, Ronnie Moran, Bob Paisley and Roy Evans in the mystical Boot Room where Liverpool's successes were plotted. It was little more than an enlarged cupboard, 12ft by 12ft. But it was hallowed ground. This was the nerve centre of Anfield. It was here that the so-called "Liverpool Secret" nestled. An ordinary room full of boots, wall-pegs and laundry skips in the dressing room corridor, next to where the kits were dried

A to Z | Greatest Pictures

Greatest Pictures | A to Z

There's a lot to cover in an A-Z of Anfield life but the 2004-05 programmes did their best to get through a lot of it.

From A for 'abandoned matches' through to Z for 'zany' pictures, the feature was a great chance to showcase some fantastic pictures from the archives.

This small selection of what was on offer that season includes B for 'boot room boys', E for 'European nights', K for Kennedy (Ray) and L for Lawrence (Tommy) and Lawler (Chris).

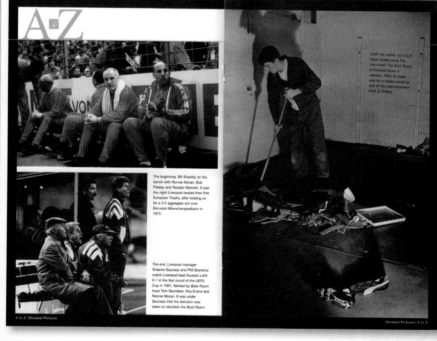

# A-Z

Over the rubble, but you'll never forget the memories! The Boot Room is knocked down in January, 1993, to make way for a media centre as part of the redevelopment work at Anfield

The beginning. Bill Shankly on the bench with Ronnie Moran, Bob Paisley and Reuben Bennett. It was the night Liverpool landed their first European Trophy, after holding on for a 3-3 aggregate win over Borussia Mönchengladbach in 1973

The end. Liverpool manager Graeme Souness and Phil Boersma watch Liverpool beat Kuusysi Lahti 6-1 in the first round of the UEFA Cup in 1991, flanked by Boot Room boys Tom Saunders, Roy Evans and Ronnie Moran. It was under Souness that the decision was taken to refurbish the Boot Room

A to Z | Greatest Pictures

Greatest Pictures | A to Z

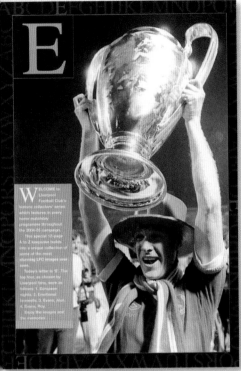

## VERY SUPERSTITIOUS

From boozers to bird watching to bench coats, we do some strange things to bring the team luck...

In March 2002 fans shared their odd matchday superstitions, including using the same Mersey Tunnel booth and buying from the same chippy

# THEY STOOD ON THE KOP

Nine famous people who practised the cult of the spec in the old days. And Robert Kilroy-Silk

The first programme of 2002 featured famous Kopites while there was a cartoon montage for the game before the 2007 European Cup final

by Bob Bond and Ed Chatelier

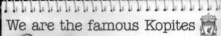

## We are the famous Kopites

**Name:** Paul Gilfoyle
**Age:** 24

'We Are The Famous Kopites' was a platform for fans to take the spotlight, these ones featuring in October 2009 (above) and August 2008 (top)

with...

SAMI HYYPIA

**What was the** LAST **sporting event you went to outside of football?**

I went to Donington Park to see the Moto GP in the summer.

That was in June and was the last event I went to other than football.

I'm very keen on motor sports. I like watching them on the television but when you are there at the live event you can really appreciate the speed they go. You just can't capture that on television.

**What is the** LAST **thing you do before you leave the dressing room?**

I'm not sure there is anything I do specifically.

I just try to focus and go through my own game in my head.

When I get on the pitch the first thing I always do is bend down to tighten my laces. I suppose that's a bit of a ritual.

I tie them before I leave the dressing room but then I do them tighter when I run out on to the pitch.

I always feel that, although I've already tied them in the dressing room, they are a bit too loose so I always do them again.

It must be a mental thing with me as it has become a habit.

**When did you** LAST **cook the Sami Hyypia fish dish, as revealed, eaten and enjoyed by your old team-mate Erik Meijer?**

(Laughs) I don't really cook that much so I'm not sure if that was just Erik having a joke.

I can't remember ever cooking it. I suppose it depends on whether he liked it or not.

It might have happened but it's that long ago I really don't remember.

As I say, I don't cook that much so I definitely don't have a fish dish as my speciality.

There must have been another chef there!

*Famous*
## LAST WORDS

'Our job is to make the fans happy. When we win 45,000 people go home happy. When we lose, it not only affects them, it affects their cats as well'

GERARD HOULLIER

The parting editorial page in 2007-08 programmes was a player Q&A called 'The Last Word'

## LIVERPOOL'S 7000th LEAGUE GOAL

"**M**O MO MO, SISSOKO!" The chant is heard on a regular basis during the season but last Saturday the travelling Kop performed it with even more enthusiasm than usual.

It had been preceded by a second of silence as those inside the Stadium of Light paused for confirmation that the Malian had finally found the back of the net.

Like the rest of us, Momo had waited over two years and 75 games for the moment his name would finally appear on the scoresheet. When it did he picked a perfect time as his strike set us on the way to a fine away win.

In doing so he followed in the footsteps of Gordon Hodgson, Roger Hunt, Kenny Dalglish and Jan Molby as the men who have helped us reach various thousand-goal landmarks.

And he copied the example of Jack Parkinson who netted our 1,000th goal, also against Sunderland way back in 1909.

### THOUSAND GOAL MILESTONES

**1,000TH:** 12/04/09 Jack Parkinson
vs Sunderland (Anfield)

**2,000TH:** 29/12/28 Gordon Hodgson
vs Bury (Gigg Lane)

**3,000TH:** 24/12/49 Kevin Baron
vs Everton (Anfield)

**4,000TH:** 08/12/62 Roger Hunt
vs Sheffield Wednesday (Hillsborough)

**5,000TH:** 25/03/78 Kenny Dalglish
vs Wolves (Molineux)

**6,000TH:** 23/03/91 Jan Molby
vs Derby County (Baseball Ground)

*Jan Molby plants in a penalty in 1991 for a Liverpool milestone, while Roger Hunt (above) netted the Reds' 4000th league goal.*

### QUOTES:

"Momo deserved his goal, we were happy for him and really excited.

"It was funny for him I could hardly believe it – it was a great goal. Some other times he was close like the Barcelona game at home."
– PEPE REINA

"I am very happy, not only because I've got my first goal for the club, but also because the team won. This was a very good result.

"It's been a long time coming – I'm in my third year here! I was very surprised to score but I want to go on and score many goals for Liverpool."
– MOMO

"It was special for Momo to score our 7,000th goal and he's now in the record books."
– RAFA BENITEZ

"I need to score goals. My aim for this year is to score maybe two, three or even four goals. Rafa has not set me a target but I always put pressure on myself to do it."
– MOMO SPEAKING IN SEPTEMBER 2006

The Derby County programme in September 2007 included a feature on the Reds' landmark league goals after Momo Sissoko had scored the club's 7,000th at Sunderland a few days earlier

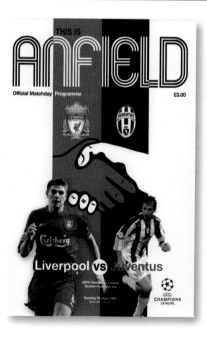

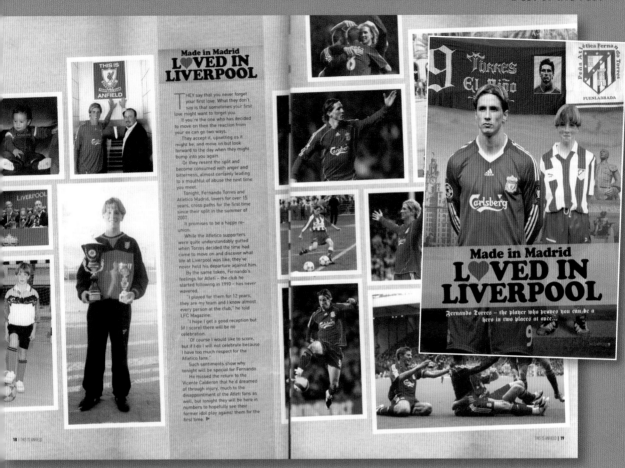

### Made in Madrid
# L♥VED IN LIVERPOOL

THEY say that you never forget your first love. What they don't say is that sometimes your first love might want to forget you.

If you're the one who has decided to move on then the reaction from your ex can go two ways.

They accept it, upsetting as it might be, and move on but look forward to the day when they might bump into you again.

Or they resent the split and become consumed with anger and bitterness, almost certainly leading to a mouthful of abuse the next time you meet.

Tonight, Fernando Torres and Atletico Madrid, lovers for over 15 years, cross paths for the first time since their split in the summer of 2007.

It promises to be a happy re-union.

While the Atletico supporters were quite understandably gutted when Torres decided the time had come to move on and discover what life at Liverpool was like, they've never held his departure against him.

By the same token, Fernando's feelings for Atleti – the club he started following in 1990 – has never wavered.

"I played for them for 12 years, they are my team and I know almost every person in the club," he told LFC Magazine.

"I hope I get a good reception but [if I score] there will be no celebration.

"Of course I would like to score, but if I do I will not celebrate because I have too much respect for the Atletico fans."

Such sentiments show why tonight will be special for Fernando.

He missed the return to the Vicente Calderon that he'd dreamed of through injury, much to the disappointment of the Atleti fans as well, but tonight they will be here in numbers to hopefully see their former idol play against them for the first time. ▶

18 | THIS IS ANFIELD

THIS IS ANFIELD | 19

### Made in Madrid
# L♥VED IN LIVERPOOL

*Fernando Torres – the player who proves you can be a hero in two places at once…*

'His armband proved he was a Red…' The visit of Atletico Madrid in October 2008 was a chance to celebrate the career of Fernando Torres from beginnings back home in Spain to a new hero-status on Merseyside

---

Building bridges and friendships for 20 years . . .

memoria e amicizia
JUVENTUS

Gianfranco Giancarlo Giovanni Giavacchino Giuseppina Giancarlo
Rocco Domenico Luciano Domenico Francesco Antonio Mario Bruno
Nino Roberto Alberto Barbara Tarcisio Roberto Gianni Claudio Nisio
Andrea Amedeo Franco Mario Eugenio Sergio Loris Tarcisio Benito

When Juventus visited for a Champions League quarter-final in April 2005, the theme was 'friendship' with the teams having not faced each other since the 1985 final that was marred by the Heysel Stadium tragedy. The programme highlighted that theme with a special cover and content

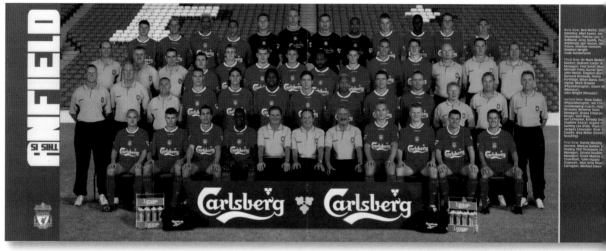

A fold-out team poster nestled within the pages of the Newcastle programme in September 2002

In 2006 the Kop was 100 years old, a fact celebrated in the West Ham programme of August that year

A few months after winning a cup treble, Reebok had a new kit out and explained its origin in September 2001

With an FA Cup final on the horizon, the Reds' U18s were celebrating FA Youth Cup success in April 2006

A mosaic designed for stricken boss Gerard Houllier was explained in the Barcelona programme of November 2001

There was a 'Stadium Special' in the Manchester City programme of 2004 – but the Stanley Park plan ultimately fell through

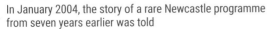

In January 2004, the story of a rare Newcastle programme from seven years earlier was told

In 2006-07 fans could send in pictures from their travels with the Reds following 'Rafa's Army'

## Is this the way to ISTANBUL?

*(To the tune of Tony Christie's "Amarillo")*

Sha la la la la la la la
Sha la la la la la la la
Sha la la la la la la la

On a Tuesday evening
Every stand in Anfield was heaving
Luis scored a magic goal
Jamie played a pivotal role

Every expert tipped Chelsea
When we came out of the hat
Said they'd win the treble
Well we put paid to that

Is this the way to Istanbul
Hear the Kop singing when it's full
Dreaming dreams of Istanbul
Lifting the cup with Stevie G

Show me the way to Istanbul
We don't care if the hotels are all full
Get me a ticket for Istanbul
And we'll see you all in Turkey

Sha la la la la la la la
Sha la la la la la la la
Sha la la la la la la la
Lifting the cup with Stevie G

The final whistle blowing
Got all the celebrations going
All the fans were in heaven
Like St Etienne in '77

Now out on the runway
There's a big old plane
And it means we're going
To a European Cup final again

Is this the way to Istanbul
Hear the Kop singing when it's full
Dreaming dreams of Istanbul
Lifting the cup with Stevie G

Show me the way to Istanbul
We don't care if the hotels are all full
Get me a ticket for Istanbul
And we'll see you all in Turkey

Sha la la la la la la la
Sha la la la la la la la
Sha la la la la la la la
Lifting the cup with Stevie G

Sha la la la la la la la
Sha la la la la la la la
Sha la la la la la la la
Lifting the cup with Stevie G

Sha la la la la la la la
Sha la la la la la la la
Sha la la la la la la la
Lifting the cup with Stevie G

*Penned by Carl King*

Ten days before the trip to Istanbul, fans were given lyrics to a new song in the Aston Villa programme of May 2005

In the Sunderland programme of November 2001, six types of Reds fan were whimsically profiled, from 'The Leader of the Kop' singing at the top of his voice with arms out wide, to 'Kirkby Under-10s' who are known only by their surnames!

*Opposition sections are a staple part of the programme diet. Some great examples from the 2000s include the head-to-heads for Barcelona's visit in March 2007 to a preview of a Borussia Dortmund match in September 2001 that featured the fans and cuisine of the German giants*

THE ANFIELD ROAD SHOW

LFC museum curator Stephen Done introduced fans to some unique artefacts from the club's archives in the Borussia Dortmund programme of October 2001

"Our next caller is..."

The Grimsby Town programme of October 2001 included an interview with Radio Merseyside's John Keith on the joys of hosting post-match phone-ins

## MASTER RED

Liverpool fans are renowned for their knowledge of the game, but Reds supporter Mark Kerr took it to extremes recently when he appeared on Mastermind to answer questions on his specialist subject: the history of Liverpool Football Club.

Mark, a chartered surveyor from Rainhill, did the club proud. He answered every question correctly and, combined with his general knowledge, won his heat to go forward to the next round.

"I don't think my knowledge is better than any other typical fan," says Mark. "It's just I've been going to Anfield since 1965. When I got back I asked the lads who I sit with in the Centenary Stand the questions I had, and they all got them right."

The show is now on the Discovery Channel, with Clive Anderson as the question master.

Fancy yourself as an Anfield Mastermind? Pull up a black leather chair and see if you can answer the questions Mark faced on the show...

1 Which non-league team beat Liverpool 2-1 in the FA Cup in January 1959?
2 Liverpool's first cup final was in 1914 against Burnley. At which ground was the match played?
3 Roger Hunt is Liverpool's highest league goal scorer with 245 goals. Whose previous league record of 232 goals did he beat?
4 Liverpool have twice played in the World Club Championship. Once was against Flamengo. Name the other team.
5 Which manager is unique in managing the club only in the second division?
6 Which player was signed from Lochgeilly Violets in 1939, but played his first match for the Reds in 1945?
7 After promotion in 1962, what was the score in the first league derby match?
8 Which player was the first substitute used by Liverpool in a league match?
9 In 1968, which was the first team to beat Liverpool at home in European competition?
10 Liverpool's first European final was at Hampden Park in 1966 in the European Cup-Winners' Cup. Who were they playing against?
ANSWERS ON PAGE 14

## GUEST COLUMNIST

### Karlheinz Riedle

I'm very much looking forward to tonight's match. I'll be at Anfield, but I'm not really going to be supporting either side because it's impossible for me to choose between Liverpool and Borussia Dortmund, my heart is still at both clubs. I just hope it's a good game.

No supporters in the world can rival the Kop at Anfield. I played in Italy at LAZIO, where the fans are very passionate, and of course in Germany, where they love football. But the treatment I got from the Liverpool fans was very special and I'll never forget that. The way they back their team is amazing. I remember my debut for the Reds, we were playing at Selhurst Park against Wimbledon. I didn't think there would be that many Liverpool fans there, so I got a real surprise – there were so many people in red it was virtually a home game for us.

I also got to work with some brilliant players at Anfield like Patrik Berger, Robbie Fowler and Michael Owen, who was just becoming a first-team regular then. I still follow the team's fortunes. I watch them on television, and I often come over to see them play.

The current Liverpool side is absolutely brilliant. What Gérard Houllier has achieved is amazing, winning three cups in one season, and hopefully they can keep on improving. It's always hard to do well after a successful year because there's added expectation from the fans. But the basis of an excellent team is there, Liverpool's forwards are fantastic and the back four are a solid unit now.

I've also got great memories from my days at Dortmund. I won a lot of trophies with them, Bundesliga titles in 1995 and 96, and of course the UEFA Champions League. My best moment personally was scoring two goals in the 1997 final against Juventus that we won 3-1.

I was at the game between tonight's teams last month and I think Liverpool looked the better side that evening. Having said that, even when they're not playing at their best, Dortmund can be dangerous and you must not underestimate them. They have some skilful players at the club, like Jan Koller, but it's really the way Dortmund play as a compact unit, rather than any outstanding individuals, that makes them a good side. In that way they're similar to Liverpool, who also put the emphasis on team play, although in the likes of Michael Owen they do have some world-class individuals. So it should be an interesting match. Whoever wins it, I will be happy.

"No supporters in the world can rival the Kop at Anfield...the way they back their team is amazing"

Karlheinz Riedle was just the person to sound forth as a guest columnist when his former teams, the Reds and Dortmund, met in 2001

# Welcome to your **new look** programme

LIVERPOOL Football Club's commitment to be number one in all areas is reflected today in our new-look "This is Anfield" programme which features the new and ground-breaking "Kop 'n' Goal Years" section.

The programme, highly acclaimed by fans last season with its Shankly Gates double-folding centre spread, has been the subject of another ambitious make-over and the concept will make it one of the most unusual and sought after publications of this type in the country.

Extensive market research has highlighted the collectability of matchday programmes in general. It's a national pastime with rare editions going for considerable sums amongst avid collectors. Liverpool fans will be able to view some of these gems within our "Kop 'n' Goal Years" section. A specific year will be targeted and an 8-page facsimile programme reproduced from that season linked with the day's opponents.

Today we replicate part of an old "Anfield Review" from 1998 when Valencia came to Anfield in the second round of the UEFA Cup.

"This is Anfield" started off at a reduced £2.50 cover price. It returns to the 2001/2002 level of £3 this time out, but with the page volume leaping from 60 to 76 and featuring "The Kop 'n' Goal Years."

Within this section Robin Gowers of the Liverpool Programme Collectors' Club begins to name his own all-time top 20 LFC programmes. Interestingly, a copy of the very first publication – Liverpool v Rotherham from September 1st 1892 – sold at auction for nearly £2,500.

It shows how something that cost just one penny in its day can become such a highly valued collectors' item. No wonder programme collecting remains so popular. Clearly the intrigue in programmes and collecting has not diminished and the new Liverpool publication will break new ground with its "Kop 'n' Goal Years" section and its historic facsimile programme. On the publishing front Liverpool already boasts the only weekly club magazine in the country – "LFC".

We hope you also enjoy "This is Anfield."

If you have a great programme collection yourself and you want to tell us about your favourite edition, write to: This Is Anfield, Sport Media, PO Box 48, Old Hall Street, Liverpool L69 3EB.

When the Reds played Valencia in a friendly in August 2003, the club were keen to let people know what to expect from their new-look programme

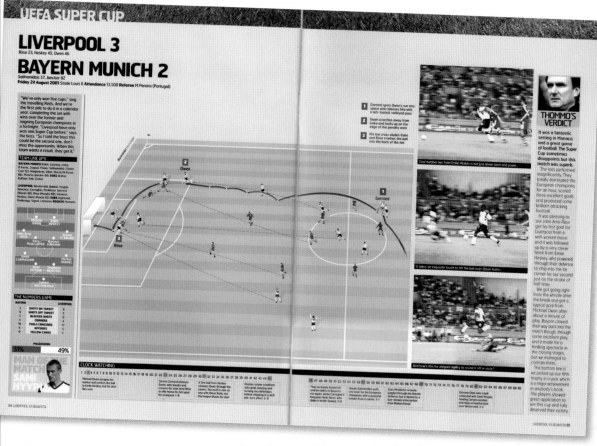

When Boavista came to town in September 2001, the Reds were still basking in the glow of winning the UEFA Super Cup a couple of weeks earlier and post-match analysis included a breakdown of John Arne Riise's opening goal in a 3-2 win

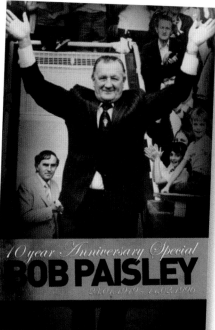

The front page of an anniversary special section, marking 10 years since Bob Paisley's death, taken from the Arsenal programme of February 2006

Far-left: How the back page of the 2001-02 programmes looked, this one being from the Leicester game in January 2002

A tribute to Anfield legend Emlyn Hughes appeared in the Crystal Palace programme in November 2004 with his mother, Ann, admitting she hadn't realised how well-regarded her son was in the football world

## Remembering Emlyn
### Shine on Crazy Horse

Turn to page 31 for a picture tribute to the life of the late, great Emlyn Hughes

# WE ARE THE CHAMPIONS

**PERFECT REWARD:** For manager John Williams and players

Liverpool Ladies were lauded in January 2004 after they had won the Northern Premier League

The introduction of an electronic scoreboard at Anfield was big news in the Arsenal programme in October 2003

## Time's up at Anfield

DON'T MISS THIS WEEK'S **LFC MAGAZINE** On sale from Tuesday...

An 'LFC Uncut' page from September 2007 saw the humour in an archive image of Sammy Lee trying to reach a ball held up by Steve Ogrizovic

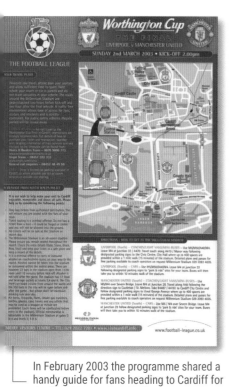

In February 2003 the programme shared a handy guide for fans heading to Cardiff for the Worthington Cup final

Kenny Dalglish picked his favourite goal of December 2004

May 2009 saw a tribute to a man who spanned the decade with the Reds

In 2009 Peter McDowall took over the mic from the late Phil Easton

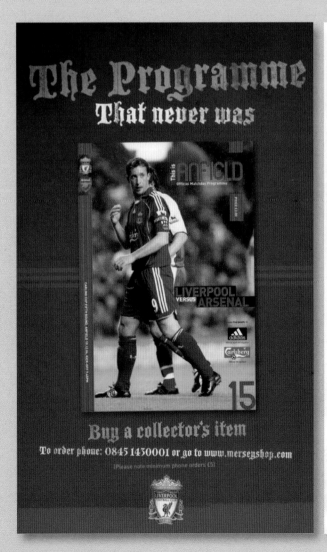
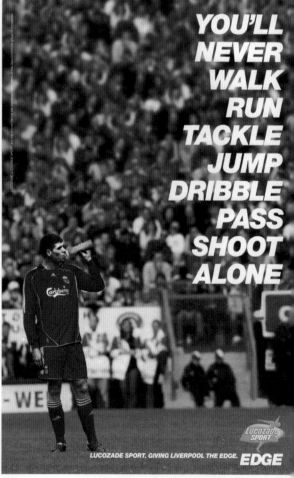

Is that really Kenny Dalglish leaning against the wall (left) outside the ground with a laptop under his arm? And can that really be Alan Hansen in the crowd with a laptop on his, er, lap…? Certainly is. The two LFC legends were helping to promote the club's official website, whose address two decades ago was www. liverpoolfc.tv. The tagline? 'You'll Never Surf Alone', of course.

Contemporary Reds stars featured in adverts, too, as the first decade of the millennium saw club partners search for ever more creative ways to appeal to fans.

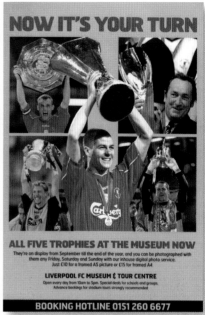

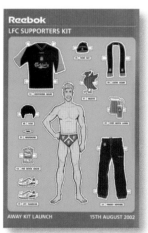

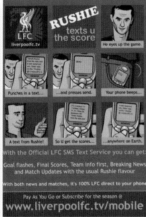

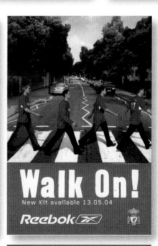

## I'M AIMING TO GET PLAYERS BELIEVING IN THEMSELVES

**After humbling reception I hope to help give fans something to celebrate**

Kenny Dalglish said he was 'humbled' by the reception he'd received as he prepared for a derby match on his return to the Anfield dugout in January 2011

*The 2010-11 and 2011-12 seasons were overseen by managers Roy Hodgson and Kenny Dalglish in turn. Both men saw the value in communicating directly to supporters through the matchday programme and their columns provided insight and analysis into recent events and a look ahead to the forthcoming fixture at Anfield.*

*Assistant-editor William Hughes compiled the columns, visiting the manager's office at Melwood for a 10-minute chat either before or after training in the days leading up to each home game.*

*"Both Roy and Kenny were always generous with their time and both helpful and supportive of the matchday programme," remembers Will. "The public perception of Kenny as a dour Scot was quite false and his trademark humour often came across in his column."*

## I HOPE FANS ARE AS EXCITED AS WE ARE

**My welcome has been superb; now I hope to make sure the team continues to earn the amazing following our supporters give us...**

Roy Hodgson used his programme notes in August 2010 to tell fans how much he'd been looking forward to leading the team out at Anfield for the first time. It was something he would do only 16 times

234

The second issue of season 2011-12 featured Luis Suarez on the cover

A Carling Cup semi-final with Manchester City was one of the biggest games of 2012

In the Blackburn programme of October 2010 Liverpool's new owners said their aim was to return the club to greatness

'Anfield Snaps' was an archive picture feature from the 2010-11 season, digging out alternative images of former stars. In the New Year's Day programme (v Bolton) the subject was legend Phil Thompson

'Where Once We Watched...' is a line from a favourite Liverpool chant and was the name of a feature from the 2011-12 season, focus

How player interviews looked in March 2012

Carling Cup success was celebrated in 2012

'Kids' Zone' aimed content towards young Reds and looked like this in 2010 and (middle) 2011

'Behind The Glass' from 2011 told the story of museum items and programmes of the past

a player of the past, on this occasion sharing pictures, a past match and a player comparison for Steve McManaman

A player Q&A with Maxi Rodriguez from 2010

A 'Just Can't Get Enough' Q&A with Dirk Kuyt in 2012

In 2011-12, opposition sections included quirky articles that linked the Reds to that day's visitors

In 2010-11, European programmes included quotes from Euro heroes of the past, while (middle) the following season there was a quiz and interactive page

# CHAPTER 8

# Modern era

In an era where high press was a key to success, the printing presses were still pretty important too – and the matchday programme captured a colourful time to be a Red

SEASON 2012/13
PROGRAMME 13

17.11.12 Kick-Off 3.00pm
**v WIGAN ATHLETIC**
OFFICIAL MATCHDAY PROGRAMME

LIVERPOOL
v ARSENAL

WE ARE LIV
THIS MEAN

VERPOOL FC
TAL PALACE FC
15/08/2022 • Kick-off 8pm

**H**as there been a more enthralling time to be the publishing team behind the official Liverpool FC matchday programme than the last decade? We're sure the spoilt-rotten programme staff from the 1970s and 80s might disagree, but as former player and regular columnist Gary Gillespie remarked during the finale to the unprecedented 2021-22 season, "We've got to be so grateful for what we're seeing now because this is very special, this group of players and the manager at this moment in time – let's just enjoy the ride."

As it happens, the last two managerial appointments at LFC have coincided with a spot of baton-changing between publishers: ProgrammeMaster had the publishing contract between 2012 and 2015 when Brendan Rodgers was boss, and Reach Sport have been the stewards ever since the arrival of Jürgen Klopp and throughout his thrilling, trophy-laden reign.

From the summer of 2012 the editorial team from ProgrammeMaster were housed in the same office building as LFC's city-centre, administrative HQ, albeit on a different floor, with a view of a famous old Liverpool pub, The Pig and Whistle – not that there was much time for a swift half as each issue was assembled to a strict production schedule with an attractive new monthly club magazine thrown in for good measure.

Back then, Brendan Rodgers had succeeded Kenny Dalglish in the dugout and over his three-year tenure, like any manager, he made his own signings – among the most notable of whom were Joe Allen, Daniel Sturridge, Philippe Coutinho, Simon Mignolet, Adam Lallana, Emre Can, Dejan Lovren and Divock Origi. Others, like Fabio Borini, Iago Aspas and Mario Balotelli, seemed to find the burden of expectation more troublesome.

All appeared regularly in the matchday programme with interviews conducted by its writers along with action and portrait photography taken by the club's own resident 'snappers': John Powell and son Andy, and Nick Taylor.

One of the most popular features was the guest column 'At the match with...' which would evolve in the Klopp era into 'Anfield Review with...' The premise remained the same: a platform for everyone, from LFC legends to Reds-supporting sports stars, musicians, actors or simply local heroes, to tell their stories and have their say.

Towards the centre of each issue from season 2012-13 to 2014-15 was the (usually) five-page 'Anfield Spotlight'. Frequently it told the story of a former player with a personal anniversary or an interesting link to the opposition on that particular matchday; now and again it was something completely different, like the untold tale behind the birth of the Shankly Gates outside Anfield.

For the last dozen or so years the programme has been perfect-bound (i.e. with a proper spine and not stapled). For the Brendan Rodgers period it was called 'THIS IS ANFIELD' with the masthead on the front cover rendered in white (2012-13), red (2013-14 when the team came so close to winning the Premier League title) and yellow (2014-15) successively.

The front cover for the latter season, 2014-15, featured action images of players stencilled-over for an illustrative effect, and there was a graphic on each spine which, when all the issues were lined up together, spelt out 'YOU'LL NEVER WALK ALONE'. This was for Premier League fixtures only; covers for domestic cup ties in recent years have tended to look a little different, as have those marking special club-related occasions or the death

Jamie Carragher played his last match for the Reds in May 2013 – and was captured on the QPR cover

There was only one possible choice as the main image on the cover of the last programme of the 2014-15 season – and even the title changed

of a famous former player or notable figure connected with Liverpool Football Club.

Also that season: the introduction of large-format, magazine-style issues for the UEFA Champions League as the Reds returned to Europe's top table. The front cover for the group fixture against Real Madrid had an artistic effect intended to make it look scuffed or 'pre-loved', although some readers actually thought that their copies were dirty!

Other special covers included send-off tributes for Jamie Carragher (Liverpool v QPR, May 2013) and Steven Gerrard (Crystal Palace, May 2015); a '96' bouquet marking the release of the Hillsborough Independent Panel report (Manchester United, September 2012); Bill Shankly's 100th birthday celebrations (Manchester United, September 2013); and 50 years since the original release of *You'll Never Walk Alone* by Gerry and the Pacemakers (West Bromwich Albion, October 2013).

In the summer of 2015 the publishing contract was awarded to Sport Media, now Reach Sport, which had a fine tradition

anfield spotlight

## GORDON WALLACE

# "I scored Liverpool's first goal in Europe"

G ordon Wallace only played 90 minutes in the European Cup, as it was, but he needed just three of them to become a Liverpool Football Club trailblazer.

The Reds have scored 317 goals in the European Cup/UEFA Champions League, many of them memorable, yet the very first was a shank! As Gordon recalls the moment, less than 180 seconds into the club's European Cup debut at the Laugardalsvollur Stadium in Reykjavik, a wry smile stretches across his face.

"I remember the goal vividly. I shouldn't really say this, but I mis-hit it. There was about a six-man passing move and Roger Hunt went to the by-line and squared it back to me. It came on my left foot and I was more or less at the near post and the Reykjavik goalkeeper [Gisli Thorkelsson] was too. In theory I should have hit it about six yards to the left.

"Fortunately the goalie must have thought that too and he went that way and I put it in between him and the post! But I hold my hands up, it was a slight mis-hit."

Gordon, who was born in Lanark but moved to South Wales with his family when he was five, admits that he'd been pleasantly surprised to be named in the starting line-up in the first place. He'd only started one game as Liverpool had clinched the league title in 1963/64 but came into the reckoning when Ian St John was ruled out of the early games of the 64/65 campaign.

"The Saint had undergone an operation so luckily for me I got into the team. I didn't really know if I would because Alf Arrowsmith was also in the squad and the club had also bought Phil Chisnall at the end of the previous season from Manchester United. So we were vying for places and I only got to know I was playing on the day of the match.

"Phil and I were involved in certain aspects

Gordon in League action for Liverpool

## "I shouldn't really say this, but actually I mis-hit my shot against Reykjavik!"

of training during the build-up to the match, but I had played in the Charity Shield the weekend before. In the end Bill Shankly selected both Phil and myself for the game."

There had been a huge sense of intrigue around the club ahead of the trip to Iceland to take on part-timers KR Reykjavik in the first leg of the preliminary round tie.

When the European Cup was first staged in 1955/56, the Reds were playing in the Second Division and the prospect of rubbing shoulders with the cream of the continent seemed a distant one. Liverpool had ended that season with a 2-0 defeat at Lincoln City, six weeks later Real Madrid were crowned as Europe's inaugural club champions after beating Stade Reims 4-3 in a thrilling final at the Parc des Princes in Paris.

"The 1964/65 season was our first time in Europe and everyone was excited. Obviously after winning the title the previous season, we were all looking forward to it and Shanks, of course, motivated the players."

It has been well documented that Liverpool's journey to Iceland was unconventional. The team travelled six hours by bus to Prestwick in Scotland and stayed at Butlins in Ayrshire at the suggestion of Bill Shankly.

Gordon's team-mate Willie Stevenson recalled: "Nobody knew we were staying in a holiday camp until we actually arrived at the gates. From the front of the bus, Bill stepped forward and informed the security guard: 'We are Liverpool Football Club and we are on our way to Europe'. The guard responded: 'I think you're on the wrong road!'"

From Scotland, the Liverpool party caught the weekly chartered flight over the North Atlantic Ocean. Gordon says: "One of the main highlights for me was being on the plane and looking down and seeing a volcano erupting. That is a vivid memory – flying there and seeing the lava spilling from the volcano was an unbelievable sight.

"There was a crowd of more than 10,000 and it was still 1-0 at half-time even though

The 'Anfield Spotlight' shone on Gordon Wallace, scorer of the Reds' first goal in Europe back in 1964, during the 2014-15 season

previously producing the LFC matchday programme. The [exi]sting editorial staff relocated to Old Hall Street in the city [ce]ntre, firstly with a view of the River Mersey through the [win]dows, then one of the redeveloped St Paul's Square in a [bra]nd new office complex also housing the *Liverpool Echo* [ne]wspaper. New publisher, new-look matchday programme…and [wit]hin a couple of months of the start of the 2015-16 season, [a n]ew manager. Along came Jürgen Klopp and everything [ch]anged.

[B]y February 2016 he'd guided Liverpool to the final of the [Lea]gue Cup, then known as the Capital One Cup. In the League [the] team had won 4-1 at Manchester City, 3-1 at Chelsea, 6-0 [at A]ston Villa and 5-4 at Norwich City. At home they'd lost to [Cry]stal Palace and laboured to a draw with West Brom which [pro]mpted a Kop-end love-in roundly trolled by rival supporters – [wel]l, who's laughing now?

[T]he 2015-16 matchday programme ran to 31 issues: 19 for [the] Premier League, two in the FA Cup, three League Cup and [sev]en Europa League. The 'THIS IS ANFIELD' masthead on the

front featured player shots on a red background with lyrics from famous songs: 'Oh when the Reds', 'Liverpool we love you', 'We all live in a red-and-white Kop', 'Fields of Anfield Road', 'By far the greatest team', 'Oh I am a Liverpudlian' and so forth.

Jordan Henderson's engaging captain's column made its debut and Jürgen Klopp's own charismatic manager's notes proved to be an instant hit.

There was a new fans section in the middle of the programme entitled 'Anfield Extra' which housed tributes and dedications plus a memorabilia/collectors page ('Got Not Got') and 'screenshot' footage of famous moments from Anfield history.

Also well-established by now was coverage of the LFC women's team, winners of back-to-back titles in 2013 and 2014.

Among the special covers in the Europa League campaign: Rubin Kazan in October 2015 when Klopp's first home game in charge was commemorated by a Barack Obama 'Hope'-style image; Manchester United in March 2016 with the tie promoted in the manner of a heavyweight boxing poster; and Borussia Dortmund in April 2016 on the anniversary of Hillsborough.

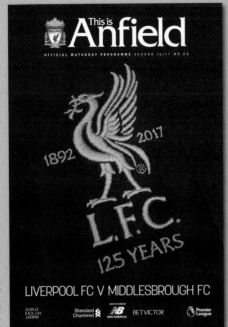

The club's 125th anniversary celebrations began on the cover of the final programme of the 2016-17 season with a close-up of the crest for the new home jersey

**THE SKIPPER'S NOTES**

jordan henderson

Whenever we begin a League Cup campaign it takes me back to my first season at this football club, when we won the competition - defeating Cardiff City on penalties at Wembley.

That trophy win in February 2012 meant a lot to all of us who were involved and is something every player wants to sample. Last season we were very close to again making the final, only to lose in extra-time in the last four.

Now we set out with the long-term aim of eventually lifting this cup. But before that can become a reality we will have plenty of opponents to overcome. The first of those are Carlisle United who arrive here tonight. I'm sure some pundits are looking at this tie on paper: Premier League team at home to a side from League Two, and saying it's a foregone conclusion.

I've been playing football long enough to know that only very rarely do knock-out ties work out in such a way. In reality they are much more difficult and I'm sure that will be the case this evening.

Keith Curle's team come here in decent form, having only suffered one league defeat so far this season. The fact they went to QPR and won in the last round illustrates that they aren't intimidated by teams from higher up the leagues. They have some dangerous individuals who can score goals. So, for us, it's about being at our best if we are to make it into the next round.

While our draw here against Norwich City on Sunday was obviously disappointing, we felt there were some positives to take from it. The first of those arrived even before the match kicked off, with Daniel Sturridge starting again after

he'd been unavailable since Ap... As his record of 40 goals in 68 g... for us demonstrates, Studge is... terrific talent. The more often h... involved, the better our chance... of success.

There was also the sight of Da... ings netting his first goal for the... club. He's a very good finisher, he demonstrated. And he brin... so much energy on to the field... he will certainly cause defende... problems with the way he press... and harries them into mistakes...

With a bit more good fortun... could certainly have had the se... goal that would have given us... points. We were encouraged... some of our attacking play and... chances we created. Tonight w... need to repeat those good as... but be more clinical. If we can... then there is no reason why we... secure a place in the next rour...

10 www.liverpoolfc.com

A new captain brought a new perspective to the 'Skipper's N... in the 2015-16 season, recording Jordan Henderson's thoug...

Defeat in the final to Sevilla may have condemned the club to a season without European football, but there was still plenty to get excited about. The first home game of 2016-17 saw an extra-special matchday programme to celebrate the official opening of the expanded Main Stand with a pull-out gatefold cover for the game against Leicester City in September 2016.

The cover concept for the season was a saturated-colour effect with strikingly vivid images of players on a red background. New features inside included 'History in Headlines', the LFC story told through newspaper reports, and 'Then & Now' which contrasted images of the same kind of scene (for example, players signing autographs for fans, aerial views of the stadium) from two distinct historical eras.

That 2016-17 season saw new arrival Sadio Mane make an instant impact in a 4-3 opening-day win at Arsenal. Other additions included Joel Matip, Gini Wijnaldum, Ragnar Klavan and Loris Karius, while among a mass Anfield exodus were Christian Benteke, Kolo Toure, Martin Skrtel, Joe Allen and Mario Balotelli.

The thriller at Arsenal was followed by a 2-0 loss at Burnley. It was that kind of season. Four points taken off Manchester City. The double over Everton. A ding-dong 4-3 defeat at Bournemouth. But home victory over Middlesbrough on Sunday 21 May 2017 secured fourth place on 76 points and Champions League qualification.

"There is one overriding message today: finish the job," wrote Klopp in his programme notes for the Boro game. "When you see a finish line you should sprint. That is what we intend to do."

Pressure, he continued, "is what we all want for seasons to come. The right sort of pressure. Pressure to achieve. Pressure to win. That is the pressure top players at top clubs embrace. I know ours have done and will do.

"These players have the attitude, character and talent to do what is required. Not just today but for the challenges of the future also. I trust them completely."

The first home programme of 2017-18, for the visit of Crysta... Palace, had a new face on the cover: Mohamed Salah. He arrived at Anfield along with Andy Robertson and Alex Oxlade-Chamberlain, with two high-profile departures in Lucas Leiva and Mamadou Sakho. The cover style was inspired by street a... with players depicted on a plaster-and-brick background.

There was also a commemorative '125' club crest to mark LFC's foundation back in 1892, and the cover for the Premier League game against Southampton featured a specially-commissioned 'Dream Scene' of Liverpool legends past and present together in a dressing room.

Back came the large-format Champions League programme... - six in total as the Reds reached the final against Real Madri... - and there was a new long feature inside called 'The Big Rea... Among its subjects over the subsequent four seasons: LFC's debut match in 1892; the club's first superstar, Alex Raisbeck; the history of Anfield Road; Johan Cruyff's two games at Anfie... for Ajax in 1966 then Barcelona ten years later; the Beatles an... Bill Shankly's boys; the fans behind the many flags and banne... on the Spion Kop; matchday with the mounted police; and the football-supporter heroes behind foodbanks.

"I've been playing long enough to know it's very rare that these kind of cup ties are a foregone conclusion"

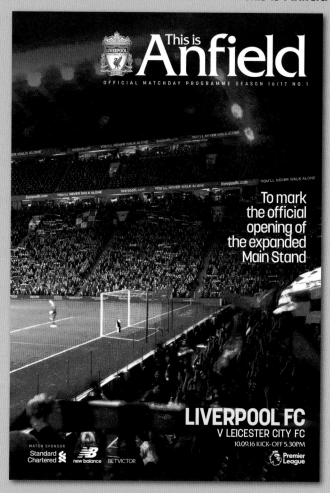

A special cover for the Reds' first game in front of the expanded Main Stand in September 2016

The Reds won four of their five opening games of 2017-18, [in]cluding a 4-0 rout of Arsenal, before they came crashing down [to] earth with a 5-0 setback at Manchester City expedited by a [fir]st-half red card for Mane.

Four months later Liverpool beat City 4-3 at Anfield in [th]e Premier League and in April they'd vanquish the same [op]ponents in the Champions League quarter-finals, 5-1 on [ag]gregate. By then Philippe Coutinho had left for Barcelona and [Vir]gil van Dijk had arrived from Southampton.

"Belief has been central to so many of the positive things we [ha]ve done this season," reflected Klopp in his final manager's [no]tes of the campaign. "We have been pushed to the limit in [re]cent weeks with the intensity of what we have been doing [but] [thi]s is what we want. It's intense because it matters."

[I]t was just about to go up another level. The programme [co]vers for 2018-19 included a new slogan: 'WE ARE LIVERPOOL. [TH]IS MEANS MORE'.

[A]head of the new campaign the Reds recruited midfielders [Fabin]ho, Naby Keita and Xherdan Shaqiri and goalkeeper [Ali]sson Becker. Out went Ragnar Klavan, Emre Can and Dominic [Sol]anke, with Lazar Markovic leaving in the winter window.

Again Liverpool's interest in the FA Cup and League Cup ended prematurely but they more than made up for it in the Premier League, remaining unbeaten until 3 January 2019 when they finally went down 2-1 at Manchester City before going on another run without defeat to the end of the season.

A quantum leap in performance and consistency. The front-three. The high-press. The Barcelona game.

Champions League nights have always given the matchday programme's designers an opportunity to take their creativity to another level, but the cover for the semi-final second leg against Barca was something else: the European Cup trophy made from colourful mosaics inspired by the famous Gaudi architecture of the Catalan capital. An instant, hugely sought-after collector's item.

Five days after his side had won 4-0 on that now-legendary night, Klopp urged his players to "run harder, jump higher and be 'in the moment' always" for the visit of Wolves, with the title race still in the balance.

Describing the fans as "our energy-source," he went on: "What we do here with our supporters has brought joy. And it's reciprocal joy, that's why it's special. The team performs for the supporters and the supporters give back to the team... This is Liverpool now: a powerful collective who looks to live in the moment and embrace the joy of it."

The Reds won 2-0. Finishing as runners-up despite a phenomenal 97 points may have demoralised lesser mortals, but Klopp's 'mentality monsters' went on to claim a sixth European Cup. They'd tasted success. They were hungry for more.

The one which really, really mattered came in July, of all months, in the unprecedented year of 2020. Between Liverpool last being crowned as top-flight champions, in 1989-90, and this latest triumph, a grand total of 11,016 days had passed.

Records were set everywhere: a club-high points total of 99; most wins in a league season (32); fewest games completed to take the title (31); three successive seasons without a league defeat at Anfield; the first team from Britain to hold the European Cup, UEFA Super Cup, FIFA Club World Cup and domestic league title at the same time.

The first matchday programme of the season had been for the Friday night Premier League game against Norwich City on 9 August 2019, in front of 53,333 spectators at Anfield. Thanks to the pandemic, there may have been no supporters inside the stadium on Wednesday 22 July 2020 to witness the 5-3 win over Chelsea and spectacular trophy-presentation, but sales of that evening's programme set new records.

After an initial print-run of 60,000, two more were needed, and ultimately over 120,000 copies were sold – phenomenal for

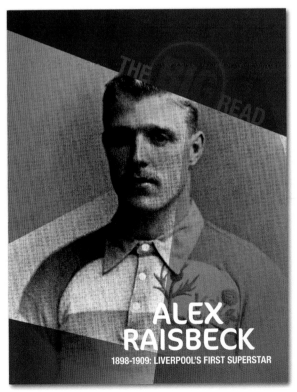

'The Big Read' provided space for special tales to be told, like the Alex Raisbeck story in LFC v Bournemouth (Feb '19)

a printed publication in the digital age. It became the fastest-selling programme of all time at Anfield.

In his notes, Klopp thanked his "remarkable staff" and the supporters – "the wind in our sails" – along with the club's owners and football-operations team, and his family. "Last season, when we came so close, I said to the players that this was not the 29th attempt for them [since 1990]. For us, it was our first proper one. I also told them I loved them, appreciated them and was so proud to call myself their manager. Everything I said in the dressing room after Wolves at home last season when we came so close, applies now but even more so.

"This group of players are giants. Tonight is their moment as a team and even though it is happening in unique circumstances the magnitude of what they have delivered stands alongside some of the greatest sides ever to grace our home."

Behind-closed-doors football persisted into the 2020-21 campaign, which duly started a little later. But the programme continued to be published and the cover – now with the simple masthead 'LIVERPOOL FC' – was to feature action shots of players inside a stadium empty but for its seats swathed in inspiring flags and banners.

There were special tribute covers for Ray Clemence, Gerard Houllier, Gerry Marsden and Ian St John, all of whom passed away during the course of the season, while 'Trending' – a more in-depth news feature – was a regular throughout 2020-21.

The season also saw a matchday programme first: an issue for a competitive home game on foreign soil, with the Reds 'hosting' RB Leipzig in the second leg of the Champions League

**OFFICIAL LIVERPOOL FC MATCHDAY PROGRAMME**

# LIVERPOOL FC

YOU'LL NEVER WALK ALONE

LIVERPOOL FOOTBALL CLUB

EST. 1892

UEFA CHAMPIONS LEAGUE

SEMI-FINAL
SECOND LEG

FCB

# FC BARCELONA

TUESDAY 7TH MAY 2019 · KICK-OFF 8PM

d-of-16 in Budapest's Puskas Arena in March 2021. On
over: a view of Anfield from the window of a passenger

the pitch there were emotional exits for Adam Lallana
Dejan Lovren while Klopp bolstered his squad with Diogo
Thiago Alcantara and Kostas Tsimikas.

Seven-nil at Crystal Palace, two-seven at Aston Villa. Injuries
at the back – with midfielders drafted into central defensive
positons – and the end of a 68-match unbeaten home run in the
league. But what an ending. The Reds won eight and drew two
of their final ten fixtures to finish third on 69 points when all had
seemed lost.

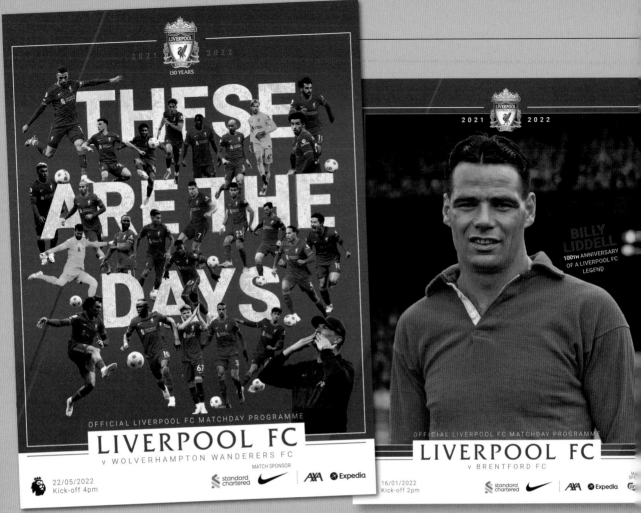

The final cover of the long and historic 2021-22 season displayed the players who had spread so much joy

The 100th anniversary of the birth of Kop idol Billy Liddell inspired the Brentford cover in January 2022

Once again, Klopp signed off in his programme notes, for the May 2021 fixture against Crystal Palace, with thanks – this time to "the amazing people [at LFC] who have guided us through what has been the most difficult period of our professional lives."

In 2021-22 another Premier League campaign (the 30th in the competition's history) was kept alive to the last week as Liverpool somehow clawed back a 14-point deficit at the top of the table. Defence and attack was strengthened by Ibrahima Konate and Luis Diaz. The team played every game possible.

There was a 'double double' over Manchester United and Everton, a treble of cup finals. The breathless pursuit of the 'Quadruple', a communion with loud, colourful, youthful LFC fan culture. And a contract extension for Klopp and his coaching team – what he described in a documentary at the time as his "Boot Room reloaded."

There were 30 issues of the programme over the course of the 2021-22 season: 19 Premier League, three FA Cup, two Carabao Cup and six UEFA Champions League. Each Premier League cover featured a player 'cut out' on a red background with two silhouettes of the same individual in different poses, for example shooting or celebrating.

The exceptions came for tributes to four LFC greats: Roger Hunt, Ray Kennedy and Peter Robinson, who all passed away and Billy Liddell, the 100th anniversary of whose birthday was celebrated in January 2022.

The domestic cup issues featured the trophies in question on their covers, and once again the Champions League programmes really caught the eye. On the front cover for the second leg of the knockout tie with Inter Milan was La Scala, legendary Italian opera house, with Anfield as its stage.

For the semi-final first leg against Villarreal there were two submarines in homage to the Spanish side's nickname and, of course, the Fab Four. The cover of the final issue for 2021-22, Liverpool v Wolverhampton Wanderers on 22 May 2022, said it all: 'THESE ARE THE DAYS'.

So to 2022-23 and another rollercoaster season with new signings like Darwin Nunez and Fabio Carvalho eager to impress and young prospects such as Stefan Bajcetic and Ben Doak dreaming of their moment. The programme cover featured ultra sharp shots of players in mid-match inside a clean white frame.

Inside, a new regular feature called 'Kop of Nations' roll-call Reds stars past and present from one distinct country, kicking off with Uruguay then the Czech Republic, Sweden, Israel,

e sad deaths of people who meant so much
the club have resulted in special programme
vers including the ones for Roger Hunt in
22 and Gerry Marsden in 2021

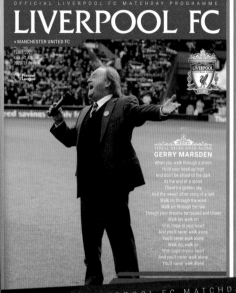

A rare home game on foreign soil led to a unique programme cover for the RB Leipzig Champions League tie in 2021 (below)

vitzerland, Portugal, Norway, Denmark and so on.
While its look and feel may change year-on-year – and
ginality is crucial in this social-media age – the Liverpool FC
ogramme continues to be the essential Anfield matchday
mpanion.

Its popularity is reflected in the huge volume of dedications
the regular fans section, 'Born & Red', and the fact that many
ople will always want a 'real', tangible souvenir of a match
ether they've attended or not. Then, of course, there are the
untless avid collectors.

There have been best-selling spin-off books, too, for
sistant-manager Pep Lijnders and head of nutrition Mona
mmer who both worked closely with the programme's
torial team; a tribute to the Jürgen Klopp era entitled,
turally, *I Feel Fine*; plus hardback titles celebrating the 2019
ampions League win and the 2020 Premier League triumph.

Above all the matchday programme strives to inform and
tertain the club's massive worldwide fanbase, providing
clusive access and insight and telling the most compelling
ries from LFC's illustrious past.

All produced and presented, we hope, in the most
ofessional and engaging way possible.

OFFICIAL LIVERPOOL FC MATCHDAY PROGRAMME

## LIVERPOOL FC
### v CHELSEA FC
22/07/2020 • Kick-off 8.15pm
2019/20 Season

CHAMPIONS

WE ARE LIVERPOOL.
THIS MEANS MORE.

Standard Chartered    new balance    Western Union WU    AXA

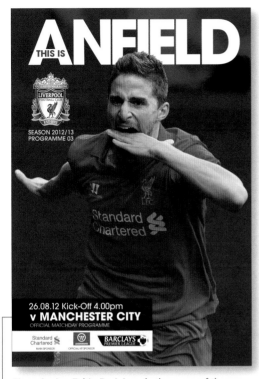

New signing Fabio Borini made the cover of the
Manchester City programme in August 2012

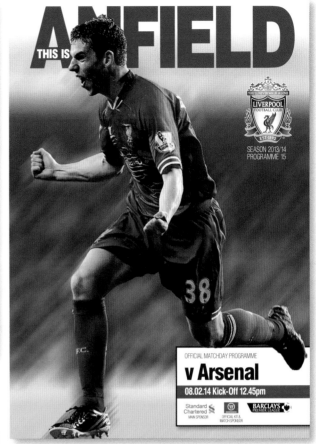

The 2013-14 season saw Jon Flanagan on the cover of the Arsenal
programme and a special Bill Shankly cover for Manchester United

*A big anniversary is always an opportunity for
something special on the front of the programme
– and the cover for the visit of Manchester
United in the Premier League on 1
September 2013 was no exception.
The next day would have been the
great Bill Shankly's 100th birthday
and an official logo (seen here on the
cover) had been created by the club
to mark the occasion.*

*Inside there were tributes from
then manager Brendan Rodgers,
author David Peace (who'd written
the Shanks novel Red or Dead) and
Bill's granddaughter, Karen Gill, plus
news of a commemorative evening at
Anfield with an authentic version of
the meal served at Shankly's thank-
you retirement dinner in 1974.*

Mario Balotelli was the cover star for the
Everton match in September 2014

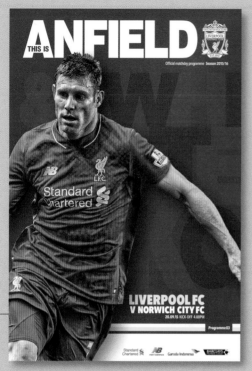

Magnificent midfielder James Milner on the cover of the Norwich City programme in September 2015

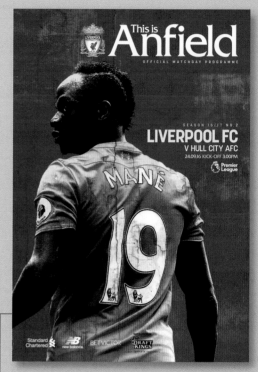

Senegalese striker Sadio Mane had only just started his Liverpool FC career in September 2016

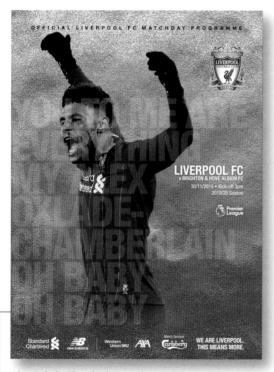

Alex Oxlade-Chamberlain on the Brighton & Hove Albion cover in the 2019-20 title-winning season

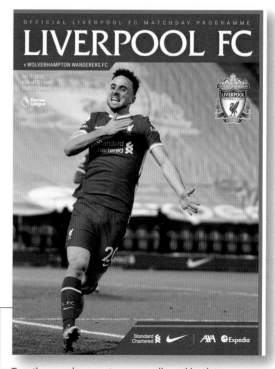

Two thousand supporters were allowed back to Anfield for this Wolves match in December 2020

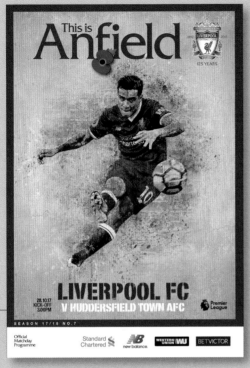

Philippe Coutinho was joined by a Remembrance Sunday poppy on the cover in October 2017

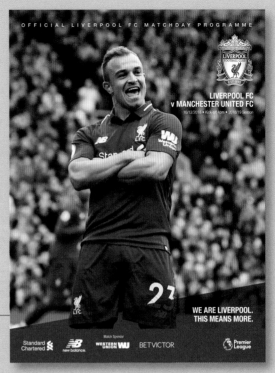

A happy-looking Xherdan Shaqiri went on to score twice against Manchester United in December 2018

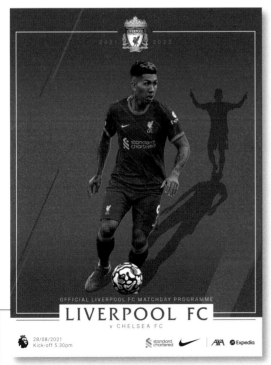

The one and only Roberto Firmino – and his shadows – appeared on the Chelsea cover in August 2021

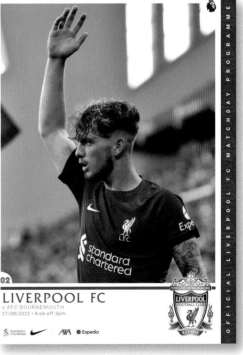

Harvey Elliott made the cover, then scored his first league goal against Bournemouth in August 2022

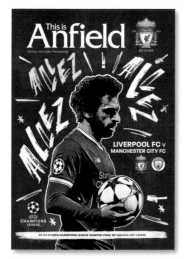

Manchester City, April 2018

Bordeaux, November 2015

Basel, December 2014

Borussia Dortmund, April 2016

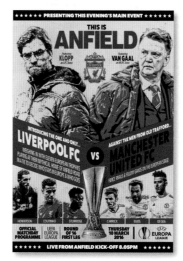

Manchester United, March 2016

Atletico Madrid, March 2020

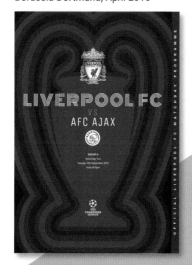

Ajax, September 2022

Real Madrid, October 2014

Villarreal, April 2022

**EUROPEAN FLAIR**
The magic of Europe has been matched by the magic of the graphic artists who have conceived some stunning covers for European programmes

OFFICIAL LIVERPOOL FC MATCHDAY PROGRAMME

# ANFIELD
## IN ASSOCIATION WITH UEFA

**PRESENTS**

SYMPHONY BY THE KOP

**FOR ONE NIGHT ONLY**

THE SECOND PART OF

## LIVERPOOL FC V INTER MILAN

**DIRECTORS**
JÜRGEN KLOPP    SIMONE INZAGHI

ROUND OF 16 SECOND LEG    08.03.22 • KICK-OFF 8PM

The visit of Inter Milan in March 2022 prompted this imaginative cover depicting Anfield on the stage at the famous La Scala opera house in the Italian city

## MANAGER'S NOTES

# BRENDAN RODGERS

## The reaction from the players this week has been excellent

Good afternoon and welcome to Anfield. It's great to be here for our first Barclays Premier League game at Anfield of the new campaign, which for me will be very special.

First of all I'd like to say a huge thank-you to the supporters who travelled to West Brom. You gave us brilliant support on the day. On the whole, we could have looked back at the day itself a thousand times and not had a worse outcome. All that could've gone wrong went against us on the day and sometimes that happens in football.

We started well and overall had a very good first half where we created chances, and the game could have been over by half time. Unfortunately we went behind just before the interval. We've no complaints abut that goal. Zoltan Gera scored with a wonderful strike and we found ourselves behind.

At half-time I asked the players to stay calm and patient and they did that but, as we know, nothing went in our favour. The most important thing is to learn from it. As a group of coaching staff and players we must learn

from the experience and build on the positives. The reaction from the players since reporting back to Melwood has been excellent. Their attitude in training has been brilliant and they are embracing everything that they are being asked to do.

These notes went to press before our Europa League

> ## Getting this club back to where we want it to be is going to take time

game at Hearts on Thursday night but I was planning to make changes for that match at Tynecastle to give an opportunity to some of the other players who have been working so hard. Hopefully we will have been able to put ourselves into a strong position ahead of the second leg here on Thursday as we look to progress to the group stages of the competition.

While I am happy with the quality in the squad

it is still a small one and we need to add numbers to it to help the players we already have. Work is continuing on that front every day as we try to make further additions before the transfer window closes next week.

The support we have received since we arrived at the club has been magnificent and has really helped everyone. We can't ask any more of the fans here at Anfield or away from home. I know the players can look forward to more of that tremendous backing this afternoon as we look to take three points off a Manchester City team who proved themselves to be the best in England last season

The process of getting this club back to where we all want it to be is going to take time and it is essential that everyone sticks together while we do this.

Our ambition is to return Liverpool Football Club to competing in the UEFA Champions League again on a regular basis but we have to understand that it won't be a quick fix. By sticking together and working together I am confident we will get there.

You'll Never Walk Alone
Brendan...

WWW.LIVERPOOLFC.COM

[ MANAGERS NOTES ]

# BRENDAN RODGERS

We must be at our best against a Palace side who have come here to win

Good afternoon and welcome back to Anfield for this afternoon's Barclays Premier League fixture against Crystal Palace.

We arrive for today's game on the back of a good performance and result away to Sunderland and looking to build on that today: the game at the Stadium of Light was a potential banana skin with the home side highly motivated to achieve a win for Kevin Ball and respond to the criticism they'd been getting.

Sunderland's performance was as we expected – fully committed and looking to prove a point. That is why we are even more delighted with how our players reacted and produced an excellent display to score three goals and secure three more valuable points.

Much of the focus was on our front two, Luis Suarez and Daniel Sturridge. That is as you would expect it, because driven, goal-

scorers and match winners always grab the headlines and dominate the talking points. And the praise both Luis and Daniel received was completely justified, because I think it was evident to everyone watching not just how well they played individually but also as a partnership.

However, they'd be the first to tell you it's only made possible by the work of the other nine on the pitch with them and the support of the rest of the squad here at Liverpool on a daily basis, ensuring our training and preparation is at the level it needs to be.

I thought the entire team last weekend were brilliant and

executed our game plan as well as we could have hoped – everyone contributed to a fine afternoon. The one disappointment is the suspension of Lucas, who picked up his fifth booking of the season in the game and therefore is unavailable for this afternoon.

Lucas is regarded as competitive but fair by his opponents. That is why he is so well respected. He is understandably disappointed not to be available today but of course his absence gives an opportunity to someone

> ## The strikers are the first to tell you their success is only possible thanks to the work of the other players

www.liverpoolfc.com

How Brendan Rodgers' programme notes looked in 2012-13 (above) and 2013-14 (left). The former Swansea City boss used his first Premier League column to state his gratitude for the welcome he'd received since arriving at Anfield – and to tell supporters that he aimed to return the club to the top table of European competition

**jürgen klopp**

## THE MANAGER

# "I ask you to believe in this team"

**G**ood evening and welcome to Anfield for our UEFA Europa League contest against FC Rubin Kazan.

First of all I would like to thank everyone for the extremely warm welcome you have given to me, my family and my staff who have also travelled to Liverpool to be part of this exciting new adventure. We have been overwhelmed by the support and enthusiasm and it has touched us greatly.

I must offer a special thanks to the owners FSG, particularly John, Tom and Mike. They have given me a wonderful opportunity. I believe they are really smart guys and I am excited about working with them.

Zeljko Buvac and Peter Krawietz extend their thanks also, having joined as members of the coaching team. They are two very important people to me and will be a big part of what we are looking to achieve here in Liverpool. I trust you will make them feel as welcome as I have.

There has been much to learn and much to experience in a short space of time, but so far it has been very positive. The staff at Liverpool FC are very passionate about the club and have shown a commitment to help us settle in and introduce our ideas. The players have also demonstrated they are committed to hard work and learning from our new ideas. This is very important because if we are to achieve success at Liverpool it will only be possible if we all take responsibility and we all work together.

It was pleasing to play a match at Tottenham Hotspur because it gave us an experience of our own

›

Jürgen Klopp spoke of the "wonderful opportunity" he had been given in his first programme notes in 2015

A small selection of Jürgen Klopp's manager's notes from his time at Liverpool shows how the design has changed through the years – though the messages have been consistent.

Ranging from the 2017-18 season through to the 2021-22 campaign, Klopp has always had something interesting to say – but the main themes have always involved respect for opponents, determination to improve, plus the understanding of the symbiotic relationship between the fans and the players.

| THE MANAGER'S NOTES |
| JÜRGEN KLOPP |

# "WE ALL KNOW OUR JOBS: THE TEAM MUST INSPIRE THE CROWD AND THE FANS MUST STAY WITH THE PLAYERS"

Good afternoon and welcome back to Anfield for our Premier League game against West Ham, our final home match before Christmas.

So, what can I say about the Bournemouth result other than for us it will serve as a lesson and we will take the information from it and develop as a team. There were so many positives from the performance and I cannot fault the players' attitude or character. They gave us everything on the pitch, but in the end we didn't get the job done and, of course, that is frustrating.

But when you can learn from experiences such as this, long-term we can take the benefits from them.

We are still a team in development. We are still learning together. We are by no means 'finished'. It would not be smart or clever if we were by this stage. Of course we did not want this lesson or experience, but we had it and now we must use it.

After the game the team and staff flew to Barcelona for a training break. I'm not sure what you would call this, I have seen 'team bonding' and other phrases used like 'warm weather training'. I suppose these descriptions are for what we did. What was take the players away so they could have some time in a different environment. They enjoyed an evening together, but the rest of the time was training and being a 'team'

away from Melwood. Of course Melwood is our headquarters of football but a change of environment and scenery is also a good thing.

Since the summer these players have given everything for us and worked extremely hard, they know we are still early in the season and early in our story and the hard work is very much in the early stages still. But I like to see them together where they can enjoy each other's company and come even closer as a group. The training was excellent and although 'warm weather' might be over-stating the temperatures it was certainly a few degrees higher than England and Merseyside.

What is absolutely clear is that our

focus today will be back on West Ham United and our only thoughts are on trying to win this game. I welcome Slaven Bilic, his players, staff, officials and supporters of West Ham to Anfield for the game today. They enjoyed some nice results against us last season and we know full well they come today not to be our friends.

Slaven has incredible managerial experience for someone of his age and I really like the way he does his job and the football his teams play. His experience across Europe and now in England makes him a top, top coach and I'm sure West Ham appreciate having someone like him, who also understands and appreciates their club. Their team is not bad also and will come to Anfield today to attack.

We have shown at home this

season we are strong, but this strength comes from the attitude we take into the games. That is all of us by the way: players, coaches and supporters. So, if our attitude is right, we have a good chance of again enjoying being at our home. If it is not – we almost certainly won't.

I think we all know our jobs and responsibilities for these home matches now. The team must look to inspire the crowd as the first and most important priority, but the supporters know their importance also in staying with the players and keeping them positive for the entire game. When we have this synergy we are a good combination.

Finally, on behalf of the team, I would like to wish all our supporters a very peaceful and enjoyable Christmas. We have a number of games to play before 25 December

but, after today, no more here at Anfield until Christmas Day itself is concluded.

I know we all have our own way of marking this time of year, it means different things for different people. For some a holiday, for others not. But I think it is a time of year, regardless of the significance or otherwise of the date itself, where people come together more and interact more. This is always a positive thing. For my family, it is a time where we always feel very grateful and blessed for what we have. It is only our second Christmas in Liverpool, but we enjoy it with friends new and old.

We feel very much at home in this country and it's amazing city and that is in a small way down to the amazing people who make it so.

You'll Never Walk Alone
Jürgen

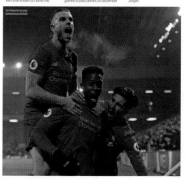

---

**FROM THE BOSS**
Jürgen Klopp

# THIS LIVERPOOL NEVER STOPS. THIS LIVERPOOL NEVER QUITS. WE DON'T DO 'IF ONLY'

Good evening and welcome back to Anfield for our UEFA Champions League semi-final second leg against FC Barcelona.

Everyone inside the stadium tonight who has Liverpool in their hearts knows the scale of the task we face.

It's not just about winning the 'game' – we are here tonight to win a 'tie' and because of what happened in Spain that will be a big challenge.

I said immediately after the first game it was not a time for shouting our mouth off about what might happen back in England – "half-time" this and "second-leg" that. I still feel this, to be honest.

Words and phrases won't win us this contest. Our fans are smart – so are Barca supporters. The situation is the situation. They have a lead and we need to strike back.

But both clubs being smart also means everyone knows we are not finished and we are Liverpool. So: let's play and let's see.

Here is one thing everyone inside Anfield knows, including our opponents. This Liverpool never stops. This Liverpool never quits.

This Liverpool gives everything at all times. Whatever happens this Liverpool leaves it all on the pitch and nothing left for regrets.

We don't do 'if only'.

It really is the story of this team and this amazing group of players. After Newcastle on Saturday night I literally have no more new expressions to use to demonstrate my love and admiration for them collectively and as individuals. What they give for this club – really, it is only to admire.

I described them after Southampton away as "mentality monsters"... I used another more inappropriate word before 'mentality' but the sentiment is as strong without it.

If what they did at Southampton made them mentality monsters, what they did at Newcastle makes them giants.

To play a game like we did last Wednesday, against the opponent we did and suffer the circumstances we did – and then to just have one short session to prepare for the weekend – and then do what we did at Newcastle. These boys are giants!

Regardless of what happens in the remaining games – and

regardless of whether our season concludes on Sunday or goes to 1 June in Madrid – this is a season of achievement for my boys.

For this set of players, failure is now off the table. And here is why: they have taken it off the table with what they have done. They have not conceded or submitted at any point. Every challenge met head-on.

No one here believes and no one will accept our journey is over and we have not got to where we want. That's regardless of what happens in these remaining days and maybe weeks.

Our journey continues and it continues together – beyond this campaign. This season they have achieved so much and yet they are still hungry.

In Newcastle we faced a side playing with the motivation and drive the likes of which is usually reserved for season-deciders. Newcastle played like their very futures were on the line. They played like we had affronted them, stolen from them.

But we found the extra yard – we went further, we battled harder, we refused to lay down and say enough. The players could have been forgiven

for thinking the tank was empty but they didn't and don't. They still find the fuel. This is why this group can only be judged against their achievements.

No one wants to deliver more than the boys in our dressing-room. I've spoken before that wanting something isn't enough on it's own – and my god, do our boys go beyond just wanting.

Tonight we ask of our boys to go again. Dig even deeper than they have already. The amazing thing is that they need no words, no encouragement, no outside motivation. They don't seek excuses.

They are ready – they want this opportunity. They want to go again and never stop. They have their own answers. This is why they are giants.

I welcome Ernesto Valverde, his players, staff, officials and supporters of Barcelona to Anfield. I also welcome them to the incredible city of Liverpool. Barca is such a cool place and I know our visitors from Spain will see that here on Merseyside we too

have a home of great culture and vibrancy.

They will enjoy their visit I'm sure – Liverpool will show its best face.

To Ernesto I offer big congratulations on winning the league title. His record and that of his team really is second-to-none. A team that entertains and thrills and wins again. Barca are world-class on the pitch and in the dugout.

I'm not going to single out players from their side in terms of labelling their qualities because the list would go beyond the page. I would, though, like to extend a warm welcome back to Luis Suarez and Phil Coutinho.

Luis I only know from brief meetings around games we play, but I know how highly he is regarded for his performances while an LFC player.

Phil, though, was my player and it will be fantastic to have him and his wonderful family back with us, albeit only briefly. I am extremely grateful for what Phil did for the team during our time together and I wish him

nothing but success in his career and life... Of course those good wishes are suspended for the duration of our game.

Finally, I would like to thank our supporters who travelled to both Barcelona and Newcastle for their amazing backing. They watched from the highest of vantage-points in both grounds but yet their voices carried down to the pitch and gave our players energy and belief.

There is no need for any rallying-calls tonight. Our players and our supporters reflect each other.

They are determined, stubborn and never ever give up. They believe in themselves and the effect they can have.

So Anfield will be Anfield tonight and we play a European semi-final – this is cool. As always our club focuses on the opportunity, what can be achieved, and we attack it together.

You'll Never Walk Alone
Jürgen

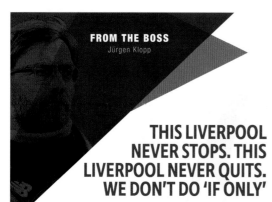

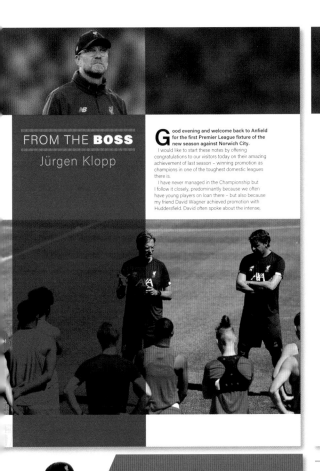

## FROM THE **BOSS**

### Jürgen Klopp

**G**ood evening and welcome back to Anfield for the first Premier League fixture of the new season against Norwich City.

I would like to start these notes by offering congratulations to our visitors today on their amazing achievement of last season – winning promotion as champions in one of the toughest domestic leagues there is.

I have never managed in the Championship but I follow it closely, predominantly because we often have young players on loan there – but also because my friend David Wagner achieved promotion with Huddersfield. David often spoke about the intense,

## SIMPLY 'GOING AGAIN' WON'T BE ENOUGH – WE NEED TO BE STRONGER, FITTER, SMARTER

relentless nature of it and how it you have to have a team with the strongest mentality to endure it and be successful.

I welcome Daniel Farke, his players, staff, officials and supporters of Norwich City to Anfield tonight.

It's not just that he achieved promotion but how the team did it that deserves so much praise for Daniel. They are brave, they are adventurous, they are organised, they are resilient. So many late and dramatic wins. They are a group who knows what it is like to win – believe in what they do – and they now have amazing shared experiences.

This is a very dangerous opponent. Tonight I have no doubt they'll be on fire.

I'm sure the away end will be full of bright colours and noise tonight as well. So, for us – as Liverpool – we know our job. We need to be better in all departments.

A new season is always about opportunity. I think this coming one presents the best kind of opportunity for all of us in the LFC fold.

As the team, we know we have the opportunity to be better than we were last season. This I love about football. Regardless of what came before you know there are new challenges and new memories to make.

This team, since I have been fortunate enough to lead them, has been all about progression collectively and individually. They know standing still means you actually fall backwards.

The Premier League, the domestic cups and Europe – all our opponents will make strides forward. Our strides can and must be bigger if we want to achieve.

I hear the words often, after a season like we just had, about how difficult or how important it is to 'go again'. I don't dislike the sentiment and there is merit to it, but simply 'going again' won't be enough. We need to be even stronger, even fitter, smarter, more committed, greater focus.

Maybe a slight change on the sentiment: 'improve again', maybe 'progress again'.

Here is what I know for certain: it will be the toughest, most challenging season we will all face, and that is because of the quality we compete with.

Starting tonight we face outstanding players, led by brilliant managers and coaches week in and week out – it doesn't stop.

But it's the challenge that makes it so fulfilling and so enjoyable. Let's never lose sight of what we are all involved in; it's about energy and joy, it's about shared experiences. There is so much in the outside world that is not to enjoy at the moment, so much that is divisive. Football at its best is the antidote to this, albeit we know it can only often be brief respite.

Football offers the chance for people from all backgrounds and all communities to come together and focus on achieving something amazing through collective effort.

Everyone – from the players to the staff to the supporters – shares equally in the joyous moment of a goal or a win. We can all experience the fulfilment that comes from helping each other. Supporters give energy to the players through atmosphere and players give energy back through their commitment and enterprise. Everyone contributes and everyone benefits.

These are the values that will shape our season. If we all look to continue this relationship – of one big community, all coming together to help the team achieve – then we can enjoy special moments again I think.

If I had one message for the coming season, to everyone who cares about this amazing club, it is that we are ready for some great times if we are prepared to work together to achieve it. We can stay together at all times if we want it this way, good times and bad.

As the team, management and players, we know what our responsibilities are and we are hungry and eager to deliver more. We know our supporters will be the wind at our backs.

The rest is about the journey and making sure you take all the joy you can from the moment.

This evening we are back at Anfield, our home. Let's cherish every moment we have in this special place together and focus entirely on this game and giving all we have to win and then enjoy that feeling together.

**You'll Never Walk Alone**
**Jürgen**

---

FROM THE BOSS JÜRGEN **KLOPP**

> Respect is an important theme on days like today but we always view the 'pressure' around these occasions as a positive – we crave it because it means we're in the race

**G**ood afternoon and welcome to Anfield for our match against Manchester City. I also welcome Pep Guardiola, his players and staff as well as the officials and supporters of our visitors.

Like most seasons any mention of Pep in my programme column must also come with congratulations. They arrive as reigning champions of our league after producing some amazing football last season in very difficult circumstances. How they performed and the consistency they showed is a testament to the quality of their team obviously, but also their character and desire. And, of course, the leadership of Pep and his coaches.

Our respect for them, as a team and club, could not be higher. The toughest opponent imaginable.

And for Pep personally, I saw he now has the most wins of any manager in the history of Manchester City.

It is clear when you meet and speak to him how much he feels for this club and despite all the remarkable accolades he has already gained in football, as a player and as a coach, I'm sure this particular one will mean a lot.

So today is a real challenge. It's a proper game. Brilliant. I love this.

We are at our home, facing the current champions and we will attack it with all we have. This is why football is such an amazing sport. Occasions like this.

I mentioned respect earlier and it's an important theme on days like today. We respect them, of course, but it is at a healthy level. It is possible to have this without needing to diminish our own qualities.

Let me be clear. I think we are a proper team also. I think we can beat any team in the world on any given day. That's how good we are also. It's two heavyweights. We don't need a puncher's chance.

We are powerful, we are ambitious, we are hungry for more and we have some of the best players in the world in our dressing-room.

We have leaders from front to back that will be heading into today with nothing other than positive anticipation. And why not?

We view the 'pressure' around occasions like this

as a positive feeling. It's opportunity!

We should start each season craving pressure games like this. It means we are in the race. It means we fight for things that are special.

This sort of pressure brings energy if you view it as such. Other players and professionals across the planet will be watching today and wishing they were part of this. It's pressure which has been earned by these amazing, talented footballers, from both sides.

I know at the time of reading this column the contest itself will have been built up to meaning something far more than 'just' three points.

This is the outside world of which we have no control. The usual rhetoric we hear around blockbuster games. Who is going to make a 'statement' and so on?

But that mentality doesn't exist in the dressing-room. All that can be won today is three Premier League points. That's it. And that's enough of a motivation for us I can tell you.

The game is worthy of hype and billing, of course it is. But not because of what it might mean come May. It's because of what it will mean on Sunday evening.

It's so cool this fixture again has a full stadium to witness it. The players deserve this. Anfield knows its importance. It will direct its energy towards us. Supporting us. The focus entirely on us and what we are doing and how they can help. We know we will need it.

Before the game, though, we will pause to pay tribute to a person who is as responsible as anyone for making occasions like today matter as much as they do to Liverpool Football Club.

Sir Roger Hunt, who died peacefully this week, was a true giant. Since I have been in Liverpool I have tried to learn as much as I can about the people who built this institution on their talent, commitment, personality and achievements. The legends whose shoulders we stand on.

CAPTAIN'S COLUMN

# WE NEED ANOTHER GREAT FIGHTBACK LIKE ALL THOSE OTHERS FROM THIS CLUB'S HISTORY

### But we'll have to be at our very best at both ends to achieve it

Last Sunday's win over Swansea was the perfect response to the defeats against West Brom and Zenit in the two previous games. We played some good football, scored a few goals and kept a clean sheet.

People will point out that Michael Laudrup's team wasn't at full strength ahead of the Capital One Cup final this weekend. That wasn't our concern. We knew whatever side they fielded we would have to perform well and we did.

The most pleasing part was five different names on the scoresheet. Earlier in the season I said all of us need to chip in. It's vital goals come from all areas and hopefully that will continue tonight.

In Russia last week we had enough opportunities to win or at least earn a draw. We didn't take them and Zenit converted their chances. In difficult conditions that was the main difference. While it was disappointing to come away with a 2-0 loss it was clear over the 90 minutes

The skipper in St Petersburg

that we can cause them plenty of problems.

Tonight we'll have to be at our best at both ends. We need to be solid but also attack well. If we do get that balance right there is no reason why we can't produce the performance and result that we need.

On many occasions we've found ourselves in tough situations such as this only to emerge victorious. Olympiacos, AC Milan, the 2006 FA Cup final, and the 2007 Champions League semi-final are some of the occasions when we've overcome the odds during my time in the first team.

There are many other examples of great fightbacks in this club's history. Tonight we need another one. It won't be easy as Zenit have some very dangerous players. But we know that with the backing of the crowd here we can do it. The tie is far from over. If we score first that changes everything and from there we can go on to get the win that would see us progress.

06 WWW.LIVERPOOLFC.COM

---

Steven Gerrard spent 12 seasons wearing the armband and this is how his 'Captain's Column' or 'Skipper's Notes' looked in 2012-13 (above) and 2014-15 (right)

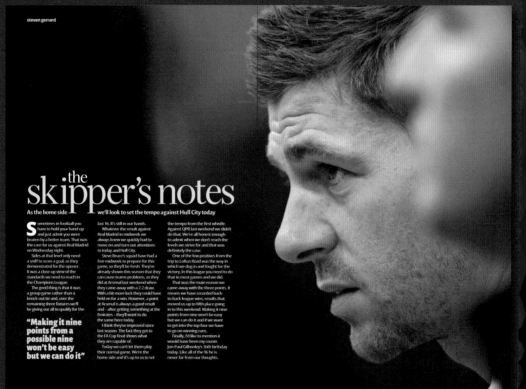

steven gerrard

# the skipper's notes

### As the home side / we'll look to set the tempo against Hull City today

Sometimes in football you have to hold your hand up and just admit you were beaten by a better team. That was the case for us against Real Madrid on Wednesday night.

Sides at that level only need a sniff to score a goal, as they demonstrated for the opener. It was a close-up view of the standards we need to reach in the Champions League.

The good thing is that it was a group game rather than a knock-out tie and, over the remaining three fixtures we'll be giving our all to qualify for the

**"Making it nine points from a possible nine won't be easy but we can do it"**

last 16. It's still in our hands.

Whatever the result against Real Madrid in midweek we always knew we quickly had to move on and turn out attentions to today and Hull City.

Steve Bruce's squad have had a free midweek to prepare for this game, so they'll be fresh. They've already shown this season that they can cause teams problems, as they did at Arsenal last weekend when they came away with a 2-2 draw. With a bit more luck they could have held on for a win. However, a point at Arsenal is always a good result and - after getting something at the Emirates - they'll want to do the same here today.

I think they've improved since last season. The fact they got to the FA Cup final shows what they are capable of.

Today we can't let them play their normal game. We're the home side and it's up to us to set

the tempo from the first whistle. Against QPR last weekend we didn't do that. We're all honest enough to admit when we don't reach the levels we strive for and that was definitely the case.

One of the few positives from the trip to Loftus Road was the way in which we dug in and fought for the victory. In this league you need to do that in most games and we did.

That was the main reason we came away with the three points. It means we have recorded back-to-back league wins, results that moved us up to fifth place going in to this weekend. Making it nine points from nine won't be easy but we can do it and if we want to get into the top four we have to go on winning runs.

Finally, I'd like to mention it would have been my cousin Jon-Paul Gilhooley's 36th birthday today. Like all of the 96 he is never far from our thoughts.

**T**he past week has been a hugely difficult one for everyone associated with Liverpool Football Club following the passing of Ray Clemence, one of the greatest players in our history and a man who richly deserved every one of the tributes that followed his death at the age of 72.

I was away with England when the news broke and although it had been pretty well known that Ray wasn't too well, it still came as a shock, mainly because of his stature for club and country and the esteem in which he was held.

It goes without saying that the thoughts of myself and everyone in our dressing-room are with Ray's family, friends and former team-mates.

I wasn't lucky enough to see Ray play, but over the years I have seen enough videos of him in action to understand why he has long been regarded as Liverpool's greatest-ever goalkeeper.

The standards he set have stood the test of time and when you see the likes of Alisson Becker, John Achterberg, Pepe Reina and so many others describing him as a legend, it tells you everything that you need to know.

In my first few years at Liverpool I often heard people say that it must be hard for the current players because we would be judged by the achievements of the players of the past, but I never saw it that way. When I look at what someone like Ray did in his famous green shirt, it inspires me rather than intimidates me.

I'm not saying I will ever achieve as much as he did because his record is unbelievable, but it reminds me of what is possible at a club like this if everyone pulls in the same direction and gives everything they can to achieve success.

I was fortunate to work under one of Ray's former team-mates, Sir Kenny Dalglish, so I know that the basic lessons that served them so well as players are the same ones that we follow today. Hard work, commitment, togetherness – none of these things ever go out of fashion.

That is the legacy of people like Ray. Whether they are at the club or not doesn't matter. Once they have been here, played their part and set new standards, they leave a legacy that stands all who follow in good stead.

There are no negatives in this. Yes it might create a pressure – but it is a positive pressure. If you are lucky enough to play for Liverpool you should relish being held to the highest standards and that means looking at what legends like Ray achieved and using it as a benchmark.

In this respect Ray's accomplishments speak for themselves. Six hundred and sixty-five appearances for Liverpool, sixty-one England caps, five league titles, three European Cups, two UEFA Cups...I could go on and on.

Each one of these feats is eye-catching in its own right and all of them tell the story of an elite footballer who thrived at the very highest level for such a long time. This is what I mean by setting standards.

Ray also played in a Liverpool team which conceded only 16 goals during a 42-game season in 1978/79, a spell which included the loss of only four goals at Anfield.

That was obviously a special team, but you don't clock up numbers like that unless you have a magnificent goalkeeper and that was what Liverpool had in Ray.

In better times the Liverpool family would come together at Anfield today to pay tribute to one of our own, but sadly we know this will not be possible. What we will do as players, though, is carry Ray's memory with us and look to be inspired by everything that he represents.

That is our duty to him and although we can never guarantee a result, especially against a top side like Leicester City, our performance can only benefit if we put into practice the lessons of those who went before us and set the standards for others to follow.

This is the least that Ray Clemence deserves.

Jordan Henderson's notes shortly after the death of Ray Clemence (left) and during the 2022-23 season (below)

10

## MAN UNITED 0
## LIVERPOOL 3

**16.03.14. OLD TRAFFORD**
**BARCLAYS PREMIER LEAGUE**

**MANCHESTER UNITED:** De Gea; Rafael, Jones, Vidic, Evra; Mata (Ferdinand 87), Fellaini (Cleverley 76), Carrick, Januzaj (Welbeck 76); van Persie, Rooney. **Subs not used:** Lindegaard, Young, Valencia, Kagawa. **Booked:** Rafael, Vidic. **Sent off:** Vidic.

**LIVERPOOL:** Mignolet; Johnson, Skrtel, Agger, Flanagan; Gerrard (Lucas 87); Henderson, Allen; Sterling (Coutinho 72); Sturridge (Aspas 90), Suarez. **Subs not used:** Jones, Sakho, Cissokho, Moses. **Booked:** Flanagan, Gerrard, Skrtel, Sturridge.

**GOALS:** Gerrard (34 pen, 46 pen), Suarez (84)
**REFEREE:** Mark Clattenburg
**ATTENDANCE:** 75,225
**POSSESSION:** Man United 48% Liverpool 52%
**SHOTS:** Man United 13 Liverpool 17
**SHOTS ON TARGET:** Man United 1 Liverpool 7
**CORNERS:** Man United 3 Liverpool 4
**FOULS:** Man United 13 Liverpool 12

## ACTION PACKED

Reds players scoring goals and celebrating them – what's not to like? The exceptional photography often tells the story all by itself

# UP AND RUNNING

*The Reds left it late against Ajax at Anfield but finally found the second goal their pressure deserved to put three precious points on the board*

Perhaps the most telling stat from last month's game against Ajax wasn't possession or shots or corners, all in Liverpool's favour, but clearances: the visitors made 30 compared to a dozen for the hosts. For the majority of the match, certainly after the first two goals, the team from Amsterdam had repelled pretty much everything that was thrown at them in an absorbing contest. In the end, though, their defence was decisively breached by a header from centre-back Joel Matip...but only just.

It was Liverpool's fifth successive group home win in the UEFA Champions League and it ended Ajax's own seven-match winning run at the same stage, putting both sides second behind Napoli in the standings. While conceding that the victory was "not yet the return of the form that made some of their players giants of Liverpool's recent past" the *Telegraph* reported that the Reds at least produced "something that resembled the best Champions League performances of the Jürgen Klopp era."

The manager made four changes to his starting XI as Matip, Kostas Tsimikas, Thiago Alcantara and Diogo Jota were brought in. Trent Alexander-Arnold meanwhile became the youngest player in club history to reach the milestone of 50 European appearances, aged 23 years and 341 days.

Alisson Becker was in goal behind a back-four of Trent, Matip, Virgil van Dijk and Tsimikas. In midfield Harvey Elliott lined up with Fabinho and Thiago, and upfront it was Mo Salah, Jota and Luis Díaz. On the bench: Adrian, Harvey Davies, Joe Gomez, Nat Phillips, Stefan Bajcetic, James Milner, Fabio Carvalho, Arthur, Darwin Nunez and Roberto Firmino.

**5-2**

MATCH REPORT

# LIVERPOOL v Everton

## DERBY WIN HAS THE BOSS PURRING

• Liverpool produce a five-star display to set a new top-flight club record of 32 league games unbeaten, eclipsing Kenny Dalglish's class of 1988. The Reds hit four sublime first-half goals, Sadio Mane playing Divock Origi and Xherdan Shaqiri in for the opening two, before Michael Keane nets for Everton.

• Origi nets his fifth derby goal after brilliantly controlling Dejan Lovren's pass and lobbing Jordan Pickford, while Mane adds a fourth after a rapid Trent Alexander-Arnold counter. Richarlison makes it 4-2 with his shoulder on the stroke of half-time, but Gini Wijnaldum seals a first five-goal haul against the Blues at Anfield since 1965 in the 90th minute.

• Mane had further chances but Jürgen Klopp, who becomes the quickest LFC boss to register 100 league wins – in his 159th game – is a happy man. "All the goals were incredible, outstanding. Wonderful goals, sensational passes, super pieces of football. I loved it a lot!"

**GOALS:** Origi (6, 31), Shaqiri (17), Mane (45), Wijnaldum (90).
**LINE-UP (4-3-3):** Adrian, Alexander-Arnold (Gomez 83), Lovren, van Dijk, Robertson, Lallana (Henderson 72), Wijnaldum, Milner (C), Shaqiri, Origi (Firmino 73), Mane. **Subs not used:** Kelleher, Keita, Oxlade-Chamberlain, Salah. **Booked:** Alexander-Arnold.

**GOASL:** Keane (21), Richarlison (45).
**LINE-UP (5-4-1):** Pickford, Sidibe (Bernard 35), Holgate, Keane, Mina, Digne, Iwobi, Davies (Schneiderlin 72), Sigurdsson (C), Richarlison, Calvert-Lewin (Kean 60). **Subs not used:** Lossl, Baines, Walcott, Tosun. **Booked:** Richarlison, Davies.

71

**MIKE DEAN**

**SADIO MANE**

**POSSESSION**
59% 41%

**SHOTS**
11 12

**SHOTS ON TARGET**
5 4

**CORNERS**
5 6

**OFFSIDE**
3 3

**CLEARANCES**
23 15

**6**
SIMPLE
QUESTIONS
ABOUT...

JOEL
**MATIP**

**1.**
Joel hopes to make his 100th PL appearance today but against which team did his league debut come in August 2016 (a) Arsenal (b) Tottenham (c) Chelsea?

**2.**
Which country has Matip previously represented in international football?

**3.**
True or false: Joel once scored against Brazil in the World Cup finals?

**4.**
Against which team did he score his last Premier League goal, in a 4-0 win last season?

**5.**
One of his five LFC goals to date came against today's visitors, Crystal Palace, at Selhurst Park but in which season (a) 2016/17 (b) 2017/18 (c) 2018/19?

**6.**
From which German club did Joel join the Reds on a free transfer in the summer of 2016?

ANSWERS: 1. (b) Tottenham Hotspur; 2. Cameroon; 3. True – in Cameroon's final group game of the 2014 tournament; 4. Wolverhampton Wanderers; 5. (a) 2016/17 – the first of his goals for the Reds; 6. Schalke 04.

75

---

**TALK US THROUGH IT...** (Martin Skrtel)

The Reds defender on the games, people and places that have shaped him

**The matches**

**Slovakia 3-0 Germany, 2005.**
This was my full international debut. I was promoted from the Slovakian Under-21s and was marking Germany forward Miroslav Klose. There had been a few injuries to our side and I took my chance. I feel honoured to have been with the nation ever since.
**Czech Republic 3-1 Slovakia, 2007.**
This was the game that Liverpool scouts first spotted me. Even though

we lost, I did well enough for them to follow my progress with Zenit St Petersburg. Within two or three months I'd signed for Liverpool. It was a very tough game and I was marking Jan Koller who is 6ft 7in. He's massive. I was young. Maybe if I hadn't played well, I wouldn't be a Liverpool player now.
**Liverpool 2-2 Cardiff City, 2012.**
The Carling Cup final was a really, really tough game. We were expected to beat Cardiff but cup finals are like this. I scored a goal to equalise

and it eventually went to penalties. Had Cardiff ended up winning, I would never have chosen the game but this is my first and only medal for Liverpool. I hope there will be more.

**"I was promoted from the U21s and here I was marking Miroslav Klose"**

'Talk Us Through It' in 2014-15 had Martin Skrtel revealing the games, people and places that had shaped his career, while there were '6 Simple Questions About' another defender, Joel Matip, in 2021-22

---

*Players like the challenge of recalling the times, places and people which have helped to shape their careers, and everyone loves a quiz too – not too hard, not too easy either. Here are three quick questions about the matchday programme, just to see if you've been paying attention...*

*1. What did it used to be called from 1969-70 to 1999-2000?*
*2. Which came first in the programme: Jürgen Klopp's first manager's notes or Jordan Henderson's first captain's column?*
*3. True or false: for one season at the turn of the millennium the programme was a larger A4 size?*

*And the answers...*
*1. It was called 'The Anfield Review' throughout that period.*
*2. Jordan's first captain's column was in August 2015, with Jürgen's first manager's notes in October that same season.*
*3. False – it was in fact for two seasons, 2000-01 and 2001-02.*

## THEN & NOW
### SUAREZ

August 2008, and 21-year-old Ajax striker Luis Suarez is taking the Dutch top flight by storm two years after his move from Uruguayan club Nacional to the Netherlands. By the time he joins Liverpool in January 2011 he's scored 81 goals in 110 appearances for the Amsterdam giants and his first full season as a Reds player yields another 17 goals in 37 games.

*My aim is to work, to show the Liverpool fans how ready I am to put the effort in for this club*

## THEN & NOW
### SUAREZ

Luis begins his second full season with Liverpool as one of the most feared strikers in the Barclays Premier League. He signs a new contract with the club, committing his future to the Reds after returning from the Olympics with the Uruguay team. He says "thank you to the fans because they are our 12th man."

*I'm pleased to be here with the club and in this city, when you're happy off the pitch you're happy on it too*

The 'Then & Now' feature from the 2012-13 season showed a Liverpool star at two stages of his career, in this case Luis Suarez

Here's to you Jordan Henderson – ten photos that tell the story of his rise from Sunderland starlet to Reds skipper

**HOT SHOTS**

**Local lad:** with his hometown club Sunderland from the age of eight, Jordan makes his Black Cats debut as a substitute in a Premier League fixture with Chelsea at Stamford Bridge in November 2008. He's 18 at the time and is loaned out to Coventry City two months later to gain more first-team experience.

**Sent to Coventry:** he makes 13 appearances for the Sky Blues, scoring his first career goal against Norwich City, before a fractured metatarsal cuts short his stay at the Ricoh Arena. "I felt it helped me progress as a player," he'll later reflect. "I was playing every week for a good club."

**Early impact:** back on Wearside he strikes his first Premier League goal against Manchester City in December 2009 and becomes a regular in midfield, winning the Sunderland Young Player of the Year award in both 2009/10 and 2010/11. By now he's also an England international.

Pictures from different eras were also the theme of 'Hot Shots' in 2018-19, including these images of Jordan Henderson

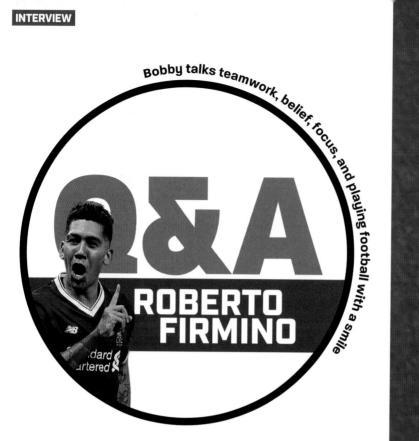

Bobby talks teamwork, belief, focus, and playing football with a smile

# Q&A
## ROBERTO FIRMINO

**Here we are in a UEFA Champions League semi-final... You must be delighted with Liverpool's progress in this tournament?**

We're happy with how things have been going. We got past another stage against Manchester City and managed to take another step.

I have to congratulate the whole team on this and I'm really happy about how things have gone. But it's not over yet – we've got two battles ahead of us and we'll give our all against our next opponent, Roma, so we have a chance of beating them. We will carry on working hard until the end of the season and we hope that we can continue on the path we're on until the very last match.

**It was an intense game at the City of Manchester Stadium. How did you feel when City scored early on – any nerves?**

We knew that they'd be giving their all in the second leg and that they'd bring all this energy to the fore, along with their supporters at home. But when they scored, we managed the pressure they put on us over the course of the match.

We learned a lot as a team as the game went on and managed to win the match. In the first half we were really withdrawn [in our own half] but before the second half the boss spoke to us and told us to just play our football and play with a smile on our faces and that's exactly what we did.

**You started the move for Mohamed Salah's goal, tracking back and robbing City's Kevin De Bruyne, and ninety seconds later the ball was in the back of the net...**

That was incredible. I hope I can keep doing this kind of thing and help the team out, not just by winning the ball back but by scoring goals so that in the end we've got a smile on our faces.

We're really happy and grateful for the wins against City. They were two really tough battles but we're in great form. But that's over now. We need to keep on battling and fighting and just keep winning games.

**How happy would you be if the season ended with a third-placed finish in the Premier League table and reaching the last four of the Champions League?**

I wouldn't be happy at all with that. I want to get to the Champions League final and we are going to fight to the end to achieve this while we still can.

All the teams are dangerous at this stage of the competition, there's no weak link and they're all top-quality sides. We all know what we have to offer so it will be really difficult, but we will fight.

We've gradually become a team that people are respecting in this way and I hope that things can carry on like this. And in the Premier League we want to end the season as strongly as we can and hopefully finish as runners-up.

# NABY KEITA Q&A

*The Guinean midfielder on the LFC family, language-learning and playing for the manager*

**How do you feel the season has gone so far for the team and for yourself?**

We have done some very beautiful things and I have done some very good things with the team. We've started the season on a good road and I am really trying to keep my concentration to keep things this way so that we can continue to play well.

**What is your objective for your first season here?**

We have a collective objective. I am not alone, we are not alone. We are a team and the objective of the team is also my personal objective. I am at the disposal of the team, I play for the team and whatever the team achieves I will achieve as well.

I want to make the effort to do my very best. I want to make the fans smile, I want to make them happy. The atmosphere when I'm on the pitch is fantastic and I am so happy to be playing with the other players so I want to fight to make the fans happy. If I can achieve success to make them smile then I will be happy.

**Are Liverpool Premier League title contenders?**

To be honest what we are trying to do is win each game we play. We want to win all of our games and

that is the path we are following. We need to concentrate because each game is important. We want to win them all and we will see what happens.

**How are you finding learning English?**

Well I am following English courses and I am really, really motivated to speak English. It is really important for me. I want to be able to speak to the coach and I want to be able to speak to the other players in the team so I am really working hard. I hope that in six months I will be able to give interviews to you in English [instead of through a translator].

**Do you know any Scouse yet?**

I am finding the Liverpool accent a bit difficult to be honest, but I am trying my best. I don't know much Scouse yet, but I have been told 'boss' means good!

*Studge has been a good pal to Naby*

27

Naby Keita used a Q&A in 2018-19 to say he was settling into Liverpool life, including learning the odd Scouse word!

Q&A with **Fabio Carvalho**

*The summer signing on settling in, linking up with Harvey Elliott again, the Anfield experience and his karaoke initiation!*

**Fabio, how did you find pre-season and the settling in process?**

It's been good. Of course it's been tough because the intensity and the quality is so high but the whole thing has been amazing.

The training has been tough but it's nothing that I'm not really used to. For the cause that we have and the ambitions that we have it's crucial to have a tough pre-season as it sets us right for the rest of the season.

Everybody at the club has taken me in so well, so it's been a good summer.

**Speaking to Harvey Elliott at the end of last season it was clear that he couldn't wait to link up with you again...**

Yes, it's been sick! We played for the same team growing up but we also went to the same school [Coombe Boys' School in New Malden] which is something that some people might not know. So me and him have been tight for a few years now, since a young age.

It's good to be back with him and it's good to be playing football with him as well because that's something I really enjoy. He's a top player.

**"ME AND HARVEY PLAYED FOR THE SAME TEAM GROWING UP BUT WE ALSO WENT TO THE SAME SCHOOL WHICH IS SOMETHING THAT SOME PEOPLE MIGHT NOT KNOW, SO WE'VE BEEN TIGHT FOR A FEW YEARS"**

**How important was the friendly against Strasbourg a couple of weeks ago in giving you a taste of the Anfield experience before tonight's Premier League action?**

I think it was crucial and it was something that I'm really proud of because I have now played at Anfield. Obviously I had heard the stories before about the crowd and so on but experiencing that live was an amazing feeling and the supporters received me so well.

Hopefully I can score goals and win games for the fans and pay back the appreciation they have shown me already.

**Tonight's game against Crystal Palace sees the start of the Premier League campaign at Anfield and hopefully the chance to make your home league debut?**

I'm looking forward to it but then I'm looking forward to every single game at Anfield! The away games too because I know the away fans are amazing as well. I just couldn't wait for the season to start.

**Did you think it was almost inevitable that the fixture-list would send you back to Fulham on the opening weekend?**

I kind of knew that we were going to get Fulham in the first few games! I didn't think it was going to be the first match but to be fair it was just business as usual and I went there with the mentality of trying to help us get the three points which we were not quite able to do. I'd had a few messages from people at Fulham leading up to it but my focus was only on Liverpool winning.

**It's going to be a busy season with the World Cup in the middle so there should be plenty of game-time available for everyone in the squad...**

There are going to be a lot of games and it's going to be a bit stop-start

How did new signing Fabio Carvalho describe linking up with his pal Harvey Elliott again? "Sick" of course!

---

interview

# LUCAS
# Q&A

The Liverpool FC long-server and Foundation trustee reflects upon his close connection with club, community and city

**You are one of the trustees of the Liverpool FC Foundation - what does being in that role mean to you?**

When I heard that Liverpool wanted a player to be one of the trustees, an ambassador for the LFC Foundation, I was very happy when my name came up. I wanted to be involved with Foundation events and be there to support local kids. I was always keen to do this so to be nominated was a privilege. A lot of people do Foundation work at the football club and I felt that I could pay back all the support the Liverpool community has given to myself and my family since we've been here.

**As a father of two yourself is it more rewarding to meet and maybe inspire local children?**

It is. Every time I go to a charity event involving kids it does make me remember how good my life is and

how lucky my own children are to have everything they want. Many kids don't have anything - they have to fight for it - so I'm not only glad to try and help but it is a learning process for me. I always appreciate everything I have, but when I see some of the kids and the problems they have, I realise that the problems I may have are nothing in comparison.

**What kinds of reaction do you get from the kids when you turn up to coach or meet them at Liverpool FC Foundation events?**

It depends. All of them are positive and happy to have myself or other Liverpool players there because they don't expect it. That reinforces what I said before. It shows how much they appreciate the opportunity and personally I'm happier to see them than they are to see me because it's a nice thing to be involved with.

54 www.liverpoolfc.com

Lucas Leiva always made time for the programme as well as the club's charity, through which he wanted to "pay back all the support the Liverpool community has given to me and my family." Each season one issue of the programme is devoted to the club's annual LFC Foundation Day

The opening pages of an interview in 2012-13 with full-back Glen Johnson makes full use of a striking image in that season's away ki

Great shot, catchy headline… This was the moment in January 2020 when Japanese international Takumi Minamino checked in at LFC

*Takumi Minamino's all about bringing goals, assists and a winning mentality to LFC*

→

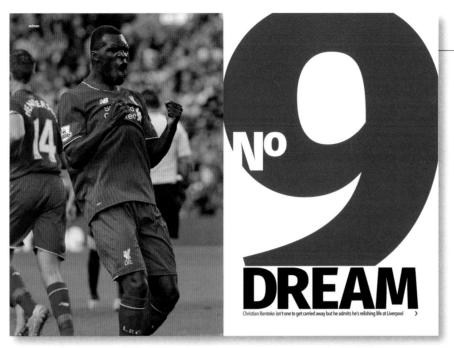

# Nº 9 DREAM

Christian Benteke isn't one to get carried away but he admits he's relishing life at Liverpool ›

Typography can bring a page – or in this case a 'spread' – to life, as shown by this impactful interview with Christian Benteke in 2015-16

# GOOD THINGS
# COME

*Virgil van Dijk says the Reds are ready to dig deeper to keep aiming high, as the demands of the season at home and abroad kick in*

**WORDS:** Chris McLoughlin

**"IN FOOTB
ANYTHING
HAPPEN,
ALL CHANGE,
WE NEED TO STAY
GROUNDED, WORK
HARD AND TRY TO
WIN EVERY GAME"**

Seven Liverpool players have been named on the 30-man Ballon d'Or shortlist but only one of them is the bookies' favourite to be named by France Football as the best player in the world.

Mo Salah, Sadio Mane, Roberto Firmino, Gini Wijnaldum, Trent Alexander-Arnold and Alisson all made the longest shortlist in football – as did Tottenham's Hugo Lloris and Son Heung-min – but it is Virgil van Dijk who is the odds-on favourite to become the first Liverpool player since Michael Owen in 2001 to lift the Ballon d'Or.

If the whispers are right then Barcelona's Lionel Messi is Van Dijk's only serious challenger with the pair sweeping up the individual accolades that have already been handed out in 2019.

Virgil was named as both UEFA Men's player of the year and UEFA Champions League defender of the year, but was pipped to the Best FIFA men's player 2019 award by the Barcelona skipper.

It now appears that, just like in last season's Champions League semi-final, Van Dijk and Messi will go head-to-head again at the glittering ceremony held at Theatre du Chatelet, Paris on Monday 2 December. However, in typical laid-back fashion, Virgil is calm as you like about the prospect.

"I was interviewed by some kids [for LFCTV] and they asked me if I was the best centre-back in the world? The thing is, with these kind of 'impressions', it's all about opinions.

"Other people in a room can think other players are the best centre-back in the world, others may think I am the one. It's just about opinions and the only thing I can do is just go out there and try to win every game, whether it is with the national team or whether it is with Liverpool, and enjoy it because you don't know when your career could be over.

"You can be at an age when your level might be dropping because the strikers are getting quicker than

you, so just enjoy the moment. That's what I'm doing, and I try to be very important for club and country."

That attitude – essentially make the best of what you have – has helped Van Dijk to develop into a player who could realistically be crowned as the best footballer of 2019, but does he think he can beat Messi to the accolade?

"There's going to be an answer to that on the second of December," he laughs. "For me to be called in the same breath, for last season's performances, to win the Ballon d'Or is something special. We'll see what's going to come out of it."

Liverpool go into today's Premier League match against Tottenham – the first meeting of the two clubs

rgil van Dijk spoke about being in the conversation for the accolade 'best centre-back in the world' in a 2019-20 interview

# "IT'S ABOUT HOW MUCH YOU WANT IT"

**Trent Alexander-Arnold hopes to progress with hard work and the right attitude**

Trent Alexander-Arnold's early displays in the Liverpool first team have shown a self-assuredness belying his 18 years of age.

His seven performances in the senior side so far have shown the kind of composure and a maturity that you would more readily associate with a seasoned professional.

The same can be said of his interview technique: his answers are calm, considered and carefully articulated and the overriding thing that shines through is just how much this West Derby lad wants to succeed as part of the Liverpool line-up.

Along with other young players to be handed debuts this season, such as Ovie Ejaria, Ben Woodburn and Harry Wilson, he's been handed most of his opportunities in the cup competitions and hopes the team's win against Plymouth Argyle in round three will afford him another 90 minutes at Anfield this afternoon.

"After the first game here, we were all expecting a difficult game going away to Plymouth," explains the full-back. "In the FA Cup both teams are obviously wanting to win and get through to the next round, but we stuck at it, dug deep and secured the result to get through to today's game against Wolves.

"Making progress is what we're all hoping for as young players and going on a few cup runs will hopefully mean some opportunities to get game-time. In the EFL Cup a few of us have had a couple of games and hopefully we will be able to get a few more in the FA Cup. We are all hoping to take our chances when we are handed them and the manager has given us a few opportunities this season.

"Every player is grateful and happy to be given those chances but it's especially been the case for me when you're a local lad and it's always been your dream. I do think it means a bit more to me in that respect. I'm grateful because the manager has really helped me develop over the past couple of months and he's given me chances and shown faith in me. I've tried to prove why I have deserved those opportunities."

As a boyhood Liverpool fan, Trent acknowledges that he was a little star-struck when he first moved up to Melwood and began rubbing shoulders with the senior squad.

"I suppose that's only natural at first. Every kid who has watched those players on TV will get star-struck, but in the end you can't let that affect your performance in training and in matches. You've got to get on with it and try and do your best.

"I've watched some of those guys playing for Liverpool for a couple of years and being able to finally play with them...well, it's a bit surreal. Coming into training every day and joining in with players that you've been used to seeing on TV is a bit strange. This time last year I was watching these guys on TV and this year I've been fortunate enough to be playing with them, but I also know that if I want to stay in and around

In 2016-17, Trent Alexander-Arnold was still hoping to be a regular first-teamer and he admitted that being a local lad meant "it means a bit more to me" but that playing with established stars was "a bit surreal"

[ REDMEN ]

# OUTINHO

**In his first full season Liverpool's Brazilian ace is just keen to keep learning while his feet do the talking**

Another example of the use of bold typography while keeping the concept clear and simple – Philippe Coutinho interviewed in the 2013-14 season

[ REDMEN ]

# THE LIVERPOOL SCOTTISH

**LFC has a history of Scots talent and new recruit Andy Robertson hopes to make a big impression**

Andy Robertson is hoping to step out at Anfield this afternoon for the first time as a Liverpool FC player.

The Scot became the club's third summer signing when his transfer from Hull City was completed last month and he is eager to experience the feeling of pulling on a red shirt in front of the Kop.

He says: "Our first home game has seemed quite far away during the past week to be honest, with the game at Watford and then a big Champions League qualifier at Hoffenheim, so those games have obviously been the focus for the players.

"But of course when you sign for Liverpool, you can't wait to play at Anfield. I think even for the players that have been here a long time, the first game of a new season back at Anfield will always be a special one."

The 23-year-old believes he has settled into his new surroundings quickly and feels the Reds' intensive pre-season training schedule has set the team up nicely for the demands of the next nine months. "When we were out in Germany there were double and triple sessions every day and it was hard on the legs," he reveals.

"From talking to the boys, Hong Kong was very hard work too especially with the humidity. All the boys found it really tough over there. Unfortunately for me

I missed that trip because the deal couldn't quite get across the line before that.

"The fitness work in pre-season was vital because we all knew that if we put the work in then, all the boys will have it in the legs and have the fitness required if we need to go that extra mile in a game or if a match goes to extra-time.

"Yes, the boys were a wee bit sore but you'd expect that and it was all worth it to get ourselves ready for the season ahead because we know how many games we will have and how hard it is going to be."

Andy's LFC bow came in the Olympic Stadium in Berlin last month as the Reds defeated Hertha Berlin 3-0 in a friendly which celebrated both clubs' 125th anniversaries.

"I will always remember how brilliant it was seeing the amount of fans that travelled over there for a friendly. Obviously I've never seen that before at any of the other clubs I've been at.

"I was just happy to get the first game out of the way. It was my first match since the Scotland-England [World Cup qualifying] match in June so it was good to blow the cobwebs away, but it was also good to pull on the Liverpool jersey for the first time and get to know the boys. You always get to know the boys a lot better by being out on the pitch with them.

"You usually feel a lot more

Andy Robertson was a new signing at the start of the 2017-18 campaign and spoke in the programme of how the first Anfield game of a new season is special for everyone, not just the new boys

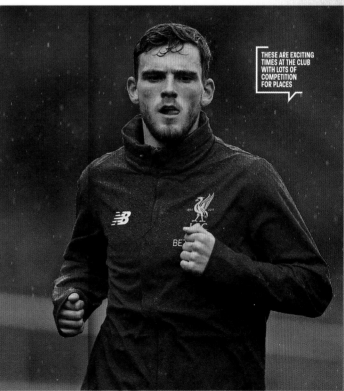

THESE ARE EXCITING TIMES AT THE CLUB WITH LOTS OF COMPETITION FOR PLACES

14

## WE ARE LIVERPOOL

> "I'VE LOVED EVERY MINUTE OF IT – AND I'M PROUD TO CONTINUE THE JOURNEY"

*Current club captain Jordan Henderson is now one of only four players to have appeared over 300 times for Liverpool in the Premier League, and this is how he and his three equally famous predecessors did it*

**W**hen Jordan Henderson led the Reds out for the game at West Ham United before the international break, he became only the fourth man to represent Liverpool Football Club on 300 occasions since the Premier League was established in 1992.

You need only to look at the other three players to have done so – all of them also team captains – to see what a fabulous milestone it is for the lad who arrived from Sunderland more than a decade ago.

Jamie Carragher leads the club's all-time Premier League appearance chart on 508. Then comes Steven Gerrard, like Jordan a Champions League-winning skipper, just behind on 504.

Third is another man who made a huge impact upon this club during a decade of service: Sami Hyypia, who played in 318 Premier League games for the Reds.

In a recent interview with the club's official magazine, Henderson said he would not focus too much on statistical milestones until his playing days were over.

He captained Liverpool for the 200th time when he wore the armband for the 3-0 home win over Crystal Palace in September. Only a handful of men have led the Reds more often. The subsequent 5-1 win in Porto also saw him clock up 400 appearances for the club in all competitions.

"Those stats are huge honours," he said. "I never take playing for this football club for granted, so to do so 400 times is pretty special.

"It may be something that when I finish my career – hopefully in a long time – I look back at and take in a little bit more. But at the moment I just want to look forward. I don't really tend to look back too often, if at all.

"I look forward in terms of what I want to achieve with this

football club and with these players, and try to give absolutely everything to do that. I don't want to waste time thinking about what I have done or what we've achieved as a team, but rather to think about the future and what we can do going forward.

"I'll have plenty of time to look back when I finish."

Another stat of which Hendo has every right to be proud is his tally of Premier League assists. The brilliant through-ball at Old Trafford last month to tee up Mo Salah for his hat-trick was Jordan's 40th

> Jordan Henderson was looking forwards rather than backwards despite reaching the 300 Premier League appearances mark during the 2021-22 season

---

**REDmen**

## BORN AND RED

*Following his impressive loan-spell last season, youngster Harvey Elliott returns stronger, wiser and steeped in the Liverpool FC mentality*

**"Football is back," says Harvey Elliott with a beaming smile about the prospect of Liverpool playing Burnley today in front of a near-capacity Anfield crowd.**

"That's the buzz around the place," he adds. "We saw it in the two friendly games at Anfield. It's a different breed to any other stadium. It gives you the motivation and the buzz to keep going, to keep trying, to give something back to the supporters – especially now that they're back.

"As a player, it makes you want to go the extra mile to excite the supporters and win games so they can walk away from Anfield today thinking: it was worth the wait – it's good to be back.

"That's the mentality we have as players here – we want to give something back to the fans."

Giving something back to Liverpool supporters is particularly pertinent to Elliott because he's a lifelong Red himself. The 18-year-old may not be Liverpool born and bred, but he is Liverpool through and through.

Elliott was just three when he sat on the Kop for the first time in 2006 as the Redmen beat Maccabi Haifa 2-1 in a Champions League qualifier. He has since travelled home and away to watch Liverpool with his dad Scott, and was in Kiev as a supporter for the 2018 Champions League final against Real Madrid.

He knows how it feels to follow his team through highs and lows, so moments such as giving his boots away to a young fan in the Main Stand, at the end of Liverpool's friendly against Athletic Club here a fortnight ago, come straight from the heart.

A few years ago, that could have been him excitedly receiving a prized memento from one of his heroes.

"It's hard to socialise with the fans at the moment because of the covid situation," he says, "but you try things here and there like giving shirts or boots away – touching moments that will make some fans happy having not been here for almost two years.

"Having the supporters back means so much to us players because they're a helping hand. I call them our twelfth man because they drive us on.

"It's hard going from being a fan to a player because you've got to be professional and put being a fan aside by not getting too excited. My family are all Liverpool fans and they still all have that excitement and buzz about going to games at Anfield and singing all the songs.

"For me personally I've got to focus on the games, but there are moments in them when I sort of think 'wow' and remind myself that I am stepping onto the Anfield pitch and playing in front of Liverpool fans. It's a dream-

> "It's a different breed to any other stadium," said Harvey Elliott as he previewed the first Anfield Premier League game of the 2021-22 season

'20 questions with...' was a quirky Q&A from the 2013-14 season. Here Welsh midfielder Joe Allen speaks about subjects as wide-ranging as meerkats, 7am alarm-calls, refereeing and the movie Ice Age!

# 20 questions with...
## Joe Allen

**Would you ever like to be a coach?**
It's a little far down the line at the moment but I'd guess that almost every player imagines themselves staying in football after they retire. It's no different for me.

**Last time that you laughed out loud?**
Probably while watching Ice Age with my son. One of the perks of being a dad is that you get to watch childish movies.

**Who is your best friend in sport?**
I'd probably say Chris Gunter who is a team-mate of mine with Wales and a good friend.

**Subject you hated at school?**
Art. I don't think I offered anything in that department.

**What time is your alarm set for?**
Normally 7am. I have a baby boy so I like to see him before I go off to work.

**Piece of clothing you've regretted buying?**
Probably every item of clothing that I've ever bought, so whatever item I bought last is the answer!

**What is your most unappealing habit?**
Probably biting my nails. I know that it's quite common but I can't seem to shake it off.

**Favourite animal?**
I want to go for something different, so I'll say a meerkat.

**Most enthusiastic member of the LFC first-team squad?**
Since day-one Kolo Toure's enthusiasm and work ethic has been refreshing. He's had a great career before coming here yet he still hasn't taken his foot off the pedal. You can see from his performances that he's been a big hit.

**Would you ever be a referee?**
No. It doesn't interest me. I think it's a specialist field and there probably aren't too many players who'd fancy all the abuse and criticism that comes with the job.

**Highlight of your time here so far?**
My home debut, against Man City, was a great feeling. We didn't win the game but the first taste of that Anfield atmosphere was special.

---

**Keeper Ryan Crump v defender Dan Cleary**

# ACADEMY CHALLENGE

**DANIEL CLEARY**

**RYAN CRUMP**

**1** Who won the British Open at Muirfield in July?
**RC:** Federer.
**DC:** Tiger Woods.
**Answer:** Phil Mickelson

**2** What first name was given to the recently born royal baby?
**RC:** George.
**DC:** Alexander or George. I'll go for Alexander.
**Answer:** George.

**3** Which full-back scored 59 goals for LFC in 650 games?
**RC:** Phil Neal or Babb? Babb.
**DC:** I can't remember but I know he won the European Cup...
**Answer:** Phil Neal.

**4** Who headlined Glastonbury this year?
**RC:** I didn't see any of it.
**DC:** Rihanna and Calvin Harris.
**Answer:** The Rolling Stones.

**5** Which goalkeeper played 628 games for LFC?
**RC:** Ray Clemence.
**DC:** Don't know.
**Answer:** Ray Clemence.

**6** Hugh Jackman plays which X-Men character?
**RC:** Wolverine.
**DC:** Wolverine.
**Answer:** Wolverine.

**7** Who was recently appointed manager of Barcelona?
**RC:** I know this but can't think of it.
**DC:** I've read about him. I'll go for Martino.
**Answer:** Gerardo Martino.

**8** Liverpool have won the Youth Cup how many times?
**RC:** I'm sure it's three.
**DC:** Six.
**Answer:** Three (1996, 2006, 2007).

**9** Who has more Twitter followers: Coutinho or Lucas?
**RC:** Lucas.
**DC:** Lucas.
**Answer:** Lucas.

**10** Which country has a bigger population: Uruguay or Argentina?
**RC:** It's got to be Argentina.
**DC:** Argentina.
**Answer:** Argentina.

**FINAL SCORE: CRUMP 6 CLEARY 4**
**REACTION:**
**RC:** I read the first question wrong. Who watches golf anyway?!
**DC:** It was just better general knowledge from him.

In seasons 2012-13 and 2013-14 the programme ran a round-by-round quiz tournament for LFC's Academy players and here it's Ryan Crump versus Dan Cleary. The grand final was shown on LFCTV with young keeper Danny Ward the ultimate champion!

*We are going to have to wait a while longer before the stadium rocks like we know it can, but today is a really positive step*

## FROM THE BOSS JÜRGEN KLOPP

There is only one place for me to start today: welcome back to Anfield. Wow. I have waited so long to say these words so for those of you who are fortunate enough to be here – I am so pleased to see you.

We have missed you and even though we never needed a reminder of how important our supporters are to us, we had one anyway.

We know Anfield will not be full and we are going to have to wait a while longer before the stadium rocks like we know it can, but today is a really positive step – not just for us as a club but for the city of Liverpool as a whole – and I hope many more will follow in the coming weeks and months.

To those who will be here, I would ask only one thing – that you support these boys to the maximum that the rules will allow. I know from experience that playing in front of small crowds in bigger grounds can sometimes be difficult because on the pitch you are able to hear individual voices so we all have a responsibility to be as positive and give as much encouragement as we possibly can.

It has been a long time since you have seen this team and I hope you like what you see. To be honest, I think you will.

This is not the easiest moment for us and we have suffered some knocks, but if anything that has brought us even closer together and made us even more determined to continue being the kind of team that this club and our wonderful supporters deserve.

It is also important that our fans who cannot be here today know that we are still playing for them. It might seem strange seeing as we have been unable to see each other since March, but we have felt you with us in everything that we have done.

We play because of our fans and for our fans. That will never, ever change.

Whether you are supporting from inside the stadium or at home, I know that you will recognise that today's opponent is one of the most difficult we can face.

Wolves are a top team. They are brilliantly coached, with brilliant players and none of us needed their win at Arsenal last weekend to educate us to this reality.

Every time we play them, it is a difficult game and I know that this one will be no different.

So I welcome Nuno Espirito Santo, his staff and players to Anfield

The Wolves game of December 2020 was a chance for a limited number of fans to see the Reds 'live' again as lockdown was eased – and the boss said, "We have missed you"

TRENDING

# NEW FOR 2020/21

Football, always football, but not quite as we knew it. Ten changes you'll notice throughout the course of this season »

**OFFICIAL LIVERPOOL FC MATCHDAY PROGRAMME**

## LIVERPOOL FC
v SOUTHAMPTON FC

## THERE IN SPIRIT

The 2020-21 season largely deprived Anfield of its driving force – fans. There were still matches, though, so there were still matchday programmes

'Trending' told fans what differences they could expect during an all-round strange season

# TICKET NEWS

## REDS BEHIND CLOSED DOORS

The 2020/21 Premier League season commences today, Saturday 12 September 2020, with all matches taking place behind-closed-doors until at least 1 October 2020.

Strict protocols have been put in place to ensure that Anfield Stadium is as safe as possible for everybody present. These protocols are to ensure that the season gets underway with the least risk possible, without adding any further strain on the NHS and other public services.

The club would like to thank the fans for supporting the teams safely during this time. Whilst restrictions and guidelines are being gradually reduced, it is important that fans continue to support the team safely. By following government and public health guidance, supporters can play their part to keep friends, family and the local community safe.

On the club's official website you can find information about the Government's 5-stage framework for the phased return of elite sport, as the club continues to work closely with the Premier League, the Sports Grounds Safety Authority and the local authorities on planning for the safe return of supporters when it is permitted and safe to do so.

Matches will be broadcast via Sky, BT Sport and Amazon Prime in the UK. Fans can also catch all the action via Liverpool FC's new Match Centre which was launched at the end of season 2019/20. Hosted on the club's official website and the official LFC App, it provides comprehensive coverage of all the build-up, action, and reaction.

Full match replays and highlights will be shown on LFCTV and on the streaming service LFCTV GO after a feedback pound. To try LFCTV GO free for a month, sign up to a monthly subscription using the code 2021GOFREE. And don't forget, matchday programmes are available to purchase for each home game from reachsportshop.com/teams/liverpool.

With safety the top priority in 2020-21, the club told fans the best ways to follow the team

## Q&A
### THIAGO ALCANTARA

Serial title-winner Thiago Alcantara, who made his Reds debut in the Premier League fixture at Chelsea, had plenty to tell LFC TV upon signing

**Why is Liverpool the right club for you at this stage of your career?**
Because at the end, when the years are passing, you are trying to win as much as you can – and when you win, you want to win more.

I think this club describes what I am as well. I want to achieve all of the goals, win as many trophies as possible. It also has this kind of family [feeling] that I need. We [like to] have a very close relationship with the club and I think I will have this feeling, with this club as well.

**Did you speak to any former Liverpool players about what you can expect here?**
Yeah, for sure, more than the football aspect because, in the end, Liverpool is what it is for the last few years.

The [team] were amazing, they have performed and it is about raising [those levels] every year as much as we can. More than that, it is the family aspect, the life aspect – how is the city, where to go, how was the life [here]? People like Philippe Coutinho and Xabi Alonso helped me a lot to take this last step. It's really good.

If I tell you the truth it was hard [to move] because I was with Bayern for seven years and from the first day until the last I was amazed with the club, with the people there, with the city. It was really difficult to leave the city, but in the end I was moving here so the decision was clear.

**What do you remember of your experience of playing at Anfield in the Champions League in 2019?**
Well, it was my second time here. The first time I was here was when I was six or seven years old, I think. My dad [Mazinho] played against Liverpool with Celta Vigo [in a UEFA Cup third round tie in December 1998]. I was never a fan of many clubs, I was just a fan of football. I was surprised with the people here, how they live football and it was really a shock for me.

My second time here was playing in a draw. We didn't plan to defend as much as we

defended because we hated just to defend a whole game, but they were stronger than us and we had to adapt. It was amazing [to play at Anfield].

**Playing against this Liverpool side then for Bayern, what stood out for you?**
At that time I just prepared for the game as I prepared for all the games I play. I watched two or three games of them, analysing them, how they attack, how they defend, where the weak points of them [were].

"I AM EXCITED NOT JUST TO PLAY HERE BUT ALSO TO TRAIN WITH MY TEAM-MATES, TO GET TO KNOW THE COACH AND WHAT HE WANTS, HOW THE TEAM PLAYS"

At that time, I didn't think much about, 'Wow I am going to be there, I want to be there'. I just faced it like another important game. In that time Bayern were not in our best condition and it was a hard defeat for us [at the Allianz Arena].

**Anfield is now your home and hopefully soon you will be playing in front of those supporters. How excited are you to make your home debut?**
I am excited not just to play here but also to train with my team-mates, to get to know the coach and what he wants, how the team plays. I want to help the guys. If I can help them to be even better then they are, and hopefully become better than I am, it would be so nice. I hope for that.

**Liverpool went on to win the Champions League in 2018/19 followed by three more trophies including the Premier League. What were your thoughts watching that from the outside?**
Liverpool deserved to win the Premier League years ago, but they didn't have the luck. In the end, they are a team that always fights for [trophies] and this year was really well deserved from a long time ago.

I am happy for the guys, happy for the coach as well and also living from a little bit of a distance, I think what you lived here must have been great.

As a football player, you look at those kinds of things like I

A Q&A in Thiago Alcantara's first season with the club revealed how he spoke with Philippe Coutinho and Xabi Alonso before joining the Reds – and that he knew Liverpool are a club that "always fights for trophies"

| LAST WORD |

## THEN & NOW

In the past it won autograph books, today it's smartphone selfies. Either way young football fans still dream of a lasting memento when they meet their heroes. The picture on the right shows Liverpool striker Roger Hunt signing for

youngsters outside the old Main Stand players entrance at Anfield after a match in December 1963. On the left a half-century later it's Reds marksman Daniel Sturridge posing with happy supporters inside the stadium at the Main Stand prior to expansion.

Cover of Goal magazine from September 1970 featuring Liverpool's Ian Callaghan, but who were 'Britain's penalty aces'? Answers on a postcard...

Joe Fagin's Pride of Merseyside single on coloured vinyl, released in 1987 and the basis for the epic fans multi-verse anthem Liverpool Upon My Chest

Metal pin badge in the shape of a football boot complete with laces and studs – talk about attention to detail!

Plate badge from late 1970s, in the days before the apostrophe had been invented, we're guessin.

Red-and-grey Adidas LFC bag from late 1980s – let's hope whoever owns it remembered to 'take those sweaty 'trabs' out...

Thanks to the LFC Museum and the Got Not Got team at Pitch Publishing

'Then & Now' from 2016-17 showed how fashions may change but not fandom – from autograph-hunters to selfie-seekers – while 'Got Not Got' from 2015-16 celebrated all sorts of memorabilia

---

## ON THIS DAY

'On This Day' in the 2012-13 programme was a memory-jogging homage to LFC history

AUG 26

**1933 Thrown to the Wolves**
The first game of another new season and it's disappointment for Liverpool who lose 3-2 to Wolves at Molineux. Benjamin Dabbs and Sam English make their Reds debuts while Dave Wright and Gordon Hodgson (left) are the scorers. Liverpool win only one of the first six games of the season and finish a disappointing campaign only four points ahead of the relegation places.

**1950 Billy's belters**
After defeating Manchester United 2-1 three days before at Anfield, the Reds entertain Sunderland. The subsequent 4-0 success is to be the club's best win of the season with two goals from Billy Liddell (right) inside 15 minutes followed by an Albert Stubbins brace.

**1961 War of the Roses**
In a memorable season for Roger Hunt, the future World Cup-winner scores the first of five hat-tricks in the 5-0 demolition of Leeds United. In total Hunt scores a club record 41 league goals as the Reds storm to the Second Division championship and a return to the top tier after eight years. Kevin Lewis (penalty) and Jimmy Melia get the other two goals.

**1967 Big Tony bags three**
In a 6-0 win against Newcastle at Anfield, striker Roger Hunt nets twice but it's the contribution of the debut scorers Tony Hateley (3) and Emlyn Hughes that raises great expectations. Hateley (right) and Hunt score 41 league goals between them as the Reds finish third, only three points behind eventual champions Manchester City.

**1985 Room for improvement**
In Kenny Dalglish's first season in charge the side start with a win, a draw and a loss which leaves the new boss asking for an all-round improved effort. The result is a 5-0 romp against Ipswich and a move to fourth in the table after four games.

**1995 Earning their Spurs**
For the first time in four visits Liverpool win at Tottenham, 3-1. John Barnes scores the first, his second before half-time is his 100th for the club, while Robbie Fowler's goal is his 50th in Liverpool red.

**2006 Agger shoots, Agger scores**
Liverpool's opening Anfield game sees them entertain West Ham who take an early lead through Bobby Zamora. The equaliser is explosive, Daniel Agger letting fly from 30 yards. It's the Dane's first goal for the club and Peter Crouch grabs the winner.

**2010 Return to Trabzon**
Liverpool fly to north-eastern Turkey to play Trabzonspor in the second leg of their Europa League tie with a 1-0 lead after Ryan Babel's goal at Anfield. The Turks, past opponents in Liverpool's glorious 1977 European Cup run, are level on just four minutes and it takes an own-goal and a Dirk Kuyt effort to secure passage into the next qualifying round.

## At the match with...

# George Sephton

**The Voice of Anfield recalls how the legend of YNWA began…**

*Words: William Hughes*

**B**y the time I took over as the stadium announcer in 1971 the tradition of *You'll Never Walk Alone* was well established.

I wouldn't like to bet any money on how many games it was played for before it became a permanent fixture, but I wouldn't have thought it was long. Gerry Marsden told me that they used to play the top 10 records before kick-off at Anfield but when YNWA fell out of the top 10, a lot of people complained. So it carried on being played and just snowballed from there and here we are now 50 years on.

In theory there was no reason why it should have caught on as it has. It was completely unlike anything that Gerry had brought out previously. His first two no.1 hits had been written for him by Mitch Murray (a famous songwriter from the 1960s). Gerry dug his heels in about *You'll Never Walk Alone* although the record company thought he was crazy. Of course he's been proved right a million times over.

Over the past 42 years I've worn through a few copies of the record. The original 7in vinyl copy is now in the museum at FC Twente in Holland. They invited me over a few years ago as they also sing YNWA before games. When I moved over to CD I thought it would be a nice gesture to give them the record. The last I heard it was still on the wall in the museum there.

Using CDs is considered old-fashioned these days but I still use a CD of the song. I also have one back-up copy on mini-disc. I'm paranoid about it now because there was one occasion in the early 1980s when I turned up to Anfield without YNWA. We were still using the vinyl versions back then. I unpacked my case and realised I'd left it at home. There was nothing I could do, so I just held my hands up and 'fessed' up to the crowd. I said: "I'm sorry. I've come without the record – you'll have to carry on." And of course they did. That was the one and only time it's happened but from that day to this I always have a couple of copies.

I consider Liverpool to be the birthplace of rock or pop – however you define it – because of what happened in the Sixties, and the Kop would always sing songs by local artists.

That's one of the reasons why I like to play records by so many local bands at Anfield. I've become renowned for it now but I am old enough to remember when the Beatles were playing for £10 a night around Liverpool – and having seen what happened to those guys I'm a great believer in encouraging talent in whatever shape or form it takes.

I have a lot of CDs and MP3 files sent to me. Some of it is not good, a lot of it is good but completely unsuitable for a football stadium but it's amazing how often you play something and you think: wow, where did that come from?

A couple of bands have said that the first recognition they had was being played at Anfield. A lot of people have also phoned and emailed me and said they've had such a reaction because I've

> **As soon as that first note is played the scarves are up and it's hair raising every single time**

played one of their songs once at Anfield. That's a pleasure to hear but it's the magic of the Liverpool Football Club name.

*You'll Never Walk Alone* has been recorded by dozens of artists and I have played a few other versions down the years. You always have to play the original but I like to squeeze in other ones as and when I can.

The Love & Joy Gospel Choir, who are based on Oakfield Road, made a fantastic gospel version which I played and played. Somebody sent me a copy of a version Elvis did and I played that once. Then there was an up-tempo disco version that I played a couple of times which was awful! I also played Katherine Jenkins' version in 2005. She came to Anfield for a charity match soon after and I got to meet her. She was genuinely chuffed that I'd played her version is probably the best of the old arrangement of YNWA – going back to its original form in *Carousel* – but obviously Gerry's is the one that we all know and love.

It's one of the great sights in football. When the Kop are in full flight singing *You'll Never Walk Alone* there's absolutely nothing like it. As soon as that first note is played the scarves are up over the heads. It's hair-raising every time.

It's frightening to think it's now 50 years since Gerry's version was released. If you'd gone back then and told Gerry what was going to happen half-a-century later – that he'd still be touring the world singing it and that football fans all over the world would be singing it – he would have thought that you were crazy.

**GEORGE IS OUR MAN BEHIND THE 'MIKE'**

---

*'At The Match With…' in 2013-14 featured stadium announcer George Sephton, affectionately known as 'The Voice of Anfield', who admitted he still gets a shiver down the spine every time fans start singing 'You'll Never Walk Alone'*

---

*'A History in Headlines' from the 2016-17 campaign told the LFC story as it was reported in the local press at the time*

1976 — LFC — 1982
*PART 15 | A HISTORY IN HEADLINES*

Season by season: the history of Liverpool FC as it was reported in the press

**EUROPEAN CUP SPECIAL**

**FAIRCLOUGH IS ANFIELD HERO**

**DAILY POST**
**CHAMPIONS OF EUROPE**

**SOCCER ACTION ON RADIO CITY TONIGHT**
EVERTON V ASTON VILLA
LIVERPOOL V ST ETIENNE

**1976/77** Champions in a tenth title for the Reds, clinched by a point from Manchester City. They narrowly lose in the FA Cup final but lift the European Cup in Rome. What a season!

**1977/78** Runners-up to surprise champs Nottingham Forest, who also beat the Reds in the League Cup final, but a second European Cup is won. Long-server Ian Callaghan retires.

1958 — LFC — 1964
*PART 12 | A HISTORY IN HEADLINES*

Season by season: the history of Liverpool FC as it was reported in the press

**Man with a mission**

**Shankly to manage Liverpool**

**1958/59** Twenty-year-old Roger Hunt signs from Stockton Heath as the Reds finish fourth in the Second Division and go out of the FA Cup at non-league Worcester City in the third round.

**1959/60** Manager Phil Taylor resigns and Liverpool FC appoint Bill Shankly, previously boss of Huddersfield Town, as his successor. The Reds come third and Hunt scores 21 league goals.

# THE BIG READ

**1964/65: JOHN, PAUL, GEORGE, RINGO, ROWDY, SIR ROGER, THE SAINT AND SHANKS**

*'The Big Read' in 2017-18 included an entertaining, in-depth look back at the 1960s*

# TOGETHER AGAIN

## TRENDING

*Last Saturday's Premier League clash with Burnley was an emotional day as supporters revelled in a full Anfield again*

"You have no idea how good it feels to say, welcome back! We've missed you like crazy"

JUST... WOW! Last Saturday saw Liverpool FC fans come together again in a capacity crowd for the first time since March 2020. The first time in 528 days. The first time since Klopp's men were crowned Premier League champions.

It was quite an occasion and not even the drizzly weather could rain on the returning Reds' parade. The whole experience lifted the spirits and heightened the senses.

There were crowds, on the walk-ups to Anfield and all around the ground, and the [once] familiar accompanying sights and sounds. 'Mind yer car, mister?' 'Get your programme, your matchday programme!' 'Hats, scarves and a badge!'

There were the tastes and aromas of pre-match food and drinks, and everywhere hugging, high-fiving mates revelling in the opportunity 'to go the game' again. All a far cry from matchdays played out against a backdrop of near-silence, and it warmed the heart. It'd been too long.

With staggered entry-times to support the club's use of NFC technology, aimed at enabling supporters to stay as safe as possible, there was plenty of pre-match chatter and the buzz of expectation as supporters waited to get behind their team in such numbers in a Premier League fixture for the first time since the Reds beat Bournemouth in L4 in March 2020.

In his programme notes Klopp had written: "You have no idea how good it feels to say, 'Welcome back!' We've missed you like crazy. And a full welcome. A full Anfield. With a full away support. Football is back and it's wonderful."

In his pre-match press conference he had spoken about the power of the Kop, too: "When you sit there, you go just for the football – if they get on their toes then the whole stadium follows. I cannot wait to feel this connection again."

Before kick-off that connection was re-established through a rousing rendition of You'll Never Walk Alone, the first time a packed Anfield had been able to share in the singing of the famous anthem for almost 18 months.

In the moments before kick-off, Anfield paid its respects to all those with a Red connection who had passed away during the COVID-19 pandemic. A poignant tribute and a moving mosaic then saluted Andrew Devine, the 97th person unlawfully killed at Hillsborough, before captain Jordan Henderson laid a wreath in front of the Kop.

Throughout the game, Liverpool's supporters worked their way through their songbook – from the previously

*The excitement of having a full-capacity Anfield again at the start of the 2021-22 season was a focus for the 'Trending' feature*

– an era when there was more than just one 'Fab Four' that were making Liverpool the place to be

## ART AND **SOUL**

*Banners on the Kop, banners in Madrid. Reds supporter*
***Peter Carney** is behind some of the finest creations*

Another 'Big Read' special, this time in 2019-20, paid tribute
to some of the famous Anfield banners, and in particular
Reds fan Peter Carney who has created some classics

### BIG READ

■ WORDS : William Hughes

## RED
## CENTURION

He only turned 22 three weeks ago but
already Trent Alexander-Arnold is on
the verge of an amazing appearance
milestone for Liverpool

In 2020-21 the focus had shifted to Trent Alexander-
Arnold, as 'Big Read' homed in on a young player
already hitting impressive appearance landmarks

# STAND & DELIVER

*A year has now passed since the Anfield Road Stand expansion project kicked off in earnest and it continues to intrigue and excite matchgoers week by week*

The previous programme for the Premier League fixture with Manchester City featured another page of photos of the expanding Anfield Road Stand, sent in by fans, and we'll have more in forthcoming issues as the redevelopment celebrates a little over 12 months since Reds manager Jürgen Klopp stuck a spade in the sand and launched the project. Ultimately it will bring 7,000 more supporters to Anfield on matchday, taking its capacity to 61,000.

To mark the year-on anniversary, drone images and time-lapse footage showed the progress made during the first year of the development. Officially on course to be completed for the start of next season, it has delivered some key milestones since the boss kickstarted the work on 30 September 2021, with more than two million people visiting Anfield for matches, concerts and stadium tours.

Four months into the build, Y-shaped columns were erected to form a safety zone allowing secure operation of the stand and access for spectators on matchdays, while construction works continue above. In July this year the 300-tonne roof truss was carefully lifted into place. Preparatory work had started in May with the erection of two huge steel towers followed by two 60ft haunches lifted into place ready to sit either side of the truss.

It took 30 skilled engineers around 12 hours, during record-breaking temperatures, to install the truss using two 600-tonne crawler cranes to take the heavy lifting. When it was all aligned, the cranes held it in position until it could be bolted in place. The towers, haunches and truss are connected by a total of 25,000 bolts.

*'Trending' from the 2022-23 season took a look at the progress being made as the expanded Anfield Road Stand took shape*

---

## ANFIELD EXTRA

From Rio to Redmen: one of the Great Britain women's hockey Olympic champions is here at Anfield to cheer on her beloved Reds

## Anfield Review with... SAM QUEK

When I got back from Rio with the rest of the GB hockey team, one of the first things I heard was that the club had invited me to today's game, and I was absolutely buzzing. I'm a massive Liverpool fan and I can't wait to see the Main Stand for this first game, having enjoyed a preview over the recent Bank Holiday. My auntie lives on one of the streets nearby and every time I've driven past the ground it's looked epic.

I was football-mad as a kid. On Saturday mornings I used to play football at Allerton for Trammere Rovers against Liverpool and Everton, then get changed and head to Chester to play hockey. I've got 20 cousins, all boys apart from one girl, and when I was younger I'd turn up in my football kit at family barbecues.

My mum is from Liverpool and all her family are Evertonians. But my dad, who's from Singapore, is a Reds fan and me and my two brothers are Liverpudlians too. I remember at primary school, in English class, writing presentations on subjects like Liverpool shirts and Liverpool managers!

I used to go to the match with the Rushes, who are family friends, and for a while I played in the same football team as J.J. one of Ian's sons. It was a boy's side and I was the only girl in the league, but I ended up captaining the team. J.J. texted me after the final in Rio to say congratulations.

I was a regular at Anfield when we won the treble in 2000/01, and I think the last game I went to was West Ham in the Champions League a couple of years ago, when they won 3-0 and Ronaldo had a blinder. I was actually in the away end in my Liverpool jacket, singing away, but the Madrid fans were great.

In the GB women's hockey squad there are a couple of other girls who follow the football. Midfielder Susie Townsend has a season-ticket at West Ham, and Kirsty Mackay, a goalkeeper, is a Man United fan, so you can imagine the banter.

I tried to keep an eye on Liverpool's results while we were away. Obviously the pre-season won over Barcelona was great, as was the result against Arsenal,

then I was cursing when we lost at Burnley. But you can't read too much into early results. At the end of June we played in the Women's Hockey Champions Trophy [in London] and just didn't perform, finishing fifth, and some people said we weren't ready for Rio. But it all came together at the Olympics. Like they say in football, it's a marathon, not a sprint.

It felt like a few things went our way in the final against the Netherlands. One of them was the kit colour. As the first team drawn, the Netherlands had the choice of strip, but we felt that the white above the orange on their kit clashed with the white tops of our change-strip. We got the verdict and played in all-red, our lucky strip. The support from our fans was like being at a football match. My boyfriend Tom had a drum and everyone was waving flags and chanting and having loads of banter with the Dutch fans.

I play as a half-back or full-back and it's probably taken two years for me to recognise my strengths in that position.

The coach told me that, one-on-one, I'm the best tackler in the game, and I take a lot of confidence from that.

My job is to tackle, win the ball and pass it to team-mates who can create chances at the other end.

There are definitely similarities between hockey and football. Penalties in hockey used to be like those in football, but three years ago the eight-second penalty-shuffle was introduced. I think it's a brilliant idea because you can scout opposing players to see how they react when they take them.

Regarding the Reds, when Jürgen Klopp was first appointed I was really excited. Last season was a transition phase for Liverpool - we've had them in hockey too - but hopefully the foundation is now there to build upon. I love Klopp's way of doing things, the passion he's instilled into the players. There's a strong team-ethic and they really play for each other, the manager and the fans. I can only see good things ahead.

*'Anfield Review' in 2016-17 included a first-hand account from Reds fanatic and Olympic gold medalist Sam Quek who explained the similarities between football and hockey, while a 'Story Board' from 2021-22 took a look at some LFC murals*

---

## STORY BOARD

*Six images highlighting some of the murals dedicated to Liverpool's finest*

1. A new mural to Hillsborough campaigner Anne Williams - mum of Kevin, one of our 97 - has been unveiled on Sunbury Road, Anfield. "Anne is someone that the city can be proud of," says artist Paul Curtis. "She's the right sort of person to have a mural, to have a tribute to her."

2. Over in Bootle, boyhood-Blue-turned-Reds-star Jamie Carragher and his 23 Foundation were thanked for raising almost £3 million for local causes since 2009 with this mural on Marsh Lane.

3. Legendary goalkeeper Ray Clemence's mural on Mylva Road was officially opened by his daughter Sarah and four grandchildren in October 2020.

4. Anfield's Sybil Road features a treble was commissioned by The Anfield Wrap and created by artist Akse in tribute to 'a normal lad from Liverpool,' Trent Alexander-Arnold.

5. Opposite Trent is Reds skipper Jordan Henderson lifting the Premier League trophy. The work of Murwalls, it was commissioned by Redmen TV to celebrate Liverpool FC's 2020 title success.

6. Next to Hendo is a mural in honour of 1965 FA Cup final goalscorers Ian St John and Roger Hunt. The Saint signed in in November 2020 and this lady made a touching tribute after his passing.

THERE ARE NUMEROUS OTHER MURALS DEDICATED TO LIVERPOOL FC HEROES ACROSS THE CITY INCLUDING ONE OF JÜRGEN KLOPP IN THE BALTIC TRIANGLE AND ANOTHER FEATURING HENDO WITH 1990 TITLE-WINNING CAPTAIN ALAN HANSEN ON OLD BARN ROAD, ANFIELD. "NICE TO BE KEEPING TRENT COMPANY ON THE OTHER SIDE OF THE ROAD," SAID THE SKIPPER OF THE ONE PICTURED ABOVE. "VERY HUMBLED BY IT."

ANFIELD REVIEW WITH...

# MONA **NEMMER**

In her fabulous new book Liverpool FC's head of nutrition takes football fans of all ages behind the scenes to show how the right food at the right times can be a recipe for success

We are so unbelievably excited and proud to finally present our lovely book – it's been a wonderful journey over the last 12 months and a dream-come-true.

My job at Liverpool Football Club is to make sure the players eat the right food at the right times. Working closely with so many friendly, talented, passionate people is an absolute privilege.

This book – I really hope – is a little way of giving something back to a special club and a special city.

My dream is to help the next generation of fans and footballers learn more about where good food comes from, why a healthy, well-balanced diet improves our wellbeing and sporting performance, and how it can be simple, easy and affordable to grow our own produce and even cook our own meals.

I'm originally from Germany where I worked for the German national team and Bayern Munich before I was appointed LFC's head of nutrition in the summer of 2016. I soon fell in love with the football club, the fans, the city.

I feel blessed because it's the hardest thing on earth to find a job which gives you so much satisfaction and you can actually integrate your work into what you love to do.

At Liverpool FC there is so much history and tradition but also a modern, open-minded perspective among the players, management and staff which has helped to give nutrition a great profile and lots of respect and makes my job so fulfilling.

Jürgen Klopp is the reason for this because he gives us a real family vibe at LFC, along with the opportunity and freedom to work hard and responsibly and achieve the highest standards we possibly can. He's a very smart leader who empowers, supports and pushes you in equal measure. None of it is possible without him. It's incredible to work with him and for him.

I will never forget the night in 2016, not long after I joined the club, during the pre-season summer tour of America when we were joking that a book might be a nice idea, and here we are – live and in colour!

Now more than ever it's important that we all try to eat well and exercise equally not only to keep fit and stay in shape but to boost our immune systems. A healthy diet means a healthy body and good mental health too.

By buying fresh, local, seasonal produce where and whenever possible, we are also supporting our own community. Local food suppliers and businesses will benefit while we reduce our 'food miles', plastic packaging and our 'carbon footprint' – helping to create a sustainable future for us all. Little changes really can make a big difference.

In the book you can learn about food types and the good things they can provide for our bodies, and even what some famous names in the LFC dressing-room have learnt about nutrition – plus a few easy and cost-effective recipes with an Anfield twist!

I have enjoyed every minute working on this project with fantastic people. We wanted to create something different for our supporters – not another recipe book and not a book that was too scientific and complicated. Instead we wanted something unique and inspiring which fans will enjoy and learn from. I hope you like it!

• A Taste of the Liverpool Way is published by Reach Sport and is available to purchase from the official LFC online store and in-store at all official LFC stores in the UK & Ireland.

*A Taste of THE LIVERPOOL WAY*

Liverpool's head of nutrition, Mona Nemmer, appeared in the 2021-22 programme to share some tips from her book about eating well

---

ANFIELD **EXTRA**

Shankly made us famous, Paisley made us sing, Rafa gave us Istanbul and Kenny is our King

## ELVIS IS **RED**

Grammy Award-winning musician Elvis Costello is back at Anfield today. He turns 65 this Sunday and watching the Reds at Anfield is the perfect birthday treat.

While he's been rightly recognised for his music since 1977, when the song *Alison* first wove its magic across the airwaves, perhaps less-known is the extent of his love for Liverpool FC.

Elvis' first visit to Anfield was auspicious, on 26 August 1961 for a 5-0 win over Leeds United, with Roger Hunt getting a hat-trick.

"My dad was very fair and took me over alternate weeks to home games at Anfield and Goodison so I could make my own mind up.

"We went to Everton and they lost then we went to Liverpool and they won, so that was it!"

Costello, who spent part of his childhood growing up in southwest London, continues: "I used to spend a lot of time with my grandmother up here on school-holidays.

"I'd plan half-term holidays just to get to the games as often as I could. We're talking about 1967 right through until the time I came to live in Liverpool in 1970. From then of course there was nothing stopping me coming every week."

For an artist famous for enthralling audiences he's surprisingly shy when face-to-face with his footballing heroes. "It's completely beyond me when I meet them. When I met Kenny Dalglish and Alan Hansen I was tongue-tied and didn't know what to say. Luckily they are great chaps and can tell some great stories."

Elvis was here last season for the Napoli game with his wife, the jazz singer Diana Krall. Let's hope the result goes our way again this evening against the Gunners.

Best wishes our kid – and enjoy the match!

Costello's kings of the early 60s

---

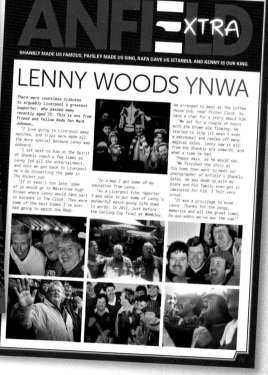

ANFIELD **EXTRA**

SHANKLY MADE US FAMOUS, PAISLEY MADE US SING, RAFA GAVE US ISTANBUL AND KENNY IS OUR KING

## LENNY WOODS YNWA

There were countless tributes to arguably Liverpool's greatest supporter, who passed away recently aged 75. This is one from friend and fellow Reds fan Mark Johnson...

"I love going to Liverpool away matches, and trips were made all the more special because Lenny was onboard.

"I sat next to him on the Spirit Of Shankly coach a few times as Lenny led all the entertainment, and once we got back to Liverpool he'd be dissecting the game in The Rocket pub.

"If it wasn't too late, some of us would go to Mavertree High Street where Lenny would take part in karaoke in The Clock. They were some of the best times I've ever had going to watch the Reds.

"In a way I got some of my education from Lenny.

"As a Liverpool Echo reporter I was able to put some of Lenny's wonderful match-going life down in words. In 2012, just before the Carling Cup final at Wembley, we arranged to meet at The Coffee House pub, near Picton Clock, to have a chat for a story about him.

"We sat for a couple of hours with the brown ale flowing. He started to sing (it wasn't even a matchday) and reeled off many magical tales. Lenny saw it all from the Shankly era onwards, and what a time he had.

"Happy days, as he would say.

"We finished the story at his home then went to meet our photographer at Anfield's Shankly Gates. He was made-up with my piece and his family even got it laminated for him. I felt very proud.

"It was a privilege to know Lenny. Thanks for the songs, memories and all the great times. Ee-aye-addio we've won the cup!"

'Anfield Extra' shines the spotlight on the supporters with these examples focusing on famous musician Elvis Costello and much-missed super fan Lenny Woods

As Steven Gerrard played his final season for the Reds, in 2014-15, the programme presented his stats with successive kits

How the 2013-14 programme celebrated Liverpool Ladies' title triumph that season

Liverpool's Champions League progress in 2019-20 was re-lived in comic-book fashion

'Anfield Spotlight' in 2014-15 took a much closer look at the Shankly Gates and tracked down their creators

# AT THE MATCH WITH...
## COLIN MURRAY

**I'm a staunch Red but I've got lots of time for the Blues too**

Both Reds and Blues are cordially invited to our Big Day Out in Liverpool at the start of June. I love coming to this city anway and this will be 5 Live's biggest-ever live event.

In the past we've been to Goodison, played Sheffield and Gateshead and thought: could we go any bigger? Well it doesn't get much bigger than the Echo Arena where we'll have a special edition

of Fighting Talk, an end-of-season 606 show and a live set from Primal Scream. We can't wait to come to town.

Today it's the derby and I don't think a single Liverpool or Everton fan really wants it to be just about this game. We all hope next season it's about more than finishing above the other team and that there's a European place at stake and even fixture congestion to worry about.

I remember vividly as a kid watching Everton in the 1985 European Cup Winners Cup final and being told by my dad that they were 'the neighbours' and our rivals but still wanting them to win.

So much about Everton FC is the same as Liverpool FC. When it comes to something like the recent Luis Suarez incident and some of the comments being made, it's only ever the five per cent you hear from. If Liverpool aren't winning, I want Everton to win. I want us to beat Everton, of course, but in a neighbourly way. Everton have

> "Of course I want us to beat Everton today but in a 'neighbourly' manner"

covered the city in glory this year. I met Bill Kenwright last season when they were playing Bolton and he said that for a 'red nose' he really liked my coverage of Everton. That meant a lot.

As far as coming here to watch my beloved Liverpool, the irony is that the more I work in football, the less matches I get to – especially this season with so many games at Anfield being on a Sunday. Previously I'd managed between 15 and 20 games and now it's nearer five to ten. I've been on the waiting list for a season-ticket for a long time and next year I'll be sharing one with a girl who's a mate. I've been kindly invited to the corporate boxes a couple of times, but nothing beats being in the crowd as an ordinary fan.

I was 16 when I saw my first

Radio personality Colin Murray wrote a piece for the 2012-13 derby programme in 'At The Match With...'

**TIME FOR COMMERCIALS**

Adverts inside the programme have come a long way since the old days and here's a selection of some of the most colourful in recent times

HERE'S TO **ANFIELD**

That calls for a *Carlsberg*

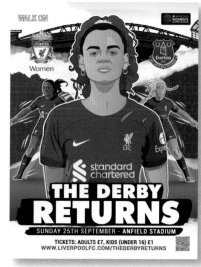

WALK ON

**THE DERBY RETURNS**

SUNDAY 25TH SEPTEMBER - ANFIELD STADIUM

TICKETS: ADULTS £7, KIDS (UNDER 16) £1
WWW.LIVERPOOLFC.COM/THEDERBYRETURNS

**SIXTY** '62 '22
STONES EUROPE 2022

THU 09 JUNE
**ANFIELD STADIUM**

TICKETS AND HOSPITALITY
PACKAGES ON SALE NOW

0151 264 2222

AEG concerts west     LIVERPOOLFC.COM/THEROLLINGSTONES

Standard Chartered

**THROUGH THE GOOD AND THE BAD, WE'VE ALWAYS HAD HOPE IN OUR HEARTS.**

WALK ON
liverpoolfc.com/walkon

18/19 TRAINING KIT

THIS MEANS MORE

IN STORES & ONLINE
LIVERPOOLFC.COM/STORE

THE **BEATLES** STORY &

**LIVERPOOL FC STADIUM TOUR**

Rock 'n' Goal Tour

ONLY £26.50 PER TICKET

**Liverpool FC Stadium Tours & The Beatles Story**

FIND OUT MORE

rockngoaltour.com

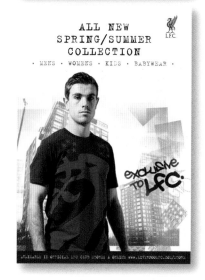

ALL NEW
SPRING/SUMMER
COLLECTION

· MENS · WOMENS · KIDS · BABYWEAR ·

exclusive to LFC.

**Alisson's header. Trent's corner. Bobby's no-look goals. Hendo's trophy shuffle...**

*Reliving 100 magical moments from the Klopp years*

The bond between manager, players and fans has always been unique at Anfield and, seven years on from Jürgen's arrival, that special relationship is as powerful as it's ever been.

A new beautifully illustrated official club book, I Feel Fine, celebrates the journey so far in 100 unforgettable, magical moments.

**BOOM!
The perfect gift book for a Liverpool fan you love**

The Klopp 100
A Modern Liverpool Love Affair

Order from: liverpoolfc.com/store,
reachsportshop.com and all good book shops

*Since the launch of the FA Women's Super League in 2011, the Reds have also produced matchday programmes for their women's team, which was known as Liverpool Ladies until a rebrand as Liverpool FC Women ahead of the 2018-19 campaign.*

In the first two seasons it was put together by then club secretary Colin Charlton before moving to LFC's publishing partner ProgrammeMaster in 2013. That coincided with a successful period as manager Matt Beard led Liverpool to back-to-back WSL title triumphs and into the UEFA Women's Champions League.

Chronicling the successes was a B5-sized matchday programme, rising from 32 pages in 2013 to 36 in 2014. Packed with columns from manager and captain, interviews, quizzes, match acton and guest columns, it charted the FA Women's Championship-winning campaign of 2021-22 and the Reds' return to the top-flight in 2022-23 with a crowd of 27,574 watching the Merseyside derby at Anfield in September 2022.

## MISSY BO KEARNS: "I DREAMT OF WINNING TROPHIES FOR LIVERPOOL"

**Missy Bo Kearns grew up dreaming of lifting trophies for Liverpool.**

So when the Scouser in this Liverpool FC Women's team gets her hand on the Championship silverware this afternoon it will be a proud moment for her and her family.

"As a kid growing up, I dreamed of lifting trophies for Liverpool and the Championship one's going to be my first," she says. "Hopefully it will be just the start. I want to keep working my way up and achieve more. This is what I've dreamt of and it's come true, so if I keep working hard and the team keeps working hard, there's nothing stopping us getting many more in the future.

"My family are proud of me. They see the ups and the downs that I go through and what every parent probably sees in their child who plays football. To see one of the highest highs you can achieve must be an unbelievable feeling for them. They come to every ground to watch me, so they probably feel like they're a part of it.

"All the girls are welcoming and always go over and speak to them. And I think that's how close of a team we are. I know everyone's parents in the team too and I think that's good because usually at the top level it's kept separate, so I think that's where we so close. I think the parents will have just as good a time today as us!"

Bo, who turned 21 ten days ago, couldn't have asked for a better script as she came off the bench to sweep home the goal that sealed the Reds' 4-2 win at Bristol City three weeks ago and with it the league title and promotion.

"It was like an early 21st birthday present but one that was for us all, for the whole team and the staff. I think it is what we've deserved for our hard work week in and week out. To have gone 19 league games unbeaten is unbelievable but it's been about hard work every week and every game.

"It took us time to adapt to the Championship. To be honest, as a team, the first season in the Championship shocked us. Some people might have thought it would have been easy and it really wasn't. This year we got together again, we got new players, new staff and it was like a breath of fresh air. We've made it look easy but it has been a lot of hard work.

"When Katie Stengel scored the third goal at Bristol, I was shaking. When you're not playing, you're more nervous. I was warming up every 10 to 15 minutes just through nervous energy because I was just sitting there watching and this season I haven't really been in a situation where I have been watching a lot. My nerves were gone! On the bench I was speaking to the girls and I said, 'If I come on, I'm going to score.' And they said, 'Well if you score, you've got to do a knee slide.' I said, 'That's a deal!' So I did a two-yard knee slide!"

Bo has been in Niamh Fahey's ear about performing the 'Hendo Shuffle' when she receives the trophy and holds it aloft before the Reds supporters but she admits the skipper has been keeping her guessing.

"I said to her, 'You are both captains of Liverpool at the same time so you should do the same shuffle. She'll laugh and mess around so I'm not sure if she'll do it. Only time will tell!"

Bo, from Allerton, is also looking forward to enjoying celebrations with the Liverpool fans who have followed the team up and down the country all season.

"Some fans haven't missed a game and it's nice that we can now go over to speak to them at the end of the games," she says. "As soon as the COVID restrictions were over, we started being able to meet them again. That was great because they're always there to support us so that's our time to give back to them. At first they wouldn't even get to say hello, but now it's great because we can meet, greet, get pictures and have chats. We couldn't have done anything without them. The fans are Liverpool Football Club and they've proved that again this season."

INTERVIEW: *William Hughes*

## SKIPPER'S NOTES
# GEMMA BONNER

*'Our run in the second half of the season has shown the standards we can set.'*

Good evening and welcome to the Select Security Stadium for our final FA WSL game of the season. We've had a long wait of four weeks for this match but now that it's here we're all looking forward to trying to finish on a winning note.

Overall, it has been a good season for us. We have welcomed a new manager and backroom staff and also had a significant number of changes to the playing squad. Taking that into consideration, it was always going to take time for things to get this year but the run we have had in the second half of the season has shown the standards we are capable of and hopefully laid down a good platform from which to move forward.

There are always frustrations when we reflect on a few results which got away from us and you look back and think there were goals that we could have avoided conceding, all of which could have meant a different end result.

But not only were we bedding in a large number of players, we were also changing the way we played. We had perhaps become a bit predictable over the past few years but now we have quite a fluid system. We have had a pretty settled back five for a while now and that has helped us at one end of the field, while at the other we have shown that we have plenty of attacking threat in the team. A number of girls have chipped in with important goals which has been pleasing to see. I know from personal experience in training how hard our attacking players can be to mark and we can be happy with the way things have gone for us since mid-May.

A win this evening would give us a top-four finish and we'll be going all out to try and secure that but we also know that Arsenal are a strong team with some great players. We managed a 2-1 win down there earlier in the season but that game was evidence of just how tough our task will be tonight.

Finally I'd like to say a huge thank you to our fans for the incredible backing you have given us this season. We never take your support for granted but as well as the vocal encouragement we receive at home, it has been brilliant to travel to Sunderland and Reading for midweek away games and be greeted by a band of fans cheering us on. We hope we give you more to cheer tonight as we aim to sign off with 3 points.

Enjoy the match, Gemma

one word answers

# EITHER OR?
**Ladies forward ASHLEY HODSON reveals her preferences**

- Twix or Mars
- Tea or Coffee
- Book or Magazine
- Barcelona or Real Madrid
- Dubai or America
- Beach or Pool
- Club or Bar
- Mac or iPad
- Corrie or Eastenders
- Pizza or Pasta
- Early bird or Night Owl
- Brown Sauce or Ketchup
- Darts or Table Tennis
- Band or DJ
- Movie or Box Set
- Twitter or Instagram
- Studs or Moulded
- Black boots or Coloured
- Chinese or Indian
- Flats or Heels

# A CHAMPION **COLLECTION**

**Tonight's issue of the matchday programme, featuring the Premier League trophy in red ribbons on the front cover, completes the set for a most extraordinary season.**

Starting with Norwich City at home on Friday 9 August 2019 to Liverpool versus Chelsea today on 22 July 2020, the issues are numbered 1 to 19 on the spine for each consecutive Premier League home fixture and on the front covers they variously feature captain Jordan Henderson and team-mates Bobby, Gini, Trent, Andy Robbo, Sadio Mane, the Ox, Naby, Divock, Mo, Joe Gomez, Alisson and Virgil, plus of course the boss.

There are also three special-edition covers, commemorating the 31st anniversary of Hillsborough, 60 years since Bill Shankly became manager, and the unveiling of a new statue to celebrate Bob Paisley in the year that he would've been 100 years old.

**01**
v Norwich City

**02**
v Arsenal

**07**
v Brighton & Hove Albion

**08**
v Everton

**09**
v Watford

**10**
v Wolverhampton Wanderers

**15**
v Bournemouth

**16**
v Crystal Palace

**17**
v Aston Villa

**18**
v Burnley

62

## COMPLETE COLLECTION

There are few better illustrations of a season's body of work than this set of covers from the 2019-20 title-winning campaign, which appeared in the Chelsea edition

**03**
v Newcastle United

**04**
v Leicester City

**05**
v Tottenham Hotspur

**06**
v Manchester City

**11**
v Sheffield United

**12**
v Manchester United

**13**
v Southampton

**14**
v West Ham United

**19**
v Chelsea

# WITHOUT WHOM...

Compiling the 'Early Years' section of this book proved the most challenging. Sourcing programmes over a century old is never an easy task with far fewer copies surviving the tests of time.

We are indebted to Phil Brough and Gerard Scully for sharing items of ephemera from their extensive programme collections. Scanning such artefacts is a time-consuming pastime that requires a great deal of care and patience. Given the perils of copying such fragile paper objects, it is a relief to report that no programmes came to harm while producing this book.

It has been a joy to work with them both – tapping into their peerless wisdom while having a front-row seat to such historical documents, rich with information relating to Liverpool FC. By the end of the scanning process, they left us with an embarrassment of riches, sufficient to create an entirely new book solely on those early years. Perhaps one day it will be produced.

**ANDY MARSDEN**